218

LDS INSTITUTE of RELIGION

Understanding

Rome

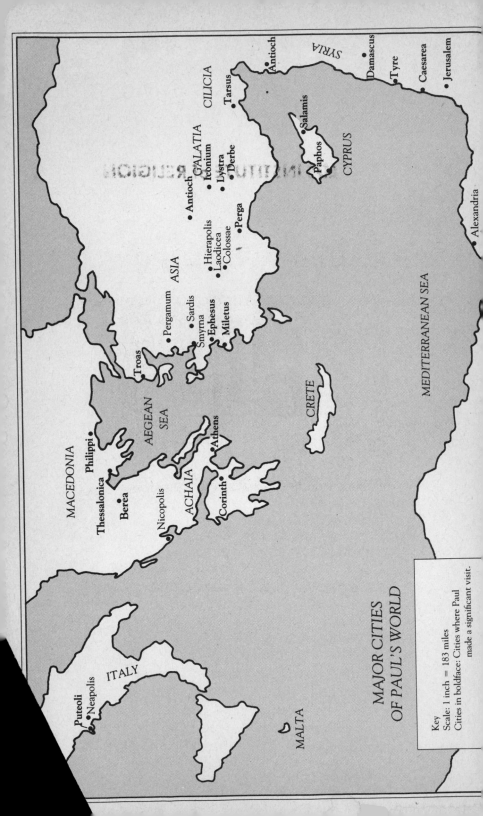

MAJOR CITIES
OF PAUL'S WORLD

Key
Scale: 1 inch = 183 miles
Cities in boldface: Cities where Paul
made a significant visit.

ITALY

Puteoli
Neapolis

MALTA

MACEDONIA
Philippi
Thessalonica
Berea
Nicopolis

ACHAIA
Athens
Corinth

AEGEAN
SEA

Troas

ASIA
Pergamum
Sardis
Smyrna
Ephesus
Miletus
Hierapolis
Laodicea
Colossae

GALATIA
Antioch
Iconium
Lystra
Derbe
Perga

CILICIA
Tarsus

CRETE

CYPRUS
Salamis
Paphos

MEDITERRANEAN SEA

SYRIA
Antioch
Damascus
Tyre
Caesarea
Jerusalem

Alexandria

Understanding

PAUL

Richard Lloyd Anderson

Deseret Book Company
Salt Lake City, Utah

First printing in paperbound edition, November 1990

Library of Congress Catalog Card Number 83-72103
ISBN 0-87579-477-7

Printed in the United States of America
10   9   8   7   6   5   4   3   2   1

Dedicated to my father
Lloyd Ernest Anderson
(1897-1970)
missionary, businessman, teacher, friend,
who taught his children the joy of work,
of learning, and of sharing the gospel

Contents

	Preface		ix
	Acknowledgments		xi
	Key to Translations		xiii
1	Two Restless Worlds		1
2	Paul's Preparation: "Fire on Earth"		19
3	The Missionary Message in Acts		39
4	Early Letters to Converts		69
	1 Thessalonians	69	
	2 Thessalonians	81	
5	Letters of Reconversion		91
	1 Corinthians	92	
	2 Corinthians	130	
6	Letters Preaching Christ		148
	Galatians	149	
	Romans	168	
	Hebrews	195	
7	Roman Imprisonment Letters		230
	Philemon	238	
	Colossians	244	
	Ephesians	259	
	Philippians	290	
8	Letters to Leaders		310
	1 Timothy	314	
	Titus	341	
	2 Timothy	362	
	Appendix A: Chronology of Paul's Life		390
	Appendix B: Two Descriptions of Paul		399
	Appendix C: Baptism for the Dead		403
	Appendix D: Glossary of Ancient Sources		416
	Scripture References		421
	Index		434

Tables and Illustrations

Major Cities of Paul's World — Frontispiece

Religions in Paul's World — 10

Coin of Augustus — 15

Paul's Recorded Visions — 30

Paul's Gentile Missions — 43

Public Miracles Through Paul — 56

Ordinances of Salvation in Acts — 60

The Writing of First Thessalonians:
Background in Acts and the Letter — 75

The Qualities of Love: 1 Corinthians 13:4-7 — 121

Two Types of Salvation through Christ — 160

The Beginning of Hebrews in the
Chester Beatty Papyri — 199

Interrelationships of Paul's "Prison Letters" — 237

Paul's Testimonies of Christ and His Mission — 250

The Constitution of Christ's Church in
Paul's Writings — 281

The Asian Apostasy During the Apostles' Lives — 370

Preface

This book started as a study of Paul and evolved to a study of Paul as a witness of the great truths of the restored gospel. It was written out of a love of Paul's commitment and his powerful impact on the mind and soul attuned to eternity. This book came from years of pondering his original words and of teaching their meaning in classes in the Church and at Brigham Young University. But reliving Paul's life and rehearing his words through intense months of writing has spotlighted for me the greatness of the man and the truth of the cause he served. Independent realities are mutually validating, and my conviction has deepened of how modern revelation adds critical insight to Paul and of how well Paul supports modern revelation. Those seeking to find or to explain Christ's true church will find the blueprint in the Acts and the writings of Paul. And those seeking to be Saints in reality will find in them a sure guide on the path to perfection.

This book is written for busy but thoughtful people, and today's author must candidly tell what he offers that hasn't been said before. The problem is how to reread Paul with insight, and this book offers these resources:

1. Can one understand Paul's criticisms of the world without knowing something about his world? The opening chapter reveals how "modern" the first century was, how the Lord sent his apostles at a most opportune time.

2. Can one understand Paul's teachings without knowing the character of the man who gave them? The Bible and Jewish

sources throw light on Paul's early life, conversion, and subsequent Jewish persecution.

3. Can one understand Paul's letters to members without knowing the doctrines they already believed? With the aid of charts, Paul's preaching in Acts is presented as the foundation of his letters.

4. Can one understand Paul's precise thoughts in a translated language? Paul wrote in Greek, and the explanations of Paul in this book are based on the author's knowledge of Greek. In the King James Version, Paul sometimes speaks like a character out of Shakespeare, obscured by the evolution of English since the King James Version. The new Latter-day Saint edition of the King James Version helps greatly with occasional word notes, but a book has space to unravel many problems of meaning.

5. Can one understand a letter of Paul without knowing why he wrote? Epistles often do not teach general doctrine but answer special questions. The letters are here presented in sequence and studied in their historical setting.

6. Can one understand a single letter without understanding the perspective of all of Paul's teachings? Here, main issues are stressed in each letter with the help of similar teachings in other letters and in the earliest Christian sources.

One is not informed about Paul without knowing how churches interpret him. For important issues, the book compares Catholic and Protestant doctrines with Paul's writings and with the restored gospel. The aim in so doing is to serve both honesty and charity, for every person seeking the Lord must admire everyone who does the same. But Paul's heritage belongs to those who know God's power to give visions and authority in the trying times that the apostle foresaw for the "last days" (2 Tim. 3:1). Wisdom and strength are now needed more than ever before to find and keep to the course—spiritual and biblical knowledge show the way. For these vital goals, concerned people will find added power in *Understanding Paul.*

Acknowledgments

Credits are fitting for a book on the apostle who writes with constant thankfulness to God and with great social awareness, another name for gratitude. A major publication is made possible by the teamwork of many, but there is space to recognize those who have made special contributions:

Hugh Nibley and Sidney Sperry, in whose former office I write; these Brigham Young University scholars opened the world of biblical languages for me and insisted on primary evidence, not parroting academic trends.

Carma de Jong Anderson, my wife, who is also a cultural historian. Her patience and encouragement extended through interminable hours of writing.

Linda Groneman, whose expert secretarial skills produced a readable manuscript and whose responsible concern for accuracy upgraded the result.

Robert J. Matthews, dean of religious instruction at Brigham Young University, whose continued friendship has significantly aided my scholarly momentum.

Others to be mentioned include the editor of this book, genial and vigilant Jack M. Lyon; capable colleague Wilfred Griggs; valued faculty friends Spencer Palmer and Gene Dalton; and Brigham Young University's efficient library staff, who keep the informational pipeline flowing. Final thanks belong to God, who has given me strength and inspiration beyond my ordinary abilities.

Key to Translations

Every New Testament quotation in this book has been checked against the Greek text. The English version selected is not the result of "shopping around" for the most pleasing reading—the criterion is always how accurately any English reading reflects the Greek original. My own punctuation and capitalization may be used to bring out the meaning of biblical and ancient quotations—and some from modern authors. Certain King James Version quotations have been used with the archaic "ye" simply to show that this pronoun was plural in Greek. Where possible, the King James Version has been favored, partly in respect for merit— its New Testament is remarkably close to the Greek text. Latter-day Saints also continue to use this translation for effective communication with English-speaking Christians. The main problem with this Bible is its frequent use of archaic terms, words vivid to 1611 readers that are little used or have different meanings today. Yet one Article of Faith commits Latter-day Saints to the Bible "as far as it is translated correctly," which leaves the option to probe the original languages for meaning, as Joseph Smith did in his Nauvoo discourses.

When no translation adequately communicates the meaning of the Greek text, my own translation is given, identified by "literal trans." Since words have objective definitions, modern translations are used where possible. Recent decades have produced bewildering numbers of versions, but six major committee translations measure up to the scholarly and group standard of the King

James Version. Their names, theological acceptance (Protestant or Roman Catholic), and abbreviations are as follows:

Revised Standard Version	Protestant and Catholic	RSV
New English Bible	Protestant and some Catholic	NEB
Jerusalem Bible	Catholic	JB
New American Bible	Catholic	NAB
New International Version	Protestant	NIV
New King James Bible	Protestant	NKJB

Undesignated quotations are from the King James Version.

After the King James Translation, the recent New King James Bible is favored because it is the only widely accepted version that uses the longer Greek text followed by the King James translators. The number of verses deleted by textual critics is not large, but it is tragic to lose anything authentic from the Early Church. Some common-sense assumptions control judgment here, but there are sharp differences among scholars. My strong view is that theological bias would more easily lead to deletions from than additions to the Bible—the latter is a much more daring and detectable act. As for straight copying, my student secretaries over a quarter of a century have proved that there is little tendency to add but great danger of losing words, phrases, and paragraphs through inattention. Thus, the basic arguments of J. Reuben Clark, Jr., deserve careful thought. These are given in his *Why the King James Version?* (Salt Lake City: Deseret Book Co., 1956). The better Greek New Testaments have full and not selective variant readings from manuscripts, and for every verse quoted here, these manuscript readings have been examined and a judgment made before translating. To help with meaning, the Greek word is often transliterated—the Greek letters are written in English script. Long "o" and "e" have been marked, and the English reader needs to know that the long "e" is pronounced like the vowel in "they." The two accents used (´ and ˆ) are stress accents and show which syllable is emphasized.

Joseph Smith's leading views on Paul are discussed with the appropriate teaching. Some of these come from Nauvoo discourses, where "it should read" is the Prophet's typical comment.

But that probably was intended as "it should *mean*," for Joseph Smith claimed to give inspired explanations; he did not present himself as an expert in Greek manuscripts. Most of Joseph Smith's insights on Paul come from the Joseph Smith Translation (JST), where major changes are infrequent compared to his treatment of Genesis or the Gospels. Since these are fully available in the new Latter-day Saint edition of the King James Version, they are not discussed here unless they affect a featured doctrine. What is said above about the discourses may also be true of the Bible corrections in the Joseph Smith Translation. As Robert J. Matthews points out, "The New Translation could be many things," two of which are "inspired commentary" or inspired "harmonization of doctrinal concepts." (*"A Plainer Translation": Joseph Smith's Translation of the Bible* [Provo, Utah: Brigham Young University Press, 1975], p. 253.) Because of these possibilities, the Prophet's comments on Paul are treated as questions of meaning, not of textual quotation.

1

Two Restless Worlds

The ultimate ignorance is unawareness of ignorance. Thus Paul sarcastically comments on "the wisdom of this world" (1 Cor. 1:20), summing up a society too egotistical to see its own shallowness. He uses similar language a dozen times as he opens 1 Corinthians, a powerful exposure of status-seeking, materiality, immorality, and a host of other false values. He expected Church members to rise to a higher standard of living—true spiritual living. He perceived men as playing games instead of facing realities, as though little children had wandered into a schoolyard for the first time and had lost themselves in enjoying the play equipment, quite unaware of the higher purpose for building the school. Virtually every letter of Paul alludes to the higher purpose in making the earth, the plan "which God ordained before the world unto our glory" (1 Cor. 2:7).

Paul's world and the modern world have learned nothing of this plan without the preaching of Christ's gospel. Jesus revealed it plainly, for, as he said, "I came forth from the Father, and am come into the world: again, I leave the world, and go to the Father" (John 16:28). A world not knowing Jesus Christ and his gospel is a world ultimately in more trouble than not knowing about sanitation or radiation. Indeed, undeveloped countries improve only through concerned people coming to teach about germs and modern farming. The technological age is not so much a time period as it is a stage of development. By the spiritual standards of the scriptures, mankind is still primitive. Christianity is visible but attenuated; lands and peoples are widely ignorant of it. And upon examination, Christian nations may be shockingly low in conviction or understanding of how to serve God. A closer survey of this modern world will show the critical need of Paul's message and that of his modern successors. We see a world today that has remarkable similarities to Paul's world, making his message the more relevant.

Earth's population is now around 4 billion people. About 1.3 billion are professed Christians, just a third of the people of the world.[1] So there are two non-Christians for every Christian living on this planet. A global map shows Christians in the majority in North and South America, Europe, Southern Africa, and Australia. But the world also has vast areas where Christianity is virtually nonexistent, as in Moslem areas and Asia.[2] Yet statistics do not address the real issue of individual commitment, for John did not see groups and nations on the day of judgment—he saw only persons: "and they were judged every man according to their works" (Rev. 20:13). Jesus compared his kingdom to a net that sweeps in all kinds. But after this gathering stage comes the judgment, when God will "sever the wicked from among the just" (Matt. 13:49). Latin America leads all continents in professed Christians, just about 94 percent of the population.[3] Yet a small fraction of that number would be found in church on an ordinary Sunday.

One spot of consistency is Ireland, where 99 percent of the population is Christian[4] and where 87 percent are found in church "at least once a week."[5] But this is not typical in Europe, where a middle-spectrum country like West Germany opens up the realities of living for self and not for God. Although 93 percent there are classified as Christians,[6] one must conclude that many European Christians are not very religious. West Germany's weekly church attendance is only 20 percent, but that is not the end of bad news. Another 20 percent of West Germans said that they attend on Easter and Christmas, but there is a more dismal figure—a full 45 percent of West Germans reported going to church "only on family occasions, as marriage, baptism, funerals, or not at all."[7] One may rationalize this inactivity by suggesting that Lutheran Christianity teaches belief, not church attendance, as the means of salvation through Christ. But a close look at belief is as distressing. In spite of the 93 percent classified as Christians in West Germany, only 79 percent went on record as believing in God.[8] And 44 percent reversed Paul's Christianity by stating that they do not believe in "a life after death."[9] This is precisely the issue that caused Paul to despair of the salvation of the Corinthians, insisting that disbelief in man's resurrection was totally inconsistent with the reality of Christ's resurrection (1 Cor. 15:12-14).

Indeed, a minority of West Germans believe in Christ, though the nation is classified as Christian. Only 33 percent committed themselves to this proposition: "God has sent his son Jesus to men in order to save them; Jesus was raised again from the dead, and I can pray to him." Even if that question was not perfectly framed, two-thirds chose the alternative of disbelief. Twenty-one percent expressed mild disbelief: "Jesus was only a man, though a great man who desired to lead men to good; thus he can still be an example for me today." But 33 percent chose stronger disbelief: "Jesus lived almost 2,000 years ago, and today we live in an entirely different world; Jesus has no meaning for me today." The final category of this recent survey expressed a degree of disbelief that no responsible scholar would support—7 percent of the West Germans expressed the ultimate skepticism that "Jesus never lived."[10]

The above survey from a respected news magazine only confirms other West German data. An independent institute recently determined that 84 percent of the populace seldom or never read the Bible, a figure moving to 94 percent of those sixteen to twenty-nine years old in the same category.[11] Surely there is a link between disbelief in Christ and ignoring the sources that speak of him. A respected English teacher bluntly explained the narrow-mindedness of many people: "You're down on what you're not up on."[12] Paul's testimony lies buried with him if no one reads his letters. And without this heritage, the youth of a great nation find no higher purpose than pleasure. They were asked to choose between the following two attitudes:

> 1. I want to enjoy my life and not trouble myself any more than is necessary. You only live once anyway, and the main thing is to be sure you get something from life.

> 2. I regard my life as a stewardship. I am here to accomplish something and must devote all my strength to it. I want to accomplish something in my life, even if that is often difficult and tiring.

Christian youth favored the first alternative, 43 percent seeking enjoyment as the controlling goal, 37 percent choosing stewardship with sacrifice, and 20 percent undecided.[13] But does such a choice bring happiness? Renate Koecher, the demographer who determined these statistics on West German youth, also found that 47 percent of young people from "very religious" homes considered themselves "very happy," whereas only 23 percent from homes "without religion" said the same. So this social scientist concluded, "The loss of religious ties and the 'liberation' which accompanied abandoning the 'coercive' quality of prescribed norms has left a poorer society in its wake."[14] But West Germany has shown a brilliant record in economics, science, scholarship, and human organization. Tragically, this proud people have lowered their flag of Christian heritage. If this standard rises again, it must come from reconversion to Christ's ancient and modern apostles.

How worldly is England, the political parent of the United States? There the same forces of apathy and skepticism are at work. Nominal Christians are 87 percent of that population,[15] but only 15 percent said they attend church once a week; 38 percent attend "several times a year"; and 46 percent attend "less often or never."[16] An old proverb runs true: "Out of sight, out of mind." For only 36 percent of the English population believe in "a personal God."[17] Christ and the Father were above all personal for Paul, so only a third of British Christians espouse Paul's doctrine recorded in their Bibles. Another 37 percent of Englanders have a vague acceptance of "some sort of spirit or life force," with agnostics or atheists comprising the other 27 percent of the population.[18] And England also is losing faith in Jesus Christ. Although 71 percent registered belief in Jesus as the "Son of God" in 1957, nearly twenty-five years later only 52 percent would make a similar commitment. "Just a man" is now the vote of another 31 percent, with "don't know" and "just a story" accounting for the remaining 17 percent.[19] In a survey of British attitudes toward the New Testament, the source of knowledge of Christ, 34 percent said that "it is mostly a collection of stories and fables." And another 13 percent said "don't know" when asked what they thought about the New Testament, making the testimony of Christ's apostles insignificant for about half of England's people.[20] Or is the problem really not with Bible testimony but the effectiveness of those who teach the Bible? For in evaluating the churches in England, extreme skepticism emerged. The following question was asked three ways: "Generally speaking, do you think that the Church in this country is giving adequate answers to:"[21]

man's spiritual needs?		problems of family life?		problems of society?	
Yes:	29%	Yes:	22%	Yes:	17%
No:	44%	No:	53%	No:	57%
Don't Know:	27%	Don't Know:	25%	Don't Know:	26%

If only a fourth see the Church as relevant in their lives, what kind of Christianity are they being taught? Certainly not the warm fellowship of the Saints surrounding every letter of Paul, certainly not the family leadership and the eternal convictions that ring in his New Testament words.

Latter-day Saints know that the Book of Mormon was revealed in the latter days "to the convincing of the Jew and Gentile that Jesus is the Christ" (title page). Latter-day Saints also know that in modern revelation God identified the trends just discussed and spoke through Joseph Smith "that faith also might increase in the earth" (D&C 1:21). Faithful Latter-day Saints identify with Paul's world missions because they are given the same world commission today. Paul testified of new revelation—that Christ was seen after his death and that his apostles received his commands through the Spirit. Paul also quoted earlier prophets accepted by the Jews and by thinking people around them. In such a way, Latter-day Saints testify to the new and justify through the old. Providentially, their headquarters is in a nation showing more healthy faith than the older countries that people left behind. An amazing number of people in the United States accept the Bible. Conservative churches make an issue out of "inerrancy," so the latest major survey was worded in this mode, but with striking results: "The Bible is the word of God and is not mistaken in its statements and teachings"—a full 42 percent in the United States agreed with that statement. And another 30 percent agreed with a less structured belief: "The Bible is the word of God but is sometimes mistaken in its statements and teachings." This means that the Bible has authoritative value for 72 percent of the people in the United States. Only 23 percent considered it a mere "collection of ancient religious philosophies."[22]

Missionaries should be aware of the strong faith of people in the United States and build upon it. A generation of Latter-day Saint Bible students should match the Bible believers in America. Few nations equal the United States in the warm generosity of its people, who contribute massive amounts to charity and still receive strangers with the hospitality descended from farm and frontier living. This is the hour to teach what the Bible says to a people who still believe in it. This does not mean that New Testament quotations will automatically change minds. A closed mind explains away evidence. A successful missionary, Brigham Young, said:

> I had only travelled a short time to testify to the people, before I learned this one fact, that you might prove doctrine from the Bible till doomsday, and it would merely convince a people, but would not convert them. You might read the Bible from Genesis to Revelations, and prove every iota that you advance, and that alone would have no converting influence upon the people. Nothing short of a testimony by the power of the Holy Ghost would bring light and knowledge to them— bring them in their hearts to repentance. Nothing short of that would ever do. You have frequently heard me say that I would rather hear an

Elder, either here or in the world, speak only five words accompanied by the power of God, and they would do more good than to hear long sermons without the Spirit. That is true, and we know it. [23]

Brigham Young does not downgrade use of the Bible, but warns against use of it without the Holy Ghost. Missionaries stress simple testimony, but capable investigators require evidence with that simple testimony. A nation of Bible believers needs a generation of missionaries able to show how the Bible points to the truth of the restored Church. If some can believe without Bible testimony, many, like John Taylor, must be led to the restored Church through it. There is no excuse for ignorance of Paul's message if a modern missionary wishes to reach all and not just part of those who hear him.

How well do people in the United States understand the Bible? They are sheep without shepherds but have deep religious feelings. About 89 percent in the United States is nominally Christian, with another 3 percent of the population Jewish, accepting the Old Testament. [24] Weekly church attendance in this country is 40 percent, a figure that has held stable for a decade, a figure twice that of England and Germany today. [25] An evidence of American faith is the responses to the question "How important is religion in life?" In the United States today, 55 percent answered "very important," with another 31 percent answering "fairly important." [26] The combined total of those who see religion as important is a little more than those who believe the Bible as basically an inspired book. So about three-fourths in the United States see religion as important and the Bible as a major source for it. Of course, there are degrees within statistics; within the 80 percent of Americans thinking religion important, there is a core of commitment—31 percent who say that religion is the "most important thing" in their lives. [27] The Lord told Paul at Corinth that he had "much people in this city" (Acts 18:10), and it is still true that "there are many yet on the earth . . . who are only kept from the truth because they know not where to find it" (D&C 123:12).

The big cities of the United States can match the worst of

Rome or Corinth in Paul's day. The movie and television industries foster that image abroad by exporting so many cheap plots. Yet United States beliefs show distinctive characteristics not only of strength but of stability over many years. Belief in God has held at 95 percent or higher over many decades.[28] United States belief in Christ has been sorted into the same general categories earlier discussed for Europe: "Do you think that Jesus Christ was God, another religious leader, like Muhammad or Buddha, or do you think that Jesus Christ never actually lived?" The percent saying "God" or "Son of God" was 81 percent in 1952, 75 percent in 1965, and 80 percent in 1978.[29] These figures show not only strong commitment, but the dip and rise shows continued religious search. The process of secularization has turned many Europeans to the state for security and happiness, accentuated by their "cradle to the grave" socialism. In the United States, most people think that life's problems will not be solved by legislation. Can religion "answer all or most of our present problems?" This is affirmed by a full 65 percent, a 1981 figure up from the 62 percent five years earlier. And 57 percent of Americans of college background agree with this position.[30] Well over a hundred years ago, Joseph Smith was consumed with the duty to present accurate religious facts to "all the rising generation, and to all the pure in heart" (D&C 123:11). What Paul called the "wisdom of this world" has failed to satisfy the sincere who are spread throughout that world. They are looking to true religion for answers today.

Paul's world and today's world have incredible parallels. This similarity opens the vision of spectacular growth for the restored gospel, a massive expansion on the model of Paul's establishing Christian strongholds in land after land. The "much people" seeking in Corinth were duplicated in a dozen locations where the book of Acts details Paul's preaching. These converts were obviously of the class who took religion seriously and were looking for answers. The first and the late twentieth centuries are both times of political and ideological transition, when people of high principles seek to replace their crumbling traditions with something more enduring. European distrust of the churches may have a positive side—a disillusionment not with true religion but with inherited ceremonialism and sterile religious bureaucracy. If someone had polled Jesus and the Twelve, they would have said that first century Judaism failed to meet "man's spiritual needs." Thus, the most religious often reject traditional religion. Western Europe is in an ideological holding pattern, culturally tied to its Protestant and Catholic heritage but not converted to it. Paul's Greek and Roman contemporaries had the same relationship to paganism. Temples were symbols of state stability, the centers of civic festivals. Thus, patriotism gave a certain vitality to public religion, even as private devotion waned. The historian Polybius was a captive Greek who wrote admiringly of the Roman system over a century before Paul, and he described how the senatorial class used mass religion as a tool for social morality, though they themselves did not believe in traditional gods. Paganism in Paul's day was vigorous, but the trend for the educated was distrust of traditional worship. (See list of religions in Paul's world on the next page.)

Greco-Roman religion blended belief in all the gods, and those rejecting it had three main options. First, there were temple traditions apart from animal sacrifice, which can be categorized as mystery religions. Their popularity escalated in Paul's century and the preceding one by offering adherents these benefits: "The object of the mystery cults was to secure salvation for men, who were subject to moral and physical evil. . . . It was effected by what may broadly be called sacramental means. By taking part in prescribed rites the worshipper became united with God, was enabled in this life to enjoy mystical communion with him, and further was assured of immortality beyond death. This process rested upon the experiences . . . of a Savior-God."[31]

Paganism had never offered immortality, traditionally the possession only of gods and heroes. Paganism reversed the Old Testament mandate by requiring sacrifice but not obedience. But mystery cults personalized religious covenants through temple drama, with the goal of immortality. This reached deeply into religious conscience and drew those in major cities and ports to the

Religions in Paul's World

Name	Strengths	Basic Beliefs
Traditional paganism	Large majority	Belief in all pagan gods State temple sacrifice No teaching on ethics or immortality Private offerings and prayers to gods Popular belief in immortality of the soul
Mystery religions	Small minority	Myth of special deities Secret initiation rites Promise of immortality Ethical duties
Stoicism	Majority of the educated	Reason exists beyond the gods Man must submit to divine reason Some belief in survival of the soul Periodic cycles of destruction Ethical duty of highest good
Epicureanism	Small minority of the educated	Gods exist but are irrelevant No survival of soul at death Ethical duty of highest "happiness"
Judaism	Minority— maximum of 10% of Roman Empire	Strict monotheism Circumcision and duty to the Law Periodic visits to Jerusalem Temple Belief in coming Messiah Ethical duty to righteous life
Judaic sympathizers	Small minority in synagogues	Belief in monotheism Perhaps belief in coming Messiah Ethical commitment to righteous life

mysteries of the goddess Isis, Egyptian in origin, and, in Paul's century, to the god Mithras, Persian in origin. Athens had long had access to the nearby Eleusinian mysteries, from which Nero withdrew in fear at the announcement of the solemnity of the coming ceremony. Obviously, secret details are known by chance descriptions, inscriptions, and the archaeology of temples of mystery religions, and enough is known to see how profound needs were met that were unfulfilled in regular sacrificial religion.

A second replacement for paganism was Stoicism. It was named for a covered porch (*stoá* in Greek) where its founder Zeno taught in Athens three centuries before Paul. Zeno and his contemporary Epicurus both reacted to paganism in terms of the meaning of life and the question of immortality, the existence of the gods, and the moral duty of man. Zeno rationalized the gods into a system, seeing reason as the practical force behind all. Man's main duty was *duty*—putting himself into harmony with his intrinsic destiny. Since this was also a basic ideal of Roman religion and literature, Stoicism flourished to become the majority view of the governing classes of Paul's day. Stoicism spoke of cycles and periodic destruction in cosmic fire, but Stoics from Paul's time strongly hinted at the survival of the soul. Popular religion included the practice of grave offerings to the souls of the dead, and surviving gravestones show widespread belief in some kind of survival of loved ones, though many inscriptions reject hope and bluntly admit the total termination of life in death. Epicurus also taught the latter, making personal obliteration a negative triumph over pain and infirmity. The Epicureans were a minority philosophy for the educated of Paul's time, perpetuating the founder's theory that gods existed but paid no attention to mankind. But both Stoicism and Epicureanism joined in upholding the Greek philosophy of the disciplined life, one dedicated to seek happiness (not cheap pleasure) through willpower and wise actions.[32] Thus, when Paul stood before Stoics and Epicureans at Athens (as Acts 17 describes), he capitalized on their rejection of religion but declared a physical immortality unknown to their thought.

If Greek philosophers had some empathy for Paul's position, only the Jews were Paul's forerunners. They were providentially placed in that role, though their conservatives detested this man who preached fulfillment of their scriptures. An unwilling voice preparing for the religion of the Lord, they were also a third reforming element in Paul's religious world. Religion and philosophy gradually reached toward monotheism, but the Jews stood as direct witnesses of Jehovah in every vital city throughout the Roman empire. Rome and Alexandria probably had a million people in each, with large Jewish populations. The third Mediterranean city was Antioch, with a population of perhaps eight hundred thousand, with an estimated 20 percent Jewish. The record of Paul's preaching rarely discloses a city without a synagogue. The dispersion of the Jews came from the earlier captivity by Babylon and by later resettlement for commercial gain. Thus, congregations were spread throughout the western world, meeting weekly to honor God and prepare for the Messiah. Expectation was high, for in the hinterland of Asia Minor, Paul mentioned without explanation how John the Baptist recently came to testify of the nearness of the Messiah: "I am not he; but behold, there comes one after me, the sandals of whose feet I am not worthy to loose" (Acts 13:25, NKJB). Jews abroad kept close ties with Jerusalem, partly because the faithful traveled to the temple for the great feasts of Passover, Pentecost, and Tabernacles. Thus, the deep expectation of the Messiah, intensified by John, was dry bark into which the sparks of Paul's testimony fell. Believing Christians today are not in a different situation, for threatening world catastrophe makes vivid the judgments that Christ promised before his second coming. And Latter-day Saints ask pointedly, will a loving God not raise up prophets to warn and ready every faithful person for these great events?

Ancient Judaism was leaven, permeating the world and stimulating serious thought toward God. Its synagogues preselected faithful Jews but also thoughtful Gentiles who sought Moses' morality and the God who transcends mythology. Ancient sources, including the New Testament, show two types of

Gentile affiliation. First, there were full converts, who took the burden of ceremonialism, including circumcision for males. The Pentecostal pilgrims were "Jews and proselytes" from all lands ringing the Mediterranean (Acts 2:10). As the plain preaching divided the Asia Minor synagogues, "many of the Jews and religious proselytes followed Paul" (Acts 13:43). "Proselytes" came from a wider circle of Gentile worshippers not burdened by the law, and Paul included all in the synagogue by addressing "men of Israel, and you who fear God" (Acts 13:16, NKJB). These uncircumcised "God-fearers" are also designated by a Greek term broadly meaning "religious," which is also translated "devout" and "worshippers" in the King James Version. Paul's Jewish preaching is sprinkled with references to these principled people who affiliated with the synagogue. In northern Greece the apostle's message of Christ brought fierce opposition, but there was also belief of "some" Jews and "of the devout Greeks a great multitude, and of the chief women not a few" (Acts 17:4). These Jewish sympathizers were not always on Paul's side, as earlier when persecution arose, because "the Jews stirred up the devout and honourable women, and the chief men of the city" (Acts 13:50). Thus, Jewish preaching generally included this wider audience. At Athens Paul first met "in the synagogue with the Jews, and with the devout persons" (Acts 17:17).

These sincere seekers of Paul's world should remind Latter-day Saints how many honest in heart are today found waiting in all places of worship. Ancient wickedness and shallowness was one layer of society, but there were others of straighter grain and strength.

The history of mankind holds ages of faith. Republican Rome was religiously solid, and Medieval culture was confident of its convictions. On the other hand, there are ages of doubt and troubled questioning. The first century moved from skepticism to positive replacements of its old creeds. Deeper religions and new philosophies were gaining ground. The twentieth century is also such a world. Skepticism for its own sake is not respected by the thoughtful. They have watched science long enough to value it for what it can do, and they do not pretend that it can solve the moral problems of mankind. When traditions and values were anciently challenged, Christianity gave strong answers, and the restored gospel offers the same in this age of doubt. The gospel that revolutionized the ancient world did not come from the political capitals or the intellectual centers. Instead, it was revealed to prophets rising above "the wisdom of the world," for God has "chosen the foolish things of the world to confound the wise" (1 Cor. 1:27).

God's preparation of the world is plain in the first spread of Christianity. Paul's biography is an awesome illustration of the efforts of many, known and unknown, to carry out Christ's commission to preach the gospel to "all nations" (Matt. 28:19). And where there is God's will there is God's way. The political system furnished more security, and the economic system allowed more effective communication, than was available in the centuries before Christianity's spread. Rome's civil wars had ended as Augustus bested Anthony and Cleopatra in 31 B.C. (See coin of Augustus on next page.) Grandnephew and political heir of Julius Caesar, Augustus founded the imperial system by shrewd use of power and wise restraint. The empire was a potential dictatorship, as careers of the worst first century emperors show. But Augustus and his wiser successors carefully ruled by Roman due process, the closest thing to extended constitutional government that the ancient world knew. Moreover, the empire was a political system of experienced civil servants, so that the moral breakdown of an emperor did not generally disturb the fair government of the provinces. Augustus left his own political autobiography with instructions to engrave it on the entrance pillars to his mausoleum. A combination of his achievements and his aspirations, the long testament has language like this: "I extended the boundaries of all the provinces which were bordered by races not yet subject to our empire. The provinces of the Gauls, the Spains, and Germany . . . I reduced to a state of peace."[33] He wove this major design into this document, stressing the triple closing of the temple of Janus in his lifetime, an event honoring peace that had

COIN OF AUGUSTUS

Augustus, founder of the Roman Empire and ruler from 31 B.C. to A.D. 14. He was the adopted heir of Julius Caesar. His coin inscription reads, "Caesar Augustus, Divi F[ilius], Pater Patriae." This translates, "Caesar Augustus, Son of the Deified Caesar, Father of His Country." Gold aureus in National Museum, Naples; photo in Laura Breglia, *Roman Imperial Coins* (N.Y.: Praeger, 1968), p. 39.

occurred only "twice in all since the foundation of the city."[34] Moreover, he added, the senate had honored him with the altar to "Augustan peace" (*pax Augusta*).[35] Modern archaeologists have dug it up and have repositioned its dramatic symbols of security and prosperity—Augustus' expression of gratitude for the blessings of heaven upon the new empire, its leaders, and its people.

This propaganda was true for the citizens of the inner empire, as shown in the letters of Peter and Paul that gave their government credit for being divinely blessed. If Augustan peace was not absolute, at least civil strife ended and war was exported to the frontiers. Paul traveled some thirteen thousand miles in Roman territory with less danger of bloodshed than one could meet in the same lands today. Rome's economic lifeline was tied to Egyptian grain, so shipping lanes were clear and travel largely secure. The sea was in the middle of the lands (the meaning of "Mediterranean"), giving easy access that would have been impossible on a landlocked continent. And peace stimulated Roman commerce, making travel easier and cheaper than ever before. Most of Paul's missionary miles were traveled by the relatively fast ships of that time. In addition to peace and the efficiency of travel, Paul's mission was eased by the common language, Greek. Paul was divinely called to leave his base of operations in the Near East and carry the gospel ever westward. Three centuries before, the brilliant Alexander the Great felt divinely impelled to march from Greece ever eastward until he had spread Greek troops and traders throughout the Near East. Politically, Alexander was a brilliant meteor, extinguished after an awesome trajectory. But his generals stabilized Greek dynasties around the eastern Mediterranean, so his real conquest was cultural, establishing Greek as the world language. Rome issued its decrees to that part of the world in Greek, a language also exported westward by trade. Paul's missions and letters to converts would have been impossible without this international language.

This chapter has quickly reviewed Paul's world. Paul's world doubted its pagan heritage and actively sought new answers; it was sprinkled liberally with Jewish centers, where the message about the Messiah was best understood; it was peaceful, with smoothly working transportation and an international language. Many historians, generally a fact-bound and unsentimental lot, are forced to ask how such a combination of favorable circumstances for the spread of Christ's gospel could come about by chance. Was it an accident that Paul was the right man at the right time with the right message? And is it for no purpose now that man's power to spread ideas has never been greater?

NOTES

1. See David B. Barrett, *World Christian Encyclopedia* (Oxford: Oxford University Press, 1982), p. 4.

2. Compare ibid., p. 865, Global Map 1.

3. Ibid., p. 796.

4. Ibid., p. 394.

5. *Emerging Trends*, vol. 4, no. 6 (June 1982), p. 5. (Published by Princeton Religion Research Center, Princeton, N.J.)

6. Barrett, p. 314.

7. *Der Spiegel*, Dec. 24, 1979, p. 71. Compare the source cited at note 5 above, which agrees with the 20 percent weekly attendance figure, but has 53 percent for "several times a year" and 24 percent for "less often or never."

8. Ibid., cited with thanks to BYU German Professor Marvin H. Folsom.

9. Ibid.

10. Ibid.

11. Renate Koecher, "The Alienation of Young People from the Church," unpublished news release from the Allensbach Institute of Demoscopy, Allensbach, Germany, p. 7 of the translation of Gordon Whiting, BYU communications professor, who generously shared this study.

12. Oral comment of former Ricks College teacher Edna Ricks.

13. Koecher, trans. Whiting, p. 15.

14. Ibid., pp. 16-17.

15. Barrett, p. 699.

16. 1982 source cited in note 5 above.

17. *Emerging Trends*, vol. 3, no. 6 (June 1981).

18. Ibid.

19. *Emerging Trends*, vol. 3, no. 5 (May 1981), p. 3.

20. *Emerging Trends*, vol. 3, no. 6 (June 1981). The chart incorrectly prints the 34 percent "fables" figure, which is given clearly in the introductory sentence.

21. *Emerging Trends*, vol. 3, no. 9 (Nov. 1981), p. 4.

22. Gallup Poll sponsored by *Christianity Today* and reported in part in the issue of June 6, 1980, p. 32.

23. *Journal of Discourses* 5:327, also cited in John A. Widtsoe, ed., *Discourses of Brigham Young* (Salt Lake City: Deseret Book Co., 1977), p. 330.

24. Barrett, p. 711.

25. *Religion in America, 1981*, Gallup Organization Report no. 184 (Jan. 1981), p. 32.

26. Ibid., p. 39.

27. Ibid.

28. The 1968 figure was 98 percent. See *Religion in America, 1971*, Gallup Organization Report no. 70. Compare the 95 percent "yes" by U.S. teenagers to the question "Do You Believe in God or a universal spirit?" George Gallup, Jr., and David Poling, *The Search for America's Faith* (Nashville, Tenn.: Abingdon Press, 1980, App. A). Compare ibid., end of appendix, for those who pray to God, 92 percent in 1952 and 1965 and still 89 percent in 1978.

29. Ibid.

30. *Religion in America, 1981*, p. 53.

31. C. K. Barrett, *The New Testament Background: Selected Documents* (New York: Harper and Row, 1961), p. 91.

32. See ibid., pp. 61-75, for a sampling of Stoic and Epicurean writings.

33. Frederick W. Shipley (trans.), *Res Gestae Divi Augusti* ("The Acts of Augustus," Loeb Classical Library) 5:26.

34. Ibid., 2:13.

35. Ibid., 2:12.

2

Paul's Preparation: "Fire on the Earth"

"Before I formed you in the womb I knew you, before you were born I set you apart; I appointed you as a prophet to the nations" (Jer. 1:5, NIV). Paul, the former Pharisee, easily recalled God's words to Jeremiah, and so he used parallel language about his call from God, "who separated me from my mother's womb" (Gal. 1:15). That "separation" was Paul's life mission, related to his call to the Gentile mission. The Lord said to the prophets and teachers of the Church in Antioch, "Separate me Barnabus and Saul [Paul] for the work whereunto I have called them" (Acts 13:2). Several modern versions give a freer translation suggesting a premortal existence: God "set me apart before I was born" (Gal. 1:15, RSV). Christian interpreters do not have the vision of man's pre-earth life, so in their view Jeremiah before birth was merely "a thought in the mind of God."[1] But Jewish and Christian traditions were far more literal. Philo lived in Paul's day and, like Paul, was a cultured Israelite in a Gentile city. This Alexandrian Jew said that souls "descended" into bodies and that the faithful would leave the earth and go "back to the place from whence they came."[2] Joseph Smith boldly taught, "Every man who has a calling to minister to the inhabitants of the world, was ordained to that very purpose in the grand council of heaven before this world was."[3] Much of Paul's language fits this restored concept of premortal life and calling.

"Fire on the earth" is the theme of Paul's early manhood. The Lord used this unfamiliar phrase (Luke 12:49) to describe the difficulty accepting his gospel, church, and values in the face of hostility from loved ones. "Do you think that I have come to give peace on earth? No, I tell you, but rather division" (Luke 12:51, RSV). We know little of the reaction of Paul's family to his conversion, but much of the reaction of his people. They treated him just as he treated Christians before he became one. At the exodus the Jewish religion and state were one, and corporal punishment continued in the later synagogues for many infractions of Jewish law. Paul was not yet converted when the Lord warned the Twelve before their mission to Israel, "They will deliver you up to the councils, and they will scourge you in their synagogues" (Matt. 10:17). The Lord also prophesied that Jewish leaders would take Christian "prophets" in the synagogues and drive them "from city to city" (Matt. 23:34). That language well summarizes Paul's first two missionary journeys described in Acts.

Fiery conflict followed Paul not only in missionary labors but in Church leadership. Jews and Jewish converts, feeling betrayed by Paul's modification of their traditions, sought to undermine the leadership of the "apostle of the Gentiles" (Rom. 11:13). Finally, false accusations reached the state, which unjustly executed him. The great apostle was fervent, but for good reason: "Necessity is laid upon me; yea, woe is unto me, if I preach not the gospel" (1 Cor. 9:16). Paul cannot easily be understood without accepting the supernatural knowledge that he claimed. As he remarked, the life of ease was as available to him as to others, yet he chose to risk danger "every hour" (1 Cor. 15:30). Paul was not some distorted soul who thrived on conflict, for he penned sensitive lines on love and displayed constructive relationships with his friends in the faith and beyond. He faced outer conflict because of the inner fire of conviction. His sacrifices convincingly show the reality of his divine visions.

This devoted convert was trained both to know the Jewish community outside Israel and to move easily in Gentile society. His credentials gave him immediate avenues of communication, as shown by his statement at his arrest in the temple riot that he was "a Jew of Tarsus . . . a citizen of no mean city" (Acts 21:39).

In Greek that is "no insignificant city," a label used in ancient literature for a place with distinguishing marks. Tarsus could boast of its size, commercial importance, and educational tradition. The largest city in its province, its fame compared well with the two dozen provincial centers of the empire. River and harbor developments gave Tarsus a sea trade, and it stood squarely on the east-west land route, which wound out of the nearby rock-walled canyon called the "Cilician Gates," the way through the Taurus Mountains. Xenophon, who, before Paul, marched east with a hired Greek army, labeled Tarsus "a large and prosperous city,"[4] and nothing altered that situation for centuries. Biographies of Paul comment on its "university," a misleading term, for ancient culture favored private schools and private tutors. Strabo, the geographer of Paul's world who knew the Near East well, commented that in Tarsus were "all kinds of schools of rhetoric."[5] His educational ideal was clearly the ancient blending of philosophy, literature, and eloquence. It is tempting to associate Paul's verbal ability with such training, for Strabo comments on "that facility prevalent among the Tarsians whereby [one] could instantly speak offhand and unceasingly on any given subject."[6] But Paul's speeches and writings are far from standard orations filled with flattery and classical allusions. The above environment simply influenced him in the same way that intelligent people are exposed to excellence in their culture. Paul no doubt heard able men in public and thus set a high standard of capability for himself in speech and writing. Since Tarsus exported educated teachers, this no doubt influenced Paul's preparatory schools and tutors. Paul's writing is correct, articulate, and informed.

In antiquity, educated people came from families able to pay for education. At the temple riot, the tribune who rescued Paul was stunned that Paul spoke Greek, which showed Paul's level in Jerusalem. Soon he was to be examined under the lash, but he cut that treatment short with the question, "Is it lawful for you to scourge a man that is a Roman, and uncondemned?" (Acts 22:25.) This immediately brought the commanding officer, who heard Paul insist, "I was free born" (Acts 22:28). How Paul's family acquired citizenship interests biographers, but there are no firm answers to this secondary issue. Likely someone had given Rome needed support in influence or money, which focuses on what citizenship tells about Paul and what it did for him. Like education, citizenship was a social distinction reaching down to the upper middle class in the first century. Citizenship protected Paul in his ministry, as we have just seen when Paul successfully demanded a fair hearing before punishment. Earlier in northern Greece he was beaten under protest but successfully demanded an official apology (Acts 16:37-39). Such confrontations suggest that Paul's effectiveness in any city stemmed partly from his confidence in fair protection of the law. Another feature of Roman citizenship is known to a generation that has seen the U.S. Supreme Court overturn local courts to uphold civil and criminal rights. Provincial governors could be brought to account for unfairness, and thus Paul was allowed an appeal to Rome after his Jerusalem arrest.

Discussing Tarsus and Roman citizenship is not a digression, since Paul would not have been Paul without their impact on his work. The same is true of his Jewish heritage. At his Jerusalem arrest he spoke Greek to the centurion and then turned to address the crowd "in the Hebrew tongue" (Acts 21:40). In subsequent speeches he defended himself as "a Pharisee, the son of a Pharisee" (Acts 23:6) and called the Pharisees the "strictest" party in Judaism (Acts 26:5, NKJB). Recent committee translations agree on that term, which means "most exact" or "most careful" in this context. The Mishnah, the Jewish law written down about A.D. 200, preserves the thinking of the Pharisees, whose fundamental tradition was, "Be deliberate in judgment, raise up many disciples, and make a fence around the Law."[7] Thus, Paul walked in the path of his father and of the fathers of his people, who sought to protect the Mosaic code, which was the central "Law." Josephus, a young Pharisee who lived at the time of Paul, explains, "The Pharisees had passed on to the people certain regulations handed down by former generations and not recorded in the Laws of Moses."[8] The Mishnah summarizes these rules about rules, condensing and compacting them into some eight hundred pages in the standard English translation. The Pharisees studied definition, analogy of one commandment to another, and weight of authority of great rabbis and their schools. For Jesus Christ, the process had gone too far, as he accused the Pharisees of cluttering the meaning of God's greatest commandments: "Ye hold the tradition of men, as the washing of pots and cups, and many other such like things ye do. . . . Ye reject the commandment of God, that ye may keep your own tradition" (Mark 7:8-9). But the young Paul did not yet know the meaning of such words.

Paul leaves no doubt about his orthodox training: "Circumcised the eighth day, of the stock of Israel, of the tribe of Benjamin, an Hebrew of the Hebrews; as touching the law, a Pharisee" (Philip. 3:5). His parents obviously had pride in their heritage, as shown by their naming him "Saul" after the first king of Israel, the most brilliant star of Benjamin. In Acts this is Paul's proper name before he gave his life to the Gentile missions.[9] The Mishnah outlines the education of the orthodox boy, who began studying scripture at five and advanced Rabbinical interpretation at fifteen.[10] Paul went from Tarsus to Jerusalem; when arrested there, he reviewed his training: "Born in Tarsus . . . yet brought up in this city at the feet of Gamaliel, and taught according to the perfect manner of the law of the fathers" (Acts 22:3). Tarsus itself broadened Paul, for Jews of the dispersion knew many sincere people outside their faith. And in Jerusalem Paul studied with a rabbi whose character shows a combination of devotedness and breadth. Grandson of Hillel, whose teaching also combined these elements, he towers in the early Mishnah tradition: "When Rabban Gamaliel the Elder died, the glory of the Law ceased, and purity and abstinence died."[11] And when the Sanhedrin was close to sentencing the apostles to death, "a Pharisee named Gamaliel" arose, "a doctor of the law, had in reputation among all people" (Acts 5:34). His advice was blunt—impostors will fall of their own weight, but religious leaders cannot risk fighting "against God" (Acts 5:39). This event poses searching but unanswerable questions.

Gamaliel's tolerance for Christian leaders was not long after the crucifixion. Was he also a member of the Sanhedrin that condemned Jesus? Since he surely heard Jesus sometime, had he been so shaken by Jesus' manhood that he entertained the possibility of godhood? An inner-circle Pharisee, he knew many resurrection stories behind the public testimony of Peter and John. And where was Paul during these events? And did he ask Gamaliel about his cautious tolerance of Christian leaders? Paul was born about the beginning of the Christian era, since Acts calls him a "young man" when Stephen was stoned about A.D. 33 (Acts 7:58).[12] His formal study under Gamaliel would fall before A.D. 20, long before Jesus' public ministry began. Paul nowhere hints that he saw or heard the earthly Jesus. Perhaps he was pursuing family and business interests at Tarsus during the ministry of the Lord. Perhaps he was called to Jerusalem afterward for his religious commitment and skill in practical affairs. Was he nominated by a troubled Gamaliel?

Paul's credentials illuminate the debated question of his marriage. He is mislabeled a bachelor or chauvinist, for careful study of 1 Corinthians strongly suggests his marriage. There are three elements of this problem in Paul's early life: the Jewish ideal of marriage as a religious duty; Paul's obedience to every possible Jewish duty; Paul's acceptance into high Jewish councils. The last point is often stated as though Paul was a member of the highest Jewish council, the Sanhedrin, whose members supposedly were married. Yet the evidence for marriage of Sanhedrin members is the same as for any other successful Israelite—religious and cultural conformity. Wisdom and trustworthiness came only through marriage; in the time of the Mishnah "an unmarried man may not be a teacher of children."[13] The Mishnah includes marriage in the life pattern of the male, who was fit "at eighteen for the bride chamber."[14] No one could fault Paul for disobedience to any commandment, he insisted, "touching the righteousness which is in the law, blameless" (Philip. 3:6). In Paul's view, no one exceeded him in keeping every requirement, none of his "peers" or "equals of age," the key term in his autobiographical survey—"I advanced in Judaism beyond many of my own age among my people, so extremely zealous was I for the traditions of my fathers" (Gal. 1:14, RSV). Since he had done everything right in his religion up to that point, he must have been married.

Against accused Christians Paul gave his "voice," a Greek word meaning "vote," as modern translations recognize (Acts 26:10). But the full Sanhedrin would not supervise details of Christian persecutions, so Paul's vote is probably that of a trusted assistant in small executive sessions. As mentioned, he was then a "young man" (Acts 7:58), which must be put in the Jewish context of thirty for temple service and mature status in the Dead Sea community. The Mishnah lists the age of "twenty for pursuing [a calling]," an age when Paul might have terminated his Jerusalem studies and returned to Tarsus for business. The Mishnah continues with "thirty for authority," a point after which Paul might be called to Jerusalem to meet the Christian threat as thousands of Jews converted to Christianity after the Crucifixion (Acts 2:41; 4:4). But the "young man" reference contradicts the idea of Paul as an elder statesman; the Sanhedrin member would be middle aged on the Mishnah's maturity scale. There, a man is ready "at forty for discernment, at fifty for counsel, at sixty for to be an elder."[15]

Paul represented the Sanhedrin's inner circle, as he said of his power as persecutor "in Jerusalem"—"and many of the saints did I shut up in prison, having received authority from the chief priests . . . and I punished them oft in every synagogue" (Acts 26:10-11). Years before, the Savior warned his first apostles of the misplaced zeal of oppressors: "The hour is coming when whoever kills you will think he is offering service to God" (John 16:2, RSV). That is just how Paul explains himself—he carefully concluded that duty required persecution of Jesus' disciples (Acts 26:9); out of "zeal" for God, he persecuted Christians (Philip. 3:6). He later obtained forgiveness, he said, because he had persecuted "ignorantly in unbelief" (1 Tim. 1:13). He was a formidable foe, using every tool except moderation (Gal. 1:13). He forced some to renounce their faith (Acts 26:11), but many firmly faced pain and punishment because of their inner certainty. Short of the death penalty, the Romans freely allowed Jewish councils the right to discipline as a sort of common law. This meant that Paul supervised investigation, interrogation, and sentencing. Of this last role, he says, "I imprisoned and beat" the believers "in every synagogue" (Acts 22:19). Moses had allowed a maximum of forty stripes (Deut. 25:1-3), and the Mishnah shows that such punishment was widely used for a variety of legal transgressions, including breaking vows. The Gospels also portray Jesus as close to stoning for blasphemy on more than one occasion, and Paul was an official observer at the unauthorized execution of Stephen, for the crowd took Stephen from the council "out of the city, and stoned him, and the witnesses laid down their clothes at a young man's feet, whose name was Saul" (Acts 7:58). Luke thus introduces Paul into the Christian story, significantly not with a vision, but with the persecution before the vision.

What visible effect did these experiences have on young Paul? Perhaps little, for his journey to Damascus to continue Christian punishment came afterward. But the inner story, if largely untold, is not to be avoided. Paul was a feeling, caring man. With intellectual certainty he faced men and women who wrote their spiritual certainty in discomfort, pain, and blood. At his first vision, Paul was told that it was hard for him "to kick against the pricks" (Acts 26:14), the last word referring to the sharp jab of the pointed stick against which balky animals fought. So Paul was resisting spiritual impressions prior to his Damascus vision. He had heard Stephen's testimony before his death: "Behold, I see the heavens opened, and the Son of man standing on the right hand of God" (Acts 7:56). Saul was prepared not by the mere mechanics of emotional reversal, but by the direct example of Stephen's vision. Not yet digesting the significance of what he had seen, Paul continued "breathing out threatenings and slaughter" (Acts 9:1). He started for Damascus with written authority from the high priest to bring Jewish Christians back to Jerusalem for judgment, whether men or women (Acts 9:2). The 150-mile journey took about a week, and David O. McKay saw Paul's conscience weighing the correctness of his course and Paul reviewing his impressions of Stephen.[16] Nearing Damascus at high noon, Paul saw the brilliant light, a celestial power not confined to Paul, for he said, "They that were with me saw indeed the light, and were afraid" (Acts 22:9).[17] But only Paul was struck to the heart by the sight of the glorious Christ, and the core account of the message is preserved in Paul's words in Acts: "And I fell to the ground and heard a voice saying to me, 'Saul, Saul, why are you persecuting Me?' And I answered, 'Who are You, Lord?' And He said to me, 'I am Jesus of Nazareth, whom you are persecuting.' . . . And I said, 'What shall I do, Lord?' And the Lord said to me, 'Arise and go into Damascus, and there you will be told all things which are appointed for you to do.' And since I could not see for the glory of that light, being led by the hand of those who were with me, I came into Damascus" (Acts 22:7-11, NKJB).

All three accounts of Paul's vision make clear that he not only experienced the voice and the light, but that he saw the Lord. "I have appeared to you," the Lord said during the vision (Acts 26:16, NKJB). The first Acts account says the same, as Ananias gave Paul his blessing in the name of "the Lord Jesus, who appeared to you on the road as you came" (Acts 9:17, NKJB). And Paul heard Ananias saying that Paul was called to know God's will "and see the Just One, and hear the voice of his mouth" (Acts 22:14, NKJB). Like Joseph Smith, Paul did not tell all the details of this profound experience at any one time. Years later, in the situation where his Gentile ministry was in question, Paul recalled how the Lord also outlined his mission to the non-Jewish "nations": "But rise and stand upon your feet; for I have appeared to you for this purpose, to appoint you to serve and bear witness to the things in which you have seen me and to those in which I will appear to you, delivering you from the people and from the Gentiles—to whom I send you to open their eyes, that they may turn from darkness to light and from the power of Satan to God, that they may receive forgiveness of sins and a place among those who are sanctified by faith in me" (Acts 26:16-18, RSV).

With such favor from the Lord, how did Paul relate to the existing Church? He did not resemble the revivalist, Bible-appointed or claiming to be God-appointed without affiliation with others earlier authorized by God. In Jesus' parable of the early and late workers, each group waited in the marketplace until the Lord called them to join the laborers already in the vineyard (Matt. 20:1-16). Although Paul talked personally with Christ, an independent revelation to his leader Ananias authorized the new convert's baptism and preaching. Christ did not first tell Paul to preach, but to go to his Church and get instruction. After Ananias laid his hands on Paul, healing his temporary blindness, Paul "was baptized" (Acts 9:18). Thus Paul was obedient to Christ's Church and its requirements. Soon he began to build up what he tried to tear down. Paul was then over thirty, and there lay before him three decades of labor, persecution, and at last martyrdom. Why did this brilliant and successful young Jew forsake the world and its rewards? All of his life he gave but one answer: "Have I not seen Jesus Christ, our Lord?" (1 Cor. 9:1).

The book of Acts highlights Paul's achievements, but one must piece together years of preparation before Christ's words would be fulfilled concerning his primary mission to "the Gentiles" (Acts 26:17). The Greek term *éthnos* is usually "Gentiles" in the plural, though often it is given its primary meaning of "nations"; occasionally it is translated as "heathen." Throughout the King James Old Testament these same terms translate the Hebrew *gôy*. These English renditions reflect just one concept for ancient Christians and Jews—that of the non-Israelite peoples. Isaiah repeatedly spoke of Jehovah's strange work to enlighten "the nations." Paul would be a pathfinder in this extended drama, but the Lord tempered him first in the fires of conflict. Acts portrays the young Pharisee as eager and able, for "immediately" (Acts 9:20, RSV) he "preached Christ in the synagogues" (Acts 9:20). Acts pictures the work with the Gentiles unfolding after this. Paul's early missionary success brought such Jewish antagonism that he had to be let down over the Damascus wall at night to save his life. Some biographies romanticize Paul as meditating for a long period after conversion, but Acts leaves no room for this. Paul's days of quiet study were long over; he summed up his years after conversion: "I laboured more abundantly than they all" (1 Cor. 15:10). The meditation image comes from one phrase about Paul's post-conversion labors: "I went into Arabia, and returned again unto Damascus" (Gal. 1:17). But "Arabia" need only mean the Damascus and transjordan areas, probably controlled then by the Nabatean kings at Petra. No source mentions remote Arabia or mentions any other activity than proclaiming the gospel. Then, after "three years," Paul "went up to Jerusalem to see Peter, and abode with him fifteen days; but other of the apostles saw I none, save James, the Lord's brother" (Gal. 1:18-19). Since this language was written after A.D. 50, Paul evidently refers to James' later calling as an apostle. These were the first of many interviews with the brethren who had walked with the Lord. In the speeches of Acts and in 1 Corinthians, Paul gives many details of Jesus' last night with the apostles, of his trial, crucifixion, and resurrection. He knew all this long before any Gospel was written. Thus, Paul had the double strength of knowledge from Christ's revelations and from conversations with the earlier apostles.

Paul's meeting with Peter dramatizes the centralized leadership of the Church. Paul had labored years in an outlying area and then counseled with two of the three presiding apostles, the acknowledged "pillars" of the Church along with John (Gal. 2:9). Paul's forthrightness in Jerusalem took him to the edge of martyrdom, for he spoke "boldly in the name of the Lord Jesus, and disputed against the Grecians, but they went about to slay him" (Acts 9:29). This is clearly the same group that engineered Stephen's death (Acts 6:9). None of that mattered to Paul, but it mattered to the Lord and his apostles that Paul stay alive to testify outside of Israel. While Paul prayed in the temple, he again saw the Lord, who commanded: "Make haste and get out of Jerusalem quickly, for they will not receive your testimony concerning me" (Acts 22:18, NKJB). Even then Paul could not easily drop the logic of preaching to those who were acquainted with his zeal for God, and that explains why this second vision was necessary. Telling the Lord

Paul's Recorded Visions

Estimated Year (A.D.)	Source	Who or What Seen	Purpose
33	Acts 9, 22, 26	Christ near Damascus	Paul's conversion; direction to go to the Church
36	Acts 22:17-21	Christ in Jerusalem Temple	Direction to leave Jerusalem for Gentile areas
43	2 Cor. 12:1-4	"Third heaven" and "Paradise"	Comfort in persecutions; possibly confirmation of call to apostleship
49	Acts 16:9-10	Man from Macedonia	Direction to preach in northern Greece
50	Acts 18:9-10	Christ at Corinth	Direction to remain in southern Greece
58	Acts 23:11	Christ in Jerusalem fortress	Comfort in imprisonment; direction for Roman visit
60	Acts 27:23-24	An "angel of God"	Promise of safety in shipwreck; preparation to stand "before Caesar"

how impressed the Jews would be with the change of the former persecutor, Paul was corrected with the command, "Depart: for I will send you far hence unto the Gentiles" (Acts 22:21). Yet the full Gentile missions were still years away, and the complete fulfillment of that prophecy would wait on Paul's growth through accepting the Lord's assignments. In the meantime, the "Ananias principle" was still at work, for the converted Jew still needed lessons on asking instead of telling the Lord. His temple vision did not show Paul where to go, but it prepared him for the inspired decision that Church leaders now gave him. Acts frequently calls presiding priesthood leaders "brethren," and in this first Jerusalem visit, they are "the apostles" that Paul first came to (Acts 9:27). Because these "brethren" knew the threats on Paul's life, "they brought him down to Caesarea, and sent him forth to Tarsus" (Acts 9:30). Paul's first three years of missionary labors had been under Damascus authorities, who were to tell Paul "all things which are appointed for you to do" (Acts 22:10, NKJB). Later, the apostles supervised Paul's further assignments, since they "sent him forth to Tarsus" (Acts 9:30). At the beginning and end of every major mission thereafter, Paul had contact with the Twelve. He was indeed a bright star shining throughout the Church, but he was nevertheless a part of the constellation of leaders. Paul's direction by God included direction through God's earthly priesthood authorities.

What did Paul do in his post-conversion years in Tarsus? The time span is known, and that he did missionary work is probable. Paul said that after his Jerusalem visit he "came into the regions of Syria and Cilicia" (Gal. 1:21). This fits the Tarsus stay and the Antioch ministry in Acts, since Cilicia and Syria were headed by these two cities. Paul later visited the Cilician churches (Acts 15:41), and their most likely establishment was during Paul's Tarsus stay. The chronological chart in the appendix shows that Paul was in Tarsus for up to five years, no doubt a period of faithful labor at his assignment, one of growth through untold sacrifices and persecutions. Paul's intense desire to share the gospel, which nearly brought his death at Jerusalem, surely continued powerfully in these years. Later, he summed up his life of danger and persecution to the Corinthians, reaching back to the Damascus years in his survey (2 Cor. 11:32-33). In Paul's list we can identify his stoning (Acts 14:19) and one beating (Acts 16:22-23), but the remaining ten torments are elsewhere unrecorded. Since Acts gives great detail on Paul after this period, some of these difficulties must have come at Tarsus and Antioch: "Five times I have received at the hands of the Jews the forty lashes less one; three times I have been beaten with rods; once I was stoned; three times I have been shipwrecked; a night and a day I have been adrift at sea" (2 Cor. 11:24-25, RSV). The instructions to the judges supplement the memory of the prisoner, for the Mishnah describes Jewish punishment. As mentioned earlier, the Old Testament maximum was forty stripes, and to avoid a mistake, thirty-nine were authorized. Paul would have received these lashes in the synagogue, since the Gospels mention this practice (Matt. 10:17). The Mishnah describes what Paul suffered:

> How do they scourge him? They bind his two hands to a pillar on either side, and the minister of the synagogue lays hold on his garments . . . so that he bares his chest. A stone is set down behind him on which the minister of the synagogue stands with a strap of calf-hide in his hand, doubled and redoubled, and two [other] straps that rise and fall [are fastened] thereto. The handpiece of the strap is one handbreadth long and one handbreadth wide, and its end must reach to his navel. He gives him one-third of the stripes in front and two-thirds behind. And he may not strike him when he is standing or when he is sitting, but only when he is bending low . . . And he that smites, smites with his one hand with all his might. And the reader reads, "If thou wilt not observe to do . . . the Lord will make thy stripes wonderful and the stripes of thy seed . . ." [Deut. 28:58 ff.], and he returns again to the beginning of the passage.[18]

Events now moved rapidly to fulfill Paul's destiny in the Church. He was transferred from Tarsus to Antioch because the apostles saw the need to supervise Gentile converts there. Strangely, Paul had contributed to the circumstances that brought this transfer, for those "scattered abroad upon the persecution that arose about Stephen" came to the areas adjoining Israel, and one city is named prominently, Antioch, capital of

Syria, the province to which Judea was technically allied (Acts 11:19-20). Josephus tells of the huge Jewish colony in this metropolis, some three hundred and fifty miles north of Jerusalem. The same reasons that made it attractive to dispersing Jews brought in the dispersing Christians. As they arrived from Judea, they first preached "unto the Jews only" (Acts 11:19). But soon Greek-speaking Christians arrived at Antioch and contacted "the Grecians, preaching the Lord Jesus" (Acts 11:20). Such gospel expansion was first seen on a smaller scale in Samaria, where Philip had great success in baptisms. When news of widespread conversions came back, "the apostles which were at Jerusalem . . . sent unto them Peter and John" (Acts 8:14), which was all the more dramatic because Peter and John were two of the three "pillars" in the Council of Twelve. Their part in laying on hands for the Holy Ghost will be discussed later, but their role in determining how the gospel should extend to semi-Jews is significant here. The Samaritans believed in the Mosaic books, in circumcision and sacrifice, and their assimilation into the Church was managed by general authorities.

Similar procedures were now followed in distant Antioch. After the first Jewish preaching there, Greeks were reached, "and a great number believed, and turned unto the Lord" (Acts 11:21). News of this came to "the church which was in Jerusalem" (Acts 11:22), a phrase that does not stress the members of a congregation, for undoubtedly many congregations were there. "The church . . . in Jerusalem" implies the leaders who presided over the churches there and elsewhere. When Antioch representatives went to Jerusalem later for a policy decision, "the apostles and elders" were contacted (Acts 15:2). As a result of the Antioch preaching to Greeks, Barnabus was "sent" to Antioch by "the church which was in Jerusalem" (Acts 11:22). Barnabus, the devoted Jew from Cyprus (Acts 4:36-37), was obviously chosen as a man like Paul who knew Greek culture outside of Israel. On arriving at Antioch and finding things in order, he immediately traveled over one hundred miles west "to Tarsus to look for Saul" (Acts 11:25, RSV). One can imagine their reunion, for Barnabus had earlier taken Paul "to the apostles" in Jerusalem after the Damascus ministry (Acts 9:27). Now he came from the apostles with the commission to direct the work in Antioch. The intended parallel is clear—the man assigned to Tarsus by the apostles was now transferred to a new field by a trusted leader coming directly from the apostles. During Paul's first vision ten years before, the Lord outlined his mission to the Gentiles, but the assignment was gradually fulfilled as directed through the Church leaders.

Barnabus now brought Paul "to Antioch, and it came to pass that for a whole year they assembled with the church and taught many people" (Acts 11:26, NKJV). Since Jewish Christians at Antioch later objected to Paul baptizing Gentiles without ties to Judaism, Paul was first preaching mainly to Jews and the "God-fearers" or "devout persons" in the synagogues. Antioch's size is estimated as high as eight hundred thousand, with a guess of a Jewish population about 15 percent of that.[19] So gospel expansion went from semi-Jews at Samaria to Jewish sympathizers at Antioch before Paul later preached to Gentiles without prior Jewish roots. Josephus describes the Jewish society at Antioch in which Paul and Barnabus moved:

> The Jewish race, densely interspersed among the native populations of every portion of the world, is particularly numerous in Syria, where intermingling is due to the proximity of the two countries. But it was at Antioch that they specially congregated, partly owing to the greatness of that city, but mainly because the successors of King Antiochus had enabled them to live there in security. . . . Continuing to receive similar treatment from later monarchs, the Jewish colony grew in numbers, and their richly designed and costly offering formed a splendid ornament to the temple. Moreover, they were constantly attracting to their religious ceremonies multitudes of Greeks, and these they had in some measure incorporated with themselves.[20]

The Antioch labors of Paul and Barnabus were interrupted after a year as a result of prophecy of famine and the assistance sent Jerusalem from the richer saints at Antioch, whose wealth parallels the Jewish society just described. One coming from Jerusalem with warning was Agabus, who later prophesied Paul's captivity on nearing the holy city. Church members sent welfare supplies "to the elders by the hands of Barnabus and Saul" (Acts 11:30). Acts shows its survey nature by simply noting that these two finished this service and returned to Antioch. Nothing is said of the seven-hundred-mile round trip, nothing of meeting with the presiding "elders" at Jerusalem, which they certainly did, nothing of plans discussed there for the expansion of the Gentile mission to Asia Minor, which took place immediately on returning. Was Luke obeying Paul's mandate of modesty in writing about his missionary leader? On the mission immediately following the Jerusalem return, Paul and Barnabus are twice called "apostles" (Acts 14:4; 14:14). The term occasionally preserves its general sense of "one sent" in nonformal New Testament references, so some have thought that Paul and Barnabus were only "messengers" and not members of the Twelve. But Luke uses *apostle* thirty-four other times in his Gospel and Acts, and every time this word designates the Twelve or its members. Indeed, his first mention seems to define what he means, since out of all Christ's "disciples," only twelve were called, and these were named "apostles" (Luke 6:13). And Paul certainly puts his office on a parity with the Twelve, speaking of those who were "apostles before me" (Gal. 1:17) and humbly calling himself "least of the apostles" after mentioning the Twelve (1 Cor. 15:9). His confident authority as "an apostle of Jesus Christ" in the openings of ten of fourteen letters matches the similar assertion of Peter beginning both of his preserved letters.

Because no apostolic ordination is preserved, some doubt that Paul was one of the Twelve. But Paul gave Timothy guidelines on conferring priesthood by the laying on of hands (1 Tim. 5:22), which shows a practice that Acts and the Letters do not need to detail. The book of Acts is a story of missionary labors, not primarily a record book of ordinances, as we shall see more plainly. Paul could have been ordained an apostle when Barnabus first came to Tarsus with his transfer to preside at Antioch, or when Barnabus and Paul visited Jerusalem with the welfare supplies before the Gentile mission to Asia Minor. And there are really more possibilities, in spite of Paul's listing only two visits to Jerusalem between his conversion and the Jerusalem Council seventeen years later.[21] We must not ration Paul's Jerusalem trips as though there was some barrier to travel. The fact that he was shipwrecked three times in his early ministry shows how frequently he traveled by sea. We do know that Luke calls Paul an apostle, that the term is strange if Paul is not a member of the Twelve, and that there are clear opportunities for ordination in connection with Paul's Antioch ministry.

Perhaps the ultimate reward of Paul's life came about this time, a great vision that in itself showed God's approval. About A.D. 57 Paul looked back on this sacred experience "fourteen years ago,"[22] about A.D. 44, at the end of his Tarsus ministry or during his labors at Antioch. Significantly, this was just before Luke called Paul an apostle and just before the great Gentile missions began. Paul only mentioned the vision to shame the Corinthians into humility, trying to refute their ridicule of his leadership. This subject is prefaced by the apostle's willingness to match credential with credential by showing the shallowness of their boasting: "I will glory also. . . . I am bold also" (2 Cor. 11:18-21). Eleven verses follow, giving personal achievements and sacrifices, followed by, "I will come to visions and revelations of the Lord" (2 Cor. 12:1). Then Paul's "visions and revelations" follow, even though narrated with the modesty of third person, for he continued to comment on his own "abundance of the revelations" (2 Cor. 12:7). The point of this vision is how the Lord blessed Paul:

> I know a man in Christ who fourteen years ago—whether in the body I do not know, or whether out of the body I do not know; God knows— such a one was caught up to the third heaven. And I know such a man— whether in the body or out of the body I do not know; God knows—how he was caught up into paradise and heard inexpressible words, which it is not lawful for a man to utter. (2 Cor. 12:2-4, NKJB.)

Paul had seen the Lord near Damascus, and publicly talked about his message. But 2 Corinthians tells of a vision beyond that in sacredness, since Paul was not permitted to repeat the "inexpressible words" given him. Paul's "third heaven" is the highest heaven, also called "paradise" here—the time and phraseology of seeing both is the same. As a young Pharisee, Paul turned away from the sophistication and materialism of his secular world. Then as a new Christian he also renounced false status, even in religion, for the true sacrifice of humility and diligent labor for the Lord. He spoke with authority to his world and so speaks through the Bible record today. Paul saw the resurrected Christ near Damascus, saw the same Lord three years later in the Jerusalem temple, and saw the celestial glory of God some eight years afterward. Not only was he strengthened by these for the crowning two decades of his life, but his revelations offer sure knowledge beyond the limitations of this world.

NOTES

1. John Paterson, "Jeremiah," in Matthew Black and H. H. Rowley (eds.), *Peake's Commentary on the Bible* (London: Thomas Nelson, 1962), p. 541.

2. Philo, *On the Giants* 12-13. For the extent of Philo's advocacy of premortal existence, see David Winston, "Preexistence in Hellenic, Judaic, and Mormon Sources," in Truman G. Madsen, ed., *Reflections on Mormonism* (Provo, Utah: Religious Studies Center, Brigham Young University, 1978), pp. 26-29.

3. Andrew F. Ehat and Lyndon W. Cook, *The Words of Joseph Smith* (Provo, Utah: Religious Studies Center, Brigham Young University, 1980), p. 367.

4. Xenophon, *Anabasis* 1.2.23.

5. Strabo, *Geography* 14.5.13 (Loeb Classical Library).

6. Ibid. 14.5.14.

7. Herbert Danby, trans., *The Mishnah, Aboth* 1:1.

8. Josephus, *Jewish Antiquities* 13:297.

9. "Saul" appears seventeen times in Acts, from its first introduction at 7:58 to its last appearance in 13:9, which is the first of the many appearances of "Paul" thereafter. "Saul" appears in no other New Testament book.

10. Danby, *Mishnah, Aboth* 5:22.

11. Danby, *Mishnah, Sotah* 9:15.

12. In Greek and Jewish cultures centering authority on middle age, "young man" easily moves from the teens to the years before about forty. Josephus uses the term of a young officer with junior authority. See William F. Arndt et al., *Greek-English Lexicon of the New Testament*, 2nd ed. (Chicago: University of Chicago Press, 1979), *neanías*, where the editors survey usage and conclude the "young man" category spans "about the 24th to the 40th years." There is some control in Paul's case, for the chronological chart in the appendix shows that his church career lasted some thirty-six years after conversion, which could not be much after A.D. 33. Writing to Philemon in about A.D. 61, Paul called himself "aged" (Philem. 1:9).

13. Danby, *Mishnah, Kiddushin* 4:13.

14. Ibid., *Aboth* 5:21.

15. Ibid.

16. David O. McKay, *Ancient Apostles* (Salt Lake City: Deseret Sunday School Union, 1918), pp. 140-41.

17. There are three accounts of Paul's vision: Luke's narrative (Acts 9) and Paul's speeches on the temple steps (Acts 22) and before King Agrippa (Acts 26). On the reaction of Paul's companions, the Joseph Smith Translation superimposes Acts 22:9 on Acts 9:7, logically preferring the first person over the third person account. Paul's first person accounts are followed here. Minor conflict of detail is normal for historic reconstructions that preserve the integrity of their sources. Acts 9:7 indicates that Paul's companions "saw no man," though Acts 22:9 indicates that they were conscious of the light, which is not a contradiction. But these two verses conflict on whether the men with Paul heard a voice. A tempting parallel is John 12:28-29, where the astounding experience produced different reactions to God's voice in the temple. The conflict between Paul's companions standing (Acts 9:7) or falling to the earth in fear (Acts 26:14) might also be a case of individual response. Luke obviously used several sources, and his trustworthiness is enhanced by his unwillingness to smooth over these peripheral conflicts. All accounts agree in the great reality of the place and time of the vision, the basic message to Paul, and the incredible glory of the heavenly vision. Its physical effect of blinding Paul should sober anyone who thinks it can be easily explained away.

18. Danby, *Mishnah, Makkoth* 3:12-14.

19. See Bruce Metzger, "Antioch-on-the-Orontes," in David Noel Freedman and Edward F. Campbell, Jr., eds., *Biblical Archaeologist Reader*, vol. 2 (Garden City, N.Y.: Anchor Books, 1964), p. 316, where the basis for calculation is given. Fourth-century John Chrysostom (*Homily on St. Ignatius* 4) speaks of the difficulty of governing "a hundred, or even fifty men," adding that "so great a city" has a "citizenry" of two hundred thousand. A population estimate must add women, children, slaves, and aliens and take into account extensive suburbs. For the Jewish population, see Metzger, p. 324.

20. Josephus, *Jewish War* 17.43.45 (Loeb Classical Library).

21. As will be seen later, the council on circumcision of Acts 15 and the Jerusalem visit on Gentile requirements of Galatians 2 are different versions of the same episode. Since Galatians gives only Paul's first Jerusalem visit, three years after his conversion (Gal. 1:1), and no other until the council visit, fourteen years after that (Gal. 2:1), many scholars want to equate the latter with Paul's second Jerusalem visit in Acts, the famine visit with Barnabas as companion (Acts 11:29-30; 12:25). But Galatians is not attempting to give a full history; it is written to explain how the apostles all agreed on the circumcision question, making the Acts 15 council central to its point. Thus, in Galatians Paul mentions his first visit to Peter, making his point that he knew the gospel before that by revelation; then he naturally jumps to the next relevant episode for his purpose, the gathering to settle the requirements of the law for the Gentiles. The "famine visit" of Acts 11 is not relevant to Gentile requirements and is therefore omitted in Galatians 1:22. Paul says he "was unknown by face unto the churches of Judaea," but this is not talking about the whole time from his first visit with Peter until the Jerusalem council seventeen years afterward. In context it talks of the "Syria and Cilicia" ministries (Gal. 1:21). That is, Paul was so suddenly sent to Tarsus that he did not have time to be known by the Christian communities about Jerusalem. This does not preclude the famine visit some eight years later, or other visits, since being "unknown" refers to his early post-conversion years in the Tarsus area.

22. The King James phrase is unnecessarily vague here: "above fourteen years ago." The Greek text has a single preposition; thus all recent committee translations of 2 Corinthians 12:2 read simply, "fourteen years ago." (For dates, see appendix A.)

3

The Missionary Message in Acts

The Early Church did not produce "Meditations of the Apostles" or the "Philosophy of the Apostles," though many such books circulate about modern Christian leaders and thinkers. Luke's real title says much about the apostles' real message. The "Acts of the Apostles" suggests that their message is not only in their letters but also in their work. Christ sent not mystics but practical men of conviction with his gospel. And what they did is a clear definition of what they taught. Paul's fourteen letters would be isolated and abstract without Luke's sixteen chapters on Paul's deeds as an apostle. The letters briefly mention many doctrines and ordinances and rarely discuss the organization of the early Church. That is because they were written to believers who had seen all this. But the modern Christian, who never observed the early Church, may easily misread the letters. Could he turn time back and walk one week with Paul, he would understand Paul's hints and reminders. The book of Acts vividly turns time back. Its descriptions are the most effective definitions. No one should open a letter of Paul without first seeing the gospel in action in Acts.

Acts is the key to the letters in many other ways. Half the book is a biography of Paul as a missionary apostle. His first dozen years in the Church must be pieced together from isolated texts. After that, the modern biographer can move from detective work to digesting work, for Acts fully reports the next sixteen years. This detail begins with the first Gentile mission and ends with

Paul's custody in Rome to be heard by Caesar's court. Thereafter, the apostle to the Gentiles lived only a handful of years, writing only three known letters in this final period. That means that the earlier eleven letters were written in the time when Acts gives Paul's full history. So there are background facts behind most of Paul's letters, many coming from Acts. This chapter will finish the survey of Paul's life with two goals in mind—understanding the general circumstances that throw light on Paul's letters, plus understanding what was taught in Church branches before Paul wrote them letters.

This last point needs emphasis. Reading Paul's words gives a false sense of completeness. He sometimes writes comprehensively on Christian doctrine—more formal letters like Ephesians and Hebrews are near that end of the spectrum. But Paul's typical letter is like a personal letter to a friend who doesn't need full explanations. After reexplaining the apostasy in one of his shortest letters, Paul asked why he needed to repeat himself: "Do you not remember that when I was still with you, I told you these things? (2 Thes. 2:5, NKJB.) Modern Christians get their doctrine from Paul's letters, but Paul did not write to explain Christ's gospel to later generations. Paul encouraged early Christians who already knew Christ's gospel. Thus, the letters and Acts each stress part of the whole. The letters contain little of the first message because they are written to those who have already believed and obeyed. Acts gives this first message—the first preaching that offered salvation through membership in Christ's Church. But since Acts is a missionary record, it says little of how members should perfect themselves. So the New Testament sequence is sound. Acts prefaces Paul's letters because it shows what the converts believed before reading Paul's letters; the letters complete Acts because they erect the superstructure resting on the first principles.

Acts vividly replays scene after scene of Paul's preaching. But Acts is also accurate, for its author was with Paul through a great many of these events. He writes "we" as a fellow missionary, this language first appearing in connection with events in about A.D. 49 as the missionaries first sailed to Greece (Acts 16:10). "We" then resumes about A.D. 58 as Paul returns to Jerusalem after two long and productive missions in the Greek cities of the homeland and Asia Minor (Acts 20:5, 13). This "we" language carries the author into Israel, where Paul was imprisoned two years, with the final "we" sections sketching Paul's exciting voyage and arrival in Rome about A.D. 61 (Acts 27:1; 28:16). Thus, the author of Acts shared Paul's missionary experiences through a dozen-year period. Though his book does not carry his name, the opening verses of Acts identify the writer by referring to his "former account" (Acts 1:1, NKJB); a comparison with the similar preface to the Gospel of Luke identifies Luke as the author. "When we came to Rome" (Acts 28:16) gives a correct impression, for Luke sends greetings in two Roman letters, one of them picturing Luke as "the beloved physician" (Col. 4:14.). Though obviously not trained in modern science, the best educated Greek physicians had a scientific attitude and a better grasp of anatomy than was possible in the Middle Ages. Thus, it is powerful testimony when Luke reports miraculous healings by Christ and his apostles. Luke's writing reflects quality education, for it is the most polished Greek of the New Testament. Luke insists that he investigated everything carefully; what he had not seen himself came from "eyewitnesses and ministers of the word," that is, the apostles who had walked with the Lord (Luke 1:2). Thus, Luke signals that he is a second-generation convert, and his Greek and Gentile interests signal that he is probably not a Jew. He was perhaps converted at Paul's missionary base of Antioch, since he begins to give details about Paul after the apostle came there.

Luke guides his readers through three missionary journeys of Paul, but numbering them first to third makes sense only if it is understood that Paul had been a Christian some twelve years before the "first mission." As we have seen, he had already done intense missionary work at Damascus, Jerusalem, Tarsus, and Antioch. Thus, the "first mission" is the first after Paul became an apostle, the first that Luke could give personal detail about, or simply the first Gentile mission. All these options have value, but we know that Luke sought to present the Gentile missions as a fulfillment of

Christ's prophecy to the apostles before his ascension: "Ye shall be witnesses unto me both in Jerusalem, and in all Judaea, and in Samaria, and unto the uttermost part of the earth" (Acts 1:8). The first half of Acts tells how the original apostles extended the work through Judaea and Samaria, and its second half tells how Paul and his companions extended the work to the nations beyond. The chart on the next page outlines the times and locations of the three Gentile missions. They need not be fully detailed here—a full reading of Acts will accomplish that. But this chapter will focus on Paul's missionary doctrines in their proper settings, adding relevant parallels from the first apostles in the earlier part of Acts. Luke had a higher purpose than merely writing exciting narrative—he wrote to solidify Theophilus in "the certainty of those things in which you have been instructed" (Luke 1:4, NKJB), a purpose that clearly carried into Acts, the continuation of this work on Christian basics (Acts 1:1-2). Acts typically gives double examples of doctrines to show that they were preached both by Paul and by the original apostles.

All the apostles had the same message: "Whether it were I or they, so we preach, and so ye believed" (1 Cor. 15:11). Paul had just insisted that the Corinthians would not be saved if they disbelieved the gospel he preached to them (1 Cor. 15:1-2). In this letter Paul began to outline that gospel, but he stopped at the great doctrines of Christ to reconvert the Corinthians to the Resurrection. Paul was in harmony with Peter and those before: "I delivered unto you first of all that which I also received" (1 Cor. 15:3). He bore this first testimony of Christ to the Corinthians: "Christ died for our sins, according to the scriptures; and . . . he was buried, and . . . he rose again the third day, according to the scriptures" (1 Cor. 15:3-4). So two foundation doctrines were the atonement and the resurrection of Christ. But Paul gave more complete articles of faith in a letter not arguing the Resurrection so intently. In Hebrews he reminded the converts that they must never forget "the first principles of God's word" (Heb. 5:12, RSV). The Greek phrase reads literally, "the basics of the beginning of God's words." Paul lists them: "The foundation of repen-

Paul's Gentile Missions

Approximate Years	How Begun	Main Locations	Main Companions
First mission, 45-47	Revelation by the Spirit after visit to Jerusalem: "Separate me Barnabus and Saul for the work whereunto I have called them" (Acts 13:2)	Cyprus and south central Asia Minor	Paul Barnabus John Mark
Second mission, 49-52	Visiting new churches with the apostles' revelation on circumcision (Acts 15:36; 16:4)—and then revelation by vision: "Come over into Macedonia, and help us" (Acts 16:9)	Mainland Greece	Paul Silas Luke Timothy
Third mission, 54-58	Invitation of Ephesian Jews, accepted after mandatory Jerusalem visit (Acts 18:20-21); compare the earlier revelation delaying preaching in Asia (Acts 16:6)	Roman province of Asia (western Asia Minor)	Paul Timothy Titus Gaius Aristarchus
Roman Custody, 61-63	Appeal to Caesar when life endangered (Acts 25:9-10) after vision of Lord: "you must bear witness also at Rome" Acts 23:11, NKJB)	House arrest at Rome	Paul Luke Aristarchus Timothy

tance from dead works, and of faith toward God, of the doctrine of baptisms, and of laying on of hands; and of resurrection of the dead, and of eternal judgment" (Heb. 6:1-2). These central missionary doctrines correlate with the first message to the Greeks at Corinth—Christ's resurrection appears in both, and his atonement discussed in Corinthians obviously relates closely to the "eternal judgment" mentioned in Hebrews. But Hebrews spells out the plan of forgiveness—exactly what Latter-day Saints know from modern revelation as the first principles of faith, repentance, baptism, and the laying on of hands for the gift of the Holy Ghost. Acts shows the same plan of salvation, not lying inert in pieces on the dissecting table but in action as a living whole. It is clear why Paul insisted that those sent by God would preach a single gospel: "If any man preach any other gospel unto you than that ye have received, let him be accursed" (Gal. 1:9).

In Paul's first mission, that gospel began to be preached to populations of non-Jews. The Christian leaders of Antioch assembled with Saul and Barnabas, appointed to preside over the work at Antioch. During their meeting, "the Holy Ghost said, Separate me Barnabas and Saul for the work whereunto I have called them" (Acts 13:2). When did God call them to the Gentile mission beyond Antioch? The apostles sent Barnabas to preside there in the first place, and a man of his obedience and loyalty would not quit the assignment without similar direction. Significantly, he and Paul had just returned from taking the Antioch welfare supply to the Jerusalem "elders," a term that includes the apostles. Just as the Twelve had directed the extension of the Samaritan mission, just as they directed the extension of the Antioch mission to the Gentiles, so they are visible in the expansion of preaching to non-Jewish lands.

The regional leaders at Antioch helped Barnabas and Paul set apart the other, an interesting parallel to priesthood blessings today in which lesser authorities can assist in a blessing. Laying "their hands on them, they sent them away" (Acts 13:3). Acts gives just this instance of laying on of hands for Paul, but that is just the point—the writer draws on the experience of his readers to fill in like details in like circumstances. Paul reminded Timothy about the laying on of hands for authority (1 Tim. 4:14); though Timothy appears in Acts, his laying on of hands does not. But earlier Luke explained how the apostles delegated authority. It was felt that Jewish-Greek widows were slighted in the welfare distribution. So the apostles requested the appointment of "seven men of honest report" (Acts 6:3). These welfare assistants had to please the Greek element of the Jerusalem church. So their nomination was delegated to the "brethren," though direction came through the apostles, who also retained their right of approval when the seven men were "set before the apostles" prior to ordination (Acts 6:6). Then authority was given when the Twelve "prayed" and "laid their hands on them" (Acts 6:6). So Luke gave two examples of laying on of hands for authority in Acts, one from the first Twelve and one as Paul embarked on his first Gentile mission. Modern readers may wish for more documentation, but Luke was clearly satisfied with representative instances of a Church practice.

Paul and Barnabas next sailed the hundred miles to Cyprus. They took Barnabas's relative John Mark with them (Acts 13:5) and no doubt sought out contacts known to Barnabas, who was from Cyprus (Acts 4:36). They began in the largest city on the east side and then traveled another hundred miles through the island to New Paphos, the Roman capital on the west. This whole itinerary appears in two verses, which may have taken weeks or even months. Cyprus had a huge Jewish population, and initially at Salamis they sought out many congregations: "They preached the word of God in the synagogues of the Jews" (Acts 13:5). What did they preach? The careful reader of Acts need not wonder, for "the word of God" regularly means the missionary message, which Luke illustrates from time to time. For instance, soon after the account of Paul's leaving Cyprus, one finds the longest synagogue speech of Acts, after which Paul said he had declared "the word of God" (Acts 13:46). Luke presented examples, not microhistory. Repeated synagogue preaching on Cyprus takes up one sentence, but as the work began on the mainland, Luke traces synagogue preaching in twenty-eight careful verses. Then afterward, synagogue preaching in a dozen major cities is reduced once more to summary verses each time. This type of writing could work only in a church with a constant message, where the doctrines and practices did not vary.

Although the missionaries concentrated on Jewish congregations in eastern Cyprus, their western success was the conversion of the Roman governor. And Luke signals the transition by here introducing the Gentile name of the former Pharisee. He says simply that Saul is also Paul (Acts 13:9), and thereafter the Jewish name is not mentioned. Did the new name come in honor of the believing governor, Sergius Paulus? Perhaps, yet the source may simply be the similarity between "Saul" and "Paul."[1] When the missionaries arrived in the provincial capital of New Paphos, they found a city known for its "harbor and well-built temples."[2] Perhaps working first with the Jewish population, they were summoned by the "proconsul," a name that Luke gives in Greek, the proper title of the Cyprus governor (Acts 13:7, NKJB).[3] Although ultimately Paul faced four provincial governors, Sergius Paulus alone appears as "prudent" and interested in hearing "the word of God" (Acts 13:7). His court magician, however, "opposed" the missionaries until Paul was moved to rebuke him by the power of the priesthood, prophesying that he would be blind "for a season" (Acts 13:11). The apostle who was led blind into Damascus knew well what he was saying. His closeness to the Lord is seen not only in visions but in miracles, as the chart in this chapter shows. The ability to stop the magician from his tirade against God's servants was like the power to cast out devils, which Christ promised to his priesthood holders (Mark 3:15; 16:17). The honest governor was humbled by this power, and he "believed, being astonished at the doctrine of the Lord" (Acts 13:12).

The second stage of this initial mission began after the missionaries sailed from Cyprus to the southern coast of Asia Minor. Before going far inland John Mark left them and "returned to Jerusalem" (Acts 13:13). His leaving at the outset of full Gentile preaching is no doubt related to his conservatism about it.[4] Paul and Barnabas took the roads north from the coastland to Antioch in Pisidia, a hundred miles away. The mountains and broad valleys must have been picturesque, but the unescorted travelers would also have had to watch for danger. Such routes were mentioned in Paul's catalog of risks— "perils of waters, in perils of robbers . . . perils in the wilderness" (2 Cor. 11:26). Arriving at the Antioch in Asia Minor, Paul and Barnabas went to the synagogue on the Sabbath and were invited to speak as visiting brethren. Here, Luke gives the full synagogue preaching—as just noted, the most complete report in the book of Acts. The reader virtually joins the audience to hear the emotion-charged review of Israel's history and how Jesus fulfilled it as the Messiah. Paul stood to address all Israelites and God-fearing Gentiles present. He reviewed the call of Israel, its deliverance out of Egypt, the age of Kings, and the promise of the Messiah through the seed of King David. Then he called to mind John the Baptist as forerunner, reviewing his "baptism of repentance" and testimony that one greater would follow. Here we see how John had impressed the dispersion as well as Israelites in his land, a situation verified by Josephus naming John as one of the three Christian leaders in his history of the first century. Paul next reviewed Christ's unjust death under Pilate and testified that "God raised him from the dead," calling on the testimony of the first apostles as "his witnesses unto the people." Paul's conclusion was personal: "Through this man is preached unto you the forgiveness of sins, and by him all that believe are justified from all things, from which ye could not be justified by the law of Moses" (Acts 13:38-39).

This central message has outlasted the hostility that it caused toward Paul and Barnabas, who were forced to leave Pisidian Antioch because of Jewish antagonism. This full example of preaching gives perspective on Paul's missionary message. It perfectly fits Paul's "first" doctrines at Corinth (1 Cor. 15:1-4). Paul there furnished names of those seeing Christ after the Resurrection (1 Cor. 15:5-7), and in the Pisidian synagogue he said that the Lord was seen by those who "came up with him from Galilee to Jerusalem" (Acts 13:31). Paul preached Jesus as the Messiah to a Jewish congregation with faith in a Messiah. He had done the same from conversion, soon after which he "confounded the Jews who lived in Damascus by proving that Jesus was the Christ" (Acts 9:22, RSV). This is a critical point, for every synagogue speech in Acts has a form of the same message. But how can Luke be consistent in reporting Paul's offer of remission of sins through Christ in Acts 13:38 as against Peter's offer of remission of sins through repentance and baptism in Acts 2:38? Peter had preached on Christ at Pentecost, so both apostles agreed that forgiveness comes through Jesus' sacrifice. And Paul preached repentance through Christ, so that is not a conflict. Paul expected a change in thinking and action, though this was not technically mentioned in the synagogue. On the second journey in Athens he stressed that God "now commands all men everywhere to repent" (Acts 17:30, NKJB); ending the third journey, he summed up his message to Jew and Greek as "repentance toward God, and faith toward our Lord Jesus Christ" (Acts 20:21).

Thus, the apparent conflict between Paul at Pisidia and Peter on Pentecost is the latter's baptism "for the remission of sins" (Acts 2:38). Though Luke does not mention baptism during Paul's entire first journey, he stresses baptism on the second and third missions. Paul's message was consistent, but Luke features different parts of it on different missions. Whereas the "principles" of faith, repentance, baptism, and the laying on of hands were always the foundation (Heb. 6:1-3), Luke is selective in reporting them. He stresses Christ and faith in him on the first mission, makes baptism prominent in the second, and features the laying on of hands for the gift of the Holy Ghost in the third.

In Acts Paul is not only preaching the gospel of Christ but establishing the Church of Christ. As he and Barnabas were forced to leave Pisidian Antioch, they left behind local branches: "The disciples were filled with joy, and with the Holy Ghost" (Acts 13:52). *Disciple* is a strong term, literally a "learner" in the sense of being a serious student or apprentice. Acts follows the Gospels in using this term for baptized members of Christ's church. For instance, after Peter's call for repentance and baptism on Pentecost, "they that gladly received his word were baptized, and the same day there were added unto them about three thousand souls" (Acts 2:41). Afterward Luke summarized Church growth: "The number of the disciples was multiplied" (Acts 6:1)—his original description holds, for "disciples" came through baptism. Paul was likewise a "disciple" after conversion—on first coming to Jerusalem, he tried to "join himself to the disciples," but they feared him, doubting "that he was a disciple" (Acts 9:26). Paul had recently been baptized (Acts 9:18), later reviewing Ananias's challenge: "Arise and be baptized, and wash away your sins, calling on the name of the Lord" (Acts 22:16, NKJB). Thus, in Luke's record, baptism was required for discipleship, so Paul's baptisms are implied by "the disciples" who were left behind in the cities of the first mission (Acts 13:52).

After receiving threats of violence, Paul and Barnabas took the dusty road east of Pisidian Antioch, and eighty miles brought them to Iconium. In a few verses Acts summarizes the synagogue preaching, conversions, anger, threats, and again leaving under duress. Yet these events took a "long time" (Acts 14:3), an indication of how many details are left out of Acts. Arriving at nearby Lystra, the "apostles" (Acts 14:4) preached in an area dominated by the old pagan religion. Here a notable miracle took place. Long before Paul was converted, the Lord commanded the Twelve to take their first mission, combining the command to preach with the promise that they should "heal the sick" and "cast out devils" (Matt. 10:7-8). The seventy were given the same double command to preach and "heal the sick" (Luke 10:1-9). And every gospel closes with the Lord's command to the Twelve to take the gospel to the world, which implies that they would hold these priesthood powers. Christ's teaching follows this pattern in the close of Mark, where the Lord commanded the Twelve to preach and promised the signs following (Mark 16:15-18). But such incredible promises were not made to just any believers. These were believers with Christ's delegated priesthood. Paul's unusual spiritual gifts followed his special calling as a general authority. Seeing a cripple "who never had walked," Paul was inspired as Peter earlier at the temple gate. Paul was impressed that the lifelong Lystran cripple "had faith to be healed." So he firmly commanded, "Stand up straight on your feet." And the man "leaped and walked" (Acts 14:8-10, NKJB).

This event was a sign to believers, for unbelievers either misunderstood or misused the miracle. The superstitious populace tried to sacrifice to these visiting "gods," considering Barnabas Jupiter, since he was perhaps taller and more imposing. Paul was called Mercury "because he was the chief speaker" (Acts 14:12). The apostles prevented an idolatrous sacrifice by bearing a simple testimony of the true and living God, who, because of man's agency, had allowed superstitious religion (Acts 14:14-18). But soon they faced a crowd manipulated by angry Jews who followed their trail from earlier cities. Paul was indeed the more eloquent, for the crowd picked him to be stoned and dragged him out of the city presumably dead. But the Lord had again protected his servant in violence. And the next morning Paul left with Barnabas for Derbe, the farthest point of the first mission. Yet this final city was not the final scene of the mission. If conversion were salvation, following up of converts would not be necessary. The close of the first mission was revisiting, a process that Paul later repeated when he had opportunity. Obviously, he considered growth in the gospel as much a critical part of salvation as first belief. Years later he would write to the Ephesians that general and local priesthood offices were given "for the perfecting of the saints" (Eph. 4:12), a constant goal for Paul in addition to conversion. Such work could continue only by the general authority raising up local authority. Thus, at the risk of their lives, Paul and Barnabas returned to the cities of opposition and violence, "confirming the souls of the disciples, and exhorting them to continue in the faith, and that we must through much tribulation enter into the kingdom of God. And when they had ordained them elders in every church, and had prayed with fasting, they commended them to the Lord, on whom they believed" (Acts 14:22-23).

Thus Paul and Barnabas established branches of the Church of Christ in every city of their converts, returning to Antioch not with some sort of mailing list but after the bold achievement of organized local churches with priesthood leaders. The missionary message came through men approved by the Twelve. In turn the new believers were organized into branches of the Church in harmony with the Twelve.

But soon conflicts arose about Paul's first mission. On returning, Paul and Barnabas called the Antioch disciples into conference to report how God "had opened the door of faith unto the Gentiles" (Acts 14:27). They must have rejoiced at the news, for the missionaries continued laboring there for a "long time with the disciples" (Acts 14:28). But the first mission did not please "certain men which came down from Judaea," who insisted, "Except ye be circumcised after the manner of Moses, ye cannot be saved" (Acts 15:1). This problem would always plague Paul and be a topic in many letters. So reading Paul requires clear understanding of it. The problem was not salvation by faith alone; it was not a question of freedom from gospel requirements and ordinances. Instead, it was a question of whether Gentile converts to Christianity had also to obey the law of Moses. As we have seen, the Gentile "disciples" had already been baptized and taught strictly to "continue in the faith" as a condition of salvation (Acts 14:22). But this did not satisfy Jewish Christians strictly observing the Law of Moses. Circumcision symbolized this issue, but Judaizers were talking about hundreds of obligations beyond circumcision. The orthodox Jews count 613 commandments in the five books of Moses, and the Rabbinical rules of the Mishnah multiply the commandments to thousands. So it is a gross simplification to see Paul advocating a gospel without rules. Instead, he opposed a tradition of too many rules.

The first debate at Antioch was whether Gentile converts had to be circumcised as well as baptized—whether they obligated themselves only to Christian rules or whether they were also obligated to Jewish law. The Antioch apostles argued vigorously against that additional burden, and after "no small dissension and disputation," it was decided that the leaders of each persuasion "should go up to Jerusalem unto the apostles and elders about this question" (Acts 15:2). Similar problems today in most churches have no solution — only an uncomfortable truce between conservatives and liberals or a split into two churches. The solution of the Early Church was to take the question to the inspired general authorities for an answer.

Luke's detailed report of the Jerusalem Council is like his other detailed reports — representative of regular Church procedure. Luke opens the council room so we can see revelation in action as the "apostles and elders came together" to deliberate (Acts 15:6). Four spoke: Peter, Barnabas, Paul, and James. This James probably became an apostle after John's brother James was killed (Acts 12:1-2). James proposed the solution and is therefore commonly credited with presiding over the council. But it was Peter who spoke first, for he held "the keys of the kingdom of heaven" from Christ (Matt. 16:19). James' name appears in Acts only once prior to this, whereas Peter's name appears fifty-seven times, beginning with leadership in naming a new apostle right after the ascension of Christ. One of the impressive marks of Peter's authority was his receiving the revelation that the Gentiles should be admitted to the Church, an earlier step that he had to defend at length before the Jewish Christians (Acts 10, 11). And standing to open the Jerusalem Council, Peter reviewed God's revelation to him about baptizing Cornelius, the Roman officer who was the first baptized Gentile. Why add to baptism, Peter argued — why "put a yoke upon the neck of the disciples"? He continued with the same reasoning Paul would develop in Romans and Galatians: "We believe that through the grace of the Lord Jesus Christ we shall be saved, even as they" (Acts 15:10-11). Peter stressed God's approval of Cornelius by the Holy Ghost falling upon him, and Barnabas and Paul next testified that the same happened to the Gentiles on their recent mission (Acts 15:12). Finally, James made his proposal, a logical step because his view would persuade Jewish Christians, for whom he later spoke when Paul returned again to Jerusalem (Acts 21:18-24). From this proposal came the decision that the Gentiles should obey only the moral law and also cooperate with dietary restrictions of their Jewish brothers and sisters.

The apostles' letter to Antioch was specific. The moral law was to avoid idolatry and adultery; Jewish conciliation took the form of abstaining from "blood, and from things strangled" (Acts 15:29), since this blood prohibition predated Moses (Gen. 9:4). The goal of all, including James, was not to "trouble" the converted Gentiles with Jewish requirements (Acts 15:19). But Jews were apparently free to live as many of their former requirements as they chose. The apostles' letter to Antioch underlined not only the decision, but how the decision was reached: "It seemed good to the Holy Ghost, and to us, to lay upon you no greater burden than these necessary things" (Acts 15:28). Few Christians today see the implications of this powerful ruling of the Twelve. Conservatives today search the Bible for answers, but had the apostles done this, they would have required circumcision for the Gentiles, since it is commanded in the Bible. The apostles were inspired to go beyond the Bible, to reverse the lesser law given earlier and to extend the higher law through Christ. In other words, not past scripture but new revelation was the foundation of the Church of Christ. What guided the apostles was not the New Testament, for their acts created it. The Bible does not make the true church, but the true church makes the Bible. Past scriptures are a guide to truth, but living prophets give new scripture.

Paul's remaining missions round out the picture of the living gospel taught by the living Church. Biographies start the second mission with Paul's desire to visit "every city where we have preached the word of the Lord" (Acts 15:36), but the Jerusalem council is in the background. As Paul revisited these branches, he gave them the "decrees" of the "apostles and elders" (Acts 16:4). "Decree" mirrors Luke's Greek here, since he uses the term of the official edicts of the Roman emperor (Luke 2:1; Acts 17:7), which shows that the Twelve gave doctrine to the Church just as the centralized Roman government ruled the empire. Paul and Barnabas had returned to Antioch with Silas and Judas Barsabas, "leading men among the brethren" (Acts 15:22, NKJB). And Silas took Barnabas's place when the two former companions disagreed sharply over taking Barnabas's relative, Mark. The two added Luke and Timothy, the latter on the way in Lystra, where he and his family had probably been converted by Paul on the first mission. Since his family was part Jewish, Paul had him circumcised to avoid the charge that Christian Jews about him were disobedient to their heritage (Acts 16:1-3).

After visiting the first mission churches, the missionary group had a decision to make. The nearest populous area was Ephesus, chief city of the Roman province of Asia, on the coast two hundred miles west. But they "were forbidden of the Holy Ghost to preach the word in Asia" (Acts 16:6). In perspective, they were delayed in preaching there until they had done other things the Lord had in mind, for later the third mission was spent in Ephesus and its surrounding Asian province. But at this point they were inspired only on what *not* to do, for revelation often shines a small light in the dark before the whole problem is illuminated. Shifting northwest they finally arrived at the Aegean coast at Troas, where the next revelation awaited them. In a "vision" Paul saw the man of northern Greece appealing to him: "Come over into Macedonia, and help us" (Acts 16:9).

Without such direction, would the missionary group have ventured over a hundred miles of open sea to Greece? Disembarking on the coast, they proceeded ten miles inland to Philippi, a prosperous center settled heavily by Roman veterans. On the Sabbath the missionaries found the Jewish place of prayer (a term also meaning "synagogue") and reached the heart of the businesswoman Lydia, who is called "devout toward God" (Acts 16:14, literal trans.). Acts says that this remarkable woman paid attention to "the things which were spoken by Paul" (Acts 16:14), and the result was Lydia being "baptized, and her household" (Acts 16:15).[5] Luke also stresses the baptism of the jailor.

Paul's arrest came from commanding an evil spirit to depart from a possessed girl. This act enraged her masters, who stirred up a mob in the marketplace before the city officials. And they pleased the crowd by stripping and beating Paul and Silas, and by binding their feet in the inner cell of the jail. But God freed his servants through a terrifying earthquake. Since the jailor had been warned about their security, he assumed their escape and drew his sword for suicide when he failed to see them. But Paul called to the confused man, who felt the power of God in Paul's presence. The man's question is every man's question: "What must I do to be saved?" (Acts 16:30.) But the answer is regularly perverted through oversimplification; Protestant tracts, road signs, and sermonizing often quote part of Paul's answer: "Believe on the Lord Jesus Christ, and thou shalt be saved, and thy house" (Acts 16:31). "Believe on the Lord Jesus Christ"? That was the beginning, not the end of the requirements for salvation. The next verse says that Paul taught the jailor and his household "the word of the Lord" (Acts 16:32), which in Acts always suggests the first principles and ordinances. And the following verse rounds out the answer to the jailor, who was taken "the same hour of the night . . . and was baptized, he and all his" (Acts 16:33). The question of salvation was as much answered by the act of baptism as by Paul's first words.

Paul next traveled to the Jewish synagogue in Thessalonica, where a branch of the Church was forged in persecution. That story forms the background to the Thessalonian letters. Moving west again, Paul faced the same circumstances of success and Jewish agitation at Berea. There, he decided to go to Athens, leaving Silas and Timothy in the area and perhaps leaving Luke, since "we" passages stop and do not resume until Paul later revisited northern Greece. The King James Version implies that Paul then traveled to Athens by land: "The brethren sent away Paul to go as it were to the sea" (Acts 17:14). But the traditional Greek here means "intention to go by sea." The logic of speed, convenience, and safety dictated that Paul sail the two hundred miles to Athens, a point reinforced by the urgency suggested when "they that conducted Paul" were told to return and tell Silas and Timothy to come as quickly as possible (Acts 17:15).

Athens was a spectacular, if temporary, stop. Modern translations add realism to Paul's visit to the center of classicism. The narrative breathes the spirit of Athenian life, as F. F. Bruce observes: "Classical students feel that they are on home ground, and

Public Miracles through Paul

Jesus' Promises	Powers	Miracles through Paul
"In my name shall they cast out devils" (Mark 16:17)	Rebuking evil	Blinding of Elymas the magician (Acts 13:6-11) Casting out of evil spirit from young woman at Philippi (Acts 16:16-18) Evil spirits cast out at Ephesus (Acts 19:12)
"They shall speak with new tongues" (Mark 16:17)	New tongues	"I thank my God, I speak with tongues more than ye all" (1 Cor. 14:18)
"They shall take up serpents, and if they drink any deadly thing, it shall not hurt them" (Mark 16:18)	Protection	"No harm" from viper's bite, though Paul "should have swollen, or fallen down dead suddenly" (Acts 28:3-6)
"They shall lay hands on the sick, and they shall recover" (Mark 16:18)	Healing	Healing of cripple at Lystra (Acts 14:8-10) Healing of diseases at Ephesus (Acts 19:12) Healing of Publius's father from fever and bleeding when Paul "prayed and laid his hands on him" (Acts 28:8) "Others also, which had diseases in the island, came, and were healed" (Acts 28:9)

the scene and the argument have all the appearance of authen-ticity."[6] Paul was depressed to see a city overfilled with idols. The view is confirmed by other ancient travelers and by rich archaeo-logical finds; there were temples, altars, public statues of the Olympians, and special images to lesser divinities at houses and roads. The ancient joke ran that it was easier to find a god than a man in Athens. Paul began in the synagogue with Jews and "the devout persons" (Acts 17:17) and then moved to the "market" (*agorá*), now the broad excavated area lying below the Acropolis. It was then filled with buildings for government, commerce, en-tertainment, and worship. Chapter 1 of this book discussed Paul's confrontation with the Stoics and Epicureans, the latter believing that "when death comes, then we do not exist," and the former seeking duty in the face of a future that might perpetuate the human soul.[7] Both operationally rejected the mythology of the gods, so they were confused by the apostle who rejected paganism but taught the strange physical resurrection. They brought him to "Areopagus" (Acts 17:19), which can be translated either the "hill of Ares" or as the proper name of the civic council that had met there in earlier centuries. In the King James translation, Paul stands "in the midst of Mars' hill" (Acts 17:22), but the Greek is still "Areopagus." So many modern translations add "council" or "meeting," since "in the midst of" prefacing the speech (Acts 17:22) is the same Greek construction for Paul leaving "from among them" at the end of the speech (Acts 17:33). Paul prob-ably spoke to the Athenian governing body, which then met in the market and which would inquire into the possible harm-fulness of the "new doctrine" that he taught (Acts 17:19).

This Athenian background is useful because Acts gives Paul's speech at length. Aside from Paul's later public defenses, Acts gives one long speech on each missionary journey, and their ideas and vocabulary have close relationships to Paul's letters. In addi-tion to the typical Jewish speech in the Pisidian synagogue, the Athens speech adds Paul's typical words to educated Gentiles. Though delivered in Athens, it could be titled "Paul's Letter to the Stoic Philosophers," since he quoted their poets.[8] When

Strabo listed famous philosophers of Tarsus, most were Stoics, a pattern for the empire. Paul began with a local detail; in the city known for divine images, he discovered an altar dedicated to an "unknown god." A traveler in Paul's time also reported seeing "altars to the gods named unknown" in the Athenian harbor area.[9] Paul used this theme as the cutting edge. Paganism was unsure of itself, realizing that there may be other deities still not placated. But Paul appealed to the sense of his educated audience. Temples symbolized pagan mythology, which was inherited from times of ignorance—times of "lack of knowledge," which God had "overlooked" (Acts 17:30, literal trans.). Stoicism and Epicureanism both denounced pagan superstition. But if they knew enough to criticize paganism, they were still ignorant of the true God and his revealed son. Paul appealed to the conscience of his audience as he warned of a coming day of accountability, proved by the mission of Christ and the reality that God had "raised him from the dead" (Acts 17:31). Paul's reasoning cuts as sharply through confusion today: without revelation men do not know the true God and his wishes for them. Surprisingly, some commentators see the Athens speech as an experiment in intellectualism, one abandoned as Paul taught the simple gospel again at Corinth. But the opposite was the case, for Paul diagnosed the shortcomings of intellectualism and challenged the Athenians to leave speculation for scripture.

Few converts are reported at Athens, but then Paul did not stay long. He probably planned it that way on his arrival, for he sent Silas and Timothy the message to come from northern Greece, and he had gone west to Corinth before they arrived. There, the ministry of belief in Christ was also the ministry of baptism, for synagogue ruler Crispus "believed on the Lord with all his house; and many of the Corinthians, hearing, believed and were baptized" (Acts 18:8). In fact, Paul later mentioned Crispus among those he remembered baptizing when he wrote to the Corinthians (1 Cor. 1:14). But Jewish conversions brought intense ill will; Paul was forced to testify plainly and to leave off preaching to Jews. Was he to leave Corinth at this point? He had left three cities in northern Greece in similar circumstances. But a vision of the Lord came in the midst of this genuine need, for there are no pointless miracles in Paul's ministry. The Lord commanded, "Do not be afraid, but speak, and do not keep silent; for I am with you, and no one will attack you to hurt you; for I have many people in this city" (Acts 18:9-10, NKJB). The prophecy came to pass. After Paul preached a year and a half, a new governor was appointed. This aristocratic Gallio scorned the Jews and upheld the Roman rights of Paul—an incident critical for dating Paul's Corinthian ministry because Gallio's name appears on an inscription.[10] The Greek has Paul staying at Corinth "many days afterward" (Acts 18:18, literal trans.). The promise of protection and of rich harvest had been fulfilled. Paul then cut his hair, terminating his special "vow," perhaps one taken in solemn gratitude for the promise of the Lord in vision or for the fulfillment later when the tables were turned on his accusers. The Corinthian letters show how much leadership these new converts continued to need and how Paul insisted on the divine authority of his calling. Acts lays the background for the powerful Corinthian drama.

The third mission fulfilled Paul's hopes "to preach the word in Asia," whereas an earlier revelation had essentially said, "Not yet" (Acts 16:6-7). But after the second mission the time was ripe, and Paul's third mission in Acts powerfully illustrates the missionary message in its opening scene. On the way to Jerusalem after closing his Corinthian labors, Paul made a promise to return to the inquiring Jews at Ephesus. Months later he returned to find "about twelve" who were "disciples," a word clearly meaning baptized Christians in Acts, as we have seen. Paul's questions and their answers can be verbally diagrammed:

Question 1: Have ye received the Holy Ghost since ye believed?
Answer 1: We have not so much as heard whether there be any Holy Ghost.

Question 2: Unto what then were ye baptized?
Answer 2: Unto John's baptism.

Paul's response: John verily baptized with the baptism of repentance, saying unto the people that they should believe on him which should come after him, that is, on Christ Jesus.

Ordinances of Salvation in Acts

Ordinances	Directed by First Apostles	Directed by Paul
	(Leaders baptized by John: John 1:35-42)	(Baptized by Ananias: Acts 9:18; 22:16)
Baptism	Acts 2:38: Jews at Pentecost Acts 8:12: Samaritans Acts 8:38: Eunuch Acts 10:48: First Gentiles	Acts 16:15: Lydia and household Acts 16:33: Jailor and household Acts 18:8: Corinthians Acts 19:5: 12 "disciples"
Confirmation (gift of Holy Ghost through laying on of hands)	Acts 8:17: Samaritans	Acts 19:6: 12 "disciples"
Ordination or setting apart (authority through laying on of hands)	Acts 6:1-6: 7 assistants to the Twelve	Acts 13:1-3: Paul and Barnabas
Sacrament of the Lord's Supper	Acts 2:42, 46: Church at Jerusalem after Pentecost	Acts 20:7, 11: Church at Troas at Paul's farewell

These dozen were then rebaptized "in the name of the Lord Jesus," and "when Paul had laid his hands upon them, the Holy Ghost came on them; and they spake with tongues, and prophesied" (Acts 19:1-6). Luke uses this impressive incident to make several doctrinal points. First, the laying on of hands is necessary for the gift of the Holy Ghost. In another case, Luke clearly makes imposition of hands a necessary and regular procedure. After Philip's baptisms, the Holy Ghost had "fallen upon none of them: only they were baptized in the name of the Lord Jesus" (Acts 8:16). Even the proper baptism, Luke says in this parenthesis, will not bring the gift of the Holy Ghost until the completing ordinance is performed. Next, the apostles laid "their hands on them, and they received the Holy Ghost" (Acts 8:17). At a later time, the power of the Holy Ghost came upon Cornelius before baptism, but the Prophet Joseph Smith rightly stressed Cornelius's special circumstances as the first Gentile to be baptized. So the outpouring of the Spirit prior to his baptism was a sign of God's approval; had he not later "received the gift of the Holy Ghost by the laying on of hands," Joseph Smith said, the power of the "Holy Ghost, which convinced him of the truth of God, would have left him."[11] This distinction between the power and the gift is sound, for Jesus blessed the apostles, saying, "Receive ye the Holy Ghost" (John 20:22). In Joseph Smith's terms, they received the gift of, or right to receive, the Holy Ghost, but its spiritual force fell upon them later on the day of Pentecost (Acts 1:8, 2:4). It is true that Acts has only two examples of giving the Holy Ghost by the laying on of hands, but one example from Peter and one from Paul obviously show that the laying on of hands was part of the missionary message of both. Unlike the healings in Acts, there are no cases where this post-baptismal gift comes any other way (Acts 8:16).

These stories about Samaria and Ephesus are bound together by another cord. Simon the magician "saw that through laying on of the apostles' hands the Holy Ghost was given" and offered money for "this power" (Acts 8:18-19). This last word (*exousía*) could as easily be translated "authority," its regular meaning for Luke, who through this language shows the apostles with authority from God and Simon Magus without it. Luke made authority a major issue in Peter's giving of the Holy Ghost, so Paul's similar ministry must not be read without looking for true and false priesthood. The Ephesian "disciples" had to be rebaptized, which means that their first baptism was flawed, either in form or in authority. And at Ephesus, Luke highlights authority by telling about the Jewish magicians. Commanding an evil spirit to depart in the name of Jesus, they were ignored with the question, "Who are ye?" (Acts 19:15.) Only a few verses before, Paul put a similar question to the dozen disciples: "Unto what then were ye baptized?" John's baptism had the same form as that of Jesus. So the issue of who had the right to baptize is raised a little before the associated issue of who had the right to cast out an evil spirit. In these cases, Paul represented God whereas others did not, just as Simon Magus earlier recognized that Peter had "power" that he did not.

A glance back at Paul's dialogue on page 59 will show that he treated the twelve Ephesians as Christians, asking if the Holy Ghost came when they "believed" (Acts 19:2). In the words of one commentator, such a phrase must mean "when you believed in Jesus."[12] Many others agree that the same point is made by Luke's use of "disciple": "In Luke's writings this word used absolutely, always means Christians."[13] Yet Paul asked the dozen "disciples" to be rebaptized, explaining that John the Baptist always taught belief "on him which should come after him, that is, on Christ Jesus." Paul's words about belief on Christ must mean more than accepting Christ; in the words of a good analyst, "this his hearers had already done."[14] So what else from Christ should these "disciples" accept? Obviously, Paul as a true servant of Christ. In Jesus' words when the Twelve were first sent: "He who receives you receives me, and he who receives me receives him who sent me" (Matt. 10:40, NKJB). The confusion of asking believers to believe is solved by the fact that in Acts the true priesthood is shown with others waiting to counterfeit it. So at Ephesus Paul did not ask the dozen "disciples" to start to believe in Christ, but to accept Christ's true servants and their ordinances as the fulfillment of the work begun by John.

In Paul's final response, the first baptisms were deficient because John always promised the coming of the Christ. When we look at John's language in doing so, the Holy Ghost was an inseparable part of the promise, for three Gospels give the exact thought: the one coming afterward "shall baptize you with the Holy Ghost, and with fire" (Matt. 3:11). Since ignorance of the Holy Ghost was ignorance of what John taught, the dozen at Ephesus certainly had not heard him or one understanding his message. Thus, Joseph Smith went to authority as the point of the rebaptism: "No, John did not baptize you, for he did his work right; and so Paul went and baptized them, for he knew what the true doctrine was, and he knew that John had not baptized them."[15] Thus, Luke made a second point in both cases of laying on of hands for the gift of the Holy Ghost. The outward ceremony might even be imitated, but God's power will follow only God's delegated priesthood. Watching Peter and John at Samaria was Simon Magus, who had previously overwhelmed the Samaritans with his religious charisma, but even he knew that he could not give the Holy Ghost on whomever he would without the apostles' ordination (Acts 8:19). And at Ephesus the same point is made through baptism: defective teaching proved defective authority. John had not baptized the dozen at Ephesus, and whoever did lacked legitimacy. Thus, the priesthood is contrasted with false authority but proved by God's sending the gifts of the Spirit when Paul rebaptized and laid on hands.

The baptisms at the beginning of the third mission were the firstfruits of hundreds more. Paul had built up the Church at Corinth, where ships came to and from Ephesus and its sister ports of Asia Minor. These coastal cities were economic outlets for Roman Asia, roughly the western third of Asia Minor. That province exceeded most in population and prosperity, as Cicero said a little before Paul: "Asia indeed is as wealthy as it is fertile, so that it easily exceeds all lands in the richness of soil, in the variety of products, in the extent of pastures, and in the number of its exports."[16] Ephesus was a main political and religious center, and the Jewish community there probably learned of Paul's work while he was in Corinth, for they encouraged him to teach in their synagogue. Their interest lasted for three months after his return, a record in the book of Acts. When resistance and antagonism hardened, Paul next moved to a public hall, his daily forum and mission headquarters for two years (Acts 19:8-9). Paul would never have stayed this long without substantial harvest, which is indicated by the dramatic phrase that "all they which dwelt in Asia heard the word of the Lord Jesus, both Jews and Greeks" (Acts 19:10). Such wide exposure suggests widespread conversions, and the brief record of Ephesus bristles with clues on the numbers of conversions. A believers' bonfire was fed by astrological and magical books altogether worth 50,000 silver coins, each coin a day's wage for a common worker (Acts 19:19). Such a quantity could easily represent 5,000 who renounced superstition at conversion. And this momentum continued: "So mightily grew the word of God and prevailed" (Acts 19:20). The Ephesian stay closed with public protest led by idol makers, whose business was fading because converts ceased to worship in the great temple at Ephesus. The chief agitator shouted to the mob, "Throughout almost all Asia, this Paul has persuaded and turned away many people, saying that they are not gods which are made with hands" (Acts 19:26, NKJB). Nowhere else do we read of such impact.

Here Paul's view of the Church's future is highlighted—the paradox of greatest success and greatest pessimism. Here Acts fits the New Testament trend—the later the letter, the stronger the skepticism on the continuation of the true Church. And Paul's last letters are validated by Luke's report of Paul's farewell on his last mission. Paul's final letter combines the joy of celestial reunion with sadness about the future of God's work on earth. And so does Paul's last speech to the Church in Acts, the farewell to the Ephesian leaders. After the silversmiths' riot, Paul sailed to Greece to spend months in final visits to his converts as he traveled to Jerusalem with strong premonitions of captivity there. Returning by the Asian coast, he passed Ephesus under pressure of time, but stopped at the next large port and "sent to Ephesus, and called the elders of the church" (Acts 20:17). These must be "presiding elders," since Paul spoke to them of how the Holy

Ghost had made them overseers (Acts 20:28). The last word here is the Greek *epískopos,* elsewhere translated "bishop."[17] The speech to these priesthood leaders is similar to the Last Supper discourse of the Lord. It is the closing speech to the third mission. In Luke's record of the first two, there are examples of public preaching to Jews and also to educated Gentiles. But the end of the Asian mission illustrates Paul's personal views to Church leaders he was leaving.

Paul loved God's work and his converts more than his life. He reviewed his three years of labor at Ephesus, warning "every one night and day with tears" (Acts 20:31). A man who had built up the work so successfully would surely promise similar success to the local leaders with a tone of optimism for further growth and achievement. That would follow as a principle of successful leadership, and Paul was a successful leader. But he did none of this. The tears were not in thankfulness for new generations of Christians but in sadness in realizing that all that he had worked for would be spoiled. He bluntly warned of apostasy soon after his time: "For I know this, that after my departure savage wolves will come in among you, not sparing the flock; also from among yourselves men will rise up, speaking perverse things, to draw away disciples after themselves" (Acts 20:29-30, NKJB). "Perverse" literally means "turned around," the exact translation of Paul's Greek (*diastréphō*). Thus, Paul left the astounding testimony that local Christian leaders would reverse the apostle's doctrines. In the words of other translations, "distortion" would follow Paul's teaching of truth. Who would walk in Paul's steps? Not Christian leaders, he said; the successors of the apostles would be "savage wolves," words close to the Savior's portrayal of sheep who are really "ravenous wolves" (Matt. 7:15, NKJB). In both cases, only the appearance is Christian. Paul's point is that the Church itself will be corrupted. He does not say that part of the Church will remain faithful. He simply speaks of the factions of different disciples and leaves it at that. Paul expresses no hope for the continuation of the Church that he labored to create.

Paul's missionary work did not end with the third mission, for he lived another vigorous decade for the Lord. But Luke's detailed record of what he taught ends there, so the closing speech at Ephesus is Paul's last testament to the Church in Acts. That book carries on with the incredible Jerusalem-Rome odyssey, starting with the witness of the Holy Ghost "that bonds of afflictions" awaited him (Acts 20:23). On leaving the Ephesian elders, he already had plans "to go to Jerusalem, saying, After I have been there, I must also see Rome" (Acts 19:21). Did he know at that time that imprisonment would be the means of bringing his testimony to the leaders of his nation and of Rome itself? At Paul's conversion, the Lord told Ananias that Paul was "a chosen vessel unto me, to bear my name before the Gentiles, and kings, and the children of Israel" (Acts 9:15). He would defend his testimony before the Jewish Sanhedrin, governors, and King Agrippa, and would finally be brought before the imperial court. To Paul's credit, he never spoke on narrow legal issues but opened up the real source of conflict—visions and testimony of the Resurrection. After his arrest and first speeches at Jerusalem, Paul received his final known vision of the Lord, who commanded courage at the beginning of years of imprisonment, and prophesied, "As you have testified for me in Jerusalem, so you must bear witness also at Rome" (Acts 23:11, NKJB). This Roman imprisonment is the background of Paul's later letters. God's revelations had come to him in moments of deep trial with the assurance of the purpose in his persecution. But years of effort lay between each vision and its realization, a perspective to remember when reading Paul's teachings about "grace."

Paul wrote to those who had joined the Church of Christ through baptism and the laying on of hands for the gift of the Holy Ghost. Protestants downgrade ordinances and the Church because the Bible is their source of doctrine. Acts shows that the Church created the letters, the Church led by the Twelve, led by revelation, centralized in leadership and with common doctrine and practices. The letters are generally snapshots of branches of the Church at given times with their special problems, but the functioning Church is found in the moving pictures of Acts. The most successful individual translator of the New Testament today is J. B. Phillips. He has a Church of England background and is scholarly in capacity but disdains scholasticism of the scriptures. As he finished translating Acts, he wrote in awe of what he had watched at close range; he was "profoundly stirred" by the Early Church, which indeed raises serious questions now:

> Yet we cannot help feeling disturbed as well as moved, for this surely is the Church as it was meant to be. It is vigorous and flexible, for these are the days before it ever became fat and short of breath through prosperity, or musclebound by overorganization. These men did not make "acts of faith," they believed; they did not "say their prayers," they really prayed. They did not hold conferences on psychosomatic medicine, they simply healed the sick. . . . We in the modern Church have unquestionably *lost* something. Whether it is due to the atrophy of the quality which the New Testament calls "faith," whether it is due to a stifling churchiness, whether it is due to our sinful complacency over the scandal of a divided Church, or whatever the cause may be, very little of the modern Church could bear comparison with the spiritual drive, the genuine fellowship, and the gay unconquerable courage of the Young Church.[18]

Phillips asks why churches do not have revelation today. The answer lies with God and his ways of working. He ignored the university and religious centers of Paul's day in favor of calling his servants anew from all walks of life. Latter-day Saints testify that the visions of Joseph Smith remarkably parallel Paul's in number and content—that the powers of the Early Church are now restored in The Church of Jesus Christ of Latter-day Saints. Its members will find inspiration and evidence in Paul's letters to the Early Church.

NOTES

1. Compare the case of Silas, sent from Jerusalem with the apostles' decision on circumcision and substituting for Barnabas on Paul's second mission (Acts 15:27-40). But when Silas joined Paul in opening the two Thessalonian letters, he used the adapted name "Silvanus."

2. Strabo, *Geography* 14.6.3 (Loeb Classical Library).

3. From the settlement of Augustus just before Paul, Cyprus was a senatorial province and therefore ruled by a proconsul, an example of Luke's care and accuracy in political and geographical matters.

4. Those who think Mark was physically sick or homesick are underestimating the moral judgment that Paul made on this act, for he totally refused to take him on the next Gentile mission (Acts 15:38). Paul later forgave Mark, whose outlook no doubt broadened in following years. Later he was "profitable to me for the ministry" (2 Tim. 4:11), but the opposite was true when

Paul faced a second Gentile mission and must have felt that Mark was too conservative for that work.

5. "Pay attention to" is my translation of *proséchō*, a strong word of mental concentration and conversion. Both the account of Philip at Samaria and of Lydia indicate that baptism was preached as part of acceptance of Christ. NKJB makes the language consistent in English, as it is in Greek. The Samaritans were baptized after they "heeded those things which Philip spoke" (Acts 8:6). And Lydia was baptized after she "heeded the things which were spoken of Paul" (Acts 16:14). "Preaching Jesus" is also preaching baptism, as Luke also makes clear on Pentecost (Acts 2:38) and with the Ethiopian eunuch (Acts 8:35-39).

6. F. F. Bruce, *Commentary on the Book of the Acts* (Grand Rapids, Mich.: Eerdmans Co., 1964), p. 354. For a survey of Paul in Athens, see Richard Lloyd Anderson, "Paul and the Athenian Intellectuals," *Ensign*, Feb. 1976, pp. 50-55.

7. Epicurus, *Epistle to Menoeceus*, cited in C. K. Barrett, *The New Testament Background: Selected Documents* (New York: Harper and Bros., 1961), p. 74.

8. For specific phrases, see Bruce, pp. 359-60.

9. Pausanias, *Description of Greece* 1.3.4 (Loeb Classical Library).

10. See appendix A for this inscription and application to dates in Paul's life.

11. Andrew F. Ehat and Lyndon W. Cook, *The Words of Joseph Smith* (Provo, Utah: Religious Studies Center, Brigham Young University, 1980), p. 108. Since spiritual powers are gifts from God, Acts uses "gift" of Cornelius's prebaptismal sign, one that all prepared converts experience in some degree. But the additional gift of the permanent right to receive the Holy Ghost is what the Prophet discusses, one Acts defines as given by the laying on of hands.

12. F. J. Foakes-Jackson, *The Acts of the Apostles* (New York: Harper and Bros., [1931]), p. 175.

13. G. W. H. Lampe, "Acts," in Matthew Black and H. H. Rowley, eds., *Peake's Commentary on the Bible* (London: Thomas Nelson and Sons, 1962), p. 796e.

14. Foakes-Jackson, p. 176.

15. Ehat and Cook, p. 328. Compare the Burgess notebook on the same version: "Unto what were you baptized? And they said unto John's baptism. Not so, not so my friends—if you had you would have heard of the Holy Ghost. But you have been duped by some designing knave who has come in the name of John, an imposture. How do you know it, Paul? Why John verily baptized with water unto repentance, always telling the people that they should believe on him that should come after him—he would baptize with fire and with the Holy Ghost. John's baptism stood good, but these had been baptized by some imposture" (ibid., p. 333). "Impostor " may be intended where "imposture" appears.

16. Cicero, *On the Command of Pompey* 6.14.

17. The large numbers of conversions in Ephesus probably necessitated multiple branches of the Church there. Writing from Ephesus during the third mission, Paul includes greetings from "the churches of Asia" (1 Cor. 16:19), which might include several in Ephesus and its suburbs. Romans 16:1-16 suggests branches of the Church grouped around several of the people greeted there.

18. J. B. Phillips, *The Young Church in Action* (London: Collins, 1955), pp. 11, 20-21.

4

Early Letters to Converts

Paul's fourteen letters are arranged in the Bible in a rough order of length, but here they will be studied in their chronological order. Their basic sequence is quite clear, except for Hebrews, which will be grouped in chapter 6 with the great epistles on Christ. Translator J.B. Phillips printed his translation as "Letters to Young Churches," a title particularly apt for the Thessalonian letters studied here. These "Letters to Recent Converts" show an intense personal relationship, for Paul had been away from Thessalonica only a short time. But he was still in communication, writing about 250 miles away as messengers brought word of the personal and doctrinal struggles of the new members. Thus he taught Church doctrines and encouraged living by Christ's standards. Paul created relationships similar to the powerful ones that the Savior created while on earth. The opposite of distant abstractions, these letters reach out not only with the truth, but also with an intense desire that these converts live up to the truth.

1 THESSALONIANS

Profile

Sent from: Paul, at Corinth, joined by Timothy and Silvanus (Silas).

Sent to: Converts at Thessalonica, largest city in northern Greece.

Date: Probably early in A.D. 50.

Purpose: To express gratitude for their faithfulness and give encouragement after Timothy and Silas brought word from them.

Main themes: The meaning of conversion; missionary leadership; Church standards of living; resurrection and Christ's coming.

Background

The City

Today, Thessalonica is the largest city in northern Greece, a busy port and manufacturing and marketing center with a population of nearly half a million. Similar economic forces made it a major business and political center in Paul's time, though the population was not as great. It was the capital of Roman administration in northern Greece, the province of Macedonia. And Strabo says that Thessalonica was "more populous than the other" Macedonian cities.[1] It stretched below the coastal hills and had port-city characteristics that fit the mob scene in Acts, where some Jews struck back in resentment by stirring up "some of the evil men from the market-place" (Acts 17:5, NKJB). The market area or forum has now been discovered, with paved remains of ancient buildings lower than street level of the modern city. The major highway across Greece ran through Thessalonica; Strabo describes the Egnatian Road as starting from the ports opposite Italy and winding about five-hundred miles to the eastern side of Macedonia.[2] Jews at such a major center would have had wealth and influence.

Church Members

Paul's first conversions at Thessalonica are briefly but impressively told in ten verses opening Acts 17. At Philippi, Paul and Silas had been beaten, jailed, and miraculously freed. After receiving a lame apology from the city fathers, they judged it better to let the Lord and his earthquake have the last word. So they left their new but determined converts and went west on the Egnatian road to Thessalonica. They might have stopped at other cities along this eighty-mile route, but obviously they aimed to do missionary work where the greatest number of people were. Luke, reporting patterns and standard practices of the early apostles, says that Paul went into the synagogue and preached "as his manner was" (Acts 17:2). Three Sabbaths of Paul's plain testimony was all that most of his fellow-Jews could tolerate. Nevertheless, Paul had converted "some of them" and also a large group of the seeking non-Jews that associated with the synagogues — "and of the devout Greeks a great multitude, and of the chief women not a few" (Acts 17:4). Such numerous conversions are similar to those made today, which include "not a few" women. Though that phrase and "a great multitude" can scarcely be defined, some minimum can be guessed at. The Thessalonian church was surely numbered in the hundreds. The predominance of Greeks among them is indicated in Paul's recollection of "how ye turned to God from idols to serve the living and true God" (1 Thes. 1:9).

Two missionary companions of Paul were probably from this harvest. At the Ephesian riot, the crowd seized "Gaius and Aristarchus, men of Macedonia, Paul's companions in travel" (Acts 19:29). And those escorting him to Jerusalem after the third journey were "of the Thessalonians, Aristarchus and Secundus" (Acts 20:4). Aristarchus later went to Rome with Paul (Acts 27:2), where he joined those "of the circumcision" in sending greetings (Col. 4:10-11). But the convert pictured in Acts is Jason, who was perhaps wealthy enough to share a large house with the new branch. His home was the target of the violent demonstration instigated in anger by those resentful Jews. Failing to find the missionaries, the mob dragged Jason and "certain brethren" before the city magistrates (Acts 17:5-6). Luke's word here is "politarch"; though generally not a regular title for civic officials in the Roman Empire, it has turned up in about twenty inscriptions, many from Macedonia, including Thessalonica itself.[3] These magistrates heard the accusation that Christians believed in Jesus as king, not Caesar, a distortion that Jesus answered before Pilate. Perhaps the Greek officials saw through this verbal fog as Jason explained his beliefs. In any event, they made Jason pledge property that could be forfeited—in case of guilt, or perhaps in case of further disturbance. Paul, Silas, and Timothy left their converts in these circumstances, no doubt considering it best to allow a cooling off period before returning. "As his manner was" applies to Paul's preaching at the outset (Acts 17:2), but it also suggests leaving elders set apart to preside over the new branch of the Church, which was done in every city on the first mission (Acts 14:23). Paul mentioned these local leaders in his letter asking the Thessalonians to recognize those who "are over you in the Lord and admonish you" (1 Thes. 5:12).

Reason for Writing

One may be misled by the King James Version notes at the end of every letter. These little postscripts are called "subscriptions" from the fact that copyists wrote them underneath or after the letters. But the sentence notes appear very late—their earliest form is fourth century, so they are merely scribes' opinions. Why Paul wrote any letter must be learned from reading that letter, related ones, and in many cases the book of Acts. The general reason for all of Paul's letters was his desire to keep his converts strong in the faith and to guide them in perfecting their lives. He wrote always as an apostle, a term of special authority, since its Greek meaning is "one sent." His first sentence generally identifies him as an "apostle" by divine appointment, or an "apostle of Jesus Christ." This is true in the openings of nine of his fourteen letters. The exceptions include Hebrews, Philippians, and Philemon, each of which have special reasons of caution or affection for not using "apostle" in the lead sentence. The others without this characteristic are the two Thessalonian letters, perhaps because Paul joined Silas and Timothy in the salutations of each, or more obviously, out of special affection. Yet Paul makes clear that "we might have been burdensome, as the apostles of Christ" (1 Thes. 2:6). So the Thessalonian letters give his authority, though not in the openings.

Does the phrase "apostles of Christ" include Silas? We have
seen that Barnabas and Paul were called apostles on the first mission, after Barnabas came from the Twelve to direct the Antioch
Gentiles. Silas likewise started the second mission after coming to
Antioch from the Twelve with the Jerusalem council decision
and could have been ordained an apostle.

The story of 1 Thessalonians is the story of what Paul did in
the weeks after leaving the converts after Jason's mobbing. Slip-
ping away at night, Paul and Silas left Thessalonica and went
forty miles west to the next main city, Berea, where they entered
the synagogue and made converts as they had done at Thessalonica. But Jewish enemies from that city followed the missionaries to cause trouble, and when the people at Berea were
"stirred up" (Acts 17:13), Paul left for Athens, as surveyed in the
previous chapter. He fully expected to return to Thessalonica
from Berea, since he wrote that he would have returned before
going to Athens, "but Satan hindered us" (1 Thes. 2:18). Paul did
what he could to nurture the new converts in the unforeseen need
to go two hundred and fifty miles away: "Silas and Timothy remained there" (Acts 17:14, NKJB), an Acts sentence referring to
the general area of Berea. But Paul added a detail in writing, saying that he "thought it good to be left in Athens alone, and sent
Timothy" to Thessalonica (1 Thes. 3:1-2, NKJB). Yet Paul's plan
to send Timothy would logically be developed before leaving for
Athens, avoiding the strange result of taking his companion to
Athens only to send him back because he had not made up his
mind before. Since Acts has Paul come to Athens alone and send
for his companions, the best reconstruction is to have Paul plan to
leave, sending Timothy to Thessalonica before departing from
Berea, and probably keeping Silas at Berea. Thus, both sets of
new converts would be supervised in Paul's absence.

As indicated earlier, Paul's stay in Athens was dramatic but
not fruitful. Depressed at first by the city full of idols, he sent word
back for "Silas and Timothy to come to him with all speed" (Acts
17:15, NKJB). But in the meantime he completed what he intended at Athens and went west fifty miles to Corinth, political

and economic capital of southern Greece. There, Silas and Timothy arrived "from Macedonia" (Acts 18:5). Paul opens his first letter to the Thessalonian converts with gratitude that they are strong in the gospel. His concern shows how important following through is in all leadership in the Church and family. Timothy was sent "to *establish* you, and to *comfort* you concerning your faith" (1 Thes. 3:2, italics added). The italicized words are not strong enough in today's English—Timothy was to "strengthen" *(stērízō)* and to "encourage" *(parakaléō)*. All Christian religions see the importance of faith, but Paul knew that without continuing leadership, faith could fail. So after assigning Timothy to build up faith, he was anxious to receive a report. He repeats his concern twice: he could "no longer *forbear*" (1 Thes. 3:1, 5, italics added) to wait at Athens without news. Again, the italicized word is traditional but inadequate; Paul says that he could no longer "endure" the suspense *(stégō)*. He worried that conversion would be pointless if they failed to follow through. But the two companions came from northern Greece with "good news of [their] faith" (1 Thes. 3:6, NKJB), at which point the apostle penned gratitude and further encouragement to strengthen that faith. Such circumstances show the incompleteness of mere belief in Christ. The sequence appears on the chart on the next page. (For a discussion of dating, see appendix A.)

Main Teachings

The Meaning of Conversion

"For our gospel came not unto you in word only, but also in power, and in the Holy Ghost, and in much assurance" (1 Thes. 1:5). Recounting his preaching at Thessalonica, Paul also reviewed the courage of those receiving "the word in much affliction, with joy of the Holy Ghost" (1 Thes. 1:6). The blend of joy and persecution challenges all who are comfortably converted, for in Greece great spiritual power was generated in conflict. Paul said that the Thessalonians became his and the Lord's "followers," a term *(mimētḗs)* that specifically means "imitator" in

The Writing of First Thessalonians:
Background in Acts and the Letter

Acts	1 Thessalonians

1. Paul's Exile from Northern Greece

17:10: "And the brethren immediately sent away Paul and Silas by night unto Berea"

2:17: "Being taken from you a short time in presence"

17:13-14: "But when the Jews of Thessalonica . . . stirred up the people . . . the brethren sent away Paul to go . . . to the sea"

2:18: "We would have come unto you, even I Paul, once and again; but Satan hindered us"

2. Paul's Plan to Be in Athens Alone

17:14: "But both Silas and Timothy remained there" (NKJB)

3:1-2: "We thought it good to be left at Athens alone"; Timothy sent "to comfort you concerning your faith"

3. Paul's Request at Athens for His Companions

17:15: Those conducting Paul "brought him to Athens; and receiving a command for Silas and Timothy to come to him with all speed, they departed" (NKJB)

3:5: "When I could no longer endure it, I sent to know your faith, lest by some means the tempter had tempted you, and our labor might be in vain" (NKJB)

4. Arrival of Paul's Companions at Corinth

18:1, 5: "Paul departed from Athens, and came to Corinth. . . . Silas and Timothy were come from Macedonia"

3:6-7: "But now that Timothy has come to us from you, and brought us good news of your faith . . . we were comforted" (NKJB)

Greek literature. Paul wrote with years of experience in facing antagonism, rejection, and violence. And the new Christians proved themselves worthy of such leaders and of Christ himself in making their love for the gospel first and what might happen to them secondary. Modern missionaries know many who reverse these priorities—converted but cowardly. Such decisions for the Lord are not easy, but the Saints' intense love for one another is increased by their suffering together for the high ideals of the kingdom. Paul alluded to the first persecutions of Peter and the early disciples after the Resurrection. The Thessalonians faced a similar trial by becoming "imitators" (the same word as above) of the Judean "churches"; they "suffered like things of your own countrymen, even as they have of the Jews" (1 Thes. 2:14). And this example powerfully aided Paul in his work in southern Greece, which he calls "Achaia," the technical name for that province. Thus in north and south, the Thessalonians' sacrifices declared the gospel without words (1 Thes. 1:7-9).

Missionary Leadership

Paul dedicated his life and then gave his life for the reality of his visions and the certainty of the life to come. His testimony rings true because he shares his inmost convictions that honest people must recognize. There is a close correlation between Paul's discourse in the Thessalonian synagogue in Acts and his sketch of his message and feelings in giving it. Reasoning out of the scriptures, Paul declared "that Christ must needs have suffered, and risen again from the dead; and that this Jesus, whom I preach unto you, is Christ" (Acts 17:3). The angry mob searched for him because these words reached so many. In writing, Paul told the Thessalonians that he knew the cost of plain words because of his recent experience at Philippi, where he had been publicly beaten. But that did not make him more cautious, for at Thessalonica "we were bold in our God to speak unto you the gospel of God with much contention" (1 Thes. 2:2). His only fear was failing to fill a divine commission: "But just as we have been approved by God to be trusted with the gospel, so we speak, not as pleasing men, but

God, who proves our hearts" (1 Thes. 2:4, literal trans.). When in Paul's life did he waver from that attitude? When did he ask odds of a world pouring out scorn and physical abuse? When did he show an ounce of self-doubt about his calling? Paul was a thinking, functioning, productive person. There can be no reasonable question about his sanity. So one studying him must face a life that points to the visions motivating and sustaining him. This feat was accomplished in a world where he and his fellow apostles could rarely meet to sustain each other. His leadership was the leadership of the Lord, who called and directed him. He knew that past persecutions would be repeated. "We told you before," he reminded the Thessalonians, "that we would suffer tribulation, just as it happened, and you know" (1 Thes. 3:4, NKJB). That was the apostles' calling, as the Savior told the original Twelve. Their total sincerity is written in their willing suffering for the truth.

Most of Paul's letters have substantial sections that are personal, not doctrinal. Paul was certainly capable of writing long letters on the vast gospel message, but his converts did not need a total diet of celestial truths as much as they needed a sustaining relationship with their file leader in the priesthood. In short, Paul's goal in writing the new members was brotherhood, not brilliance. This approach casts much light on what Jesus meant in telling and retelling Peter to feed his sheep. A little before that conversation after the Resurrection, Jesus simply said that the great evidence of the gospel is not logic but the inspired love that Church members have for one another: "By this shall all men know that ye are my disciples, if ye have love one to another" (John 13:35). Paul says so much about his gratitude for the wonderful news that the Thessalonians were still faithful; about half the letter speaks in some way to this point. Thus, 1 Thessalonians preserves valuable doctrine and an invaluable example. Paul's concern teaches today's leaders to communicate and in those communications to personally express the righteous feelings of their hearts. And Paul's concern was not just an occasional letter to those he led. He planned to revisit them when possible (1 Thes. 3:11), but while absent he prayed "night and day" for their progress in the faith (1 Thes.

3:10). Sincere love begets sincere prayers, so Church members were to "pray without ceasing" (1 Thes. 5:17) for themselves, their families, their brothers and sisters in the faith, and their leaders: "pray for us" (1 Thes. 5:25). Old and new scriptures command teaching one another, to which must be added helping one another and praying for one another.

Church Standards of Living

New Church members who "turned to God from idols" (1 Thes. 1:9) also turned from a worldly to a godly life. Midway through and closing 1 Thessalonians, Paul reminded them of the high standards of Christlike living. "The will of God" for Church members is their "sanctification" (1 Thes. 4:3), a term meaning "holiness" that will be explored in depth later. Step one toward that goal, Paul says, is to "abstain from fornication" (1 Thes. 4:3). Nine of Paul's fourteen letters have direct instruction on this subject, as did the apostles' letter that Gentile converts must "abstain . . . from fornication" (Acts 15:29). The term in Greek (*porneía*) refers to unlawful sexual intercourse for single or married people. Thus, the Early Church commanded sexual self-control. Man-made religion had no such standard, but the apostles taught God's way. Paul added the command that each use "his own vessel in sanctification and honor, not in passion of lust, like the Gentiles who do not know God" (1 Thes. 4:3-4, NKJB). Some modern translations substitute "wife" for "vessel," an inaccurate idea; the Greek means "vessel," a household jar or any equipment, its regular New Testament use. But a person can be the instrument of God—Paul was a "chosen vessel" (Acts 9:15). Thus, one's "vessel" is his person. Each body is a tool for its owner, who is commanded to control it righteously. One freer translation interprets Paul's thought in this way: "Each one of you must learn to gain mastery over his body" (1 Thes. 4:4, NEB).

Paul reminds the Thessalonians of a number of other gospel ideals: honesty, respect for other children of God, "brotherly love," forgiveness, self-reliance, helping the needy, and cultivating spiritual gifts. Like other letters, 1 Thessalonians closes with encouragement to seek good and to avoid every evil. But Paul did not attempt to catalog every duty, for their appointed leaders would be counselors and guides in their progress in gospel living. The Early Church was serious about the moral development of each convert, so it was also serious about the need of having and respecting priesthood leaders: "And we urge you, brethren, to recognize those who labor among you, and are over you in the Lord and admonish you, and to esteem them very highly in love for their work's sake" (1 Thes. 5:12-13, NKJB).

Resurrection and Christ's Coming

Before closing his letter, Paul answered a problem that the missionaries communicated from Thessalonica. It concerned deceased loved ones and their status in the Resurrection. Paul began by correcting any ignorance about those "which are asleep, that ye sorrow not, even as others which have no hope" (1 Thes. 4:13). This telling contrast of Christian faith and ancient agnosticism shows another higher standard preached by the missionaries. A little before Paul there was Catullus, a sophisticated and educated Italian poet, an example of the young man who had everything that his culture could offer. Writing verse to his lover "Lesbia," he sought for gentle pleasure now, for "When once our brief light sets, there is only the sleep of eternal night."[4] But Paul told both the Thessalonians and Corinthians that Christ's sure resurrection meant that those who "sleep in Jesus will God bring with him" (1 Thes. 4:14). What is the place of dead loved ones at Christ's coming? Some form of this question was the Thessalonians' problem, for Paul's words translate, "For this we say to you by the word of the Lord, that we who are alive and remain until the coming of the Lord will by no means precede those those who are asleep" (1 Thes. 4:15, NKJB). Paul uses a common Greek verb (*phthánō*) with the basic meaning of "be first." Thus, the King James Version uses an obsolete Latinism—the living "shall not prevent them which are asleep" means that the living shall not "come before" (*pre* [before] plus *venio* [come]) the dead. In what way could the living "come before" or have a better status than the dead? There is no objective answer, but the logic of the question is revealing to Latter-day Saints, for no hint is given that the Thessalonians doubted the Resurrection—when the Corinthians later did, Paul wrote one of the longest and most passionate New Testament chapters on their inconsistencies. So the Thessalonians' worry about the status of their dead must not stem from doubt that they would be resurrected. Their worry must have been about *how* they would come forth. Paul goes on to speak of the glorious coming of the dead "in Christ" first, with those on earth afterward caught up to meet them. But who would seriously ask in what order the living or dead come forth on resurrection day, since they share eternal glory at nearly the same time? If the Thessalonians would not be worried about the Christian dead, what about the immense problem of their relatives who died before the gospel arrived? Would they come forth afterward, in the last resurrection? (1 Cor. 15:23-24.) We do not know their precise concerns, but this is the most logical area for their serious questions. In 1 Corinthians 15, baptism for the dead was associated closely with the Resurrection in Paul's mind, and the acceptance of the gospel by the dead may be suggested in 1 Thessalonians 4. Peter mentions preaching the gospel in the spirit prison (1 Pet. 3:18-20); Paul could refer to prior teachings that those not hearing of Christ on earth may hear after death and be "in Christ" by the time of the Resurrection.

No description exceeds Paul's of the dramatic moment of the glorious coming of the Lord. Here and in 1 Corinthians 15 is mentioned the piercing call of the "trump of God"; there is also the "voice of the archangel"—literally the mighty "ruling angel" (1 Thes. 4:16). [5] Paul refuses to discuss the "times and the seasons" (1 Thes. 5:1), the same language the Lord used to tell the Twelve that it was not for them to know the timetable of the restoration of Israel and of his second coming (Acts 1:6-7). But Paul vividly outlines how unprepared the world will be when "the day of the Lord" bursts through mortal walls "as a thief in the night" (1 Thes. 5:2). Yet that brilliant day is not something to be feared, Paul assures his brothers and sisters, for "ye are . . . the children of the day"

(1 Thes. 5:5), preparing for "salvation by our Lord Jesus Christ, who died for us, that, whether we wake or sleep, we should live together with him" (1 Thes. 5:9-10).

This last verse says that Paul does not know whether or not he or the Thessalonians will be alive at Christ's coming. Yet many commentators ignore this for the urgency of the earlier language: "We which are alive and remain unto the coming of the Lord" (1 Thes. 4:15). But that is only a manner of speaking, not prophecy, since Paul so plainly avoided speculating on when Christ would return. Describing the same scene later, Paul spoke of "they that are Christ's at his coming" (1 Cor. 15:23). Joseph Smith avoided any misleading impression by revising 1 Thes. 4:15 to read, "They who are alive at the coming of the Lord" (JST).

2 THESSALONIANS

Profile

Sent from: Paul, at Corinth, joined by Timothy and Silvanus (Silas).

Sent to: New members at Thessalonica, largest city in northern Greece.

Date: Probably midyear in A.D. 50.

Purpose: To correct the belief that Christ would come soon and to motivate members not to use Christ's coming as an excuse for idleness.

Main themes: Christ's coming and judgment; the imminent apostasy; the commandment to work.

Background

The City

See the sketch under First Thessalonians.

Church Members

The Thessalonians' conversion and first communication with Paul was discussed under 1 Thessalonians. Why were they singled out for a second letter above the other two Macedonian churches? One answer is that the Thessalonians had problems that did not exist at Philippi or Berea, the other northern groups described in Acts. It is also possible that Paul was speaking to all those Saints through the Thessalonian letters, since Thessalonica lay between the other two and the traveling distance was not great either way. The Thessalonians lived in the commercial and political center of the province and were possibly the largest Macedonian church. Thus, Thessalonica may have been the stake center or location of regional Church authority in northern Greece. What Paul sent to Thessalonica was surely shared with the other two major churches in their area. Ships from this port city made regular trips to Corinthian harbors, the busiest in southern Greece, where Paul stayed to preach.

Reason for Writing

The Thessalonians had a doctrinal problem as well as a practical problem growing out of it. Silas and Timothy had joined Paul at Corinth (Acts 18:5), and Paul immediately sent his first letter back to the Thessalonians, perhaps by one of these companions. At some point word came back from the north that the Thessalonians were "shaken in mind" with the false idea that Christ would come in the very near future (2 Thes. 2:2). Paul wrote that they were "soon" or "quickly" shaken, so a short time had passed since Paul had been with them. Thus, Paul was still at Corinth, where he continued to preach for some two years (Acts 18:11, 18). From there he authored a letter of correction and instruction. Appendix A shows that Paul arrived at Corinth about the beginning of the year A.D. 50. He wrote 2 Thessalonians some time later, after several communications had gone back and forth between southern and northern Greece.

You must not be troubled, Paul insisted, "by spirit, nor by word, nor by letter as from us, as that the day of Christ is at hand"

(2 Thes. 2:2). This very literal translation incorporates the Greek "as," which removes the responsibility for an idea away from the writer. Paul says that the idea of Christ's immediate coming is not his: "as if from us" (NKJB), "purporting" (RSV, NEB) or "supposed to have come from us" (NIV). But there are two possibilities. Paul does not deny writing a letter but denies writing a letter that says that the coming of the Lord is near. Some commentators imagine a forged letter, linking that idea with Paul's own signature at the end of 2 Thessalonians, his proof of authenticity "in every epistle" (2 Thes. 3:17). But instead of proving an earlier forged letter, these words show that Paul regularly signed to identify his views plainly. Indeed, Paul names a letter and two other options as the source of this notion of an imminent Second Coming. What was quoted above can be paraphrased: "Wherever you learned this false concept, it is wrong, whether from someone's prophecy [by spirit], or from someone's preaching [by word], or by letter misread to mean that such doctrine came from us." If Paul knew of a forged letter, he would likely have said so instead of generalizing about an atmosphere of excitement that included the use of his name. This sounds more like a false interpretation of 1 Thessalonians than a forged letter.

Paul earlier described Christ's coming in this way: "For when they say, 'Peace and safety!' then sudden destruction comes on them" (1 Thes. 5:3, NKJB). The Greek "sudden" (*aiphnídios*) basically means "unforeseen" or "unexpected." But "sudden" does not here mean "soon"—Paul had used no time estimate in teaching about Christ's appearance. Thus he wrote again to the Thessalonians to explain clearly that the apostasy would come first. But Paul worried about more than false ideas, for misconceptions breed wrong actions. In this case, Paul identified the problem while answering it: "For we hear that some of you are living in idleness, mere busybodies, not doing any work" (2 Thes. 3:11, RSV).[6] In Greek there is a play on words between working (*ergázomai*) and working aimlessly (*periergázomai*), which some translations try to reproduce: "They are not busy; they are busybodies" (2 Thes. 3:11, NIV.)

Main Teachings

Christ's Coming and Judgment

The letter on Christ's second coming starts with a broad panorama of it, for Paul's message is not that the coming is unimportant but that certain events and preparations must precede it. Paul wrote that "the Lord Jesus shall be revealed from heaven with his mighty angels, in flaming fire taking vengeance on them that know not God, and that obey not the gospel of our Lord Jesus Christ" (2 Thes. 1:7-8). Here the apostle sums up a basic doctrine linked in language and idea with the Savior's own testimony of it: "For the Son of man shall come in the glory of his Father with his angels; and then he shall reward every man according to his works" (Matt. 16:27). The point of knowing of the coming of the Lord is to be ready for his judgment, whenever it occurs. That view contradicts the attitude of passive waiting criticized by Paul at the end of this letter. What works prepare one for judgment? At Athens Paul answered generally by declaring God's command to "all men every where to repent" before Christ "will judge the world in righteousness" (Acts 17:30-31). Jesus counseled the Twelve specifically after opening the future "when the Son of man shall come in his glory, and all the holy angels with him" (Matt. 25:31). There on the Mount of Olives he emphasized feeding and clothing and fellowshipping. Paul's letters were all written to prepare the early Saints for judgment. The book of Romans, the great epistle on grace, also begins with a vivid picture of judgment and the need to prepare for it, later adding detailed instructions on Christian living. Paul weaves faith in and out of his Thessalonian letters, but always against the pattern of action. He prays that God will strengthen the Saints "in every good word and work" (2 Thes. 2:17) and makes them responsible to bring this about. Judgment implies freedom to make choices, so the goal of Paul's letters is stronger faith plus righteous action. Joseph Smith put that same burden on Latter-day Saints in teaching that the horizon of death should "prove as a warning to all men to deal justly before God and with all men—then we shall be clean in the day of judgment."[7]

The Imminent Apostasy

Paul reviews the false belief that "the day of Christ is at hand" (2 Thes. 2:2). Replacing it with the truth, Paul insists that there must "come a *falling away* first" (2 Thes. 2:3, italics added). In Greek, "falling away" is *apostasía*, derived from "standing" and "away" in the sense of evading and opposing authority. Closely related is *stásis*, a central word in Greek history that often had the same meaning of standing alone in civil war. And Josephus uses the related *apostasía* to describe the Jewish uprising against Rome.[8] Thus, modern translators have Paul speak of a "great revolt" (JB) or "rebellion" (RSV, NEB, NIV) that must precede Christ's coming. Paul, of course, means a religious departure, just as the Greek translation of the Old Testament uses *apostasía* for a hypothetical "rebellion" of all Israel against God (Josh. 22:22). In Paul's prophecy God is openly opposed by "that man of sin" (2 Thes. 2:3), so careful commentators do not treat the coming "apostasy" as just a minor thorn in the side of Christianity. A Roman Catholic translation has "mass apostasy" (NAB), and seasoned Protestant scholars talk of a "worldwide rebellion";[9] it is unmodified by Paul and therefore total: "By and large, the visible Church will forsake the true faith."[10]

But Christian scholars do not think of Paul's prophecy as undermining Catholic or Protestant churches, because they generally view the prophecy as yet to be fulfilled just before Christ's coming. It is true that Paul foresaw Christ coming to end the worldwide apostasy (2 Thes. 2:8), but that does not prove that the apostasy was at a late hour in Christian history. Although Paul said the apostasy would come in its time (2 Thes. 2:6), he defined the time as beginning then, saying "The mystery of iniquity is already working" (2 Thes. 2:7, literal trans.). Paul wrote to get the Thessalonians to face their problems and quit daydreaming about the future. The Second Coming was not at hand; their real worry was the apostasy. Paul said that he had stood in their midst and "told you these things" (2 Thes. 2:5). Commentators regret that what Paul spoke personally about this has been lost.[11] But what was important enough to explain in his first brief stay at Thessalonica would likely crop up again. And it did when Paul stood before the Ephesian elders to warn, "After my departure savage wolves will come in among you, not sparing the flock" (Acts 20:29, NKJB). Thus, Paul's typical speech about the coming apostasy was not about the distant future, but about dangers then threatening the Church: "Therefore watch, and remember that for three years I did not cease to warn everyone night and day with tears" (Acts 20:31, NKJB). What was vital at Ephesus must have been spoken at Thessalonica.

Paul's central symbol of the apostasy is the man of sin or lawlessness sitting "in the temple of God, shewing himself that he is God" (2 Thes. 2:4). Pounds of pages have been written about this being the Jerusalem temple, but that would be destroyed within two decades and would have no one sitting in it. And what did that temple mean to the Greek Gentiles or even to apostles in terms of their own religion without Mosaic sacrifices? The real question is how Paul used the word *temple* in his writing.[12] Almost always he used it figuratively—occasionally the body is a temple for God's Spirit, but usually the Church is the temple of God. The members ("ye," older plural English for the plural Greek) are "God's building" (1 Cor. 3:9), with Christ its foundation (1 Cor. 3:11), or, in summary, "the temple of God" (1 Cor. 3:16). Elsewhere Paul teaches about Christ as cornerstone, apostles as foundation, and members fitting into their places as a "holy temple in the Lord" (Eph. 2:21). And in one of his last letters, Paul still spoke of "the house of God, which is the church of the living God" (1 Tim. 3:15). Paul must define Paul, and his own words show that he was here referring to the Church.

The structure of the Church would remain, but the presence of God would depart. Paul warned at Ephesus that the false teachers would come from "your own selves"; leaders then hearing Paul would reverse the truth "to draw away disciples after them" (Acts 20:30). Thus, the Church would not disappear, but would be captured by the enemy. Who that enemy is need not be debated, for there is only one. Paul uses various terms that are appropriate names for Satan, the mastermind of evil. No wonder that

John would soon say that the prophecy of the coming of "anti-christ" was fulfilled, for "even now there are many antichrists. . . . They went out from us, but they were not of us" (1 Jn. 2:18-19). Despite centuries of theories about the identity of Paul's "Man of Sin," the New Testament leaders indicated no one but Satan with such power to oppose God.

Common sense demands that prophecies be integrated, not isolated, and the Lord's earlier words to the Twelve gave a sweep of events, of which Paul's concise sketch is part. Paul said the "lawless one" (2 Thes. 2:8, NKJB) would show "signs and lying wonders" (2 Thes. 2:9). And Jesus earlier said there would be "false Christs and false prophets" who would show "great signs and wonders," and that, if possible, "they shall deceive the very elect" (Matt. 24:24). Both surveyed the same era of apostasy, with the difference that Christ stressed the many under Satan's influence, while Paul stressed the source—the "lying wonders" would be "after the working of Satan" (2 Thes. 2:9). In Jesus' prediction, the era of apostasy would be preceded by the era of apostles. But they would be hated and killed (Matt. 24:9), and Jerusalem would be destroyed (Matt. 24:15-16). And right after these first-century events would come "great tribulation" (Matt. 24:21); then men would seek the true Christ in vain (Matt. 24:23) but find only false teachers and their false wonders (Matt. 24:24). Paul explains this transition between two eras more obscurely. Something "withholds," or more accurately in modern transla-tions "restrains" (2 Thes. 2:6). In the next verse the same Greek term is translated as "lets," but this also means "restrains."[13] In terms of Jesus' prophecy, the true apostles restrain or delay the coming of the false ones. But this insight is incidental to the great point of both prophecies—that the truth and true authority held by the apostles would disappear until God would once again show his power in the latter-day events surrounding the Second Com-ing.

The Commandment to Work

Paul closes 2 Thessalonians with words of command (2 Thes.

3:4), expressing strong feelings about the report that "some" were idly wasting their time, "working not at all" (2 Thes. 3:11). As mentioned, Paul opened the letter by stressing the moral responsibility to prepare for the Second Coming. He knew that lazy thinking brought lazy waiting for God to care for everything. But the Early Church taught a morality of money. Paul insists on the Lord's way in specific "commands" on working for a living. Such language elevates practical affairs to high ethical responsibility. One verbal parallel is the earlier language of the Ten Commandments, containing specific instructions on property in the commands not to steal (Ex. 20:15) and not to covet (Ex. 20:17). Paul spoke for the Early Church in explaining the duty to be industrious and shoulder one's share of the cost of life. It is part of the New Testament perspective of coming to earth for a purpose and therefore receiving time as a stewardship.

Paul's "commands" use the terms of Greek military and court orders. He gave the first one when preaching at Thessalonica: "This we commanded you, that if any would not work, neither should he eat" (2 Thes. 3:10). That bluntly states the ideal held up to new converts—not social seclusion but financial responsibility: "Aspire to lead a quiet life, to mind your own business, and to work with your own hands, as we commanded you, that you may walk properly toward those who are outsiders, and that you may lack nothing" (1 Thes. 4:11-12, NKJB). Self-reliance is so important that Paul later "commanded" the Thessalonians "in the name of our Lord Jesus Christ" to avoid the person who would not work for a living (2 Thes. 3:6). The traditional translation of "withdraw" is too strong, for Paul returned to the point, saying that the lazy person should not be treated as an "enemy" but admonished "as a brother" (2 Thes. 3:14-15). Church membership would not be withdrawn, but idlers were not worthy of full fellowship, partly to avoid the danger of others being drawn to an aimless life. Appealing directly to the offenders, Paul again used his authority: "We command and exhort by our Lord Jesus Christ, that with quietness they work, and eat their own bread" (2 Thes. 3:12).

Paul also taught by example in Thessalonica: "Nor did we eat anyone's bread free of charge, but worked with labor and toil night and day, that we might not be a burden to any of you" (2 Thes. 3:8, NKJB). This labor was going on while "we preached unto you the gospel of God" (1 Thes. 2:9). He wrote these letters while he still continued his tentmaking work at Corinth, for Acts describes it (Acts 18:1-3), and Paul vigorously told the Corinthians that he was never a financial burden to them (2 Cor. 11:9). Of course, he accepted the hospitality of Lydia at Philippi and gifts of support from time to time, for he knew how to receive as well as to give. But through his incredible example of working while teaching, he proved that he was on the Lord's errand of helping people spiritually, not profiting from them financially.[14] This practice continued through the third mission at Ephesus, for Paul reviewed his time there with the eloquence of action: "I desired no one's silver or gold or clothing. You yourselves know that these hands served my needs and the needs of those with me. In everything I showed you that by thus laboring, you must help the weak and remember the words of the Lord Jesus. For he said, 'It is more blessed to give than to receive'" (Acts 20:33-35, literal trans.).

These words catch the impact of a principle spoken from the soul of one who had made it his own. They show that insistence on work was taught on the level of what each could do, for sustaining those in need was a core principle in Paul's philosophy and in the regular welfare contributions of the Early Church. "If any *would* not work, neither should he eat" (2 Thes. 3:10, italics added) is treated as a common motto by commentators, but it may well have been an operating rule measuring when to give help. It sounds like a curt formula, "No working, no eating," but the italicized "would" is a separate Greek verb, meaning "to desire" or "to want to." Paul is saying that one should not eat if he is unwilling to work; he is speaking to those who can but do not.

Administrative problems of welfare are later discussed in 1 Timothy 5. All these passages show that a church not concerned with the morality of earning and the charity of sharing does not have the full philosophy and program of the Early

Church. Paul quoted a saying of Jesus that it is more blessed to give than to receive (Acts 20:35). Although Paul applied this to working with his hands, living that principle made him the great missionary that he was.

NOTES

1. Strabo, *Geography* 7.7.4 (Loeb Classical Library).
2. Ibid.
3. See the summary in James Hope Moulton and George Milligan, *The Vocabulary of the Greek Testament* (Grand Rapids, Mich.: Eerdmans Publishing Co., 1980), p. 525. Compare William F. Arndt et al., *Greek-English Lexicon of the New Testament* (Chicago: University of Chicago Press, 1979), p. 686.
4. Catullus 5:5-6: *"cum semel occidit brevis lux, nox est perpetua una dormienda."*
5. The only other "archangel" reference in the New Testament is to "Michael the archangel" (Jude 1:9). The equivalent Old Testament concept is "Michael the prince," who labors for Israel in the events just before the second resurrection (Dan. 12:1-2). Similarly, in modern revelation "Michael, mine archangel, shall sound his trump" before the second resurrection (D&C 29:26). He is "Michael, or Adam, the father of all, the prince of all, the ancient of days" (D&C 27:11).
6. The word translated "idleness" in the RSV is translated "disorderly" in the King James Version (*ataktōs*). It fundamentally means "out of ranks" or "out of order" but was used in ancient apprenticeship contracts of not keeping a promise to work a certain number of days a year. George Milligan, *St. Paul's Epistles to the Thessalonians* (Grand Rapids, Mich.: Eerdmans Publishing Co., 1953), pp. 153-54.
7. Andrew F. Ehat and Lyndon W. Cook, *The Words of Joseph Smith* (Provo, Utah: Religious Studies Center, Brigham Young University, 1980), p. 113.
8. Josephus, *Life of Josephus* 43 (Loeb Classical Library).
9. F. F. Bruce, *Word Biblical Commentary: 1 & 2 Thessalonians* (Waco, Tex.: Word Books, 1982) 45:166.
10. William Hendriksen, *New Testament Commentary: Exposition of I and II Thessalonians* (Grand Rapids, Mich.: Baker Book House, 1979), p. 170.
11. For example, Leon Morris, *The Epistles of Paul to the Thessalonians* (London: Tyndale Press, 1963), p. 128 (commenting on 2 Thes. 2:5): "The imperfect tense *elegon* may have the meaning 'I used to tell you' . . . Paul had evidently spoken much of the second coming in his original preaching, and he expected the Thessalonians to recognize his allusions accordingly."
12. Since Paul earlier taught the Thessalonians about this subject (2 Thes. 2:5, 15), the vocabulary of the letter was not unique and should be found in other letters.
13. The Greek term in both verses is *katéchō*; an example of its use is Josephus's description of John of Gischala trying to "restrain" or "hold back" the revolt against Rome at its outset. (Josephus, *The Life* 43.) The King James usage is seen in Shakespeare's *Hamlet* (act 1, scene 4), where Hamlet's friends try to keep him from following the ghost of his father, and he answers, "Unhand me, gentlemen. By heaven, I'll make a ghost of him that lets [restrains] me."
14. For a survey of Paul's self-support and support by others, see Frank J. Goodwin, *A Harmony of the Life of St. Paul* (Grand Rapids, Mich.: Baker Book House, 1960), pp. 207-8.

5

Letters of Reconversion

"Moreover, brethren, I declare to you the gospel which I preached to you . . . by which also you are saved, if you hold fast that word which I preached to you—unless you have believed in vain" (1 Cor. 15:1-2, NKJB). In these words Paul virtually wrote his own introduction to the Corinthian letters. The Saints at Corinth had believed, prospered, and divided, with parties opposing Paul and many doctrines he had taught. Because Paul had to correct so much, he wrote more to Corinth than to any other branch on record. The two Corinthian letters contain more than a fourth of the content of all fourteen of Paul's letters. They include much interaction—answers to letters, references to the faithfulness and unfaithfulness of the Saints, even quotations from skeptics and critics in connection with Paul's replies. Hence, these letters candidly picture a troubled branch of the Church and Paul's logical and spiritual convictions in response.

First Corinthians is Paul's most valuable letter of reconversion. His follow-up letter also has great personal and practical insights, but 1 Corinthians contains an incredible range of doctrine. Here we see the essence of the true Church in its revelation, inspired organization, and knowledge of the life to come. Although Galatians and Hebrews are also reconversion letters, they are more specialized. They are really deconversion letters against Jewish interpretations of Christ. But the Corinthian letters, particularly 1 Corinthians, cover Christ's mission plus a broad spectrum equaled by few of Paul's letters. So 1 Corinthians is treated in unusual detail because it furnishes unusual detail on Christian beliefs and practices. Most of what Paul taught in all the letters is set on larger foundations in 1 Corinthians. By thoroughly repreaching the gospel, Paul in 1 Corinthians gives special insight into what was commonly believed by the Church members to whom Paul's many special letters were written.

1 CORINTHIANS

Profile

Sent from:	Paul, at Ephesus, joined by Sosthenes.
Sent to:	Members at Corinth, provincial capital of southern Greece.
Date:	Not long after the Passover, about A.D. 57.
Purpose:	To correct dissension in that branch, to correct many wrong beliefs and actions, and to prepare them for Paul's future visit.
Main themes:	Appeal for unity; revelation and man's wisdom; Paul's apostleship; sexual standards; marriage questions; true and false worship; Church organization and spiritual gifts; pure love; the Resurrection.

Background

The City

Paul's Corinth still stretches under Greek skies and looks down on the blue water of the Corinthian gulf. Some of its marble remains come from later periods of remodeling, but the site has not changed much, thanks to the resettlement of the modern village so that archaeologists could continue to unravel the past. Paul looked up at the Acrocorinth, the blocky mountain watching over the city, which in pre-Roman times was a nearly invincible fortress. The visitor today can walk into the small museum and see the stone block that sat over the doorway of the Jewish synagogue. Half of the letters are intact, reading "Synagogue of the Hebrews" in rough cuts that could easily date to Paul's time. Back in the main marketplace, he can look at the long stone platform that was probably where the new governor sat when Paul was accused before his tribunal.

When Corinth was alive, it flexed powerful muscles. Strabo said that it was "always great and wealthy."[1] Rome made southern Greece into the province of Achaia and made Corinth its capital, as readers know from the Gallio incident in Acts. Trade passed to and from the southern section of Greece through a Corinthian funnel, and cargoes to and from Italy were regularly routed through Corinth in days when ships navigated near the shores rather than risked open sea. Thus, Paul was at a communications center while at Corinth and was accessible to Corinth in his Asia Minor stay afterward. The city was a few miles from the narrow passage where Mediterranean waters nearly turned the south into an island. This land bridge was about five miles wide, and today a straight-cut canal makes it unnecessary to ship around dangerous southern shores, saving miles of circuitous travel. In Paul's day cargoes and small ships were pulled across this isthmus. This symbolizes Corinth's prosperity, which Strabo said came because "it is situated on the isthmus and is master of two harbors, the one leading straight to Asia and the other to Italy."[2]

This trade center was also a center of wickedness, as 1 Corinthians clearly shows. In its early success, the Greeks coined a verb "Corinthize," meaning to enjoy worldly pleasures. The big cities of the Roman Empire were like today's big cities in offering the best and the worst, though there was no general Christianity then to temper society. The Romans had destroyed Corinth in the Greek wars, but it was refounded a century before Paul with a strong Roman influence—first-century inscriptions are heavily Latin. Ancient sources picture a city with the vitality and seductiveness of the Chicago pictured by Carl Sandburg's poem. Immorality problems are more visible in 1 Corinthians than in any other letter of Paul except that to Rome itself. Plutarch attacked predatory bankers, and those from Corinth led the list.³ Yet the existence of bad society does not make all society bad. The Lord stood before Paul in vision and commanded him to stay and gather his people out of this worldly center. Because Corinth has so many parallels to any major modern city, what Paul wrote to the Corinthians has great relevance to Saints today.

Church Members

Acts 18 describes Paul's conversions at Corinth on the second mission. He bore plain testimony and left the synagogue when Silas and Timothy first came from Macedonia. Crispus, the "chief ruler of the synagogue" had been converted "with all his house" (Acts 18:8), and Paul baptized him (1 Cor. 1:14). The rich harvest followed in which "many of the Corinthians hearing believed, and were baptized" (Acts 18:8). Several gave possessions and time to the work. Justus was a devout Gentile who also left the synagogue and opened his neighboring home as a meeting place (Acts 18:7). Paul's missionary companion Erastus was apparently from Corinth. He was sent with Timothy back to Greece on the third mission (Acts 19:22) and remained at Corinth at the end (2 Tim. 4:20). Perhaps he was the official thought to be "treasurer [oikonómos] of the city" at Corinth, from which Paul sent Romans (Rom. 16:23, NKJB). An inscription at the large Corinthian theater mentions an Erastus that donated the pavement when he was aedile, a secondary civic office. It is tempting to see the same man in all of the above.

Paul also baptized two others. Gaius (1 Cor. 1:14) was perhaps the "host" when Paul later visited Corinth (Rom. 16:23). Paul also baptized "the household of Stephanas" (1 Cor. 1:16). The apostle insisted that they be recognized as "the firstfruits of Achaia, and that they have devoted themselves to the ministry of the saints" (1 Cor. 16:15, NKJB). If his family had shared service positions, Stephanas stands out as one with presiding authority in Corinth. For Paul uses the masculine pronoun next with these words —"so you may also be subject to such men and to each fellow-laborer and worker" (1 Cor. 16:16, literal trans.). Wherever there are adequate sources, local priesthood officers emerge, with Paul encouraging the Saints to support them. The character of the Corinthian branch can be appreciated only by reading the Corinthian letters. Some ridiculed Paul, promoted factions in their branch, aggressively dominated the meetings, and doubted major doctrine. Paul's patient but firm leadership is constant in his Corinthian letters. Here was a branch in need of strong local and general authorities.

Reason for Writing

First Corinthians was not the first letter to the Corinthians. Their earliest known problem is bluntly stated: "I wrote to you in my letter not to fellowship sexual transgressors" (1 Cor. 5:9, literal trans.). So problems of living gospel standards went along with problems of doctrine. One could expect as much from their worldly environment. When Paul first wrote to the Corinthians, he was probably at Ephesus, due east across the Aegean, for in Acts he left Corinth to visit Jerusalem and returned to Ephesus to begin the third mission. He was still there when writing 1 Corinthians, for he sent greetings from "the churches of Asia," the province of Ephesus; and he intended to "tarry" (*epiménō*) in Ephesus until Pentecost, after which he would visit the Greek churches (1 Cor. 16:5-8). (See appendix A for the date of these plans.) Paul received word from those sent by Chloē, evidently a woman of prominence, that there were factions in the Corinthian branch. Some were loyal to Paul and some to Cephas (Peter's Aramaic name; 1 Cor. 1:11-12; John 1:42). Peter had probably visited Corinth, since Paul talks about Peter's travels with his wife as being well known to the Corinthians (1 Cor. 9:5). A third group followed Apollos, the brilliant Jewish convert with Alexandrian polish, whose intense Corinthian missionary work is known (Acts 18:24-28, 19:1).

So there was deep dissension at Corinth, but it is important to see this lack of unity as really an authority problem. Is it an accident that most of the local leaders known at Corinth were then at Ephesus with Paul and joined to support his correction of the Corinthians? Apollos sent greetings but deflated his faction by staying to work with Paul in a clear showing of unity with the apostle (1 Cor. 16:12). Priscilla and Aquila, who had worked faithfully as missionaries with Paul before going to Ephesus, sent their greetings through Paul to Corinth (1 Cor. 16:19). The strange joining of Sosthenes with Paul in opening 1 Corinthians surely has some purpose. He is possibly the Jewish synagogue leader who was beaten by the anti-Semitic crowd when Paul was accused before the governor (Acts 18:17). Was he now converted and associated with Paul to show to the faction "of Cephas" that faithful Jewish converts should follow the apostle then in their region? Stephanas is identified in the above sketch of members, a leader to whom the Corinthians should "submit." He and two associates came to discuss Corinthian problems with Paul, for they were returning to the branch with Paul's command: "Give recognition to such men" (1 Cor. 16:18, RSV). Paul does not merely teach Christian unity in 1 Corinthians; unity must come through following local officers supervised by apostolic authority.

First Corinthians is a doctrinal gem, ranging through the ancient gospel with a scope unmatched by most of Paul's letters and equaled by only one or two. Were the Corinthians especially worthy of receiving such a letter? The opposite is the case, for the most faithful branches did not need reconversion. And 1 Corinthians is a letter detailing the basics that were disbelieved and giving testimony and evidence to bring the full truth again to the Corinthians. The letter is so specific because the Corinthians were so confused. One can hear Paul preaching in 1 Corinthians better than in any other place except Acts. He repreaches the Resurrection to doubters and repreaches sexual morality to those who had reverted to worldly ways. He takes modern readers into the meetings and homes of early Christians to correct their carelessness in eating meat of pagan sacrifice, not eating the Lord's Supper with reverence, and allowing zeal to run uncontrolled in open meetings. He answers doctrinal questions and shows that the ultimate answers to all these problems are true spirituality, respect for priesthood leaders, and Christlike love.

Main Teachings

Appeal for Unity

"Is Christ divided?" (1 Cor. 1:13.) That searching question demands a look at Christ's goal for his Church. Setting apostles over it (Matt. 18:17-19) and naming a presiding prophet in their midst (Matt. 16:18-19), the Lord trained them carefully in leadership and at the end prayed for them and all the believers they would direct:

> And now I am no more in the world, but these are in the world, and I come unto thee. Holy Father, keep through thine own name those whom thou hast given me, that they may be one, as we are. . . . As thou hast sent me into the world, even so have I also sent them into the world. . . . Neither pray I for these alone, but for them also which shall believe on me through their word—that they all may be one; as thou, Father, art in me, and I in thee, that they also may be one in us: that the world may believe that thou hast sent me (John 17:11, 18, 20-21).

As chapter 1 of this book shows, a minority in the world believes in Jesus Christ, and the wrangling of Christians has certainly contributed to skepticism in the message and mission of the Master. Indeed, if the energy spent attacking other Christians had been seriously spent on uniting and teaching non-Christians, Christ's goal would have been much further along—"that the world may believe that thou hast sent me." For Paul, it is self-evident that a divided Church violates Christ's will.

Christ commissioned preaching to the nations and envisioned the unity of all converts under the apostles, but the apostles faced the practical era of putting these plans into operation. In Paul's case, there is not a letter without mention of the ideal of unity. One striking thing about his letters is how often problems of dissension arise and how firm he is in not allowing separations into different Christian groups. A dozen major verses elsewhere match his plea to the Corinthians "that ye all speak the same thing, and that there be no divisions among you; but that ye be perfectly joined together in the same mind and in the same judgment" (1 Cor. 1:10). Christian leaders have immersed themselves in the Bible and know this. Their public regret at the loss of unity is as common as Paul's frequent insistence on God's requirement of unity. The problem is widely admitted, but the solution evades all.

Yet Paul did not raise major questions without giving clear answers. The solution to the problems of factions discussed in chapter 1 of 1 Corinthians is the Church's inspired central leadership discussed in chapter 12. Paul's answer is not harmonious with official Protestantism, which divided from Rome because it perceived in the Roman church central authority without inspiration. Latter-day Saints are now asking the world if God cannot bring together what history divided. Christ's prayer for unity included a special prayer for the inspired central leaders who would direct that unity. Without Paul the branches constantly fragmented. It was his work to resolve conflict—to direct, teach, and correct. He did not ask the Corinthians to debate differences in a church council or ecumenical conference. Unity would come by harmony with the apostles' doctrine and leadership.

However, many Christians read the Bible without seeing the original Church of Christ in it. They sometimes explain away baptism because it is a church ceremony, sometimes using Paul's words: "For Christ sent me not to baptize, but to preach the gospel" (1 Cor. 1:17). In this explanation, one is saved by believing the preaching of Christ, but baptism is secondary and nonessential. But what happened at all the cities of Greece in Acts 16 and Acts 18? Upon belief, Lydia and the jailor were baptized at Philippi, and the Corinthians "believed, and were baptized." Early Christians did not profess Christ and treat baptism as optional; for them, baptism was the commanded method of showing belief. Paul seems to minimize baptism for one reason—the Corinthians were using his personal baptisms to promote their factions. In these circumstances he did not reduce the importance of baptism, but the importance of who baptized them: "I thank God that I baptized none of you, but . . ." (1 Cor. 1:14). He readily remembered Crispus and Gaius, then recalled Stephanas's household, and faded away with not remembering "whether I baptized any other" (1 Cor. 1:16). He obviously made the point that whom he baptized was insignificant, but it indeed mattered that the Corinthians *were* baptized. Later he reviewed how one achieved salvation through the true Church, and the first step was baptism: "For by one Spirit we were all baptized into one body— whether Jews or Greeks, whether slaves or free" (1 Cor. 12:13, NKJB). If there were no exceptions, baptism was not optional. And Paul, the enemy of useless religious requirements, would not have taught "all" a principle unessential to salvation.

As Paul explained his relationship with Apollos, he said they were co-workers on the same building, God's temple or Church. He added the image of farming: "I have planted, Apollos watered; but God gave the increase" (1 Cor. 3:6). Thus "he who plants and he who waters are one" (1 Cor. 3:8, NKJB), a verbal construction identical to Jesus' language, "I and my Father are one" (John 10:30).

There is no more biblical reason for merging the Father and Son than for thinking that Paul and Apollos physically merged. In his prayer for unity, already quoted, Jesus equated the oneness of believers with the oneness of the Father and Son. And at the end of 1 Corinthians, Paul teaches the glorious resurrection of individuals; so like the believers, the Father and the Son exist in glory now as individuals. Otherwise Paul could not sensibly close his plea for unity with the verbal separation of the Father and Son: "and ye are Christ's; and Christ is God's" (1 Cor. 3:23). If the members of the Godhead have achieved such intimate cooperation as individuals, the challenge of family and Church members to do the same also seems possible.

Revelation and Man's Wisdom

Unity requires humility. Indeed, Jesus said that one entering the Kingdom must "humble himself as this little child" (Matt. 18:3-4). Paul sought to humble the Corinthians for their own good, as the arrogance of some led them to dictate to God instead of being taught by him. Pride is the opposite of humility—pride of status, pride of wealth, and pride of having all the answers. The apostle who used his talents and intellectuality for the Lord did not teach the glory of ignorance, but he showed that man's highest knowledge, without revelation, falls short of preparing him for eternity. "Christ, and him crucified" (1 Cor. 2:2) was the beginning of his message, which blended with "Christ and him resurrected," as Paul says in 1 Corinthians 15. Paul reviewed the human scoffing at this revelation in order to warn the Corinthians against their own feelings of superiority to revealed doctrines. Men of great success tend to be too smug to accept the gospel, Paul observed; in modern terms, the highly educated, the powerful in business or government, and those born to privilege did not generally accept the gospel (1 Cor. 1:26). Paul gave a Thessalonian-like review of how he came to Corinth, a picture seen well either through the synagogue testimony beginning in Acts 18 or through Paul's memories beginning in 1 Corinthians 2. Paul did not preach with the skill of human persuasion, but by the power of God's Spirit, "that your faith should not be in the wisdom of men but in the power of God" (1 Cor. 2:5, NKJB).

This is no small point. At the beginning of a long letter of instruction, Paul went back over the Corinthians' belief in his message. Their Greek philosophy taught no resurrection; their native religion did not feature an atonement and the call to obey the first principles. The gospel came by revelation and had to be validated by the witness within. Faith and reason ultimately harmonize, but human reason knows little of the eternal dimension that the gospel brings. Paul used Isaiah's verbal picture of God's power and kingdom, which will transcend what eyes have seen and ears have heard (Isa. 64:4). People instinctively explore and inquire, reaching beyond their limited world through books, newspapers, television, radio, conversations with visitors, and travel. Eternity and its requirements can be learned only through these heavenly counterparts: scriptures, prophets, revelations of the spirit, angels, and visions. So Paul as a living prophet reminded the Corinthians that they must seek for the Holy Ghost to raise them above the ignorance of arrogance. Regarding the things of eternity, he wrote, "God has revealed them unto us by His Spirit. For the Spirit searches all things, yes, the deep things of God" (1 Cor. 2:10, NKJB). The whisperings of eternity are near the one with the Spirit. God's reality and God's will for that person are within reach. Those seeking a higher way will find constant refreshment and challenge in Paul's review of the power of the Holy Ghost in the second half of 1 Corinthians 2.

Paul's Apostleship

Several times in 1 Corinthians 4, Paul calls his detractors "puffed up," a Greek word meaning just that, inflated ego, filled with pride. Later in his defense he states his position vigorously (1 Cor. 9:1): "Am I not an apostle? am I not free? have I not seen Jesus Christ our Lord?" Paul answered accusations of exploiting the Corinthians for his own gain, his point being that any apostle had the right to be supported by the Church, though he had not used that right out of his love for the Corinthians. The power of his apostleship stands out, for his revealed calling was so sure that "necessity is laid upon me" (1 Cor. 9:16); willingly or unwillingly, he was responsible for a "dispensation" (1 Cor. 9:17), a powerful word of delegation translated "stewardship" in the Gospels. Paul asked the Corinthians to whom stewards were accountable. He noted that priesthood leaders are "the ministers of Christ, and stewards of the mysteries of God" (1 Cor. 4:1). The Corinthians, Paul said, had no right to judge him, for "He who judges me is the Lord" (1 Cor. 4:4, NKJB). In the Early Church men were appointed to low and high office by divine authority, and apostleship was delegated from God. The agent was responsible to the one who appointed him. Thus, backbiting could not diminish Paul's right to come and set affairs in order (1 Cor. 4:21): "Shall I come unto you with a rod, or in love in the spirit of meekness?"

Modern revelation teaches the balance between divine authority and common consent. After Joseph Smith's death, Brigham Young presented himself and the Twelve to the Church for sustaining, saying that the people had the right to accept or reject their leadership, but that the Twelve had authority and would, if necessary, raise up a people elsewhere.[4] Yet Christ's priesthood is delegated with his example of forthright but unselfish leadership. Paul later taught that pure love is constant, and he refused to be rejected by those he was called to lead. Although he criticized them, they were literally "his children" (*tékna*); he was their father in the gospel (1 Cor. 4:14-15). Parents are often hurt by rebelliousness and lack of appreciation by their children, but in that role Paul did not complain. He listed inconvenience, strain, and danger constantly suffered to bring the gospel to new souls. If they rejected him, he would speak plainly but not cease to love. He personifies the role of the priesthood (and by implication motherhood) repeatedly outlined by Jesus—the higher the office, the more generous the sacrifice of time and concern (Luke 22:26).

Sexual Morality

No one exceeds Paul in being candidly positive about sexual love in marriage (1 Cor. 7:1-6). But Paul unites with all true prophets in restricting sexual intercourse to marriage. Nothing so quickly brands today's man-made prophet as his permissiveness on sexual relations. Some politicians frequently place popularity over principle, disguising their compromises with noble words. So do some religious leaders who ignore, explain away, or dispense with the commandment of chastity as given through Moses and repeated by Christ and Paul and Joseph Smith in modern revelation. Another form of religious avoidance is teaching a standard of morality but looking the other way. The Early Church countered serious sexual transgression with action. Paul was shocked to hear of a case of incest and simply said that local leaders should meet and deliver the offender to Satan and his powers of "destruction of the flesh" (1 Cor. 5:5). The chapter later clarifies that as excommunication of "that wicked person" (1 Cor. 5:13); and later in life Paul spoke of two whom he had "delivered unto Satan, that they may learn not to blaspheme" (1 Tim. 1:20). This last phrase is the point, for consequences are lessons. Which churches today have a court system for serious transgressions? Which churches by their actions teach cheap forgiveness and repeated sin? In a half-dozen major places, Paul lists the sins that will keep one out of God's kingdom if unrepented, whether before or after conversion. Included are the major sins of dishonesty and physically or verbally harming one's fellowmen. And such lists never fail to include sexual relations outside of marriage. If God will really exclude the unrepentant on that basis, how honest is a church with its members if it will not? The false prophet is one who teaches a false expectation. The integrity of the Early Church and the restored Church is shown in their discipline of immorality in wise but firm court decisions on membership. Anything less misrepresents the kingdom of God. "Do you not know that the unrighteous will not inherit the kingdom of God? Do not be deceived" (1 Cor. 6:9, NKJB). Paul then gives two terms for unlawful sex between man and woman and two for homosexuality. The King James Version frankly translates these latter words "effeminate" and "abusers of themselves with mankind." The former does not refer to the tender qualities of woman that might well be shared by men, but means "soft" with the connotation of a male perverted to a female role with other men. And the second word is bluntly "men lying with men." The current propaganda of self-justification avoids Paul's words here and in Romans 1.

With the logic of Christ, Paul's sternest chapter on sexual sins is also the most hopeful about repentance. After discussing the above sins and others that bar one from the kingdom of God, Paul refers to the repentant, buried past: "And such were some of you; but you were washed, but you were sanctified, but you were justified in the name of the Lord Jesus and by the Spirit of our God" (1 Cor. 6:11, NKJB). The purifying forgiveness of Christ and sanctifying power of the Holy Ghost came only after baptism and was retained only through a moral life. Yet the astounding power of the gospel provides the path up from the valley of darkness. The invitation of the gospel is not condemnation but change. If some Corinthians were guilty of serious sins, were they in the Lord's mind when he told Paul to labor there at length because he had "much people in this city" (Acts 18:10)? Paul's ministry at Corinth is a sober warning to avoid immorality and a serious motivation to repair the damage done by it. Paul's blunt words to the Saints expose the inconsistency of incontinency and set an eternal value on sexual purity: "Your body is the temple of the Holy Ghost which is in you" (1 Cor. 6:19).

Marriage Questions

Paul's discussion of marriage is incomplete and was written for special circumstances, and the controversial half on unmarried or engaged women is labeled as Paul's opinion, not as a "commandment of the Lord" (1 Cor. 7:25). Joseph Smith throws refreshing perspectives on the chapter that scholars should seriously consider. Most translations have Paul begin with the grim generalization, "It is good for a man not to touch a woman" (1 Cor. 7:1). This is a strange statement for a scripturalist who elsewhere relies on Genesis, which commands man to leave parents and be "one flesh" with his wife (Gen. 2:24), a passage cited by Christ himself (Matt. 19:5). But Joseph Smith's translation makes "not to touch a woman" part of the Corinthian's letter of inquiry and not Paul's answer. That rings true to other sentences in 1 Corinthians that translators surround with quotation marks. For Paul clearly quotes views and communications of others to refute them (for example, 1 Cor. 10:23, RSV, NEB, JB, NIV). In this case Paul's refutation would be the tender picture of married love in the next four verses, exactly reversing the mood of "not to touch a woman." That phrase and the whole chapter is prefaced by, "Now concerning the things whereof you wrote to me" (1 Cor. 7:1, NKJB), which simply means we have here some answers to unknown questions. Listening to only half of a conversation is frequently misleading. So it is better to outline key issues rather than give a false impression that the full chapter is well understood.

What does Paul think of marriage? The parties are free to choose to be married (1 Cor. 7:36), and marriage is righteous (1 Cor. 7:28). These verses add that duties of marriage may compete with serving the Lord, conflicting somewhat with the positive views of the family in Ephesians. The skepticism on widows remarrying (1 Cor. 7:39-40) is directly contradicted by the young widow's duty to marry and raise a family noted in 1 Tim. 5:14. So 1 Corinthians 7 seems to relate to special circumstances. Following Christ, Paul warns against easy divorce (1 Cor. 7:10-11). Throughout the chapter is a steady theme of loyalty to a married partner once that relationship is made.

Was Paul an example of celibacy? Chapter 2 of this book discussed the firm Jewish ideal of marriage and Paul's repeated claim that he failed in no religious duty. Thus, he must have been married as a young man. He gives himself as an example to the "unmarried and widows"—"it is good for them if they remain even as I am" (1 Cor. 7:8, NKJB). One tendency here is to see Paul as a widower, serving the Lord rather than remarrying. But another option is persuasive; he was using himself as an example of sexual self-control (1 Cor. 7:7). "With consent for a time" (1 Cor. 7:5) did he leave his wife to pursue a dangerous mission at Ephesus? Clement of Alexandria wrote about A.D. 200 and responsibly worked from earlier sources. He claimed knowledge of Paul's marriage, identifying his wife with the "yokefellow" of Philippians 4:3: "Paul himself does not hesitate in one of his letters to address his yokefellow, whom he did not take about with him in order to facilitate his mission."[5] The apostles as a group were examples of both marriage and companionship in the ministry, for Paul said that he had "power to lead about a sister, a wife, as well as other apostles, and as the brethren of the Lord, and Cephas" (1 Cor. 9:5). That whole chapter argues that Paul could have required the Corinthians to support him but didn't. But Paul stresses his literal "authority" to ask for support for self and for wife. Would he renounce a right of support that was never a possibility? That passage really takes for granted Paul's marriage and the Corinthians' knowledge of it.

Was Paul giving regular rules for marriage? Paul discourages marriage only "for the present distress" (1 Cor. 7:26). Elsewhere in the Bible this last word is "necessity" (*anágkē*). Paul next says that "the time is short" (1 Cor. 7:29), following with the conclusion that normal marriage relationships and business activity should be suspended. Commentators quickly leap to Paul's supposed belief that Christ's coming loomed on the horizon, which completely violates what he said on the subject in 2 Thessalonians 2. Yet Paul is certainly concerned about doing the Lord's work under a deadline, whether that deadline is coming persecution, coming apostasy, or just the "necessity" of facing the huge task of reaching so many with such small resources. The Joseph Smith Translation says simply that this "necessity" was missionary work, a situation that today would delay marriage for a time, an exception to the regular rule of the Church: "But I speak unto you who are called unto the ministry. For this I say, brethren, the time that remaineth is but short, that ye shall be sent forth into the ministry. Even they who have wives, shall be as though they had none; for ye are called and chosen to do the Lord's work" (1 Cor. 7:29, JST).

True and False Worship

Preserved among the "waste papers" of antiquity are invitations to private dinners, wedding feasts, and dining at pagan temples.[6] All touched the daily life of the Corinthians, and church members had to decide on the morality of eating at the table of a god. Animals sacrificed to the "idol" were available for temple feasts with the surplus marketed for food. Paul partly agreed with Corinthian rationalizers—the gods were mythical, and the pagan priests offering sacrifices were powerless. Yet the principle of eating in pagan worship was wrong, even if the motivation was food, not worship. What kind of an example was being set, Paul asked, for the weaker brother? (1 Cor. 8:10.) After reviewing Israel's idolatry at the exodus from Egypt, Paul made the critical point that walking the borderline of any principle is not living the principle: "Ye cannot drink the cup of the Lord, and the cup of devils: ye cannot be partakers of the Lord's table, and of the table of devils" (1 Cor. 10:21). At the other extreme was the surplus sacrifice that was sold in the market (the obsolete "shambles" of 1 Cor. 10:25). When commercially offered, that would be simple food and not a matter of conscience (1 Cor. 10:25-26). But the case was reversed if a person was invited to a private home and someone identified the food as "offered in sacrifice," for no Christian could consciously honor any god but the true one and his Son (1 Cor. 10:28). Temples of Zeus and Athena have long ceased to operate, but the temples of drinking, gambling, pornography, and questionable entertainment invite worshipers and visitors alike. "Partakers of the Lord's table" today must still avoid every "table of devils."

With their lack of judgment on idol worship, would some do better in Christian meetings? Paul opens Corinthian doors wide for the answer. The letter begins with their "divisions" based on cults of personality; then more "divisions" erupted in their most sacred worship, the commemoration of the Lord's Supper. Indeed, they mocked its purpose by gluttony, each one virtually eating "his own supper" (1 Cor. 11:21). Their greed is clear, whether it was gorging on the consecrated bread and wine or on a common meal held in connection with the ceremony. Paul's correction is also clear—church was not the place to satisfy physical appetite; the Saints should eat at home and wait patiently for each other and the Lord's spirit in the Christian meeting (1 Cor. 11:33-34). The sacrament of the Lord's Supper is a solemn moment, Paul insists, putting over his point by telling the story of Christ first establishing it (1 Cor. 11:23-26). The reader of the Gospels takes this for granted, but when Paul wrote this letter there were probably no Greek Gospels. His account is very close to Luke's record of Christ's blessing of the bread and wine (Luke 22:19-20). The Gospels of Mark and Luke were likely written a few years later, but 1 Corinthians reports specific facts about Christ's last instruction and his resurrection. This shows that the Gospels were based on carefully preserved data, which one would suspect, knowing the value of both truth and the memory of the Lord to the Early Christians.

But there is so much more here than the retelling of the Last Supper and the Corinthians' abuses. Paul gives the most detailed Biblical insight into the purpose of this ceremony. Those who ate and drank thoughtlessly were told what to think about: "But let a man examine himself, and so let him eat of that bread, and drink of that cup" (1 Cor. 11:28). Before taking these symbols, one is obligated to consider the Lord as well as whether one's life is in harmony with the Lord's will: "This do in remembrance of me" (Luke 22:19; 1 Cor. 11:24). But does Christ merely ask for adoration? At the Last Supper he solemnly challenged those who had partaken of the consecrated bread and wine: "If ye love me, keep my commandments" (John 14:15). One must not read Paul's Corinthian correction narrowly, for to "examine yourself" is a general teaching for all, not merely for the greedy offenders. The same is true of the warning not to eat and drink "unworthily" (1 Cor. 11:27).[7] For Paul, the "cup of blessing" and the broken bread are visible signs of "communion" with Christ (1 Cor. 10:16). That term (koinōnía) means a "common sharing" and is usually translated "fellowship." In the letters one has "fellowship" with heaven and with the Church if one's life is in order. There is a "fellowship" or "communion of the Holy Ghost" (2 Cor. 13:14), but it comes only "to them that obey" God (Acts 5:32). Paul states this general principle (2 Cor. 6:14): "And what communion hath light with darkness?" Thus, the sacrament of the Lord's Supper was a symbol of visible relationship to God through Christ, accompanied by self-examination of the worthiness of one's life. These simple but profound relationships characterized the Church after Pentecost, which faithfully continued "in the apostles' doctrine and fellowship, and in breaking of bread, and in prayers" (Acts 2:42).

All of this means much to a Latter-day Saint, with the revealed sacrament prayer calling for remembrance through being called by the Lord's name, with the obligation to "keep his commandments," and with the eternal promise of his Spirit.[8] Contemporary with the last books of the New Testament, a literate Roman governor examined Christians carefully and wrote the emperor that the central act of their worship was "a solemn oath . . . never to commit any fraud, theft or adultery."[9] A few decades afterward, Christians prayed in the sacrament meetings "that we may be counted worthy, now that we have learned the truth, by our works also to live good lives and be keepers of the commandments, so that we may be saved with an everlasting salvation." Then just before the distribution of the bread and wine, a prayer of thanks was offered "for our being counted worthy to receive these things."[10] From Paul through another century, the emphasis is the same as the restored ordinance—to "always remember him and keep his commandments which he has given them."[11] Why do Christians today celebrate the sacrament of the Lord's Supper? One should ask his Protestant and Catholic friends. Many see a sacramental value without grasping the motivational value of gaining strength to lead a righteous life. Typical answers show a lack of focus, a tendency to participate in a mystical drama or share a ceremony without the covenant of obedience distinctly stressed in the Early Church. Here is another mark of the restored gospel with sobering obligations for believers in it.

Early Christian worship involved organization and participation. Standardized ceremonies today tend to create a passive Christian audience, but attending the Early Church was anything but a "spectator sport." Paul insisted that there be worship, not chaos. The difference came from priesthood leadership. In Paul's writings, we glimpse the common elements of meetings in several branches of the Church: "Quench not the spirit; despise not prophesyings" (1 Thes. 5:19-20). Where he had never been, Paul could mention prophecy, teaching, and exhortation (Rom. 12:6-8). An early Christian might speak by revelation, knowledge, prophecy, or teaching (1 Cor. 14:6). "Teaching" can also be translated "doctrine." Meetings also included psalms, the praise of God in poetry, sometimes set to music (1 Cor. 14:26); the use of psalms is emphasized in letters to Ephesus (5:19) and Colossae (2:16). And at Corinth Paul adds speaking in tongues and the interpretation of tongues (1 Cor. 14:26), listed as general gifts of the Spirit (1 Cor. 12:10) but discussed in no letter except

1 Corinthians. Paul's correction is long, matching the seriousness of their difficulties.

The first apostles spoke in tongues at Pentecost; pilgrims from over a dozen lands heard untaught Galileans speak "in our tongues the wonderful works of God" (Acts 2:11). Missionaries of the restored Church have reported the sudden gift of language or the miraculous temporary gift to communicate in a language never learned. Using a known language is the main purpose of the gift of tongues, Joseph Smith said: "preaching among those whose language is not understood, as on the day of Pentecost."[12] This fits Paul's correction, for in 1 Corinthians 14 spirituality is equated with understanding. Some Saints at Corinth were speaking unknown tongues without interpretation, and in their ecstasy were speaking out of turn or simultaneously with others. Paul, the man of visions, said that he also excelled in speaking with tongues; "yet in the church I would rather speak five words with my understanding, that I may teach others also, than ten thousand words in a tongue" (1 Cor. 14:19, NKJB). The apostle sharply criticized uncontrolled sound and excitement. No one was to speak in tongues without an interpreter to give the message publicly; a few should speak, but only one at a time (1 Cor. 14:27-28). These rules were then rephrased to apply to anyone speaking by prophecy.

Thus, the meeting does not give a mystic display of power, but a rational message, transcending human reason but meshing with it. How many religious fakes trade on the unknown, straining to generate a climate of emotion without judgment? Jesus talked quietly with Nicodemus and reasoned with his disciples instead of overwhelming them. Then the Lord promised his apostles special gifts to further their missionary work: "They shall speak with new tongues" (Mark 16:17). In this spirit, the latter-day prophet Joseph Smith bluntly said, "It is not necessary for tongues to be taught to the church particularly, for any man that has the Holy Ghost can speak the things of God in his own tongue, as well as to speak in another, for faith comes not by signs but by hearing the word of God."[13] The approaches of Joseph Smith and Paul would argue strongly for learning world languages to communicate the gospel, for conversion comes through understanding. But the modern Prophet reinforced Paul's caution to the Corinthians: "If any have a matter to reveal, let it be in your own tongue. Do not indulge too much in the gift of tongues, or the devil will take advantage of the innocent. You may speak in tongues for your own comfort, but I lay this down for a rule—that if anything is taught by the gift of tongues, it is not to be received for doctrine."[14]

Are women more susceptible to emotionalism disguised as religion? Joseph Smith gave the above caution to the Relief Society, and Paul gave a rule for the sisters that seems harsher without knowing the context: "Let your women keep silence in the churches: for it is not permitted unto them to speak" (1 Cor. 14:34). This raises the double question of what Paul meant and what relevance it has today. Both issues are met by comparing chapter 11 with chapter 14. In the former, Paul insists that a woman ought not to "pray and prophesy" without being veiled (1 Cor. 11:5). This proves that women did participate in Christian meetings, which is also known through the names of several faithful, participating sisters mentioned in Acts and the letters. This suggests that Paul had a particular kind of speaking in mind in the later chapter. Some ask whether Corinthian women were interrupting meetings with questions. Or were they "speaking out" in the sense of "leading out," loudly correcting the presiding elder? The Joseph Smith Translation interprets "speak" in that official sense, saying that women were not permitted to "lead." That is certainly one thrust of the chapter, since men and women are both told to be silent whenever someone else is speaking (1 Cor. 14:28, 30). And just before mentioning women, Paul directed that the local authorities must manage both tongues and prophecy: "And the spirits of the prophets are subject to the prophets; for God is not the author of confusion, but of peace" (1 Cor. 14:32-33). Some things in Corinthians are culturally dated, for Greek women were particularly cloistered and seem to have moved beyond self-control in the new social freedom of the Early Church. So hair length and veiling in 1 Corinthians 11 seem to have little relevance today in everyday life, though faithful Latter-day Saints realize that some issues of dress may have renewed significance in temple worship. Symbolism is paralogical in that it suggests truth rather than defines it. Woman's mission has a depth far beyond her attractive appearance.

Church Organization and Spiritual Gifts

Good analysts have called 1 Corinthians 12 the "Constitution of the Church," for nothing in the New Testament better describes God's plan for Church structure and operation. Two-thirds of the chapter develops the comparison of the parts of the "body," the institution all "members" were baptized into (1 Cor. 12: 12-13), and lists the officers that God has placed "in the church" (1 Cor. 12:28). Ephesians also calls the Church the body of Christ, with the understanding that Christ is the "head." This has nothing to do with Christ's resurrected body, which Paul also talks about in 1 Corinthians 15. In Paul's illustration, the organization of the Church would be lifeless without the inspiration of God's spirit. Thus 1 Corinthians 12 begins by surveying the power of the Holy Ghost within the Church.

Paul's mixing of priesthood offices with spiritual gifts is confusing unless one remembers the criticisms that Paul gave on speaking in tongues. Since "tongues" is one of many gifts mentioned in 1 Corinthians 12, Paul is obviously trying to extend Corinthian horizons on other spiritual gifts that they should seek. At the end of the chapter, these gifts of the spirit are mingled with priesthood offices, but in a sequence of priority, with the major priesthood functions listed first. Paul is clearly saying that Church leaders must direct the use of gifts in each branch of the Church. Modern revelation relists the spiritual gifts and makes Paul's point of supervision more directly: "And unto the bishop of the church, and unto such as God shall appoint and ordain to watch over the church and to be elders unto the church, are to have it given unto them to discern all those gifts lest there shall be any among you professing and yet be not of God. And it shall come to pass that he that asketh in Spirit shall receive in Spirit; that unto some it may be given to have all those gifts, that there may be a head, in order that every member may be profited thereby."[15]

Christian leaders have traditionally compared spiritual gifts to watering a tree—they teach that only a young Christianity needed these special gifts to nourish growth. But the devout of all ages have never believed that explanation. For instance, Bible Protestants developed a vigorous Pentecostal movement in the United States from the beginning of this century. And at mid-century, international gatherings were seeking the "renewal of the Spirit" as they conferred on unity. More recently the "charismatic movement" has reached for personal gifts in the structured faiths, Catholic and Episcopalian. But God works in his own way and own time, and he has already restored the primitive gospel with its primitive gifts. After all twentieth century attempts, the full range of personal and public revelation of 1 Corinthians is impressively lacking. Yet the restoration of these gifts is found in the public history and the private journals of the Latter-day Saints. Joseph Smith bluntly said, "No man can receive the Holy Ghost without receiving revelations—the Holy Ghost is a revelator."[16] The real charter for Christian gifts came from Christ, who promised certain powers of the Holy Ghost to the apostles at the Last Supper. As discussed in chapter 3 of this book, the Lord also associated spiritual signs with true preaching when he sent out the Twelve in his lifetime and in the Resurrection. Thus, Paul's spiritual panorama closely reflects Christ's promises, as well as documenting their complete fulfillment.

Paul's first spiritual gift stands independent of his list, perhaps because it is the essential gift for each Church member—no one "can say that Jesus is the Lord, but by the Holy Ghost" (1 Cor. 12:3). Christ promised that the Holy Ghost would come and "testify" of him (John 15:26). This reward of faith either brings one into the true Church or holds him there, for a lifetime of purposeful sacrifice cannot rest on guesswork. Paul no doubt assumed that one saying that Christ was the Lord would do so with knowledge, but Joseph Smith did not like a verbal loophole here; he thought it should read, "no man can know, etc."[17] Modern revelation also emphasizes the gift of testimony at the head of the list: "To some it is given by the Holy Ghost to know that Jesus Christ is the Son of God, and that he was crucified for the sins of the world" (D&C 46:13). Others rely on those who know, which should be seen in a dynamic sense of a learning stage in the gospel. These will also have eternal life "if they continue faithful" (D&C 46:14), which is virtually to say that continued faithfulness will bring a testimony, for no one enters the kingdom on borrowed light.[18]

Paul's short list of spiritual powers stretches wide with possibilities. The Holy Ghost comes to each Church member, but with different results in each member's life. Such a reality makes meeting together all the more significant because all the gifts of the Saints come together when the Saints come together, teaching "one another the doctrine of the kingdom" (D&C 88:77). The gifts are grouped in pairs, with the exception of faith, one that supplements many others. Heading the list is the "word of wisdom" and the "word of knowledge" (1 Cor. 12:8), the capacity to teach, for "word" in 1 Corinthians is generally the expressed message, variously translated in the first two chapters of the letter as "utterance," "preaching," and "speech." In these same chapters, the knowledge and wisdom of man conflict with the gospel, but spiritual gifts include knowledge and wisdom higher than human logic. Gospel reason is still reason, but set in eternal perspective with eternal premises. Joseph Smith felt the point deeply when he gave this heartfelt comment: "Every word that proceedeth from the mouth of Jehovah has such an influence over the human mind—the logical mind—that it is convincing without other testimony; faith comes by hearing."[19] Is it by accident that Paul lists faith right after the gifts of explaining the gospel? All the above is concisely summed up in modern revelation: "To another is given the word of knowledge, that all may be taught to be wise and to have knowledge" (D&C 46:18).

Paul lists gifts of healing and working of miracles after faith; Jesus also taught clearly that they do not come without faith. The apostle was not spinning theories, for the chart on Paul's miracles in chapter 3 of this book shows how much experience is behind these short comments. Tongues and their interpretation are last, as we have seen above, because they are least. And just before them are the more important gifts of prophecy and the "discerning of spirits" (1 Cor. 12:10), more important because Paul said so as he began to correct the excesses on tongues: "Desire spiritual gifts, but rather that ye may prophesy" (1 Cor. 14:1). Prophecy in the New Testament is normally discerning the future, as Jesus said of the Holy Ghost: "He will show you things to come" (John 16:13, literal trans.). God's Church is like responsible institutions in the professional and business world—it can capably advise because it is in touch with trends that will affect people in the future. Only the Holy Ghost can speak about what kind of future mankind will face and about what kind of people will succeed in the future. That is why the gift of "discerning of spirits" is verbally and logically linked to prophecy. There is a discerning of the validity of the gifts as a whole, or of a given prophecy (1 Cor. 14:29-30). But there is also a discernment of the motives and potential of individuals, and Paul calls this a form of prophecy. A nonmember might come into a meeting and hear the "prophecy" of several reveal the "secrets of his heart," at which he would know "that God is in you of a truth" (1 Cor. 14:25).

Jesus used that power repeatedly, as in his first telling Nathanael what kind of a person he was and afterward what he was doing just before they met (John 1:47-48). Being spiritually responsive, Nathanael at once knew that Jesus was "the King of Israel" (John 1:49). Latter-day Saint patriarchs are blessed with these powers, as are other priesthood holders who give personal blessings apart or in connection with ordinances of naming a child, confirmation, marriage, setting apart, ordination, or the laying on of hands for healing the sick. In 1946 I sat in the office of a new apostle named Spencer W. Kimball, who had been assigned to set apart about ten missionaries, of which I was one. After hearing a few blessings, I realized that he spoke appropriately to the different needs of each one, though he had not seen them before. "Learn a new word each day" was one of his inspired directions to me, instruction given to no other missionary in that group and given years before a career of teaching and writing was anticipated. And Elder Kimball's prophecies concerning missionary work were just as inspired, for they were fulfilled. The body is incomplete without all its spiritual powers, Paul argues, and without all of its appointed officers. The foot by itself does not constitute the body (1 Cor. 12:15). Thus no church is the true Church of Christ without all the offices that Christ appointed in his Church. Excluding the mingled spiritual gifts, Paul lists these offices in this order: "First apostles, second prophets, third teachers, after that . . . helps, administrations" (1 Cor. 12:28, NKJB). Clear truth needs no verbal scaffolding to prop it up. And Paul plainly outlines the general and local levels of Church government. The overall point is that Christ's Church must be governed by inspired officials. Concerning prophets, modern churches have advanced many vague ideas, since Christianity has been deprived of prophets for centuries. Prophecy does not constitute an office by itself but is a common function of every office. Thus an apostle is also a prophet, just as the regional leaders at Antioch were called "certain prophets and teachers" (Acts 13:1), for they were both. Concerning "helps," there are parallels; but the commonsense question is, "Helpers of what?" Since the subject is organization and not welfare, the "helps" assisted those first named, the presiding apostles. Literal translations keep "helps," though the word could also be accurately translated "helpers" (RSV) or "assistants" (NAB). Concerning "governments," the final term, local authorities supplemented the general authorities. The term is clear—*kubérnēsis*, the quality held by the Greek *kubernétēs*, in Acts the pilot or shipmaster of Paul's vessel (Acts 27:11). This and the equivalent Latin *gubernator* extended from seafaring to life, meaning a manager or director in political or business affairs. Modern translations use some form of "administrators" (RSV, NAB), "administrations," (NKJB), or even "good leaders" (JB).

Paul repeatedly asks how the body can survive if its parts are missing. Without apostles and without all the spiritual gifts, the Christian churches are strictly unconstitutional today. Like Paul's synagogues, they contain groups of the most sensitive and sincere seekers in today's wicked world. But honest Bible students must admit the discrepancy between the Early Church and modern Christianity. In the last century a competent and classical biblical scholar squarely faced this issue with the best explanation he could offer:

> We have seen that according to the scriptural view the Church is a holy kingdom, established by God on earth, of which Christ is the invisible king—it is a divinely organized body, the members of which are knit together amongst themselves, and joined to Christ their head by the Holy Spirit, who dwells in and animates it. It is a spiritual but visible society of men united by constant succession to those who were personally united to the apostles, holding the same faith that the apostles held, administering the same sacraments, and like them forming separate, but only locally separate, assemblies, for the public worship of God. This is the Church according to the divine intention. But as God permits men to mar the perfection of his designs in their behalf, and as men have both corrupted the doctrines and broken the unity of the Church, we must not expect to see the Church of Holy Scripture actually existing in its perfection on earth. It is not to be found thus perfect, either in the collected fragments of Christendom, or still less in any one of those fragments; though it is possible that one of those fragments more than another may approach the scriptural and apostolic ideal which existed only until sin, heresy, and schism had time sufficiently to develop themselves to do their work.[20]

Pure Love

First Corinthians 13 is the most moving chapter of the New Testament outside of Jesus' teachings, a fact that suggests its real source. Many non-Christians are inspired by it. Israeli statesman David Ben-Gurion was an intense student of the Old Testament prophets and was drawn to Paul; blending truth and humor, he told a reporter, "1 Cor. 13:1-13 ought to be in the Hebrew Bible— I asked the rabbis about this, but they said no."[21] Like uplifting music, Paul's profound sentences can raise spiritual vision again and again. Like the Sermon on the Mount, it treats the disease, not the symptoms. In the latter category were the Corinthians' lack of unity, immorality, misuse of spiritual gifts, and disrespect for leaders. In the rest of 1 Corinthians, Paul answered questions and corrected attitudes logically, but 1 Corinthians opens a stunning vision of a world of pure love. One who understands even part of it has glimpsed the glory of the hereafter. In less than three hundred words Paul outlines the gospel priority of love, how to love, and the eternal power of love.

Realizing that they walked on sacred ground, the King James translators recognized the Christlike love of 1 Corinthians 13 and rendered it "charity." Since this is not a vivid word today, translators follow consistency and write "love" here as elsewhere. The Greek term is a powerful religious word for love, *agápē*, which has generated some uninformed mythology.[22] Jews and Christians preferred this term for love, since it was used less in Greek writing. The verb is *agapáō*, which is almost always "love" in its 142 uses throughout the King James Bible. "Charity" is translated only from the noun *agápē*; yet this is still translated "love" 86 times in the King James Bible and "charity" only 27 times, 9 of them in connection with 1 Corinthians 13. The word by itself does not elevate Paul's discussion of love. It is the other way around—Paul's high view of love elevates the word. But it is important to know that Paul's "charity" is the same Greek word used by Jesus for love. Otherwise, one would not necessarily correlate their teachings.

In the Book of Mormon, Moroni equates "charity" and profound love: "Charity is the pure love of Christ" (Moro. 7:47). Since Moroni's presentation is so similar to Paul's, skeptics cry fraud on the ground that Moroni postdates Paul by centuries. But deeply religious people will not quickly agree, since the Book of Mormon tells of a God powerful enough to reveal himself on two hemispheres instead of one. The Book of Mormon people were entitled to the special revelation of Christ and his finest message, the Sermon on the Mount, and they were entitled to the inspiration of the finest Christian teachings on love. And who is the ultimate source of such Christlike thoughts? Clement of Rome wrote to the Corinthians forty years after Paul and quoted Paul's words: "Love endures all things; love is long suffering in all things."[23]

Clement added eight other striking statements about love not known elsewhere. But Clement did this without using Paul's name. And talking of love earlier, Clement asked the Corinthians to remember "the words of the Lord Jesus which he spoke when he was teaching gentleness and longsuffering." Is this an unrecorded sermon in Christ's life? Part of Clement's following quotation from the Lord contains a striking term from 1 Corinthians 13: "As you are kind, so shall kindness be shown you."[24] On the basis of this, respected scholars have wondered whether part of 1 Corinthians 13 might come from the earliest Christian record of Jesus' sayings.[25]

Indeed, Jesus gave the same priority to love that 1 Corinthians 13 does. The Lord said that loving God and one's neighbors was the essence of "all the law and the prophets" (Matt. 22:36-40). Jesus also gave a distinguishing mark of the true church—having "love one to another" (John 13:35). After writing on spiritual gifts, Paul encouraged "the best gifts" and introduced love as "a more excellent way" (1 Cor. 12:31). The Greek phrase is more dramatic—translated literally as a way "immeasurably better." Then phrases of comparison rapidly follow; the main spiritual gifts again pass in review and are found wanting unless they lead one to deeper service in love. Tongues alone are as empty as the fading vibrations of the cymbal, which was sometimes used at noisy private parties.[26] Paul adds prophecy, understanding mysteries, and moving mountains by faith—and even martyrdom and giving away one's property. Here is an astounding judgment: one can do all these things without love and not be accepted of God. The concept of love is not dramatic sacrifice but steady relationship. It is not a giant gift on a special occasion but the continued support of personal caring. Above all, it is not the theological achievement of becoming an information bank, but of steadily helping others up steep slopes.

As Paul moves from the priority of love to the actions of love, the significance of his approach must not be missed. "If ye love me, keep my commandments," Jesus said (John 14:15). Christ's measure of love is action. Doing is also the measure of loving in

Paul's examples of love. But those who aspire to follow their steps must love enough to tell the truth. Jesus commanded a disciple who was wronged to go to his brother "and tell him his fault" (Matt. 18:15). And Paul added 1 Corinthians 13 to his letter that condemned the Corinthians' faults but was not faultfinding. The difference was Paul's absolute commitment to the Corinthians and his total faith that they could solve their problems. Out of this framework of love come the following descriptions of love.

Love *"suffers long."* "Suffers long" is a literal translation of the Greek word, which is translated "patience" in modern translations. Love has the confidence not to demand an immediate accounting, not to judge failure prematurely. Good manners reflect a willingness to take extra time in small things. The opposite of "suffering long" is to be quick-tempered or overanxious. The New Testament letters strongly emphasize the duty of "longsuffering" or patience.

Love *"is kind."* The main modern translations retain this interpretation, but it needs clarification. The root here is "useful," implying that love serves the needs of others, giving them "goodness," "gentleness," and "kindness," all King James Version translations of the equivalent noun (*chrēstótēs*). Paul elsewhere stresses God's goodness and kindness to men in saving them, and he is here asking people to deal in a similar way with each other.

Love *"envies not."* Modern translations have Paul prohibit either envy or jealousy, two words for the same evil. After twice illustrating positive concern for others, Paul adds a number of things a loving person will not do. Jealousy is personal frustration at another's success. It would restrict the growth of others to match the narrowness of the jealous. Caring parents emulate a caring God in helping their children to expand and develop.

Love *"vaunteth not itself."* The Greek term used in this description is not used elsewhere in the New Testament. It refers to being a braggart. Thus, modern translations tend toward describing love as "not boastful." Whereas jealousy is egotism turned inward, bragging is egotism turned outward. The opposite is Christlike generosity turned outward, the goodness and kindness identified above.

The Qualities of Love: 1 Corinthians 13:4-7

King James Version	Personal Characteristics	Literal Translation
Charity suffereth long	Patience	Love is patient
and is kind	Kindness	It is kind
charity envieth not	Generosity	Love is not jealous
charity vaunteth not itself	Modesty	Love is not boastful
is not puffed up	Humility	nor conceited
doth not behave itself unseemly	Self-control	nor dishonorable
seeketh not her own	Unselfishness	seeks not its own interests
is not easily provoked	Even temper	nor is irritable
thinketh no evil	Tolerance	does not count up evil
rejoiceth not in iniquity, but rejoiceth in the truth	Empathy	does not rejoice in unrighteousness but rejoices with others in the truth
beareth all things, believeth all things, hopeth all things, endureth all things	Steady trust	bears all things, trusts all things, hopes all things, endures all things

Love *"is not puffed up."* "Puffed up" is the precise Greek meaning and metaphor. What is one called who has an inflated sense of importance? Translations give "arrogant," "conceited," "proud," and "snobbish." Paul earlier told the Corinthians, "Knowledge puffs up, but love builds up" (1 Cor. 8:1, RSV, NIV). Real achievements in building others bring the deepest satisfactions for self. The gratitude of others for pure love brings true importance that never fades: "Without compulsory means it shall flow unto thee forever and ever" (D&C 121:46).

Love *"does not behave itself unseemly."* The best recent translations agree that love is not "rude," but that rendition settles for etiquette, not the morality of behavior. The Greek term is *aschēmoneō*, literally meaning "to be disordered," the opposite of the New Testament *euschēmoneō* word group, which refers to fitting, proper, or decent conduct. Thus, in his letter to the Romans, Paul commands the Saints to walk "properly" (Rom. 13:13, NKJB) or "decently" (Rom. 13:13, JB, NIV)—and there the contrast is to those who are drunken, immoral, and filled with "strife and envying." So these things are in Paul's mind for "unseemly," clearly a moral term. Love preserves integrity and righteousness and does not exploit and debase. "Love does no evil to its neighbor" (Rom. 13:10, literal trans.).

Love *"seeks not her own."* Translations only vary the words here, for Paul says literally that love does not "seek its own interests." In a word, love is unselfish. Counselors in human relations stress a good self-image; one cannot give to others without self-worth and self-respect. But such strong people have generally been loved by generous parents. Thus, the selfish may emotionally cripple those dependent on them with the constant message that they are not worth time and attention. Unselfishness generates emotional strength in an eternal dimension.

Love *"is not easily provoked."* Here Paul gives the opposite of his first quality, patience or long-suffering. The main translations agree in concept: love is not "irritable" (RSV), not quick to "take offense" (NEB, JB), not "easily angered" (NIV), or not "prone to anger" (NAB). Some who are successful in church and community have this private characteristic but excuse it as insignificant.

But if love is the finest achievement of gospel living, one cannot live the gospel without changing abrasive irritability. Drummond painted "evil temper" in its true colors: "For embittering life, for breaking up communities, for destroying the most sacred relationships, for devastating homes, for withering up men and women, for taking the bloom off childhood; in short, for sheer, gratuitous, misery-producing power, this influence stands alone." [27]

Love *"thinks no evil."* This translation is too abstract, for love exists in a social setting. Some interpreters think this refers to dwelling on injuries. But Paul's phrase closely repeats the Greek of Zechariah 8:17: "And let none of you imagine evil in your hearts against his neighbour." Thus people build themselves up by tearing down those around them. The narrow jealousies in Paul's other phrases yield the fruit of suspicion and false accusation. This is the opposite of trust, another word for love.

Love *"rejoices not in iniquity, but rejoices in the truth."* What translations miss here is the social dimension of the second "rejoice"; it adds a prefix that is "rejoice with" (*sugchaírō*) in its other New Testament appearances. If the worldly enjoy thinking and talking of evil, the Saints should delight together in the truth. To thus "rejoice together" is to be in harmony, to be free from suspicions and false accusations. "Rejoicing together" also takes place after forgiving others, a duty stressed by Christ and his prophets.

Love *"bears," "believes," "hopes,"* and *"endures all things."* The main translations do not differ on the last three qualities, but are confused on the first. They should not be. In the first place, this is the recurrent speech pattern called chiasm, where two middle terms mean the same thing and the beginning and ending terms are basically the same. A second reason is clear by itself, for Paul's word means bearing up under pressure (1 Cor. 9:12) or being able to stand emotional tension (1 Thes. 3:1, 5). Thus "bearing up" and "enduring" are the negatives, and "believing" and "hoping" are the positives. As we have seen, Paul told the Corinthians that they might waver in their relationship with him, but that he was their father in the gospel and would never stop caring for them (1 Cor. 4:12, 14-15). Thus, pure love is steady love—it does not quit at insult or rejection.

The tragedy of many unloving people is that they only imagine they love. In truth they want to love but do not pay the price to move from wishful thinking to reality. As a good teacher, Paul confronts the Saints with their inconsistencies. The impatient jerk on a child, the harsh word to someone trying to assist, or the cold shoulder to a spouse all reveal a smallness of soul. Paul sketches gross egotism, but it is subtly disguised in appearing to care but being too busy, or in blaming others for not caring. Here Paul challenges believers to believe. He closes his panorama of the loving and unloving by asking for patience with human inconsistency and faith in divine possibility. One can remain cynical, as H. L. Mencken was when he remarked that love was the triumph of imagination over intelligence.[28] But that is the point of the gospel, which gives a vision of what may be if imagination is put to work. Parents in tune with their divine calling know that eternal potential is wrapped up with their helpless and uncoordinated infant. Parents of resistant teenagers are wise if they remember that the potential is still there, and gospel brothers and sisters with this vision will do the same. The future is unlocked by pure love, which "believes" and "hopes all things."

Those who have unselfish love know that they work with the most powerful creative force in the universe. Paul's conclusion stresses the fragmentary nature of prophecy and knowledge. God gives or allows what is necessary for man's survival in being tested on this earth. Paul never doubts that he brings enough knowledge to prepare mankind for eternity, but in 1 Corinthians 13 he warns the Saints not to be overconfident in claiming all knowledge. In the King James Version, his words are, "We see through a glass darkly" (1 Cor. 13:12), which weakly translates Paul's Greek. The more literal translation "We look into a mirror with obscurity" was vivid in a culture with polished metal mirrors. For Paul, knowledge must be supplemented and revised, but love never fails (1 Cor. 13:8). The gospel experience of unselfish love is closer to eternity than anything else. It may be counterfeited by immorality and cheapened in superficial society. But genuine love is a taste of eternity. An unsophisticated child said, "I like people to love me—it makes me feel shiny."[29] In the restored gospel, pure love is expressed in families, friendships, and righteous service; family relationships are sealed for eternity. Like Paul, Joseph Smith taught that pure love on earth would not change but be added upon: "That same sociality which exists among us here will exist among us there, only it will be coupled with eternal glory, which glory we do not now enjoy" (D&C 130:2).

The Resurrection

Human hopes never exploded with more power than in Paul's doctrinal climax of 1 Corinthians 15. Can the Resurrection be doubted? This chapter's brilliant beginning, middle sequences, and final completeness become vivid realities as one perceives its blending of prophecy and clear knowledge of the apostles. These truths can be ignored or ridiculed but not refuted, for here they come from an eyewitness who soberly reports personal knowledge and that of the Twelve. The fiery dawn of immortality glows in the triumphant words of the apostle. Who can be indifferent to the future that all will meet? What intelligent choice remains but to learn and prepare? Paul's rich explanations reveal how weakly modern Christian theologians understand the rich knowledge possessed by Paul.

"How do some among you say that there is no resurrection of the dead?" (1 Cor. 15:12, NKJB.) Paul's whole discussion centers around this clear question and one other. Reminding the Saints of the certainty of Christ's resurrection, he asks how one could believe in that without believing in the resurrection of mankind. Before the Gospels were written, Paul lists resurrection appearances to leading apostles, to all the apostles, and to "above five hundred brethren at once," most of whom were still alive (1 Cor. 15:6). These were not vague rumors, but virtual challenges to ask available people about their personal experiences. The Early Church knew firsthand from living witnesses. And one was Paul, who added last but not least that he had seen the Lord (1 Cor. 15:5-8). We are not "false witnesses," he insists (1 Cor. 15:15). He is not accusing the Corinthians of doubting Christ's resurrection, but jolting them with its reality for consistency's sake. That is the key to the chapter, for doctrines of salvation turn to jarring contradictions if they do not include the resurrection of mankind. If "there is no resurrection" (1 Cor. 15:12)—if "the dead rise not" (1 Cor. 15:15), then the central realities fail. And Paul lists them in order: (1) Christ's own resurrection (1 Cor. 15:13); (2) the apostles' integrity (1 Cor. 15:15); (3) forgiveness through Christ (1 Cor. 15:17); (4) the value of baptisms for the dead (1 Cor. 15:29); (5) the value of Paul's sacrifices and risks (1 Cor. 15: 30-32). This perspective is critical in understanding baptism for the dead, for many commentators toss it aside as a local practice that Paul did not accept. Such an argument is simply nearsighted—the other four points on the above list are not only true but interlocked in Christ's plan of salvation. Baptism for the dead cannot be moved from its rightful relationship by skeptics' shrugs.

Paul started 1 Corinthians 15 with the testimony that "Christ died for our sins" (1 Cor. 15:3, also 17), but his real subject was the resurrection of mankind that must follow Christ's own resurrection: "For as in Adam all die, even so in Christ shall all be made alive" (1 Cor. 15:22). Thus there will be a general or universal resurrection, and death itself will disappear (1 Cor. 15:26). Thus Paul refutes the terrible thought that those who have "fallen asleep in Christ" might have perished (1 Cor. 15:18). But what of those who have "fallen asleep" without Christ? The universal resurrection must include them. Is this apparently missing group really missing? The powerful section on the general resurrection is prefaced by the category of those "fallen asleep in Christ" (1 Cor. 15:18) and concluded by concern over those dead for whom baptisms are being done (1 Cor. 15:29). Paul's thinking is strictly logical if he is saying that the universal resurrection will bring forth both believers and those dying as unbelievers, whose work was being done for them. The Resurrection is not universal unless that majority without Christ are resurrected. And the Resurrection is unjust unless the dead without Christ have the opportunity to accept him. Thus, baptism for the dead is not incidental to Paul's argument. Nor is it casually thrown into the chapter; everything else in 1 Corinthians 15 is strict and relevant truth. Peter's first letter shows that the Early Church knew a good deal about the gospel in the spirit world. (Appendix C discusses early Christian convictions about preaching to and baptizing for the dead.) Most of the recent translations change "baptized for the dead" to "baptized on behalf of the dead," supporting Joseph Smith's revelations on this subject.

"How are the dead raised up—and with what body do they come?" (1 Cor. 15:35.) This second question raises issues of the timing and kinds of resurrection. The plural here is scripturally necessary, for no one responsibly interprets Paul's three glories in 1 Corinthians 15 without correlating them with Paul's three heavens in 2 Corinthians 12. Also, Paul unites with John in teaching a resurrection of those that are "Christ's at his coming" and a final resurrection later (1 Cor. 15:23 and Rev. 20:6-13). Are not these two distinct "glories"? Joseph Smith and Sidney Rigdon puzzled over this problem in John 5:29, reasoning that various degrees of faithfulness should bring various rewards. And their resulting vision (D&C 76) became the basis of the detailed knowledge of the life to come held by Latter-day Saints. That revelation does not depend on Bible interpretations, though Paul's words contradict the traditional idea of a heaven and hell and support Joseph Smith's revelation of the three degrees of glory. So does a remarkable early Christian source. Irenaeus, bishop of Lyon, wrote about A.D. 170, often quoting his teacher Polycarp, who had seen John the Apostle. Apparently referring to this transmission of information, Irenaeus quotes "the elders, the disciples of the apostles," about distinct heavens in the hereafter. Such traditional information would not necessarily be accurate in detail, but that the Early Church believed in three heavens is striking:

> As the elders say, then also shall they which have been deemed worthy of the abode in heaven go there, while others shall enjoy the delight of paradise, and others again shall possess the brightness of the city; for in every place the Savior shall be seen, according as they shall be worthy who see him. They say moreover that this is the distinction between the habitation of them that bring forth a hundred-fold, and them

that bring forth sixty-fold, and them that bring forth thirty-fold; of whom the first shall be taken up into the heavens, and the second shall dwell in paradise, and the third shall inhabit the city; and that therefore our Lord has said, "in my Father's house are many mansions."[30]

Paul pictured multiple glories in answering what kind of body could come forth in the Resurrection. Some scoffed, claiming that physical imperfections were inconsistent with a physical resurrection (1 Cor. 15:35). Paul's sharp answer was that the insignificant seed was left behind as the new crops flourished, a symbol of human change from mortality to "incorruptible" immortality. But there must be more than that simple metaphor, for Paul took time to develop the varieties of the harvest. The mortal planting stage is singular in his language ("body"), but the Resurrection yields "celestial bodies" and "bodies terrestrial." Since these adjectives usually mean "heavenly" and "earthly," some translations write that alone, suggesting that Paul is simply contrasting the sowed earthly bodies with the resurrected, heavenly bodies. But that causes a severe problem of definition. Generally in Paul, and in this chapter, "glory" is the stage of resurrection: "It is sown in dishonour; it is raised in glory" (1 Cor. 15:43). Thus "celestial" and "terrestrial," would be states of resurrected "glory" (1 Cor. 15:40), followed by comparisons of eternal brilliance: "There is one glory of the sun, another glory of the moon, and another glory of the stars; for one star differs from another star in glory" (1 Cor. 15:41, NKJB). And the concluding sentence summarizes all these as future: "So also is the resurrection of the dead" (1 Cor. 15:42). Sun, moon, or stars are not images of "corruption" but of "glory."[31]

Is the resurrection physical? Modern revelation plainly says so: "Every limb and joint shall be restored to its body" (Alma 40:23). But modern ministers have their doubts. One spokesman generalizes for his church but really speaks for liberal Christian ministers everywhere:

> With a few exceptions, Presbyterians do not interpret the phrase in the Apostles' Creed, "the resurrection of the body," as meaning the *physical* body. Saint Paul writes: "Flesh and blood cannot inherit the kingdom of God . . ." They understand "the resurrection of the body" as a refer-

ence to the *spiritual* body of the resurrection. Paul writes: "It is sown a natural body; it is raised a spiritual body." . . . Our Lord's sinless body . . . was transformed into a spiritual body. Saint John in his Gospel suggests that the resurrected body of Jesus for evidential purposes retained certain physical properties.[32]

Thus "physical properties" are left behind as educated ministers now define resurrection. But their position is dangerously close to the Corinthian heresy that Paul was correcting. Jesus told Peter that "flesh and blood" had not revealed his knowledge of Christ (Matt. 16:17), and Paul told the Galatians that he did not confer "with flesh and blood" right after his conversion (Gal. 1:16). In both cases, the phrase is simply a metaphor for *mortality*. Thus Paul answered Corinthian scoffers by saying that the mortal, flesh-and-blood body would not come up in the Resurrection (1 Cor. 15:50). But as a "body" it retains its physical properties. Jesus contrasted his resurrected body to a spirit: "A spirit hath not flesh and bones as ye see me have" (Luke 24:39). And instead of Christ being an "evidential" exception, Paul told the Corinthians and others that Christ was the example of the resurrection of mankind: "The second man is the Lord from heaven. . . . We shall also bear the image of the heavenly" (1 Cor. 15:47, 49).

Modern revelation gives many insights into the Resurrection. A "spiritual body" (1 Cor. 15:44; D&C 88:27) would better be called a "glorified body," for it is the mortal body perfected: "They who are of a celestial spirit shall receive the same body which was a natural body . . . and your glory shall be that glory by which your bodies are quickened" (D&C 88:28). The glorified frame will be flesh and bone, though not "flesh and blood" (mortal) for Joseph Smith repeatedly spoke "as one having authority," saying, "When our flesh is quickened by the spirit, there will be no blood in the tabernacles."[33] All will "raise by the power of God, having the spirit of God in their bodies and not blood."[34]

2 CORINTHIANS

Profile

Sent from:	Paul, in northern Greece, joined by Timothy.
Sent to:	Members at Corinth, provincial capital of southern Greece.
Date:	About A.D. 57, in the fall.
Purpose:	To express joy on the repentance of many Corinthians, to warn others of discipline for rebellion, and to plan the welfare collection for the Jerusalem Saints.
Main themes:	Christ's atonement; the principle of sacrifice; repentance; welfare contributions; priesthood authority; three heavens.

Background

The City

See the sketch above under 1 Corinthians.

Church Members

The discussion on the background of 1 Corinthians surveys the first conversions and known people of that branch of the Church. As a result of Paul's long mission there, many Greeks accepted the faith. So after the Acts 18 ministry, Paul characterized the Corinthians: "Ye know that ye were Gentiles, carried away unto these dumb idols, even as ye were led" (1 Cor. 12:2). Thus, there was a low percentage of Jewish converts, who had training in religion and discipline in the synagogue. This probably contributed to the instability and self-willed character of many members.

Reason for Writing

Paul had written 1 Corinthians in Ephesus before the early summer feast of Pentecost (1 Cor. 16:8). He then planned to visit

Corinth later that year and spend the winter there (1 Cor. 16:6). Acts tells how these plans were fulfilled. Paul visited in Macedonia or northern Greece for some time (Acts 20:1-2), and then spent three months in Greece proper, apparently at Corinth. Since his return journey back through northern Greece coincided with the spring Passover feast (Acts 20:6), he did winter at Corinth. Second Corinthians went from Macedonia, as Paul learned from Titus the good news of Corinthian faith and loyalty (2 Cor. 7:5-6, 13). This letter was sent back with Titus and another unnamed brother well-known to the Corinthians (2 Cor. 8:16-18). The time was probably the fall of the same year in which Paul wrote 1 Corinthians, about six months before. This was probably A.D. 57. (Appendix A gives further details.)

When Paul set out for northern Greece, he closed his three-year mission in Ephesus (Acts 20:31) with definite plans. He had already sent Timothy and Erastus to prepare the Greek churches for his farewell visits (Acts 19:21-22), after which he would travel to Jerusalem. He was gathering welfare contributions. Prior to leaving Ephesus, Paul had written about preparing "the collection for the saints" before he came; then it would be taken on to Jerusalem (1 Cor. 16:1-2). Afterward, Paul wrote 2 Corinthians from Macedonia, giving further detailed instructions on this welfare project. Another purpose for writing was to heal his relationship with them before he arrived. At the beginning, he worried that the Corinthians had misread his motives, mentioning there and later, "I made you sorry with a letter" (2 Cor. 7:8). This could be a lost letter, although 1 Corinthians is harsh enough in places to qualify. That detail does not matter as much as seeing the unbending determination of Paul to speak the truth but to keep a good relationship with the Corinthians. He did not attempt to smooth over difficulties with superficial politeness. This second letter is a genuine second communication of gratitude that the first letter found its mark and that lives were changed. This combination of firmness and profound love for the Corinthians throws some commentators off guard. Since they cannot understand how the same letter can combine reproof and healing outreach, the

Corinthian correspondence is often sliced into a number of letters. But this is purely artificial, for Jesus and Paul stood for love based on reality. Thus both criticism and concern can be given in the same communication. This is the case with 2 Corinthians, with an added factor. There were now two main groups in the branch, one of which had achieved the unity that Paul commanded, but the other stood defiant against him. So Paul's mood swings in the letter to match the two different groups addressed.

The mission of Titus must be reconstructed from 2 Corinthians. He left Ephesus after Timothy and Erastus, either carrying 1 Corinthians or being sent to represent Paul in working with the Corinthians. Paul expected a report north of Ephesus. The apostle left with a heavy heart because of persecution, probably the Ephesian riot and the unexpected pressure to leave (2 Cor. 1:8). As he traveled north to Troas, he was glad for the great missionary harvest but anxious because, as he said, "I found not Titus my brother." So he sailed for Macedonia with apprehension for the future (2 Cor. 2:13), a situation like his first voyage after the Troas vision called Paul to Macedonia. Now when he came to Macedonia, he had the joyful reunion with Titus mentioned in the opening paragraph above. Earlier, Paul had written 1 Thessalonians when his messengers reported their unity in the faith, and 2 Corinthians somewhat recapitulates these circumstances. Like 1 Thessalonians, 2 Corinthians is not a great doctrinal letter but an intense letter of relationship, a letter standing above all others in revealing Paul's feelings about the gospel and his converts.

The above events are straightforward and understandable, though 2 Corinthians discussions are complicated by confusion on some details. These problems seem to arise from Paul's marked skill in outlining alternatives and in reporting how the Corinthians had worried him. Keenly conscious of the ultimate authority of his apostleship, he waited for their repentance before coming: "I call God for a record upon my soul, that to spare you I came not as yet unto Corinth" (2 Cor. 1:23). For this reason, Paul made plans to come and then changed them—he would have come on a second visit but for very serious reasons abandoned that plan (2 Cor. 1:15-17). And at the end of 2 Corinthians, Paul says, "This is the third time I am coming to you" (2 Cor. 13:1). Yet this might only be the third time he planned to come, with overtones of shame that his second visit aborted because of their lack of repentance. Earlier he referred to "the third time I am ready to come to you" (2 Cor. 12:14). Acts relates only Paul's original missionary stay at Corinth and his revisit at the end of his Ephesian labors. But because 2 Corinthians has the above language, some scholars assume he made a second visit before that letter was written. On this evidence, it is speculative to say it happened, though the question is not of great significance either way.

Main Teachings

Christ's Atonement

Paul's earlier letters did not explain Christ's atonement, though it clearly is one of his core beliefs. Only when the Corinthians were confused did Paul remind them that he first preached that Christ "died for our sins" (1 Cor. 15:3). An English word stressing this phase of Christ's mission is "atonement," his sacrifice that overcame sin and placed mankind literally "at one" with God again. Though in the Book of Mormon that word often describes Christ's mission, the King James New Testament has but one appearance of "atonement" (Rom. 5:11). Yet the Greek noun and verb form appear in Romans and 2 Corinthians as "reconciliation" and "reconcile." These are expressive terms in English or Greek, meaning to restore an original relationship. That and the resurrection were the message when "the Son of God, Jesus Christ . . . was preached among you by us—by me, Silvanus, and Timothy" (2 Cor. 1:19, NKJB).

Thus the "light of the glorious gospel of Christ, who is the image of God," dawned at Corinth (2 Cor. 4:4). In the Greek, "gospel" meant "good news" or "message of happiness," a concept with the same positive tones for man as "the great plan of happiness" referred to in the Book of Mormon (Alma 42:8). Christ's atonement made it so, and Paul was one of the "ministers of the new testament; not of the letter, but of the spirit" (2 Cor. 3:6).

"Testament" here is a Greek legal term (*diathḗkē*) for the binding promise of a will, but it was used in the Greek translation of the Old Testament for God's covenant with Israel. Thus, Paul's "new testament" is the Lord's new covenant with the Saints wherein their sins are forgiven through the atonement of Christ. And 2 Corinthians 3 takes its joyful tone not from the disappearance of divine commands but from the rejoicing of the believer that the "letter"—the searching by study and the multiplicity of Mosaic rules—had been replaced by Christ's atonement and gospel, in which "my yoke is easy, and my burden is light" (Matt. 11:30). The King James Version uses "covenant" and "testament" interchangeably as Paul teaches that the work of Christ fulfills the laws of Moses.

Although Christ's atonement is more visible in the next letters to be studied, 2 Corinthians 5 explains how it works. Latter-day Saints also know its striking doctrines in the great Book of Mormon chapters on the subject and in Doctrine and Covenants 19. Paul begins with the reality that the body will be laid down, bringing a time when the Saints are "absent from the body, and . . . present with the Lord" (2 Cor. 5:8). But they are accountable for their earthly actions, since in the future "all appear before the judgment seat of Christ, that every one may receive the things done in his body . . . whether it be good or bad" (2 Cor. 5:10). But the sins of those who have accepted Christ and his gospel are taken by him "who knew no sin" (2 Cor. 5:21)—for "one died for all" (2 Cor. 5:14). This concept builds to the magnificent testimony of God, who "reconciled us to himself by Jesus Christ" (2 Cor. 5:18). This is the end of the "saved by grace" tract, but it was the beginning of Paul's life of gratitude, for 2 Corinthians 5 ignores passive Christianity and steps confidently along the path of responsible Christianity. The old sins and the old ways should be past for those who have accepted Christ's true gospel (2 Cor. 5:17); this comparison of the death of the old person and the vital new person meets readers of Romans, Ephesians, and Colossians.

Yet Christ is not only Savior for the Saints, but he is also their example on the road to perfection, where they must carefully walk by the Spirit. Christ brought about the Atonement so that those accepting his gospel "should not henceforth live unto themselves, but unto him which died for them, and rose again" (2 Cor. 5:15). Such a new life involves daily choices of self-control but is surrounded by the blessings of God.

Sacrifice

No one leads others to a higher level without experiencing unawareness, insensitivity, or even rejection from them. Few realize what it takes to help others until they also reach that higher level. How many children or students appreciate their parents and teachers before they become parents and teachers themselves? Christ and Paul both reveal the struggle to lead others spiritually, but there is a corresponding joy that is highlighted in 2 Corinthians: "For just as the sufferings of Christ flow over into our lives, so also through Christ our comfort overflows" (2 Cor. 1:5, NIV). Paul "boasts" in this letter, but only to remind his enemies of his credentials on knowing Judaism, suffering, and the visions of the Lord. He does not boast of the inner peace of the Spirit, but his inner composure emerges in 2 Corinthians as vividly as the sacrifices and hardships that he consciously reviews. This book quietly shows that God's rich blessings are sure when one performs his errands.

Paul needs no earthly status, for he is satisfied to hold heavenly treasures with other Saints in "earthen vessels," referring to the common pottery around him (2 Cor. 4:7). He validates Jesus' beatitudes, for in literally hungering and thirsting he is filled with the joy of the Spirit. Can one be "blessed" when persecuted? Paul answers that he is "troubled on every side, yet not distressed . . . persecuted, but not forsaken" (2 Cor. 4:8-9). Part of Paul's burden of sacrifice was risking danger—some of these persecutions were mentioned in the biographical chapters of this book. He wanted his Corinthian detractors to know his integrity by the measure of his discomfort and his risking his life for the gospel: whether the blows of being beaten, whether prisons, whether mobs (2 Cor. 6:5), whether fatigue, hunger, or physical discomfort (2 Cor. 11:27). But how easily he moves from such outer afflictions to anxiety over the Saints' righteousness and the criticisms of self-righteous Saints. After exposure to thieves on lonely roads, he was certain to be mobbed in the cities when he preached the gospel (2 Cor. 11:26). And after making converts, he was certain to meet problems from many and rebelliousness from some. After all perils "without," he assumed "the care of all the churches" (2 Cor. 11:28). Paul's longest letters express his deep concerns over serious problems: "For out of much affliction and anguish of heart I wrote unto you with many tears" (2 Cor. 2:4).

What parent, leader, or concerned friend has not had the same feelings? Even Jesus wept over unrepentant Jerusalem. Paul was not sacrificing for an institution but for people. The principle of sacrifice means discomfort in finding his missionary contacts, means facing any scorn in sharing the gospel, means care in leading converts through immaturity to godliness. His list of sacrifices seems inexhaustible. With this record of what one apostle gave for the kingdom, can one smugly think of going to Paul's glory without being able to turn off the television and talk with family members and fill Church assignments? Missionaries look back at the "happiest years of their lives" because they sacrificed for the Saints and for converts. Parents similarly look back at their busiest involvement with their families. Bishops and Relief Society presidents experience the same illogical combination of giving beyond their capacity and receiving unimagined joy. Latter-day Saints are deeply committed to the principle of sacrifice, and the above examples show that selflessness is not a burden but the essence of life's opportunity. Jesus said, "Whosoever will lose his life for my sake shall find it" (Matt. 16:25). Paul was in the midst of visible dangers and demanding travel when he wrote 2 Corinthians, but he could say that the "inward man is renewed day by day" (2 Cor. 4:16). And he gives a convincing glimpse of the Lord's resources and rewards that were deep wells of refreshment as he labored "by pureness, by knowledge, by longsuffering, by kindness, by the Holy Ghost, by love unfeigned" (2 Cor. 6:6).

Repentance

Speaking by the same inspiration that guided Paul, Joseph Smith took the above words and made them the yardstick of how all priesthood must be used (D&C 121:41-42). Every organization is a system of extended authority, and appointments are made to achieve the goals of that organization. Christ's church is also a system of extended authority, which is delegated to "bring to pass the immortality and eternal life of man" (Moses 1:39). Since that process moves from imperfection toward perfection, repentance is critical. Since repentance involves knowing a better way, teaching is essential. And no leader can twist away from the hard truth that teaching involves criticism. Thus, Joseph Smith faced the "reproving" function of leadership, but strictly cautioned that its motive must be "love unfeigned"; its method must be "when moved upon by the Holy Ghost"; its result must always be "showing forth afterwards an increase of love toward him whom thou hast reproved, lest he esteem thee to be his enemy" (D&C 121:43). Second Corinthians is Paul's "increase of love" afterward. This letter shows the anatomy of repentance and how one leader applied the inspired principle of steadfast love in his relationship with those he sought to help. This eternal principle is vital this hour to any Latter-day Saint leader, teacher, or parent.

The gospel seeks to alleviate guilt, not produce it. Confusion, misunderstanding, and sin all produce guilt. Christ's atonement illuminates dim human paths with the glow of assurance. Everyone is included in "God so loved the world" (John 3:16). Yet many things are implied in God's giving of his Son—not only the Atonement, but the missionary commission to spread the message and include all willing in Christ's Church. This does not mean handing people tracts and ignoring them thereafter. Paul's church was a system of caring, above all for spiritual welfare. Paul says that God set the example by "the riches of His goodness, forbearance, and longsuffering"—and that these qualities develop steadfast love, which "leads you to repentance" (Rom. 2:4, NKJB). Paul's Corinthian letters show him exercising just such concerned leadership to motivate the Corinthian Saints to repent.

Paul wrote his first letter not to wound, but "that ye might know the love which I have more abundantly unto you" (2 Cor. 2:4). He encouraged the Saints to "forgive . . . and comfort" an offender (2 Cor. 2:7); to "confirm your love toward him" (2 Cor. 2:8). Paul's "increase of love" was especially appropriate because the Corinthians had taken seriously Paul's letter and the leader sent to follow it up. The apostle's heart went out to them because of "the obedience of you all, how with fear and trembling ye received him" (2 Cor. 7:15). Thus, Paul's duty of confrontation had produced only temporary pain because lives were changed (2 Cor. 7:8). A slight modernization clarifies Paul's powerful explanation of this "first principle": "Now I rejoice, not that you were made sorry, but that your sorrow led to repentance. For you were made sorry in a godly manner, that you might suffer loss from us in nothing. For godly sorrow produces repentance to salvation, not to be regretted; but the sorrow of the world produces death" (2 Cor. 7: 9-10, NKJB).

There is indeed the bitter pain of the results of sin in a person angry because he immaturely refuses to learn. "It is hard for you to kick against the goads" (Acts 26:14, NKJB), the Lord had told Paul at his conversion. But when one sincerely reaches to God for growth, he takes the pain of sin as a lesson. This "godly sorrow" brings repentance "not to be repented of" because it rests on true principles and never needs to be changed. But the "sorrow of the world" tends to death—in one sense the actions themselves must die because they are counterfeit. The eternal way is the only permanent way to happiness. Second Corinthians shows that those accepting Christ must still struggle for righteousness in their lives, that repentance is a constant, ongoing process necessary for exaltation. Christ's atonement provided hope and forgiveness for the Corinthians but did not relieve them of the personal struggles to develop in their ability to live Christ's principles. As in modern revelation, the measure of their repentance was both regret and change of behavior. One truly repenting of sins "will confess them and forsake them" (D&C 58:43). Repentance is no more restricted to the time of conversion than is faith, for both are lifelong principles of growth in the gospel. Confession of Christ merely opens the way to learn to serve him, another name for repentance.

Welfare Contributions

The welfare program of the Early Church was operating immediately after Christ's forty-day ministry. "Not many days" after the Lord ascended, the apostles rose in the power of the Spirit to bring thousands into the Church, and the believers "had all things in common, and sold their possessions and goods, and divided them among all, as anyone had need" (Acts 2:44-45, NKJB). The perspective of Acts corrects some books that speak of Paul "taking up a collection" for the Jerusalem poor in order to bind the Jewish and Greek segments of the Church. That result followed, but Greek contributions to Jerusalem were part of a program that continued from Pentecost, both in Jerusalem and Antioch. Considerable property was laid "at the apostles' feet," with distribution continuing on the basis of need (Acts 4:35). Management was delegated to seven ordained assistants when burdens grew and bad feelings developed among Jewish widows with Greek or Jerusalem roots (Acts 6:1-6). Soon Paul was converted, and Barnabas called him to Antioch; then the Saints there were inspired to send these two with "relief unto the brethren which dwelt in Judaea" (Acts 11:29).

Welfare policies set the stage for Paul's Gentile contribution. After their first mission, he and Barnabas traveled to the Jerusalem council, where the Gentiles were required only to live principles of morality and awareness of their Jewish brothers and sisters. Paul later reviewed how the "pillars" (Peter, James, and John) assigned Paul and Barnabas to Gentile missions, reserving their own attention for the Jewish work. But at that time the leaders requested from the Gentile apostles, "We should remember the poor" (Gal. 2:10). Perhaps this was done in many ways over the years, but 2 Corinthians highlights the known efforts of Paul to fulfill the above promise. These were underway at the end of the third mission, as 1 Corinthians laid plans "to bring your liberality unto Jerusalem" (1 Cor. 16:3). While in Asia Minor, Paul was still in touch with the Galatian churches of the first mission and asked them to support "the collection for the saints" (1 Cor. 16:1). Romans and Acts show how Paul followed through, with the aid of representatives from many branches of the Church, until he finally arrived at Jerusalem to meet James with "alms and offerings to my nation" (Acts 24:17, NKJB).

The story of the early welfare program is inspiring; in spite of long distances the Early Church was a brotherhood of love in action. Their convictions on giving and rules for giving are found in Paul's insightful chapters of 2 Thessalonians 3, 1 Timothy 5, and 2 Corinthians 8 and 9. In these last two chapters, Christ's second great commandment is so visible. Paul's encouragement to generous giving recalls other "golden rules" of the Lord: "It is more blessed to give than to receive" (Acts 20:35)—"Give, and it shall be given unto you" (Luke 6:38). So Paul stresses the example of the giving Savior, who gave his spiritual riches to raise mankind from spiritual poverty (2 Cor. 8:9). The principle of sacrifice is clear. Northern Greece had given out of "deep poverty" (2 Cor. 8:2), and Paul expected prosperous Corinth to fill the wants of Jerusalem from "your abundance" (2 Cor. 8:14). But rich blessings of sacrifice are promised in this version of the law of the harvest: lean givers will reap lean blessings, and rich givers will reap rich blessings (2 Cor. 9:6). Prosperity and wealth are resources by which the faithful might increase faith on the earth (2 Cor. 9:10-12). And what greater blessing for giving than the approval of God and his Son, who said, "Inasmuch as ye have done it unto one of the least of these my brethren, ye have done it unto me" (Matt. 25:40). Paul knows that relationship and promises its warmth to the generous: "For God loves a cheerful giver" (2 Cor. 9:7, NKJB). The quotation is adapted from the Greek translation of the Old Testament: "God blesses a cheerful man and a giver."[35]

From personal knowledge Paul changed the verb—such a person God loves.

Priesthood Authority

"For his letters . . . are weighty and powerful; but his bodily presence is weak, and his speech contemptible" (2 Cor. 10:10). Thus the defiant party continued to ridicule the apostle who waited for repentance by delaying confrontation. For the most part he had been rewarded, but now on the verge of coming, he warned his detractors. Just as his letters insisted on obedience, so "will we be also in deed when we are present" (2 Cor. 10:11). Indeed, he had "authority, which the Lord hath given us for edification, and not for your destruction" (2 Cor. 10:8). Hoping to reach the rebellious, Paul warned them that division and strife could not be tolerated. The Early Church was indeed one, and its priesthood leaders had the duty to excommunicate those who attacked the doctrine and leaders from within.

The defiant party was led by "false apostles, deceitful workers, transforming themselves into the apostles of Christ" (2 Cor. 11:13). They were Satan's "ministers . . . transformed as the ministers of righteousness" (2 Cor. 11:15). Paul describes his opponents without naming them and uses two other expressions that bluntly label these false leaders. Paul quickly reviews his sacrifices, sarcastically concluding that he is "a fool in glorying." But his opponents have forced this, "for in nothing am I behind the very chiefest apostles, though I be nothing" (2 Cor. 12:11). This does not refer to his fellow members of the Twelve, since it is too debasing. He argues that he can indeed meet the qualifications of his opponents by being nothing, which not so thinly says that they are nothing. The overdone adjective with "apostles" is ironic—they are literally "overgreat apostles" (*huperlían*). Interpreters now tend to see Paul matching ridicule with ridicule. If he is a weak apostle, those without authority to judge him are "superapostles" (NAB, NIV). One of them is evidently the "thorn in the flesh" that Paul three times prayed would depart (2 Cor. 12:7). Many continue to assume that this is some sickness or affliction of Paul, one otherwise unknown in Acts and his letters. But the "thorn in the flesh" is personalized as "the messenger of Satan" (2 Cor. 12:7). Paul's triple prayer to have him removed precedes his "third time I am ready to come to you" (2 Cor. 12:14), making it quite possible that the apostle prayed for the humbling of the chief rebel every time he contemplated coming. The "thorns" of Moses (Num. 33:55) and Ezekiel (Ezek. 28:24) are the enemies of Israel.

But true signs did not follow false apostles, and Paul insists that in him the "signs of an apostle" came powerfully to Corinth (2 Cor. 12:12). His office is highlighted by exposing the "false apostles" (2 Cor. 11:13). The closing chapters of 2 Corinthians strikingly resemble 1 Corinthians 9 in vocabulary. There, Paul headlines his answer by writing "apostle" three times (1 Cor. 9: 1-2, 5). Then he spontaneously mentions his "power" six times in the same argument. Only those with real power worry about its misuse, and Paul treated the Corinthians carefully, saying, "that I abuse not my power in the gospel" (1 Cor. 9:18). "Power" here is *exousía*, regularly translated "authority." That translation appears as Paul begins to warn the rival party of his "authority," given for "edification, and not for your destruction" (2 Cor. 10:8). Paul used the same phrase and the same word for authority in closing the letter, promising "sharpness" if he had to come and exert his "power" (2 Cor. 13:10). There were not only sins of belonging to dissenting factions but also sexual sins for which "many . . . have not repented" (2 Cor. 12:21). Thus, Paul wrote plainly that on coming "I will not spare" (2 Cor. 13:2). No one at Corinth would doubt that the office of apostle had the right to direct and supervise the whole Church.

Three Heavens

"The third heaven"? (2 Cor. 12:2.) Christian literature today knows no such terminology. In recent years several books have the title *Heaven*; Protestant and Catholic encyclopedia articles continue to use the singular instead of the plural. Yet if Paul is believed, there is more than one heaven. Although commentators soften the contradiction by explaining different states of joy in one heaven, Paul's "third heaven" erases that picture. True, Paul sometimes wrote "heaven" of the place where God dwells, but he used "heavens" twice as much. Paul normally used the plural, even though the King James Version sometimes writes the singular for the Greek plural. For Paul, Christ is exalted "far above all heavens" (Eph. 4:10). If Christ is literally "higher than the heavens" (Heb. 7:26), he is in the highest heaven.

So the "third heaven" is not unexpected in Paul's letters. Indeed, it would be expected by anyone reading 1 Corinthians 15 on the rich possibilities for resurrected bodies. Answering the scoffer who asked what kind of body there could be in the Resurrection, Paul said that there is unimagined variety as God brings forth the dead: "One glory of the sun, and another glory of the moon, and another glory of the stars: for one star differeth from another star in glory" (1 Cor. 15:41-42). Why don't more commentaries mesh the three glories in 1 Corinthians with the three heavens in 2 Corinthians? Instead, we meet strange comparisons to apocryphal books where imagination runs to mythical schemes of seven or twelve heavens. Speculation is unnecessary, for Paul once talks of three glories and once of three heavens. Not only do the two Corinthian letters correlate, but the second adds the critical fact that his knowledge came not from opinion but from a mighty vision.

Was this vision Paul's? This question was concisely answered at the end of chapter 2. There, the meaning of his prefacing words was surveyed: "I will come to visions and revelations of the Lord" (2 Cor. 12:1). Paul actually linked that thought to the material just before, since chapter divisions are modern. The reader of 2 Corinthians knows that the apostle answered challengers by a long section asking whether anyone could meet his record of sacrifices for the gospel. This takes the entire second half of 2 Corinthians 11, starting with the necessity of having to boast: "Seeing that many glory after the flesh, I will glory also" (2 Cor. 11:18). And then Paul lists his trials in the first person, commenting that such things are best for boasting "if I must needs glory" (2 Cor.

11:30). But for his detractors, the real question is whether Paul represents God, so he is forced to tell how God guided him, prefacing that with the apology that literally says it is not fitting or appropriate to boast about visions (2 Cor. 12:1). But, of course, he must in order to confront his critics. The prefacing verse still speaks of "me"; Paul follows with the vision about a "man in Christ" and resumes with concern for his own humility—"Lest I should be exalted above measure through the abundance of the revelations" (1 Cor. 12:7). Someone else's vision would not answer Paul's Corinthian scoffers, and he personally ends with the "abundance" of his contact with the Lord. The "man in Christ" who saw the glories of the third heaven was clearly Paul.

What did Paul see? "Such a one was caught up to the third heaven. . . . Caught up into paradise and heard inexpressible words, which it is not lawful for a man to utter" (2 Cor. 12:2-4, NKJB). Although Paul and Luke tell of several visions, no other contains the unique language of being "caught up." So the third heaven and paradise merge as the same experience. Paul uses "paradise" of the place of God's throne, as did John (Rev. 2:7) and Joseph Smith on occasion (D&C 77:2). Paul dates the "third heaven" experience "fourteen years ago" and does not give new circumstances for seeing "paradise," another reason for seeing these parallel terms as describing the same experience. Moreover, both "third heaven" and "paradise" are introduced by the same language of "whether in the body or out of the body I do not know, God knows" (2 Cor. 12:3, NKJB). None of Paul's other visions carry such words of awe before them. Paul shares the bare reality of the most sacred event of his life.

This last point shows that the "third heaven" is the highest heaven. By the time Paul wrote 2 Corinthians, he had received three other known visions of the Lord: his first vision near Damascus, his temple vision three years after his conversion (Acts 22:17-21), and the vision directing him to stay at Corinth (Acts 18:9-10). In each of these, the words of the Lord are given in some detail. But Paul did not talk about the vision of the third heaven; he said that it was "not lawful" to talk about it (2 Cor. 12:4). So seeing the "third heaven" was more sacred than his other visions of Christ. And why did he pick this vision above all others to share with the Corinthians? Obviously because nothing else in his life matched it, and his detractors could not name another vision like it. So the vision of transcending sacredness must be of the highest heaven. Latter-day Saints commonly refer to the "first degree of glory" as the highest, and Paul makes the "third heaven" the highest, the place where God dwells. Since no heaven exists above it, Paul clearly accepted just three heavens from the sure knowledge of his most sacred revelation.

As discussed in studying 1 Corinthians 15, the earliest Christian "elders" taught the doctrine of three heavens in the hereafter, a knowledge restored by Joseph Smith in his sweeping vision recorded in Doctrine and Covenants 76. Paul's three guarded verses on his "inexpressible" revelation are doctrinally close to the 119 verses given to the Prophet. Joseph Smith was authorized to outline the future for the benefit of the latter-day world, though, like Paul, he was commanded not to record all things (D&C 76: 44-47, 114-16). Apparently Paul's detailed knowledge of the three heavens went to the grave with him. Thus, churches based only on the Bible can say little about the hereafter unless they trust to imagination rather than revelation. The views in one Protestant church are typical of today's confusion: "Ideas range from a nebulous, indefinable existence to a definite place, like a city of golden streets."[36] Yet Christian leaders say less and less on just what mankind must prepare for. One characterizes the situation: "We suffer from a silence in the pulpit on the subject of heaven."[37] Paul shows that God's plan includes the three glories of the hereafter. If not in modern revelation, where else will such knowledge be found?

NOTES

1. Strabo, *Geography* 8.6.23 (Loeb Classical Library).
2. Ibid., 8.6.20.
3. Plutarch, *On Borrowing* 831A (Loeb Classical Library).
4. See the printed minutes in Joseph Smith, *History of The Church of Jesus Christ of Latter-day Saints*, 2nd ed. rev., edited by B. H. Roberts (Salt Lake City: The Church of Jesus Christ of

Latter-day Saints, 1932-51) 7:233: "You cannot appoint a man at our head, but if you do want any other man or men to lead you, take them, and we will go our way to build up the kingdom in all the world."

5. Clement of Alexandria, *Stromata* (*"Miscellanies"*) 3.6.74-76, also cited in Eusebius, *Ecclesiastical History* 3:30. Since the Greek text is the same, I have followed Kirsopp Lake's translation in the Loeb Classical Library, changing "wife" to the literal "yokefellow."

6. See examples in A. S. Hunt and C. C. Edgar, eds., *Select Papyri, Non-Literary Papyri, Private Affairs* (Loeb Classical Library) 1:401-3.

7. This is a general mandate for how one partakes, not a narrow critique of the "unworthy manner" in which Corinthians had partaken. There is a strong moral connotation of Paul's positive adverb for "worthy." To walk "worthily" of the Lord and his calling is simply to live gospel standards (1 Thes. 2:12; Eph. 4:1).

8. The words are quoted from the prayer on the bread, Doctrine and Covenants 20:77, and the ancient Book of Mormon record in Moroni 4:3. The following prayers for the wine simplify the language but no doubt are intended to compress the ideas stated in the first prayer.

9. Pliny, *Letters* 10:96 (Loeb Classical Library). The "oath" to live righteously was part of the worship service and was likely either the prayer blessing the bread and wine or the act of partaking itself. It translates *sacramentum*, from which the Christian word developed, meaning "an act making a binding oath."

10. Justin Martyr, *First Apology* 65. The translation is from the following with one change: Alexander Roberts and James Donaldson, *Ante-Nicene Fathers*, vol. 1 (Grand Rapids, Mich.: Eerdmans Publishing Co., 1956). I have translated *politeúomai* in the general sense instead of the overly literal "be a citizen."

11. Source given at n. 8 above.

12. Andrew F. Ehat and Lyndon W. Cook, *The Words of Joseph Smith* (Provo, Utah: Religious Studies Center, Brigham Young University, 1980), p. 3.

13. Ibid., pp. 3-4.

14. Ibid., p. 119.

15. Doctrine and Covenants 46:27-29, a revelation given soon after Joseph Smith arrived in Kirtland, Ohio. Early Kirtland strikingly resembles New Testament Corinth in intense faith together with aggressive attacks on the authority of Joseph Smith and Paul. In both cases counterfeit spirituality was identified and rebuked by these leaders. Partly with this experience in mind, Joseph Smith later said, "Every spirit or vision or singing is not of God. . . . Speak not in the gift of tongues without understanding it, or without interpretation. The Devil can speak in tongues." Ehat and Cook, p. 12.

16. Ibid., p. 256.

17. Ibid., p. 115.

18. Compare Brigham Young, *Journal of Discourses* 9:279 (1862): "I say that the living oracles of God, or the spirit of revelation, must be in each and every individual, to know the plan of salvation and keep in the path that leads them to the presence of God."

19. Ehat and Cook, p. 237.

20. William Smith, *Dictionary of the Bible*, rev. H. B. Hackett (Cambridge, Mass.: Houghton, Mifflin and Co., 1887) 1:458.

21. "The Religious Newsmakers," *The Herald* (Provo, Utah), Jan. 3, 1972.

22. Christ used synonyms for *agapáō* or *agápē*, even in the resurrection questions to Peter about loving him (John 21:15-17). The more secular synonym of *philéo* was also used a couple of dozen times by Christ and Paul of pure love in relationship with God and fellowmen.

23. 1 Clement 49:5, *Apostolic Fathers* (Loeb Classical Library).

24. 1 Clement 13:1-2.

25. James Hope Moulton and George Milligan, *The Vocabulary of the Greek Testament* (Grand Rapids, Michigan: William B. Eerdmans Publishing Co., 1930), p. 692 (*chrēsteúomai*), citing Harnack.

26. Classical references to cymbals seem broader than the religious ceremonies indicated as likely by some commentators. Adolf Deissmann prints a letter about musical instruments, including cymbals, used during a sacrifice at a private feast, which Deissmann thinks might be broadened to the sacrificial dance there. He also notes the correlation in Jesus' details in the prodigal son parable. Note the "music and dancing" (Luke 15:25). *Light from the Ancient East,* trans. Lionel R. M. Strachan (Grand Rapids, Mich.: Baker Book House, 1978), pp. 164-66. One ancient mosaic shows musicians entering with flutes, percussion, and small cymbals. Instruments used in religious ceremonies were obviously available for other kinds of performances.

27. Henry Drummond, *The Greatest Thing in the World* (London: Hodder and Stoughton, 1890), p. 32.

28. See H. L. Mencken, *Prejudices, First Series* (New York, N.Y.: Octagon Books, 1976 rpt. 1919 ed.), chapter 16.

29. Llewelyn Miller, ed., *What Is This Thing Called Love?* (New York: Simon and Schuster, 1970), final page.

30. Irenaeus, *Against Heresies* 5.36.1-2, trans. J. B. Lightfoot. Compare Matt. 13:23.

31. Verbal accurateness appears in the names revealed to Joseph Smith for the three glories. The highest is the "celestial," which means "heavenly" in Greek and is the heaven proper where God dwells (D&C 76:92-94). The next is "terrestrial," which means "earthly" in Greek, and is the place for the "honorable men of the earth," who were indifferent to spiritual growth through faith in Christ (D&C 76:74-76). And the "telestial" or last degree of glory meshes with Paul's description of those in the second resurrection: "but each one in his own order: Christ the first-fruits; afterward those who are Christ's at his coming; then comes the *end*" (1 Cor. 15:23-24, NKJB). The italicized term is *télos*, meaning in this case the final resurrection. So those in the "telestial" glory have come up at the "end," for which they were delayed by lengthy preparation in overcoming their wickedness (D&C 76:103-6).

32. John S. Bonnell, "What Is a Presbyterian?" in Leo Rosten, ed., *Religions of America* (New York: Simon and Schuster, 1975), p. 205.

33. Ehat and Cook, p. 368; compare p. 255.

34. Ibid., p. 109; compare pp. 370-71.

35. Proverbs 22:8, Septuagint Version, which circulated in Paul's day and is regularly quoted by him. Proverbs 22:9 in the King James Version is based on the Hebrew text, the thought of which was paraphrased by the Greek translators.

36. William B. Lipphard and Frank A. Sharp, "What Is a Baptist?" in Rosten, p. 30.

37. James Richmond, "Heaven and Hell," in Alan Richardson, ed., *Dictionary of Christian Theology* (Philadelphia: Westminster Press, 1969), p. 151.

6
Letters Preaching Christ

Most letters of Paul emphasize Christ, but the three grouped here were written with an intensity and sustained teaching about the Lord that sets them apart. It is useful to group them topically because the dates of Galatians and Hebrews can be debated. Yet Romans appears here in probable order. It was written soon after 2 Corinthians to prepare the Roman Saints for Paul's stay at Rome, during which time he wrote the imprisonment letters discussed in the next chapter. Hebrews probably belongs to that group in time of writing, and Galatians' style argues strongly that it was written near the time of Romans. These three together explain the limitations of Jewish laws of salvation and show how Christ's sacrifice made possible the personal remission of sins.

The Protestant Reformation was erected on the foundation of Romans and Galatians. Luther stressed them, and tracts on salvation through Christ take most of their quotations from these books. These letters of Paul show the strengths of great depth but also limitations of little breadth. With Hebrews, they were written to counter a Jewish interpretation of the gospel. The theology of the letter to the Romans is not Paul's theology, but only a part of it. The atonement of Christ is the marvelous foundation of the gospel, but not the whole gospel. Belief in Jesus Christ does not save without obedience to Jesus Christ. When studied as a whole, Romans and Galatians clearly say that. And the truths about Jesus Christ do not bring salvation without the ordinances administered by the Church of Jesus Christ. Hebrews opens that issue dramatically in discussing Jesus' authority as High Priest over his Church.

GALATIANS

Profile

Sent from: Paul, probably in Greece before traveling to Jerusalem, joined by "all the brethren with me."

Sent to: Members at Galatia, the converts of the first mission.

Date: Probably written about the same time as Romans, A.D. 58.

Purpose: To correct false teachings that circumcision and the law of Moses were necessary for salvation.

Main themes: The gospel and revelation; justification by faith; moral laws of the gospel.

Background

The Location

As Paul returned to Jerusalem with the large welfare collection for the Jerusalem Saints, he surrounded himself with representatives from each Gentile missionary area in which he had worked. In reverse order of the missions, there were two from Asia, three from Greece, and two from the central Asia Minor cities of the first mission: Gaius of Derbe and Timothy (Acts 20:4). Timothy was from Derbe's neighboring city Lystra (Acts 16:1). And Paul had told the Corinthians that he was in touch with "the churches of Galatia" for their welfare contribution (1 Cor. 16:1). Without much question, Gaius and Timothy were used to communicate with their own area, as the other welfare representatives of the churches were. Thus "Galatia" in the Corinthian letter includes two of the prominent cities of Paul's first missionary journey. Indeed, one possibility for Paul hearing disquieting news from Galatia would be when the welfare representatives brought contributions from these cities at the end of the third missionary journey. Since Paul personalizes all other letters, Galatians stands out in adding an unnamed group sending the letter: "all the brethren with me" (Gal. 1:2, literal trans.). The reference makes no sense unless the Galatians knew some or all of these associates. Paul called new converts to assist him, so the Galatians would not ordinarily know all his missionary companions. But this situation was reversed at the end of the third journey when Paul sent details of how the Galatian welfare contribution would be sent to him and forwarded to Jerusalem.

Meticulous scholars have sought another Galatian location. They point to northern Asia Minor as the incoming land of the earlier migration of Gauls, who gave their name to the Galatian heartland. That may be so, but no one disputes that some cities of the first mission were in the Roman province of Galatia, which included central Asia Minor. Paul might write specifically to Derbe and Lystra, where his representatives had come from, and properly use Galatia. Or Galatia could include surrounding cities and still be a fairly accurate generalization. Luke's story of missionary work never describes Paul's preaching in northern Galatia but has this sequence: (1) conversions at Iconium, Lystra, and Derbe during the first mission, with presiding elders left over organized branches; (2) revisiting Derbe and Lystra during the second mission with the Jerusalem Council decision—this seems to be summarized as traveling "throughout Phrygia and the region of Galatia" (Acts 16:6); (3) revisiting "the country of Galatia and Phrygia in order, strengthening all the disciples" (Acts 18:23)— this took place on the third mission as Paul traveled through Asia Minor on the way to Ephesus. Luke is a clear writer and normally just mentions revisits to areas of preaching already described. Thus, he defines "Galatia" for his readers as the group of inland cities Paul reached on his first mission. Specific references in both letters and Acts refer to the cities of southern Galatia. Acts shows how carefully Paul followed through with them, and the letter shows how the apostle continued to use every opportunity to educate them in the gospel.

Church Members

Besides the men mentioned above, only Timothy's family is profiled in Acts 16 and 2 Timothy 1. So the missionary journey in Acts 13 and 14 and the Galatian letter are the sources for understanding these Church branches. Many Gentile converts are reported in Acts, and Paul recalled that they turned to the true God after serving those "which by nature are no gods" (Gal. 4:8). Intense Jewish opposition drove Paul out of Antioch, Iconium, and Lystra, and it is known from Josephus that this area had strong Jewish populations. This throws light on the chief problem of Galatians—whether Gentile converts should be circumcised. In fact, Paul had Timothy circumcised because of Jewish suspicion that he would be a lukewarm Jew in a divided home: "Because of the Jews which were in those quarters, for they knew all that his father was a Greek" (Acts 16:3). As time went on, there were probably conversions of orthodox Jews who could not deny that Jesus was the Messiah but could not adapt to the church rule relieving Gentile converts from living Old Testament rules. Jews and Christian Jews were also in contact with Jerusalem through the regular pilgrimages there to the main feasts. The Antioch experience was probably repeated as those returning from Judaea taught a stricter rule: "Except ye be circumcised after the manner of Moses, ye cannot be saved" (Acts 15:1).

Paul reminded the Galatians how they received him "as an angel of God, even as Christ Jesus"—if possible "ye would have plucked out your own eyes, and have given them to me" (Gal. 4:14-15). And this acceptance came in spite of "how through infirmity of the flesh I preached the gospel unto you at the first" (Gal. 4:13). Biographers leap to drama, in this case too quickly to the "thorn in the flesh" (2 Cor. 12:7) to conclude that Paul labored under the handicap of chronic sickness, malaria, or any number of other guesses. But part of the foundation disappears, as already discussed, when 2 Corinthians 12:7 really talks of Paul's main opponent instead of sickness. Likewise in Galatians, "infirmity" is a term (*asthéneia*) that Paul normally uses for human frailty, not sickness; "weakness" in 1 Corinthians 2:3 is the mortal "fear" and "trembling" of an imperfect person preaching a perfect message. If one is determined to look for physical disability, Paul was stoned and left for dead at Lystra, which was one reason he could remind the Galatians that his sacrifice for them was beyond reproach: "I bear in my body the marks of the Lord Jesus" (Gal. 6:17). They had been fiercely loyal to the apostles in the trials "at the first" (Gal. 4:13), which suggests some time lapse and continued faithfulness. The apostle could thus challenge them with the question, "Have ye suffered so many things in vain?" (Gal. 3:4.)

Reason for Writing

Paul aimed at a narrow target in writing Galatians: those burdening the Gentile converts with circumcision and its covenant of living Jewish rules. An ancient word used by Paul and Josephus is useful—these were "Judaizers." The threat to the Galatian churches is clear from the letter, but the manner of Paul's defense as clearly suggests that the Judaizers used the leaders of the Church against him. Such claims are cheaply made but harder to back up. When Church leaders sent their decision to Antioch after the Jerusalem Council, they noted similar rumors but denied them: "Certain which went out from us have troubled you . . . saying, Ye must be circumcised, and keep the law: to whom we gave no such commandment" (Acts 15:24). This clearing of the record not only showed their position on circumcision but also revealed the pattern of misrepresenting their position. Paul's defensiveness in Galatians 1 cannot be understood without knowing that he is correcting such a problem.

"Who has cast a spell upon you?" That is Paul's question as he moves to preach Christ over the old covenant (Gal. 3:1, literal trans.). The "foolish Galatians" are afflicted by those "that desire to be under the law" (Gal. 4:21). This is specifically the Law of Moses, for the Judaizers "constrain you to be circumcised," and

Paul accuses them of wanting to please Jews living around them to avoid persecution (Gal. 6:12). Many had begun to obey the ceremonies of the Jewish calendar: "Ye observe days, and months, and times, and years" (Gal. 4:10).

All of the above is most important in using Galatians, for it speaks to the narrow issue of false doctrine more precisely than does any other letter Paul wrote. A refutation of a single misconception is not a good source for perspective on the whole gospel. We have truth, powerfully presented, but not the whole truth. Readers should think about their reactions under the emotions of arguing against a false position. Paul can oversimplify in correcting extreme Jewish Christians. Galatians is a sharp and precise tool but created for a narrow purpose. Paul here explains the power of Christ's atonement but not all the remaining doctrines that relate to it.

No other letter of Paul has so much agreement on authenticity and so little on dating. Scholars multiply theories here, but there are important guidelines. One is the organization and style of Romans and Galatians. Midway through chapter 2, Galatians discusses the inadequacy of the Mosaic law and the need to accept Christ through baptism (Gal. 3:27). It closes with the moral duties of the Saints. Paul is too creative to make any letter the duplicate of another, but Romans follows the same format: it discusses the shortcomings of the Mosaic law, becoming Christ's through baptism (Rom. 6:3-5), and closes with the moral duties of the Saints. No two letters of Paul resemble each other so closely in content and argument. Then there are impressive phrases unique to the two: the Golden Rule as the sum of Christian duty (Gal. 5:14, Rom. 13:9) and the language of the Saints' adoption, using the Aramaic word in "crying, Abba, Father" (Gal. 4:4-7; Rom. 8:14-17). Such similarities argue for nearness in the times of their writing. As will be seen, Romans was clearly written in southern Greece as Paul was on his way to Jerusalem with the welfare contribution. His premonitions of persecution were strong, for he said that "all" of his converts "shall see my face no more" (Acts 20:25). He could not interrupt taking funds and Church representatives to Jerusalem. Had he received news of the Galatians' defection at such a time, the frustrated tone of that letter would follow. His only chance of helping would be a strong rebuke, though he really desired "to be present with you now" (Gal. 4:20).

Whatever the date of Galatians, the average Bible reader would recognize the correlation between the Jerusalem Council of Acts 15 and Paul's conference with Church leaders on his Gentile gospel in Galatians 2. Some scholars spin theories here, insisting that the Galatian conference does not give the conclusion of the Jerusalem Council decision—and Paul would have told the Galatians specifically of that decision if the Jerusalem Council had been already held. But this argument comes from modern armchair scholarship. The decision of the Twelve was taken to the Galatian churches by Paul (Acts 16:4-5), and if his converts had weakened in spite of knowing that, why should it be re-quoted? Galatians would give supplementary information in the obviously short time that Paul could write. The following discussion will show the close resemblance between the Acts 15 and the Galatians 2 councils. Since they so clearly refer to the same event, Galatians must have been written after that council and Paul's first revisit to Galatia. The Galatians accepted the council decision from Paul about A.D. 50, and one would assume some time would have passed afterward for their radical change of mind. Stylistic correlations discussed above suggest how much later Galatians was probably written—about the same time as Romans, A.D. 58.

Main Teachings

The Gospel and Revelation

Paul opened 1 Corinthians by condemning divisions in Christ's Church, and he opens Galatians by condemning changes in Christ's gospel. To paraphrase his Ephesians summary: one Lord, one Church, and one doctrine (Eph. 4:5). Most thoughtful people are impressed by young Joseph Smith's search for God, for he was puzzled by various faiths and opposing teachings before praying and finding the answer by revelation. How else can one get an answer? Contradictory doctrines have started the same way conflicting churches started—through new interpretations of the Bible. People are creative enough to produce unending differences, but who except God can say which of the hundreds of ways will please God? So Paul links the true gospel with revelation. His credentials are not those of a Pharisee, finely studying the issues. His credentials are those of a prophet relaying God's will. There is but one gospel, and neither mortal nor angel must contradict its truth (Gal. 1:8), for "I neither received it of man, neither was I taught it, but by the revelation of Jesus Christ" (Gal. 1:12).

This general principle had special relevance to the Galatians. Paul first used it to deny the gospel of circumcision, and afterward he stressed that the council had settled the question by revelation.

Paul vigorously develops the first point by denying need of an apostle to instruct him, for he had preached in power for three years before meeting Peter and James. Many Protestants see an indication of individualism here: "Paul recognizes no college of apostles above him, only Christ and the gospel."[1] But that confuses knowledge with authority. Furthermore, Paul is not opposing the Jerusalem apostles but the Judaizers' reports about the Jerusalem apostles. As noted in the Galatian introduction above, the Twelve pointed out that men had misrepresented their views on circumcision (Acts 15:24). Corinthian attempts to divide Peter and Paul (1 Cor. 1:12) were countered as Paul insisted that he and the other apostles preached the same gospel (1 Cor. 15:11). And in Galatians the leading apostles gave Paul "the right hands of fellowship" (Gal. 2:9), meaning specifically that they agreed with his procedure on his Gentile missions.

In the obviously urgent circumstances of writing, Paul had no choice but to undercut those clearly misusing the authority of the apostles "of the circumcision" (Gal. 2:8). Peter had no doubt visited Corinth (1 Cor. 9:5), and his name had been exploited there. In Galatia his name was also being exploited. In a day of poor communication, Paul made a "no matter what" argument. He could have produced letters from the chief apostles in several months, but he came to the point by insisting that even if Peter or an angel would support circumcision, that position was wrong because it was contrary to the "revelation of Jesus Christ" (Gal. 1:8, 12). Paul was not downgrading priesthood leaders; he was bluntly saying that the revelation must guide all priesthood leaders alike. Thus chapter 1 has the "even if" tone that only seems to set Paul above the Twelve; but chapter 2 is the sober appeal to the fact that Paul met with the Twelve. Thus, Galatians discloses Church order in keeping with Paul's powerful insistence on the leadership of the Twelve in 1 Corinthians 12 and Ephesians 4. Indeed, Paul valued the earthly knowledge of Christ from Peter and James; in Jewish synagogues Paul quoted their testimony of the Resurrection (Acts 13:31), as he did in his writing (1 Cor. 15:5, 7). Paul's fifteen days with Peter three years after his conversion is a symbol of correlation and supervision, not isolation (Gal. 1:18).

Galatians next reviews the only Jerusalem meeting detailed in the letters, and the point-by-point description of Acts is strikingly similar. In both, the occasion was reviewing the Gentiles accepting the gospel without Jewish rules; the location and participants are the same; circumcision was central in each, with the approval by general authorities of the "gospel of the uncircumcision" (Gal. 2:7). In both accounts Paul and Barnabas return to Antioch afterward. As noted above, close comparison is necessary because some scholars theorize that the Acts-Galatians councils are two different meetings. But the New Testament demands a single meeting. Luke narrates the Jerusalem Council as the necessary outgrowth of the first full preaching to the Gentiles. It was not needed before that, and its decision effectively settled the issue of circumcision of the Gentiles. Paul's point is just that—after the council, all should know better. Both sources have an air of urgency before the meetings, and an air of finality afterward. Acts and Galatians mesh well in view of Paul summarizing in 10 verses what Luke takes 30 to cover. Thus, Galatians should not be required to give full details.[2]

At the Jerusalem Council Paul "*communicated* unto them that gospel which I preach among the Gentiles" (Gal. 2:2, italics added); the italicized word (*anatíthēmi*) means to "lay before," and it implies "the added idea that the person to whom a thing is referred is asked for his opinion."³ Thus, Paul wanted the "pillars," Peter, James, and John, to evaluate his procedure of not circumcising the Gentile converts. The "right hands of fellowship" (Gal. 2:9) signified a ruling that Paul's methods were acceptable. Other agreements between the two records appear in outline:

Acts 15	Galatians 2
"They determined that Paul and Barnabas . . . should go up to Jerusalem" (v. 2).	"I went up again to Jerusalem with Barnabas, and took Titus" (v. 1).
"They were received of the church, and of the apostles and elders, and they declared all things that God had done with them" (v. 4).	"I . . . communicated unto them that gospel which I preach among the Gentiles, but privately to them which were of reputation" (v. 2).
Certain believing Pharisees insisted "that it was needful to circumcise them" (v. 5).	Certain "false brethren" sought to compel Titus "to be circumcised," but Paul absolutely refused (vv. 3-5).
The Twelve sent Paul and Barnabas back to Antioch with their decision and a letter to "the brethren which are of the Gentiles in Antioch and Syria and Cilicia" (v. 23 ff).	Peter, James and John "gave to me and Barnabas the right hands of fellowship, that we should go to the Gentiles" (v. 9, NKJB). Paul and Barnabas went to Antioch (vv. 11-13).

Revelation is the main point of Galatians 1 and the obvious reason for narrating the Jerusalem Council in Galatians 2. Paul sets the stage by emphasizing, "I went up by revelation" (Gal. 2:2). Of course, Acts 15:28 says specifically that the decision was made as "it seemed good to the Holy Ghost, and to us." If Paul did not consider the decision of the "pillars" made by revelation, how could he blame Peter for coming to Antioch and not eating with the Gentiles? There Peter first ate with them—an act in keeping with the dietary harmony of Jew and Gentile recommended by the Jerusalem Council (Acts 15:29). But some came to Antioch from James, which caused Peter to withdraw from Gentile tables. Paul reacted strongly and confronted Peter, who in Paul's judgment was not acting "according to the truth of the gospel" (Gal. 2:14). But Peter no doubt had his side of the story. Fear may not have been his motive, and Paul may have acted prematurely. Paul admits that the mission of the "pillars" was to the Jews (Gal. 2:9). If intense Jewish converts reacted negatively to the council decision, James and Peter may have sought a transition delay to convince the stubborn. If Peter labored to bring this about, Paul may have pushed conformity to the council's ruling ahead of its time. Paul evidently retold the story because the Judaizers used the episode to give the impression that Peter agreed with them. The incident is instructive in showing two strong leaders agreeing on a principle that came by revelation but applying it with different timing. Paul does not say that Peter permanently separated himself from the Gentiles. These candid examples show how revelation came after deep searching. Paul reviewed them, of course, to show that Church leaders stood with him in teaching salvation through the revealed gospel, not through the Mosaic law.

Justification by Faith

Justification by faith is really salvation through Christ. Galatians gives Paul's main concept, though Romans uses the words "save" and "salvation." Latter-day Saints know that there are degrees of salvation, so these terms could logically refer to salvation from death. That is part of Christ's work as Savior in 1 Corinthians 15, where Paul vividly pictures the resurrection of all through Christ. But that is a partial salvation in the case of those not entering God's kingdom in eternity. Full salvation is receiving the highest degree of glory. Full salvation is receiving the first resurrection and entering Christ's kingdom. Full salvation reverses the effects of sin and purifies one to stand in God's presence. Ancient and modern scriptures generally apply "salvation" to entering God's presence. The Prophet Joseph Smith was told to seek for "everlasting salvation in the kingdom of God" (D&C 6:3), to be "saved in the kingdom of God, which is the greatest of all the gifts of God; for there is no gift greater than the gift of salvation" (D&C 6:13). Paul consistently uses "salvation" in the same sense—those rejecting the gospel are still resurrected, but "the gospel of Christ . . . is the power of God unto salvation to every one that believeth" (Rom. 1:16). Since Paul powerfully taught salvation by faith in Christ, he is talking about how mankind may obtain full salvation, or salvation from sin.

What is justification by faith? Galatians answers like a clear trumpet call: "We have believed in Jesus Christ, that we might be justified by the faith of Christ, and not by the works of the law: for by the works of the law shall no flesh be justified" (Gal. 2:16). What does it mean to be justified? Peter and John do not use this word in the New Testament writings, though they use the concept. Luke uses it in the ordinary sense when the lawyer tried to save face in questioning Jesus: he was "willing to justify himself" (Luke 10:29). This questioner was trying to avoid the judgment of his audience. But God deals with eternal realities. The Greeks used "justify" of judges giving a decision of innocence, so Paul testifies that God through Christ holds his children guiltless. So to "justify" is to award forgiveness through Christ's sacrifice. One is justified when his sins are canceled through Christ's atonement. Luke traveled with Paul and recorded his synagogue speech saying that Christ brought about "forgiveness" or literally "remission of sins," and the same idea was repeated with different words: "By him all that believe are justified from all things, from which ye could not be justified by the law of Moses" (Acts 13:38-39).

This simple and assuring concept must not be obscured with theological theories. Justification is forgiveness. Paul simply teaches that through Christ sins are forgiven and not through Moses' laws. As noted, Paul's definition is: "By the works of the law shall no flesh be justified" (Gal. 2:16). What law? Many Protestants insist that Paul condemned *all* law as alien to justification through Christ: "Law condemns; it cannot justify. Ritual acts and

Two Types of Salvation through Christ

Salvation from Death	Salvation from Sin
General salvation	Individual salvation
Resurrection	Exaltation
Obtained by all	Obtained by some
Different glories in the Resurrection	The celestial glory
Wicked receive the Last Resurrection	The First Resurrection
Obtained through Christ's sacrifice	Obtained through Christ's sacrifice
Confession of Christ finally required	Faith in Christ required
Unrepentant evil works bring suffering	Good works required
Saving ordinances not required	Saving ordinances required

—Doctrine and Covenants 76

good works offered as the basis of salvation destroy grace."[4] But it is irresponsible to jump from Paul's criticism of *Jewish* law to a supposed criticism of *all* law. What precedes the Galatians 2 theme of justification apart from the "works of the law"? The Jerusalem Council on circumcision and Paul's rebuke of Peter for following Jewish rules of eating. Paul follows his theme of justification by Galatians 3, a spirited historic argument that reviews God's acceptance of Abraham through faith long before "the law, which was four hundred and thirty years after" (Gal. 3:17). No letter of Paul preaches justification apart from law more powerfully than Galatians, but no letter of Paul so clearly equates "the law" with the law of Moses. The best New Testament dictionary notes how many times "law" means "law of Moses" in Paul; the term "can almost come to mean *(Jewish) religion.*"[5] Because Galatians is shorter than Romans, it states justification without law more directly. Justification is plainly salvation through Christ's gospel instead of legalistic Judaism.

What did justification through Christ mean to Paul? Classical Protestantism asserts the deceptive opposition of grace versus law. But Paul is the measure of the true historical opposites that he encountered. The young Pharisee had labored for years in study. Lamplight flickered upon his manuscripts in Tarsus and at Jerusalem. Was the living God in books of history? The vision near Damascus shed a divine brilliance on all his study of scripture. The real opposites of new and old in Paul's life were love of the personal Christ versus plodding reasoning about past texts; obedience to new revelation versus the Rabbinic rules about the Mosaic rules; simplification of divine laws versus proliferation of man-made laws; the purification covenant of baptism versus daily ritual purifications; God's central moral obligations versus man's ceremonial observances that confused the central commandments. When the Mishnah was written down not long after Paul, it had sixty-three chapters containing five thousand to ten thousand rules on what a righteous Jew could and could not do. Paul was liberated from an oppressive religious system by his faith in Christ. Justification without the law was a judgment on the extreme elements of his Judaic life. The true contrasts between the old and new were simplification versus complexity and personal love of the Lord versus endless conformity to detail—in short, the new law and the new covenant over the old. The central justification passage in Galatians disagrees not with the "law" but the "works of the law" (Gal. 2:16), and Paul clearly had in mind Jewish ceremonialism in writing the phrase. Neither Galatians nor Romans is really philosophical, but practical, evaluating what is historically present, not abstract ideas. The contrast is not total grace over all law, but experience with a particular law that could not "have given life" (Gal. 3:21) versus the divine Lawgiver who sacrificed his life: "I live by the faith of the Son of God, who loved me, and gave himself for me" (Gal. 2:20).

Basic Protestantism follows a logic not supported by Galatians. Since justification comes through faith in Christ, actions and divine ordinances are theoretically irrelevant: "If people could be saved by obeying or fulfilling ritual requirements, they would be saving themselves. Lutherans believe that only God can save us."[6] But Jesus commanded baptism (Mark 16:15-16), and the apostles required it to obtain a "remission of sins" (Acts 2:38). The fundamental Protestant believes he has already obtained this by accepting Christ, so usually baptism is seen as "an outward sign of an inward grace." That is, forgiveness is already given, making baptism a righteous gesture but not a requirement for adults. For instance, over one hundred Protestant ministers of Utah were polled, and 72 percent agreed that "those who reject Christ will suffer everlasting punishment." But of these only 20 percent agreed that "baptism is essential for salvation."[7] But Paul did not reason in this fashion. One's justification through Christ required accepting Christ and his commandments: "For ye are all the children of God by faith in Christ Jesus; for as many of you as have been baptized into Christ have put on Christ" (Gal. 3:26-27). Paul did not argue the necessity of baptism because he was writing to Saints who had already been baptized. In Acts, Paul showed that baptism was essential to salvation by regularly requiring it. And according to Galatians, Paul did not consider that a person had "put on Christ" without baptism. Thus, the forgiveness of sins offered through Christ was accepted and made operational through baptism.[8]

Moral Laws of the Gospel

Are daily acts irrelevant to justification by faith? Protestant theology comes perilously close to saying so. The following story will illustrate the difference between Latter-day Saint and extreme Protestant thinking. In the second world war, a Protestant minister and a very young serviceman in the U.S. Navy were engaged in a cordial conversation in Memphis, Tennessee. The minister discovered that the serviceman (this author) was a Latter-day Saint and asked, "What do Mormons believe one must do to be saved?" The serviceman quickly thought of the war around him that many were losing, the war against unrighteousness; he also thought of the minister as an ally in making people more Christlike. So assuming their common commitment to Christ, he answered, "We believe that we must live a good life." The response of the minister? Seething anger, beginning with "You could not have given me a worse answer." The serviceman kept calm and asked questions as the minister raged in defense of salvation through faith without any responsibility for righteous acts. The final question put to him: "Do you mean to say that one can commit adultery and murder and still be saved if he has confessed Christ beforehand?" The minister's answer: "That's exactly what I mean."

If this statement is shocking, it is simply blunter than explanations that pad some Protestant logic with abstract terms. Many ordinary Protestants would be deeply troubled by belief in Christ without belief in his moral laws, and many ministers are more balanced than this Memphis crusader. Yet he gave the core Protestant interpretation of Galatians and Romans. It is based on misunderstanding Paul's command: "Stand fast therefore in the liberty with which Christ has made us free, and do not be entangled again with a yoke of bondage" (Gal. 5:1, NKJB). But "liberty" here is measured against the "yoke" of the law of Moses—what

Peter called the "yoke . . . which neither our fathers nor we were able to bear" (Acts 15:10). This world knows no liberty without law; in science, for example, exact requirements are the avenue for new discoveries and new possibilities. The God who controls the physical world through law would not ignore law in saving his children. Nothing more clearly solves this puzzle than the Book of Mormon teaching that Christ met the demands of the law of justice, enabling God to exercise mercy (Alma 42:14-15). In other words, God respects law enough to require his Son to meet the penalties of law in order to save mankind. Then does he ignore law in their personal lives after that? The object of all intelligent penal systems is to rehabilitate the criminal by effectively teaching him not to repeat his crime. Is God careless of the acts of his children who accept Christ? Protestant theory sees Galatians as teaching "the adequacy of faith without works as man's proper response to the work of Christ."[9] In this theory, God motivates the believer to good works, but human agency, decision, and self-control are irrelevant to that process:

> According to Protestant doctrine, justification is by faith alone without any merit deriving from any good work of the recipient either before or after justification. Justification is on the basis of good works—the good works of Jesus Christ. But the benefits of his redemptive work are received by the believer who has no merit of his own to contribute. Nothing which he ever does, even after justification, merits anything; because nothing which he does is ever perfectly good. That is, nothing which he does proceeds from a perfectly good motive, is directed perfectly according to the good standard, and is aimed perfectly at the glory of God. Nothing short of this is truly good. Since no justified person in this life ever does anything which meets such standards, he does no meritorious good work. Therefore, he never has any merit to claim which in any way supplements the merit of Christ.[10]

But if law and obedience to it has disappeared in Galatians, why does Paul command the Galatian Saints to bear "one another's burdens, and so fulfil the law of Christ" (Gal. 6:2)? As surely as any Jewish rule, this is a rule, a Christian rule, even if it does go straighter to the heart of religion than thousands of regulations on ritual purity. Does the believer have license to ignore the commands of his Savior? Paul consistently teaches both freedom from past rules and obedience to the teachings of Christ and the apostles: "If we live in the Spirit, let us also *walk* in the Spirit" (Gal. 5:25). The italicized term means for Paul what the believer actually does in his daily life. Walking in the spirit does not mean to avoid daily life but to carefully control it by spiritual goals and the added strength of the Holy Ghost. Over thirty times Paul used "walk" in this sense: "Walk worthy of God, who called you into his kingdom and glory" (1 Thes. 2:12, literal trans.) Will one enter that kingdom if he ignores the command to walk worthily? Paul told the Thessalonians how "to walk and to please God," measuring this by the "commandments we gave you by the Lord Jesus" (1 Thes. 4:1-2). Paul asked the Galatians to "walk in the Spirit" (Gal. 5:25) in the same way, for in that chapter and the next he weaves in commandments as examples of their Christian duty. It was Jesus who equated commandments with walking in the Spirit. He had promised the Holy Ghost, "whom the world cannot receive," after stating a requirement: "If ye love me, keep my commandments" (John 14:15-17). Both the Lord of the Gospels and the Tarsus apostle gave inspired commandments to those justified by faith: "Whosoever . . . shall break one of these least commandments, and shall teach men so, he shall be called the least in the kingdom of heaven" (Matt. 5:19).

Paul's language in Galatians shows that the Saints knew the positive commandments, though the negative ones there are most striking. They yet believed in Christ, but they added to his teaching, so Paul warned them, "You have fallen from grace" (Gal. 5:4, NKJB). If that happened by performing unauthorized religious practices, it could more easily happen through blatant wickedness. That is Paul's specific warning to the Galatian branches of the Church that were rife with rebellion and conflict: "Now the works of the flesh are evident, which are these: adultery, fornication, uncleanness, licentiousness, idolatry, sorcery, hatred, contention, jealousy, anger, selfish ambition, dissensions, factions, envy, murders, drunkenness, revelry, and the like; of which I tell you before, just as I have also told you in time past, that those who practice such things will not inherit the kingdom of God" (Gal. 5:19-21, NKJB.)[11]

Several of the ten commandments are here, reiterated when Paul teaches elsewhere of sins that will keep people out of God's kingdom. Are these to be commandments in the Old Testament but not in the New Testament? What is the distinction between the moral imperatives of the prophets and the conditions of obtaining God's kingdom in Paul? If the Galatians abused their liberty by violating these standards, they would have broken God's laws and would suffer the stated penalty. One is playing with words to deny that the above requirements are Christian laws. "Thou shalt not" is as plainly written in Paul's letters as in Moses' tablets.

Protestant theory wrestles with the answer: "Although Paul has said that we cannot by 'doing' inherit the kingdom of God . . . yet he strongly asserts here that by 'doing' we can bar ourselves from that kingdom."[12] Thus, the Protestant premise forces a "paradox," and some solve it by claiming that those doing such things "thereby show themselves to be without the transforming gift of faith."[13] That answer has some truth, but its fallacy is the effective denial of man's agency. Christian theologians define justification by faith in terms of accepting Christ's grace at conversion, but the spiritual growth in Christian virtue afterward is termed sanctification. Of great significance to Latter-day Saints, the word will be fully discussed later. The question here is the post-conversion life of the committed Christian. Paul warned the Galatians to avoid a dozen and a half serious sins. But Protestant analysis rejects that conclusion because it holds that God's children cannot share in responsibility for their own salvation: "In classical Protestantism, sanctification like justification is by grace alone through faith alone. No works of ours contribute anything to it."[14] In that theology, forgiveness first comes "through faith alone apart from works"; next, works are inspired in the faithful by God's Spirit: "Yet such works performed, as well as the faith out of which they spring, make no contribution to the soul's justification, but they are to be regarded as declarative evidences of a man's acceptance in the sight of God."[15] This leads to the idea that God arbitrarily saves those whom he will.

In summary, core Protestantism teaches that faith alone saves, that afterward God works in the believer to show the fruits of faith, but that the believers "make no contribution" to their salvation by a Christian life. In this major Christian view, "we are compelled to recognize our passivity."[16] But if the early Saints did not labor with God in their own salvation, why did Paul speak ten thousand words on living up to God's standards? His letters are not attempts to convert them to Christ but exhortations to make their lives worthy of their commitment to Christ. And they are a farce if readers then and now can do nothing toward their salvation. Obviously this theory violates the common sense of many Protestants. One only has to read the signs in front of North American churches to know that ministers exhort their members to a better life. Practical Protestantism acts as if men and women are free agents. More significantly, members of churches today seek to live up to their Christian commitment. In the United States some 75 percent rate themselves as living a "very Christian life."[17] That can be defined in terms of what is done or what is avoided, and 50 percent on this survey rated the following characteristics of a person living a "very un-Christian life" in this order: "Selfish, self-centered; does not seek or follow the will of God; unconcerned, uncaring; indulges in immoral conduct."[18] People are taught by Bible reading and spiritual impressions that Paul's list of serious sins are indeed to be avoided. Paul, of course, spoke of unrepentant transgressions, for the true gospel holds out hope, not despair. Nevertheless, it also requires individual responsibility from those who covenant with the Lord in the waters of baptism. Their lives must rise above the serious sins on Paul's list. That is why Latter-day Saint worthiness interviews deal with the sins Paul mentions.

The believers' works are a part of their salvation, for Paul closed Galatians by the challenge to work and thus receive the eternal reward: "And let us not be weary in well doing: for in due season we shall reap, if we faint not" (Gal. 6:9). The condition is literally "If we don't give out," meaning not to allow oneself to "faint" in the heat of the day. The labor is literally "doing good," and clear connotations of determined action are seen in the translations: "If we do not slacken our efforts" (NEB); "If we don't give up the struggle" (JB); "If we do not give up" (NIV). What is "well doing"? Revelation gives God's standards, his laws. Christ's atonement does suspend cause and effect to bring mercy to all who fully accept him. But the "law of Christ" (Gal. 6:2) then requires a higher life. Growth through the Atonement is not passively relying on the omnipresent Savior of theology, but on the divine person who taught new laws to his disciples on the mount. His beatitudes were conditions of receiving blessings, and he inspired a modern prophet to restate that principle: "When we obtain any blessing from God, it is by obedience to that law upon which it is predicated" (D&C 130:21). This restores perspective to Paul, who closed his "charter of Christian liberty" with the believer's "law of the harvest": "For he that sows to his flesh shall of the flesh reap destruction; but he that sows to the Spirit shall of the Spirit reap everlasting life" (Gal. 6:8, literal trans.).

ROMANS

Profile

Sent from: Paul, at Corinth.
Sent to: "All . . . in Rome . . . called to be saints."
Date: Probably early in A.D. 58.
Purpose: To prepare the Roman members for his intended visit and to refute false teachings of the Judaizers.
Main themes: God's patience and judgment; justification by faith; the baptismal covenant; conditional election; moral laws of the gospel.

Background

The City

Perhaps a million people were interlocked in Rome, city of the emperor, the aristocracy, and the masses. Augustus could claim that he found a city of brick and changed it to marble.[19] This boast had merit, for he left behind an astounding list of temples and public buildings that he built and repaired.[20] Political and geographical center of the empire, Rome had long attracted Paul as a culminating missionary opportunity. He wrote to the Saints that he had desired "these many years to come unto you" (Rom. 15:23). The Italian Juvenal lived in Rome a few years after Paul and sketched the people of the city with slashing satire. The rich are carried by in sedan chairs, while the poor elbow each other through cluttered streets. Rome is wicked but on the move with projects and ideas—an international city and a melting pot. In Juvenal's overdone complaints, one can scarcely find a Roman in Rome. Greeks were everywhere, and one famous jibe referred to Antioch's river: "For long the Syrian Orontes has flown into the Tiber."[21] And the Jews? They are also unwelcome realities in Roman satire.

Many sources report the extensive Jewish colony in Rome in the first century. Grateful to Julius Caesar for favor, the Jews were conspicuous at his funeral: "A throng of foreigners went about lamenting, each after the fashion of his country, above all the Jews."[22] There was an attempted expulsion of the Jews under Tiberius,[23] and another under Claudius, just before Paul came to Corinth, for he met the missionary couple Priscilla and Aquila, "lately come from Italy . . . because that Claudius had commanded all Jews to depart from Rome" (Acts 18:2). The imperial historian Suetonius seems to refer to Christ in a garbled way in mentioning this decree of Claudius: "Since the Jews constantly made disturbances at the instigation of Chrestus, he expelled them from Rome."[24] This intimately fits the Acts picture of angry Jewish demonstrations against Christians. But another good

Roman source suggests that Claudius's edict was modified somewhat because of the Jews' great numbers: "As for the Jews, who had again increased so greatly that by reason of their multitude it would have been hard without raising a tumult to bar them from the city, he did not drive them out, but ordered them, while continuing their traditional mode of life, not to hold meetings."[25] The decree was temporary, but its various reports give invaluable glimpses of the impact of the gospel in Rome and of the strength of the Jewish community there. Paul had reason to fear the effect of the Judaizers as he wrote Romans.

Church Members

Was the Roman branch of the Church the largest to which Paul wrote? Romans has the longest list of greetings to individuals of any letter. Part of this is Paul's desire to cultivate friendships in an important place to be visited. The fact that he knew so many shows the effective communication network of the Early Church. The faith of the Saints at the world capital was "spoken of throughout the whole world" (Rom. 1:8; also 16:19). Although Paul had not yet been there, he had no doubt met travelers and members from Rome, to whom he sent greetings. Before Paul was converted, Jewish visitors heard the apostles at Pentecost (Acts 2:10), a process of investigation open thereafter at the three annual feasts that drew pilgrims from the world. When such contacts grew to conversions or when missionaries first visited Rome is not known. Now the apostle to the Gentiles sought to visit the Gentile political center, to build up the Church "even as among other Gentiles" (Rom. 1:13).

Romans 16 sends greetings to twenty-eight individuals in Rome, about a fourth of which were women. Families and Church circles were also included. And Paul sent greetings from nine members in Greece. Although identities are mostly obscure, these names show the intense personal relationships that Christ's gospel produced. Paul's letters shared eternal ideas, but his personal messages show the effective fellowship of the Church. Even the brother who wrote the letter for Paul felt at liberty to add his greetings "in the Lord" (Rom. 16:22). The same was true with Timothy, Paul's fellow laborer, who would visit Rome with Paul (Rom. 16:21). Sisterhood is indicated by Paul's recommendation of the bearer of the letter, called "a servant of the church which is at Cenchrea" (Rom. 16:1). Reference to her town, a little south of Corinth, helps establish Paul's location in writing Romans, but her Greek title of *diákonos* is intriguing. Because this is the word sometimes translated "deacon" in the Bible, several translations want to make Phebe a "deaconess." This is not warranted, since that office is known only at a later period of Christian history, and since Paul often employs the term in the general sense of "servant," rendered "minister" in the King James Bible. When Paul used the term of himself (as in Col. 1:23), he spoke of his role of service, not his office. Phebe may or may not have had an official calling in the Church; in either event she had helped many, and Paul also (Rom. 16:1-2).

Of the remaining names, two pairs require comment. Greetings are sent to "Andronicus and Junia, my kinsmen, and my fellowprisoners, who are of note among the apostles, who also were in Christ before me" (Rom. 16:7). "Kinsmen" no doubt means that they were Jewish, since Paul used that word of four others in Romans 16 (compare Rom. 9:3). Some argue that they were apostles, a forced interpretation for two otherwise obscure Saints at Rome. Paul apparently means to say that they were converted early, had sacrificed for the gospel, and thus were respected by the apostles. Paul claimed special fellowship from his imprisonment at Philippi. The other two names are important in understanding Paul's confidence in writing to Rome. As noted above, Aquila and his wife Priscilla had "lately come from Italy" when the Emperor Claudius had expelled the Jews "from Rome" (Acts 18:2). They were strong missionaries, for they had convinced Apollos that he had only part of the truth (Acts 18:26). Paul found them so valuable that he brought them to Ephesus (Acts 18:18), from which place they sent greetings (1 Cor. 16:19). Afterward they were free to return to Rome, where Paul sent regards to these fellow laborers who had risked their lives for him (Rom.

16:3-4). Did Paul send them to Rome to survey the situation when he first left Ephesus? They had shared their knowledge of Jewish-Christian tensions at Rome when they labored with Paul on two missionary journeys after their expulsion. They probably kept in contact with the Saints there when they were away; there was a church "in their house" after returning to Rome (Rom. 16:5). Paul could write Romans to a group he had never seen in full confidence of the common brotherhood and Christian unity of belief. But he also wrote with special knowledge of the problems at Rome he had learned of from Priscilla and Aquila.

Reason for Writing

Paul's priorities had delayed his coming to Rome. He explained that God had blessed his ministry by "mighty signs and wonders, by the power of the Spirit of God; so that from Jerusalem, and round about unto Illyricum, I have fully preached the gospel of Christ" (Rom. 15:19). This was his spiritual and physical description of his missionary journeys, stretching from Israel to the western coast of Greece. This work of years prevented his "coming to you" (Rom. 15:22; also 1:13). Paul's situation then is very clear, since 1 Corinthians, 2 Corinthians, and Romans form a sequence, spaced a few months apart. The first was written as Paul planned to come on his farewell visit to Greece, and the second when Paul wrote from the north to have the welfare contribution ready to take to Jerusalem. In writing Romans he could report that northern and southern Greece had contributed their money: "For it hath pleased them of Macedonia and Achaia to make a certain contribution for the poor saints which are at Jerusalem" (Rom. 15:26). At this point, Paul was about to leave: "But now I am going to Jerusalem to minister to the saints" (Rom. 15:25, NKJB). All of this ties in intimately with the Acts return after the third journey, down to the premonition of trouble in Jerusalem both in Romans (Rom. 15:30-31) and in the farewell speech at Miletus (Acts 20:22-23). But when Paul wrote Romans, he was still in southern Greece, for the letter was sent with Phebe, the faithful sister from Corinth's southern port, Cenchrea (Rom.

16:1). Thus Paul's host Gaius (Rom. 16:23) is apparently his early convert of Corinth (1 Cor. 1:14). Since Paul hurried to return to Jerusalem for the spring feast of Pentecost (Acts 20:16), Romans was probably written early in A.D. 58 before Passover (Acts 20:6). The above discussions of Rome and the Roman members stress the Jewish population and Jewish-Christian problems. To review, Acts 18:2 mentions that Christians Priscilla and Aquila had to leave Rome because of the decree of Claudius against the Jews, and the Roman historian Suetonius indicates that continual Jewish disturbances against Christians were the cause.[26] Thus, Paul wrote Romans in full awareness of Jewish pressure on the Roman converts. Paul devoted ten chapters out of sixteen to the relationship of the Jewish law to the Christian gospel, so he was clearly apprehensive on the point. As discussed, Galatians correlates with Romans in topic and style, making likely an association in time. Romans mainly reasons against the Judaizers, and it seems to relate to the anxiety expressed in Galatians, which should be dated at or not long before the time of the writing of Romans. The latter is a more positive refutation of Judaism than is Galatians, but it is nevertheless a refutation. The Jews were intensely preoccupied with ceremonial detail, whereas the modern world has a hard time finding any standards of religion. Thus, the background of Romans suggests a caution on the modern relevance of all its reasoning about Jewish religion. Paul's powerful testimony of Christ is timeless, but his arguments against the overobedient people must not be misunderstood by under-obedient, secular cultures today.

Main Teachings

God's Patience and Judgment

Does God exist? Evidence for him is not in the fact that the majority of human beings accept a higher power but in the fact that sensitive people must take the question seriously. Intellectual proofs of God are impressive, but more impressive is the quest for God that continues in human hearts. Our spirits respond to

God because they are of his spirit. In words of modern revelation, the planets and stars speed on their appointed paths, and anyone seeing their glory sees "God moving in his majesty and power" (D&C 88:47). Yet the skeptic retorts, "Why is there cruelty and suffering in this world, if it is ruled by an almighty power?" The answer is the necessity for the agency of mankind. Modern revelation has perspective here that traditional Christian theology lacks. God does not create and dictate; he organizes and delegates. A Latter-day Saint convert watched his fellow German soldiers turn to atheism in the midst of destructive war. Before hearing of the Restoration, he simply answered in his heart, "God did not start the war—Hitler did." Paul begins Romans by discussing the majesty of God and the degradations of life by willful mortals.

God formed the earth and its opportunities, but men have invented false gods, false values, and false relationships. Paul regrets the horrible misuse of the physical body by which people dishonor themselves, seeking pleasure and the "lusts of their own hearts" (Rom. 1:24). One contrasts the powerful challenge of the Lord to be "pure in heart" (Matt. 5:8). Nor is Paul hesitant to face sexual perversion. His blunt criticism of homosexuality (Rom. 1:26-27) repeats what he said on that subject when listing serious sins in 1 Corinthians 6. Roman satirists also mentioned the gross homosexuality there in the first century, so Paul gives an inspired warning against actual evils. He moves to survey human ingratitude in action with a list of sins longer than that in Galatians 5. There members were told that such things would keep them from the kingdom of God; here Paul says those doing these things are "worthy of death" (Rom. 1:32). But Paul was not talking of criminal punishment, since society tolerated most of the sins he listed; his point was that God would not tolerate them. "Death" in Paul's letters implies Satan's power and at times equates with John's vision of the wicked receiving a "second death" (Rev. 20:6), a banishment from God's presence at the future judgment. So "worthy of death" (Rom. 1:32) means that the kingdom of God is closed to those guilty of serious sins without repentance. Paul gives a list of sins that is more than a catalog of the evils in the

Roman world—it is a solemn warning to Saints to live above the world's standards. In the King James Version, Paul's list is introduced by an archaic word: the rebellious do "those things which are not *convenient*" (Rom. 1:28, italics added). But the italicized term is clear only in Greek or older English. It refers to those things not "fitting" or "correct." These are the listed sins of aggression, immorality, and dishonesty (Rom. 1:29-31). Their common denominator is selfishness.

Romans 2 explores the moral duties of member and nonmember, Gentile, and Jew. Paul underlines a principle of Old and New Testaments: "There is no respect of persons with God" (Rom. 2:11). Protestant commentators tend to interpret this negatively—that all will be equally condemned by sin, making justification through Christ the only avenue of salvation. Paul no doubt means that but also says much more, for there was positive Gentile achievement because of "the law written in their hearts, their conscience also bearing witness" (Rom. 2:15). Thus "the Gentiles, which have not the law, do by nature the things contained in the law" (Rom. 2:14). What things? Certainly not the temple rituals of Jerusalem or the purification rituals that they do not practice. The Gentiles were obeying the moral laws of God because those were written in their consciences. And the Gentiles were accepted by God because of these works; the "righteousness" of the moral law was "counted for circumcision" (Rom. 2:26), a symbol of their acceptance as the new covenant people. And Paul argues that the Jew who violated this moral law was inferior to the Gentile who kept his covenant of conscience by his righteous actions. At the end of Romans 2, Paul seems to contrast inner attitude and outer conformity, but he really means ritual righteousness as against moral righteousness, for Paul has described the moral Gentile as one obedient "inwardly" (Rom. 2:29). Paul is clearly stating the Old Testament principle as still true: "To obey is better than sacrifice, and to hearken than the fat of rams" (1 Sam. 15:22).

It is too easy to see Romans 2 as limited to Gentile society, although Paul mingles member and nonmember together as being judged by the same standard. A check on what Paul says here is 2 Corinthians 5, where Corinthian members were told: "We must all appear before the judgment seat of Christ"; the measure is what we have "done, whether it be good or bad" (2 Cor. 5:10). The Lord said that he would then "reward every man according to his works" (Matt. 16:27), the same thing that John saw in vision of the righteous and unrighteous (Rev. 12:12-13). And Paul precisely agrees, for God "will render to every man according to his deeds" (Rom. 2:6). Some simplistically think that justification will come through Christ's atonement and condemnation by works or deeds. They ask, "How can men be saved if works count but works fall short?" But it is not up to theologians to say what is impossible with God, for the scriptures clearly teach forgiveness through the Atonement and the believers' responsibility of works. If they really take that responsibility, extreme sins will not be committed or repeated, and the rest will be minimized. God knows the heart and knows what he expects of each individual. When Paul tells the Romans that there is judgment "according to his deeds," the word "deeds" is *érgon*, translated in the King James Version 152 times as "work" or "works" and 22 times as "deed" or "deeds." Paul next applies this judgment to the Saints and to those who "do not obey the truth" (Rom. 2:8). Those who do obey will receive "immortality" and "eternal life" by "patient continuation in well doing" (Rom. 2:7), which in Greek is literally "by endurance in good work." And the cause and effect are repeated: "glory" and "honor" come "to everyone who works what is good" (Rom. 2:10, NKJB). Accepting Christ's atonement brings forgiveness, but obtaining exaltation requires continued good works.

When is it too late to repent and prepare for judgment? Paul answers that God is rich in "goodness and forbearance and longsuffering"—that these qualities must lead a person "to repentance" (Rom. 2:4). In simple terms, God waits for man to see the point of life before bringing about the judgment. Modern revelation teaches that people are sent to earth with agency and with time to develop. Peter taught the same thing, which raises the fascinating possibility that he had read Romans on this point. "The longsuffering of our Lord is salvation," said the chief apostle, "as also our beloved brother Paul, according to the wisdom given to him, has written to you" (2 Pet. 3:15, NKJB). The only place where Paul applies "longsuffering" to God is in Romans. This colors Peter's evaluation that Paul's letters contain things "hard to be understood" (2 Pet. 3:16); indeed, Romans is a special problem because of Paul's long explanations. To return to the point of God's "longsuffering," God delegates and waits. In this he is the greatest example for men and women who supervise others, in church, in the practical world, and especially in families. Paul stressed Christ's longsuffering to him, waiting for the persecutor to be led to the truth. "Longsuffering" became an important ideal for Paul in dealing with others because the Lord had treated him so. God's children are led to repentance by teaching and also by waiting until they are ready for teaching, as ancient (2 Tim. 4:2) and modern (D&C 121:41) revelations say. Neither the judgment nor this waiting for change would make sense without confidence in the individual light of conscience, to which ancient (Rom. 1:20; 2:15) and modern (D&C 84:45-46) revelations testify.

Justification by Faith

Romans is the epistle of grace through faith in Christ. It leads all New Testament books in the number of times that the words *grace* and *faith* are used. As modern revelation says, "Justification through the grace of our Lord and Savior Jesus Christ is just and true" (D&C 20:30). The problem is how to blend this center of the gospel with the other revealed doctrines. The first step in properly understanding justification is understanding Paul's terminology, partly covered in Galatians because Paul preaches the same message there. It was seen that *salvation* for Paul is not merely resurrection but exaltation with God in eternity, that *justification* is quite simply forgiveness of sins through Christ, that *law* usually means the Mosaic law. The remaining word of difficulty is *grace*, which has become a theological abstraction because it is not used in everyday speech. This word (*cháris*) was used in classical Greek to refer to the attitude or action "on the part of the doer" of "kindness, good will" or "favor."[27] In addition to this general meaning, the standard Greek dictionary adds the concrete meanings of a favor or a kindness done, or even thanks returned. Thus, grace relates to the core principle of love, God's kindness in leading his children back to him—God's favor in sending his dear Son to atone for their sins. God's grace is not spiritual substance; it is his spiritual generosity.

The slogans of the Protestant reformation were the Latin phrases *sola scriptura, sola fides, sola gratia:* "scripture alone, faith alone, grace alone." Thus, any discussion of justifying grace is really the question of whether it brings salvation by itself. Such a doctrine arose as an extreme reaction to extreme religious practices. Martin Luther was a committed monk who sought God's favor through repetitious works of fasting, prayer, and rituals. Continual penance and veneration of relics were ways of appeasing the terrifying God who demanded so much: "I had no confidence that my merit would assuage him." Yet Paul gave Luther warm hope in these cold performances. Luther reflected on the Old Testament phrase of Romans 1:17: "The just shall live by faith." In Luther's mind the loving Savior replaced the austere medieval judge of the "day of wrath." Luther explained his change: "Faith leads you in and opens up God's heart and will, that you should see pure grace and overflowing love. This it is to behold God in faith that you should look upon his fatherly, friendly heart, in which there is no anger nor ungraciousness."[28]

Righteous parents know the tension between love and rules, for out of love they establish wise rules to protect their children and to foster their growth. But does our Heavenly Parent require merely the acceptance of his love? Luther thought so, for as a translator he added a powerful modifier to Paul's affirmation of salvation through faith: "Therefore we conclude that a man is justified by faith *alone*, without the deeds of the law" (Rom. 3:28). The italicized term does not appear in English translations nor in the Greek original, though its German equivalent *allein* has been in

Protestant Bibles since Luther. What is the difference between salvation by grace alone and salvation by grace? In the one case, God's grace operates to save mankind through faith by itself. In the other case, God's grace operates to rescue them as they show faith by their own serious efforts. Truckloads of tracts have been distributed to Latter-day Saints in an attempt to prove that the latter view is wrong. These are composed with tunnel vision because they have a narrow range of quotations, using little else than Romans, Galatians, and Ephesians. Indeed, Luther said that these three books—with 1 Peter, John's Gospel, and 1 John, would "teach everything you need to know for your salvation, even if you were never to see or hear any other book or hear any other teaching."[29] Thus, oversimplification goes beyond a Bible sufficient for salvation to only six books of the Bible as sufficient for salvation. But is 20 percent of the New Testament the scripture God wants men to read? And is grace alone the intended gospel of Christ? William Temple stands for this minimal Protestant tradition in summarizing, "The only thing of my very own which I can contribute to my redemption is the sin from which I need to be redeemed."[30]

Romans 3 through Romans 5 powerfully support forgiveness through grace and faith, but these three chapters are only 20 percent of the teaching portion of Romans. The value of good works is only suggested there. But the necessity of baptism and righteous works afterward is discussed in Romans 6 and Romans 8, and the Christian commandments reach through Romans 12 beyond Romans 14. Thus, the 20 percent on grace is matched by over 30 percent on works. In this perspective, Protestant theology is not so much wrong as half right, akin to taking the oxygen out of the basic formula for water that requires two parts of hydrogen and one part oxygen. When preaching grace, Paul says that more is to follow. He asks, "Do we then make void the law through faith?" Definitely not, he answers, "we establish the law" (Rom. 3:31). This is not a metaphor, since Paul reasoned in Galatians that the law of Moses was inferior (Gal. 3:17) and at the end wrote of the "law of Christ," associating it with the Christian commands of morality and how to care for others. Roman's early chapters on grace (3-5) must not obscure the closing chapters of Christian commands (12-14). "We establish the law" (Rom. 3:31) is the bridge between these two principles.

So the Romans chapters on justification by faith must be read in connection with the entire book, and they give intense insights into Christ's atonement. Romans 4 focuses on Abraham and is extremely close to Galatians 3, where Paul reasons from Abraham's belief in God, "and he counted it to him for righteousness" (Gen. 15:6). Thus, the patriarch's faith brought him acceptance long before the law of Moses, the same point of Romans 4 with the same Genesis quotation. Throughout that chapter one reads that righteousness was "reckoned," "counted," or "imputed," to Abraham, a parallel of how the believer obtains forgiveness. All these words come from one Greek term meaning "to consider" or "to count up," and they simply say that God will accept the believer as righteous because of his faith. Nothing in this chapter adds to the simple message of forgiveness through grace. How does forgiveness happen? No one can fully merit salvation without Christ: "For all have sinned, and come short of the glory of God" (Rom. 3:23). So Christ brought the "redemption" (Rom. 3:24). Scattered through Paul's epistles, this word comes from roots meaning "buying back," used of property but also of ransoming people who were captives or slaves. Thus, in this image Christ paid the purchase price to free believers from their sins. Christ also gave his blood as a "propitiation" (Rom. 3:25). The equivalent verb form had a long Greek usage as sacrificing to bring favor of a god or to restore harmony in a human relationship. Thus, Christ's innocent sacrifice restored believers to harmony with God. And as in 2 Corinthians, Paul adds another strong term of restoring personal relationships: "We were reconciled to God by the death of his Son" (Rom. 5:10).

Joseph Smith deeply agreed. His earliest account of the First Vision has a moving assurance of forgiveness of sins through Christ. The Joseph Smith Translation changed Romans 3:24 to "being justified *only* by his grace" and Romans 3:28 to being "justified by faith *alone.*" The italicized words are verbally like Luther's change but with a clear doctrinal difference—Joseph Smith taught that forgiveness (justification) came through Christ alone but that retaining this marvelous blessing was dependent on the actions of men and women. That is clear from the Joseph Smith Translation formula for full salvation in Romans 4:16: "Therefore ye are justified of faith and works, through grace." Whether from modern revelation, the Book of Mormon, or from Paul, the logic of the atonement of Christ is awesome. But Paul stresses a personal love for the Lord that is critical in understanding grace.

The young Saul was raised to grapple with the standards of "the strictest sect of our religion" (Acts 26:5, NKJB); he studied complex rules that the Pharisees had developed for at least a century. But could such a system bring peace with God? Paul answers no in his short spiritual autobiography. His vain struggle to become perfect through the law starts in the past tense; he was vanquished by "sin, taking occasion by the commandment" (Rom. 7:11). The Joseph Smith Translation generally keeps Paul's failures with the law in the past tense. For Joseph Smith, Paul expressed the inability to keep Jewish law prior to conversion. How was the gospel different? The sheer quantity of thousands of rules for memorization and performance is one main difference. But another reason permeates the first half of Romans—personal gratitude from the apostle whose letters are a testimony of grace. This persecutor was not worthy of a vision by mortal standards, yet God "called me by his grace" (Gal. 1:15). What he preached for all was especially true for him; grace was first freely given by God (Rom. 5:15-16). And what was his reaction to Christ's free gift?

Too many see Christ's atonement in static terms at this point. The gift is given, bringing the joy of gratitude. But what about the responsibilities of gratitude? Does one ever receive a gift without moral obligation? Does the Christian remain the polite child expressing verbal thanks only, or does he develop the maturity to show gratitude in action? The issue is whether God considers salvation complete when the grace of forgiveness comes into the human soul, or whether that is the starting point. Preachers of the "decision for Christ" make salvation a choice of a moment, but all of Paul's letters explain a process of perfecting oneself through Christ after forgiveness. Grace for Paul was justification plus motivation: "His grace which was bestowed upon me was not in vain; but I laboured more abundantly than they all: yet not I, but the grace of God which was with me" (1 Cor. 15:10). Some view Paul as automatically working by God's grace, but he used "labor," a word of conscientious efforts. After diligently preaching and courageously facing persecution, he took credit for his sacrifices in 2 Corinthians 11. For Paul the first stage of salvation was realizing and receiving the precious gift of a relationship with God through Christ. That is too often held out as the end, so that church meetings are places for rejoicing of the believers. But for Paul the relationship with God was the beginning of the second stage of progression through service. At his life's end, Paul looked back as a driving runner to say, "I have finished my course" (2 Tim. 4:7). This completed his autobiography of grace, which was linked to his most intense efforts. This illustration of what grace meant to Paul must fit his doctrine in Romans. There he does not teach that grace replaces effort for salvation. It was his gratitude for grace, "the love of Christ," which steeled him to face "persecution" and "peril" (Rom. 8:35).

Paul described how justification by faith operates. Romans 5:1-5 makes it the first in a series of steps leading to the full "love of God." Protestant commentaries tend to pass this quickly, labeling the steps as "fruits of faith." But they are meant to be distinct stages in the believer's spiritual development, in growth to full salvation. For this reason 2 Peter 1:5-8 has been justly called a "ladder of salvation," and the opening verses of James and of Romans 5 show identical thinking. All these sources start with faith and show that it must be tested to be accepted by God. Paul's first rung on the ladder is "being justified by faith," which is the condition of "this grace wherein we stand" (Rom. 5:1-2). But that commitment leads to the testing of faith through "tribulations" (Rom. 5:3), a process that Paul taught as inevitable (Acts 14:22). The word for "tribulations" simply means "difficulties"; it is also translated "afflictions" or "troubles" in the New Testament. Paul says that determined faith subjected to such trials will bring about "patience," a weak translation today (Rom. 5:3). This word is the Greek *hupomonē*, literally "holding up under [stress]." Modern translations favor either "perseverance" or "endurance" here. And this endurance of faith brings "experience," a word (*dokimē*) that literally means a "tested condition." It is rendered "tested virtue" (NAB) but more frequently "character" (RSV, NIV, NKJB). Thus, the final reward of tested faith is a character worthy of sure hope in "the love of God . . . in our hearts by the Holy Ghost which is given unto us" (Rom. 5:5).

Thus, Romans establishes a progression for the full favor of God: first grace and justification through faith, followed by trials, followed by endurance, followed by a tested character. It is fiction to say that people go through such processes without using their total resolve, resources, and powers of decision. As real Gethsemanes come, only prayer and inspiration from God will bring the victory. Only gratitude to the atoning Lord can give meaning to the constant struggle. The Book of Mormon teaches that "it is by grace that we are saved, after all we can do" (2 Ne. 25:23). It is also true that God's offer of grace through Christ is incomplete until men and women grow by acting upon it. Paul's chain of progression means that the rich gift is of no benefit without every believer's total diligence in making use of it. Thus, both faith and works are required for full salvation. In his most sweeping revelation, Joseph Smith saw that those in the celestial kingdom were "just men made perfect through Jesus the mediator of the new covenant" (D&C 76:69). But they also had to "overcome by faith" (D&C 76:53). Salvation by grace could more clearly be entitled "called by grace," for the reward is dependent on a righteous life motivated by love for Christ.

The Baptismal Covenant

Paul came into the Church with the challenge, "Arise and be baptized, and wash away your sins, calling on the name of the

Lord" (Acts 22:16, NKJB). And the Book of Acts begins with the doctrine that belief and repentance make possible baptism for the "remission of sins" (Acts 2:38). Thus, baptism affects the past life of the person coming into the Church. Does it have an effect upon his future life? Paul is really asking that question in the opening of Romans 6: "Shall we continue in sin, that grace may abound?" His answer is to look to the purpose of baptism. It is like the death and burial of Christ, which clearly shows that immersion was then the method of baptism. Even the rationalizers of infant baptism admit that from this plain comparison. But the form of baptism was incidental to the purpose of baptism that Paul explained by his comparison. Christ had laid down a broken body to come gloriously from the tomb, just as the believer must bury his past sins in water and come out to a new life of purity and righteousness. "Therefore we are buried with him by baptism into death: that like as Christ was raised up from the dead by the glory of the Father, even so we also should walk in newness of life" (Rom. 6:4).

How does such reasoning apply to newly born infants who are baptized and cannot promise to live a good life? Roman Catholics and large Protestant churches are forced to that question, for they make up the majority of Christians who baptize babies. They explain that baptism is induction into the Christian community or that baptism is the symbolic equivalent of circumcision, a sign of God's calling of a new people. But scriptural authority is lacking for these arguments; baptism in Romans expresses a personal covenant of righteousness. A vocal Protestant minority insists on "believers' baptism," relating the ceremony specifically to repentance. The New Testament knows no baptism except that which follows sincere faith and repentance. Paul said in Galatians that faith preceded the baptism by which sincere believers "have put on Christ" (Gal. 3:27). In Romans 6 Paul said that baptism was tied to using grace righteously. Since "remission of sins" of Acts is the same thing as the "justification" of Romans, baptism is the means of partaking of the grace of forgiveness. Baptism is a physical commitment to "walk in newness of life" (Rom. 6:4)—the tangible demonstration of determination "that henceforth we should not serve sin" (Rom. 6:6).

If so many Christians have changed these scriptural purposes, Latter-day Saints should appreciate the restoration of baptism as an adult covenant of righteousness. The Book of Mormon stresses baptism as a "covenant" with God to serve him and keep his commandments, so that he may pour out his Spirit more abundantly upon the baptized disciple (Mosiah 18:10). Joseph Smith taught baptism only for those "willing to take upon them the name of Jesus Christ, having a determination to serve him to the end" (D&C 20:37). The purpose of baptism in Romans 6 and modern revelation is the same—it is a solemn promise not to sin. The Biblical history of Israel shows that God did not lightly regard the breaking of covenants. Romans 6 is not an exultant chapter on the joy of grace, but a severe warning about wrong decisions after baptism. And what prophet ever gave commandments without penalties attached? Paul required action consistent with baptism, showing that he valued baptism as part of the process of salvation.

Protestant theology has generally been uneasy about either accepting or rejecting works as relevant to salvation. As discussed in connection with Galatians, basic Reformation theory excludes works, but the attempt to keep them away from the front door simply means that they knock loudly at the back entrance. No self-criticism had more impact than that of Deitrich Bonhoeffer, a Lutheran minister who in 1945 courageously gave his life for opposition to Hitler. He had written on the unchristian carelessness that often came from assuming that "grace alone does everything." He called that "cheap grace, the grace which amounts to the justification of sin without the justification of the repentant sinner who departs from sin and from whom sin departs."[31] Billy Graham repeated Bonhoeffer's phrases in evaluating conservative Protestants: "Too often we have tended toward superficiality—an overemphasis on easy-believism or experience rather than on true discipleship. We have sometimes offered cheap grace and cheap conversions without genuine repentance."[32] But Reformation ideology tends to produce that result. It teaches that faith is "the only channel of justification," which "means quite literally that all works are excluded. . . . If our salvation is to remain a matter of grace alone, by faith alone, this prohibition extends no less to what are called post-regeneration works." This view holds that what is done after conversion to Christ cannot have "meritorious value" but only "evidential value."[33] Protestant leaders think that works in Christ do not help to merit salvation but are only proof that salvation has come. In early battles against medieval superstitions, "Luther had so insisted that man is incapable of contributing to his salvation as to make easy the inference that moral effort is pointless."[34] Luther wanted to allow but not count the works of morality and brotherhood, summarizing: "Good works do not make a good man, but a good man does good works."[35]

The real criticism of such reasoning is that it is fiction. Dependable people know that their acts are important, for they control them. Religious people who have successfully struggled will not believe that their daily choices mean nothing for salvation. When that is taught, radical Protestantism deserves the caricature of teaching a decision for Christ and ignoring ten thousand others. Years of labors for the Lord bring about the tested character of Romans 5:1-5. And at the root is the disciple's daily input of willpower. That term is heresy to theology because it implies self-will instead of God's will. But can there not be an inspired will in the Saint who has repented of his sins through faith, purified himself through baptism, received the gift of the Holy Ghost by the appointed laying on of hands, and has then sought inspiration and strength to serve God? This is the apostolic program from Pentecost onward in Acts, and a correct interpretation of the letters must harmonize with it. To say that a "good man does good works" is naive, for good works come only by exerting spiritual power in action. Paul puts his verbs in the imperative form, the language of command, as he counsels the Roman Saints to achieve the "newness of life" after baptism: "Therefore do not let sin reign in your mortal body, that you should obey it in its lusts. And do not present your members as instruments of unrighteousness to sin, but present yourselves to God as being alive from the dead, and your members as instruments of righteousness to God" (Rom. 6:12-13, NKJB).

Is Paul not expecting self-control and personal choice from the Romans in their post-baptismal conduct? And do such critical choices not count for salvation? In the background is Jesus' overriding command, "If you love me, keep my commandments" (John 14:15, NKJB). In the background is Jesus' explanation of righteousness in the Sermon on the Mount, ending by his commending "whoever hears these sayings of mine, and does them" (Matt. 7:24, NKJB). Protestant theory says that actions do not count for salvation but are the fruits of salvation. But after Jesus said that true disciples would bring forth those fruits, he insisted that those only confessing him to be Christ would not enter heaven, but "he who does the will of my Father who is in heaven" (Matt. 7:21, NKJB). Every one of these statements of Christ presuppose that any believer may choose wrong actions; thus, his good actions are part of his eternal salvation. Otherwise, the commands of the Savior and of his apostles are meaningless observations. Paul's letters are confusing theory without admitting that salvation comes through two causes: God's initiative and man's agency in responding.

Paul's "law of the harvest" told the Galatian members that one could sow "to his flesh" or sow "to the Spirit," with the reward of "life everlasting" (Gal. 6:8). And in Romans this same option is given after discussing the "newness of life" after baptism: "For to be carnally minded is death; but to be spiritually minded is life and peace" (Rom. 8:6). In Greek "carnally minded" is literally "the mind of the flesh," and "spiritually minded" is literally "the mind of the Spirit." Thus, the choices in Romans are the same as in Galatians. There is also the same reward, for Galatians' "life everlasting" equates with the eternity implied in Romans' "life." Being "spiritually minded" does not come automatically by justification but through honest toil for the fruits. And the general purpose of Romans is the same as Paul's other letters—to encourage Church members to develop lives worthy of their beliefs. Of course, there is the help of the Spirit, but this does not supplant the agency of men and women. As explained at the close of Galatians, to walk "after the Spirit" (Rom. 8:4) is to keep the commandments and be worthy of the guidance of the Holy Ghost. Eternal life will come to those who "through the Spirit do mortify the deeds of the body" (Rom. 8:13). "Mortify" is a simple Greek word meaning "put to death," so Paul is asking the Roman saints to destroy their evil works as a condition of living in God's kingdom. Here is a sequence to be met again in Colossians: in Romans 6:3-5 Paul reviews the covenant of a new life through baptism, he requires the death of evil practices in Romans 8:13, and he details commands for righteousness in three full chapters near the end of the book. The components of salvation through Christ are not finished until the *end* of Paul's long, dictated letter.

Conditional Election

Why did the Jews lose God's favor? Commentators say that is Paul's topic in Romans 9 through Romans 11. But he also discusses the fall of Judaism for the benefit of Gentiles, so the question is really, "What can be learned from God's rejection of his people?" These chapters digress from the subject of personal salvation and yet throw great light on it. They begin with the Jewish apostle's deep love "for my brethren, my kinsmen according to the flesh" (Rom. 9:3). Some of the best Christian minds have misread God's calling of Israel, and the harsh doctrine of predestination is the result. The proof texts mostly come from Romans 9, but Joseph Smith correctly linked that chapter to the message of the following ones: "The whole of the chapter had reference to the priesthood and the house of Israel, and unconditional election of individuals to eternal life was not taught by the apostles. God did elect or predestinate that all those who would be saved should be saved in Christ Jesus, and through obedience to the gospel. But he passes over no man's sins, but visits them with correction, and if his children will not repent of their sins, he will discard them."[36]

Predestine is used only four times in the King James Bible, and *predestination* not at all. That word can better be understood in discussing Ephesians, but the doctrine as expressed through "election" is central to Romans 9 through Romans 11. Joseph Smith rightly says that Paul discusses the calling of Israel, not of individuals. Whereas Israel received the covenant and revelation of the Old Testament, it forfeited that relationship for a time by not accepting the new revelations. Paul is pained to admit it, for his "prayer to God for Israel is, that they might be saved" (Rom. 10:1). The former Pharisee knows the strength of their "zeal for God" and their weakness of not accepting the Messiah: "For they . . . seeking to establish their own righteousness, have not submitted to the righteousness of God. For Christ is the end of the law for righteousness to everyone who believes" (Rom. 10:2-4, NKJB). John the Baptist had challenged Jews not to see their relationship with God on the superficial level of descent from Abraham. Paul does the same, indirectly suggesting that Ishmael was a son of Abraham but did not inherit his promises; then Paul names Esau as a son of Jacob who did not inherit his promises. Paul's point is that the promise had then passed over Abraham's descendants to rest for a time upon the Gentiles. They had not merited God's call from the point of view of earth life, but Latter-day Saints have the added perspective of the premortal existence in understanding God's choices. The methodical reformer John Calvin lacked this understanding and mistakenly extended Jewish and Gentile election to individual salvation: "By predestination we mean the eternal decree of God, by which he determined with himself whatever he wished to happen with regard to every man. All are not created on equal terms, but some are preordained to eternal life, others to eternal damnation. And accordingly, as each has been created for one or other of these ends, we say that he has been predestinated to life or to death."[37]

This negation of human agency is argued strongly from two examples. Paul never comes to Calvinist conclusions, but the Calvinists argue that Paul's views on Esau and Pharaoh teach predestination. In both cases one must look at notes in Bible verses to see when Paul is quoting the Old Testament. While Jacob and Esau were in the womb, Rebekah was told, "The elder shall serve the younger" (Gen. 25:23). Through this example Paul told the

Jews that God could shift the birthright from them to the Gentiles. He simply said that God made the "election . . . not of works but of Him who calls," for the children were unborn and had not "done any good or evil" (Romans 9:11, NKJB). Calvin argued that "no good works are taken into account . . . there being nothing in them, either past or future, to conciliate his favor."[38] On this view, God did not select by foreseeing the works of Jacob or Esau in life, though Paul does not rule that out. And on Calvin's view no works preceded their birth. But two centuries after Paul, the Christian scholar Origen believed otherwise, saying that Jacob must have been "beloved by God, according to the deserts of his previous life, so as to deserve to be preferred before his brother."[39]

This doctrine of premortal existence can be clearly traced to orthodox Jewish and Christian sources in Paul's time, as will be seen in studying Ephesians and Titus. So Origen's explanation must be considered. Indeed, Romans mentions the premortal existence of the righteous and suggests their worthiness by saying that God "prepared beforehand for glory even us whom he has called" (Rom. 9:23-24, NKJB). This means that Calvin developed his doctrine too narrowly. Paul simply insists on God's right to choose Jacob, without probing into why he made that choice. The story of Jacob and Esau is but a parable about God preferring Gentiles over Jews, and we have seen that Gentile election came after the apostasy of the Jews (Rom. 10:3-4). Paul's argument is from precedent and is limited by what Genesis and Exodus said. Thus, the examples of Esau and Pharaoh are not likely to include Paul's full perspective. A dozen verses from the Old Testament alternate with Paul's comments in Romans 9 as he makes a "from your own scriptures" presentation. So all comments on Pharaoh come straight out of Exodus—his being raised up to show God's power, with Paul's remark that God hardens "whom he will" (Rom. 9: 17-18, NKJB). Since Paul never elsewhere uses "harden" in this way, he is obviously using the language of Exodus to convince his "kinsmen."[40] "And unto the Jews I became as a Jew, that I might gain the Jews" (1 Cor. 9:20). No writing of Paul better illustrates this principle than this section of Romans.

Paul's argument emphasizes the responsibility of the Jews in rejecting the preaching of Christ. Jew and Gentile are both loved and accepted by God if they will only "call upon him" (Rom. 10:12). So the rejection of Israel is based on Israel's rejection of the Lord's messengers. They preach in power: "Faith comes by hearing, and hearing by the word of God" (Rom. 10:17, NKJB). And "the word of God" here means more than quoting scripture, as Joseph Smith stated in commenting on this verse: "Faith comes by hearing the word of God through the testimony of the servants of God—that testimony is always attended by the spirit of prophecy and revelation."[41] The "apostle of the Gentiles" (Rom. 11:13) moved through the basics of finding the true gospel: belief is based on hearing, which is based on those preaching the message, and they cannot preach "except they be sent" (Rom. 10:15). As in Corinthians, the true gospel comes with the authority of the true church. Paul conditions salvation on openly confessing "the Lord Jesus" and deeply believing that God "raised him from the dead" (Rom. 10:9). Some quote that verse to prove that belief alone brings salvation. But in Acts the missionary apostle required his believing converts to be baptized, and he wrote about belief and salvation here after writing Romans 6:3-5 on God's requirement to live up to the baptismal covenant.

The crescendo of Paul's treatment of election is also the crescendo of stressing agency. *Election* appears only seven times in the New Testament, and four of these appearances are in Romans. Calvinist theology gives the word a misleading ring of finality: "It assures the believer of his eternal security. . . . If he is in grace now he is in grace forever."[42] But Paul uses *election* as a term of God's conditional selection. It is equivalent to the verb *call*, which in Paul generally refers to conversion with the implied period afterward of testing for faithfulness. *Calling* and *election* refer to gospel opportunity, not to God's final determination, which for Jesus, Paul, and John the Revelator comes on the day of judgment.

Israel was originally Jacob's name, and before birth he was given the "election . . . not of works," identified as the "call" of God (Rom. 9:11). And Paul noted in the Church a "remnant" of

191

Israel "according to the election of grace," also defined as not of works (Rom. 11:5-7). But Jacob's original call was also the call of his descendants; it was made before they lived on earth. Election is without earthly works because calls are by definition prior to the task for which the call is made. Paul testifies that "Israel shall be saved," showing that the "election" or "calling of God" will not fail (Rom. 11:26-29). But that is prophecy, not predetermination. For most of Israel then had temporarily failed, suffering "blindness in part . . . until the fulness of the Gentiles be come in" (Rom. 11:25). God had not given them an election for all time that would not diminish. And why did they in large part fail? Paul answers with the image of the Jewish branches of the olive tree. They were removed "because of unbelief" (Rom. 11:20). Then the Gentile branches were grafted to the tree, but their agency to stand or fall was exactly that of Israel: "Toward you, goodness, if you continue in his goodness. Otherwise you also will be cut off" (Rom. 11:22, NKJB).

Moral Laws of the Gospel

The greatest epistle on grace is also the greatest epistle on keeping God's commandments. The magnificent close of the teaching portion of Romans beats out a sharp staccato of Christian duties. Some fifty commandments follow the challenge of being "transformed by the renewing of your mind" (Rom. 12:2). These detailed instructions fill three and a half chapters, after which Paul closes the letter by sharing his plans and greetings. No Pauline letter has as many rules of righteousness. The apostle is intent on upgrading the conduct of those Church members who have accepted Christ through baptism. These closing chapters are the capstone of this letter of grace and certainly are not intended as incidental to eternal life. Salvation may be defined in terms of theory, or in terms of the steps of what to do. Just as actions speak louder than words in real life, the actions that Paul required speak louder than interpretations of his theology.

Vital discipleship is paralyzed by the philosophy that Christ did all, that "we have no ability to win his grace or favor."[43] An example is a survey a few years ago identifying Lutherans of the Missouri Synod and the Southern Baptists as the most conservative Protestant bodies in the United States. In these groups 97 percent of the members said that "belief in Jesus Christ as Savior" was "absolutely necessary" for salvation.[44] Then these same individuals were asked whether "doing good for others" was "absolutely necessary" for salvation, and only 38 percent of the Lutherans and 29 percent of the above Baptists agreed. Thus, the majority of each group saw no contribution of service as necessary to salvation. They were also asked whether salvation depended on "loving thy neighbor," a more ambiguous question because "loving" can be an attitude instead of an activity. Yet only 51 percent of the Lutherans and 41 percent of the Baptists said that "loving thy neighbor" was "absolutely necessary" to being saved.[45] Christ said that "the law and the prophets" were summed up in loving one's neighbor (Matt. 7:12). Yet huge groups of committed Christians feel that God does not require belief in the Golden Rule or practical service applying it. But the closing teaching section of Romans jars that conclusion, for of about fifty commandments, at least a fourth pertain to loving and helping one's neighbor. Indeed, Paul repeats as binding the Savior's statement just quoted, saying that "any other commandment" is "summed up" in the rule of loving one's neighbor as self (Rom. 13:9, NKJB).

Paul's use of this highlight of the Sermon on the Mount is the clue to his message at the end of Romans. The thought of most of the beatitudes is found in Romans 12. The thrust of that chapter follows the closing challenge of Matthew 5 to return good for evil and to actively bless those who hate us. That is exactly Paul's message: "Overcome evil with good" (Rom. 12:21). Paul does not quote Jesus, but his ideas are exact applications of Jesus' principles. It should be recognized that Romans 12 through the beginning of Romans 15 is the Sermon on the Mount of the epistles. Paul should be seen, like Jesus, not coming to "destroy the law, or the prophets . . . but to fulfil" (Matt. 5:17). That should be clear from Paul's command to live five of the ten commandments (Rom. 13:9). Rather than revoking them, Jesus taught what it meant to keep them in the opening chapter of the Sermon on the Mount. Paul's epistle of grace also stresses them as Christian law, as do the modern revelations of the Prophet Joseph Smith.

Can we forget the Lord who challenged the rich young ruler to "keep the commandments" if he would enter into eternal life? (Matt. 19:17.) When asked which ones, Christ gave (Matt. 19:18-19) nearly the exact words of Paul in summing up the commandments to the Romans (Rom. 13:9). Members of the Early Church were growing and developing through obedience. As discussed, baptism brought them to "newness of life . . . that henceforth we should not serve sin" (Rom. 6:4, 6). That was the ideal, but the reality was to be won on the moral battlefields of their lives as Christians. Paul wrote Romans to lead them to avoid every sin and to "yield your members servants to righteousness unto holiness" (Rom. 6:19). This post-baptismal command was restated as a preface to the moral laws of the gospel: "Present your bodies a living sacrifice, holy, acceptable unto God" (Rom. 12:1). The next verse set the goal of membership in the Church and of every command that followed: moral transformation and renewal. Neither Christ nor Paul had a single offer of salvation but a program of growth to salvation. Jesus personified it in instructing, encouraging, and correcting his disciples. With most of his ministry spent in these activities, was he not contributing to salvation? And Paul's work as Christ's apostle was also training the Saints in living the gospel.

Paul insists on the power of prayer and of humility before God. He links his main theme of genuine love to actions of helping and to the self-control of sexual purity. Even civil obedience and the duty of paying taxes are parts of citizenship in God's kingdom. Romans opens with recognition of the spiritual conscience in all people; it closes with the appeal to live a life that will be recognized as righteous. Paul commands to do "honest" things (Rom. 12:17) and to walk "honestly" (Rom. 13:13), but these terms are used in the older English sense of "honorable" and "honorably," basically the meaning of the Greek. Thus, Paul's version of the Sermon on the Mount carries the Master's theme: "Let your light so shine before men, that they may see your good works, and glorify your Father which is in heaven" (Matt. 5:16).

HEBREWS

Profile

Sent from: Paul, in Italy and probably at Rome.
Sent to: "The Hebrews," possibly those who helped Paul in the Judean imprisonment.
Date: Possibly A.D. 62.
Purpose: To warn Jewish Christians against falling from the faith and to reconvince them that Christ and his gospel are above the law of Moses.
Main themes: Christ's authority and mission; faithfulness and first principles; Melchizedek priesthood; Christ's atonement; faith and endurance.

Background

Reason for Writing

The title goes back to the earliest Greek manuscripts: "To the Hebrews." And the contents have intricate arguments about Jewish law and the temple rituals. Who were these Jews who first read this letter? The answer must come from the letter itself, since no information on the circumstances of writing is in Acts or early Christian sources. Endurance in trial and faithfulness in temptation are the watchwords expressed throughout chapters 2-6 and chapters 10-12. Like the Corinthians, the Hebrews had to go back and relearn the "first principles" at a time when their gospel growth should have been advanced (Heb. 5:12-14). They were "dull of hearing" (Heb. 5:11), which shows that Paul had particular information that worried him. What were their problems? One was living the gospel, a problem common to most branches of the Church in the letters. But the long arguments of reconver-

195

sion center around Jewish ritual. The Hebrews overstressed the Levitical priesthood that operated the temple and the daily sacrifices that were superseded by Christ's great sacrifice. Chapters 7 through 10 are written for Jews who did not believe that Christ's coming outdated temple sacrifice. After the third journey Paul returned to Jerusalem and shared in temple sacrifice to show that he respected his Hebrew heritage (Acts 20). But it was another thing to believe that sacrifices were part of Christ's gospel, the Jewish heresy that this book combats.

Though scholars disagree on the origin of Hebrews, many see it as written prior to A.D. 70 because that year the temple was destroyed, and arguments against continuing sacrifice would have no point after that date. The present tenses of chapters 7 through 10 give the impression that the priests are then sacrificing, and the long arguments against ceremonies logically suggest a present threat rather than a past problem. Jesus predicted the destruction of the temple (Matt 24; Mark 13; Luke 21), and some hint of it is probable if Hebrews had postdated the Roman assault. These inferences place the letter within Paul's lifetime, which closed just before the temple was destroyed. And there are further clues that point to his Roman imprisonment described at the end of Acts.

After Paul's third journey he returned to Jerusalem, to be arrested and held for trial for two years; Acts closes as he waits another two years for trial under house arrest. The four letters that easily fit into his Roman custody will be studied next. In one of these Paul closes with "remember my bonds" (Col. 4:18), which is similar to the flashback recalling how the Hebrews "had compassion of me in my bonds" (Heb. 10:34). Manuscripts divide here between "my bonds" or "the prisoners," but the majority of texts have "my bonds." This fits the circumstances of Paul's loose custody in Caesarea in A.D. 58 through 60, when the governor commanded the guard to "forbid none of his acquaintance to minister" to Paul (Acts 24:23). Hebrews was probably written at Rome, because greetings are sent from the Saints "of Italy" (Heb. 13:24). [46] This places the book after about A.D. 61, for until Paul's appeal to Caesar, he had not yet been in Rome. Possibly in his

Roman imprisonment Paul wrote to correct the Jewish branch at Caesarea, where he earlier had been imprisoned, addressing the general problems of the Jewish Christians. They should "recall the former days in which, after you were illuminated, you endured a great struggle with sufferings" (Heb. 10:32, NKJB).

Authorship Evaluation

Hebrews has the same manuscript credentials as other letters of Paul, but its distinctive nature produced unnecessary skepticism among ancient and modern scholars. Yet trends are not necessarily truths. Of all the arguments against authorship, style is the most easily misused. The Gettysburg address is remarkably unlike most of Lincoln's speeches but of course was authored and delivered by him. With such cautions against prejudging, the evidence on Paul's authorship can be examined. At first glance, Hebrews must come from an early Christian leader, for it is quoted in the letter called 1 Clement, written by Clement, the bishop of Rome, about A.D. 96. This is one of several subapostolic books, mostly from bishops who had some personal knowledge of the apostles and who quoted them for authority in their arguments. Clement writes of "Jesus Christ, the high priest of our offerings" in these words: "Who, being the brightness of his majesty, is by so much greater than angels, as he has inherited a more excellent name."[47] This clear use of Hebrews 1:3-4 omits phrases but runs in strict sequence with ten exact Greek words, the remaining four being synonyms of those in that passage.

Clement's quotation shows that Hebrews was in existence and circulating by the close of the first century. That fits into its probable writing prior to the destruction of the temple in A.D. 70, as discussed above. But Clement's use of Hebrews says something more. With the exception of some quotations from the Gospels and Acts, all of Clement's New Testament quotations come from letters attributed to apostles. Hebrews is used in several places in 1 Clement because it had apostolic authority. And in the first Christian centuries, no other apostle but Paul was named in connection with it. The most dramatic proof of that is the modern discovery of the Chester Beatty Papyri, which contain portions of most books of the New Testament. The most precious jewel in this find was a nearly complete copy of Paul's letters, the oldest known. This was written in book, not scroll, form. All the letters that Paul wrote to churches are found in this collection except for 2 Thessalonians, which obviously fits in the remaining pages known to have existed prior to destruction of the first and last pages of the manuscript. Not only is Hebrews in this ancient book, but it is in a place that shows that it was considered a letter of Paul when this document was written about A.D. 175. Paul's church epistles appear there in rough order of length as follows: Romans, Hebrews, 1 Corinthians, 2 Corinthians, Ephesians, Galatians, Philippians, Colossians, and 1 Thessalonians. Commenting on the location of Hebrews in this manuscript, Kenyon said, "Its present position is a proof of the high importance assigned to it, and of the unquestioning acceptance of its Pauline authorship."[48]

Since Hebrews was widely considered one of Paul's letters a century after his death, why is there any doubt? As noted above, the essential answer is the style of the letter. The most obvious problem here may be the most superficial one: opening without the name of Paul in the text. Most modern books and many ancient ones do the same, with the author identified on a title page or a heading. The Chester Beatty Papyri do just that by listing Hebrews as the second item in Paul's letters. So the book is certainly by an identified author, though it lacks Paul's name in its opening. At its end, Hebrews mentions Timothy, whose name appears only in Acts in connection with Paul and in eleven of Paul's letters. "Grace be with you all" ends Hebrews, and this phraseology closes every other letter of Paul—it does not close other New Testament letters. Paul's other letters begin with phrasing on grace and peace from the Father and the Son; Hebrews differs in wording but begins with the testimony of the Father and the Son. Hebrews is the one letter addressed to the Jews by the apostle called to the Gentiles—perhaps Paul's consciousness of

THE BEGINNING OF HEBREWS IN THE CHESTER BEATTY PAPYRI

The oldest surviving collection of Paul's letters (about A.D. 175) places Hebrews immediately after Romans and before 1 Corinthians. The centered Greek title is "To the Hebrews"—*pròs (H)ebraíous*. The previous line is the end of Romans 16:23: "and Quartus a brother"—*kaì Koúartos (h)ò adelphós*. From the plates volume of Kenyon's publication, cited in note 49.

transcending his normal assignment caused the absence of his name, apostleship, and authority in the letter to the Hebrews.

Must the most creative writer of the New Testament fit one literary mold? Scholars dash off informal letters and also labor over elegantly worded papers of logical symmetry. Paul was capable of this careful testament of faith to his nation as well as of the spontaneous, often dictated language in the majority of his letters. Thoughts and expressions characteristic of him are prominent in the personalized final chapters of Hebrews. Other New Testament writers do not use the comparisons of the church to the body (Heb. 13:3) and of enduring in an athletic contest (Heb. 12:1). Yet these are found throughout Paul's letters. Being fed milk is a positive beginning of growth for Peter (1 Pet. 2:2), but Paul uses the metaphor to shame those weakening in the faith (1 Cor. 3:1-2), the same viewpoint as in Hebrews (Heb. 5:12-14). In explaining justification by faith, Paul favors Habakkuk 2:4— "The just shall live by his faith"—quoting it in Romans 1:17 and in Galatians 3:11. It is quoted one other time in the New Testament as Hebrews 10:38 introduces the great chapter on faith. No one stressed that principle more than did Paul, and Hebrews 11 is the greatest chapter in the New Testament on that subject. But what about sentence structure and vocabulary? Those elements follow from the subject and the occasion; since Paul wrote to the Hebrews formally and only once, natural differences would appear. Indeed, stylistic differences are regularly exaggerated, for many words in Hebrews are distinctively Pauline. [49]

The earliest information about Hebrews supports Paul's authorship. Origen, the brilliant Christian scholar who lived from about A.D. 185 to 253, furnished an irresistible quotation that some use as the last word: "But who wrote the epistle, in truth God knows." But that statement only represents Origen's judgment on the style of the penman, for he was convinced that "the thoughts are the apostle's," coming from a disciple's "short notes of what his master said." Yet Origen admitted that the historical tradition upheld Paul's authorship: "For not without reason have the men of old time handed it down as Paul's." [50] Origen's teacher was the educated Clement of Alexandria, who lived about A.D. 150 to 215. Clement in turn relied on a source, "the blessed elder," apparently his Christian teacher Pantaenus, who flourished earlier in the second century. Thus, the following views of Clement and his teacher reflect the early conviction that Paul wrote Hebrews; their views are preserved by the later church historian Eusebius, who quoted Clement of Alexandria:

> And as for the Epistle to the Hebrews he says indeed that it is Paul's, but that it was written for Hebrews in the Hebrew tongue, and that Luke, having carefully translated it, published it for the Greeks. Hence, as a result of this translation, the same complexion of style is found in this epistle and in the Acts. . . . Then lower down he adds: "But now, as the blessed elder used to say, since the Lord, being the apostle of the Almighty, was sent to the Hebrews, Paul, through modesty, since he had been sent to the Gentiles, does not inscribe himself as an apostle of the Hebrews, both to give due deference to the Lord and because he wrote to the Hebrews also out of his abundance, being a preacher and apostle of the Gentiles."[51]

It is logical that Paul would write to the Hebrews in their literary language, but Clement may have assumed translation on the narrow basis of style. What is important is that he and his teacher represent the informed conviction that Hebrews came from Paul, for they gave this view at the time when the scribe of the Chester Beatty Papyri copied Hebrews as second in its collection of Paul's letters. Thus, there is a substantial second-century conviction of Paul's authorship. On the level of inspired reaction to style and message, Joseph Smith did not claim formal revelation on the subject but consistently referred to Paul as the author.

Main Teachings

Christ's Authority and Mission

Eternal realities are unfolded in the beginning of Hebrews, and they are based on historical realities. For Paul proclaims salvation that "first began to be spoken by the Lord, and was confirmed unto us by them that heard him" (Heb. 2:3). Paul heard these eyewitnesses of the Lord, and he adds that God also testified through healings, miracles, and "gifts of the Holy Ghost" that followed the Lord of the Gospels and his apostles of Acts (Heb. 2:4). Paul had experienced these signs following but focused on how the gospel came before his conversion. If God had spoken, what kind of God was he? Most large Christian churches have formal statements defining the Holy Trinity, but their principle adjectives are not found in Paul's great testimonies of the Father and the Son. In fact, the creeds speak of a triune God, not of one glorious being in the shape of another. Paul opens Hebrews with the Father sending the Son, who is the "brightness of his glory, and the *express image* of his person" (Heb. 1:3, italics added). The italicized words translate the Greek *charaktér*, the ancestor of the English *character*, which roughly approximates Paul's meaning.

Christ is the "character" of God's being, the apostle says. This term meant the "mark" of an engraving tool—in physical terms a "stamped likeness" or "an exact reproduction."[52] Thus, Christ is not the Father, but he is stamped with his divinity and exact form. And this is not in some mystic sense of sharing the same soul, for man in his distinctiveness from God is also said to be in God's "character" in early Christian literature. Clement of Rome wrote about A.D. 96 and said that God formed man in the "*likeness* of his own image."[53] In the opening of Hebrews Christ is clearly distinct from God, standing "on the right hand of the Majesty on high" (Heb. 1:3). Commentators too smugly say that "no literal location is intended."[54] Yet the mother of James and John had a location in mind when she wanted them to sit at Christ's right and left hand in eternity (Matt. 20:21-23). But Christian scholars believe that "God has no physical right hand or material throne where the ascended Christ sits beside Him."[55] They interpret the "right hand" as merely descriptive of status or power, but how do they draw the line between explaining and explaining away? Stephen saw Christ at the right hand of God (Acts 7:55-56), as did Joseph Smith in 1820 in the First Vision. A half dozen times Paul speaks of Christ at the right hand of the Father and never hints at less than literalism.

As separate from God, Christ fulfilled a unique mission. He is God's son and God's "heir," the creator of worlds (Heb. 1:2); he is the power "upholding all things," who "brought about the cleansing of our sins" (Heb. 1:3, literal trans.). For a time he descended below angels that he "might taste death for everyone" (Heb. 2:9, NKJB). Using a form of the word of priestly sacrifice in Romans 3:25, Paul pictures Jesus as the High Priest making "propitiation for the sins of the people" (Heb. 2:17, NKJB). Thus, Hebrews opens to attest the Atonement and never moves far from this subject. Obviously the Jewish converts needed the powerful message of forgiveness through Christ instead of their purification rites. With their faith in Jehovah and his angels, they had apparently assimilated Christ into their religious system as a part but not the center. The opening two chapters of Hebrews give ten Old Testament quotations in a row on the superiority of the Son to angels. The Psalmist said that man on earth was "a little lower than the angels" (Heb. 2:7), and Christ came to share the human condition (Heb. 2:11) to raise all to celestial fellowship. The point of this reasoning is Christ's descending to lift all—the point of the Old Testament quotations is the superiority of the Son to all angels. The appearances of Moses and Elijah to Christ and to Joseph Smith are part of the evidence that angels are righteous men in postmortal glory. In authority they function under Christ, and those worthy in this life will not be lower than angels in eternity—Paul reminded the Corinthians, "We shall judge angels" (1 Cor. 6:3).

Another Jewish problem is refuted in Hebrews. Paul opened Corinthians by regretting that Christ was a "stumbling-block" to Israel because "the Jews require a sign" (1 Cor. 1:22-23). The disciples on the Emmaeus road had difficulty believing in a slain Messiah, since they looked to the prophets' words of the victorious Messiah of the day of judgment (Luke 24:20-21). So Hebrews probes the suffering mission of Christ and what it means to those who follow him. Christ is the "captain" of our salvation (Heb. 2:10) and the "author" of our faith (Heb. 12:2)—these are different renditions of a word meaning leader, founder, or originator. Thus

Christ, who brought the plan of salvation, was made "perfect through sufferings" (Heb. 2:10). This theme is resumed with the same wording in Hebrews 5:8-9: the "Son . . . learned . . . obedience by the things which he suffered" and thus was "made perfect." That is the first half of the message about Christ, for his earthly life was outwardly a defeat but really a personal victory. Jews who might stumble at his suffering must know that he filled the Father's assignment and thus completed his Godhood. Since the perfecting of the Messiah through suffering is identical in Hebrews 2:10 and Hebrews 5:8, the Joseph Smith Translation note identifying the latter with Melchizedek must not be taken superficially. "Standing alone . . . this footnote gives an erroneous impression"; the verse refers to Christ, since "Melchizedek was a prototype of Christ."[56]

What benefit could come from a suffering Savior? For many years Paul probably faced that question of ridicule or confusion. His answer is that a suffering Savior knows us better and is better known by us. Having learned obedience through mortal trials, Christ can be trusted totally to lead "all them that obey him" to "eternal salvation" (Heb. 5:9). In the Joseph Smith Translation, this verse speaks of Christ alone. The Savior does not call from a distant height but from a little ahead on the rocky path that his disciples climb: "For we do not have a High Priest who cannot sympathize with our weaknesses, but was in all points tempted as we are, yet without sin" (Heb. 4:15, NKJB). Jesus was once on this earth, fully felt its pressures, and met its challenges. He not only died for the sins of all but lived as the example for all. Could anyone believe that perfection is attainable unless someone had attained it? And could anyone have confidence in divine mercy unless the Lord knew personally the terrible realities of life? "For in that he himself has suffered, being tempted, he is able to aid those who are tempted" (Heb. 2:18, NKJB). This knowledge is behind Paul's assurance that others have faced the temptation that any person is called to face—that God "will not allow you to be tempted" beyond your ability to bear it (1 Cor. 10:13, NKJB).

Faithfulness and First Principles

"Well done," the Lord told the "good and faithful servant" (Matt. 25:21, 23). This approval was given to those productive enough to double the five or two talents given to them. In this and other parables Jesus taught that faith is shown only by being faithful, the major personal message in Hebrews. In bold strokes Paul puts forth the example of Jesus, "the Apostle and High Priest of our profession" (Heb. 3:1). "Profession" is used in the sense of what doctrines one "professes," and the better rendering is "confession." The point is that salvation comes not by professing or confessing Christ but by following through on one's commitment to Christ and his gospel: "Let us hold fast our profession" (Heb. 4:14). Christ showed the way because he was "faithful to him that appointed him" (Heb. 3:2). We shall share his kingdom "if we hold fast the confidence and the rejoicing of the hope firm unto the end" (Heb. 3:6). Paul repeats this last phrase, for it is his theme: literally "steadfast unto the end" (Heb. 3:14).

Like many New Testament letters, Hebrews is a message about crossroads. "If" permeates its teaching. As discussed in Romans, the natural branches of Israel were broken off God's olive tree because of "unbelief" (Rom. 11:20, 23). Paul takes up this theme again in Hebrews, warning the Hebrews not to fail in discipleship as Israel once failed to follow Moses—then the reward was lost "because of unbelief" (Heb. 3:19). The greatness of the ancient revelation is suggested by the language, "Unto us was the gospel preached, as well as unto them" (Heb. 4:2). There is little on this subject in the New Testament except Galatians 3:8, which says God "preached before the gospel unto Abraham." These passages may indicate the general message or revelation of God instead of the full gospel of Christ. Modern revelation shows that higher priesthood and ordinances predating Moses were offered ancient Israel through Moses, but that they "hardened their hearts" and received only lesser laws (D&C 84:19-25). The Jewish converts were well aware of the rebellion against Moses, which made effective Paul's warning on not taking the wrong spiritual road. Christ is the author of eternal salvation only to "them that obey him" (Heb. 5:9).

When many Corinthians doubted, Paul had to restate "the gospel which I preached unto you" (1 Cor. 15:1). When the Hebrews wavered, he had to declare again "the first principles of the oracles of God" (Heb. 5:12). Since "oracles" is ambiguous English, readers should know that it translates a specific term for "revealed words" or "scriptures." Thus, Paul was literally outlining their need to hear "the central principles of the beginning of God's words" (Heb. 5:12, literal trans.) And Paul's list of first principles is soon given, headed by nearly the same label: "The word of the beginning of Christ" (Heb. 6:1, literal trans.). In other words, Paul is reteaching the basis of their conversion, or in the King James phrase, "the principles of the doctrine of Christ" (Heb. 6:1). The above literal translations show that these principles were first in the two senses of being of first importance and also being taught first in sequence. Thus, Hebrews turns the clock back to the fundamental doctrines all converts accepted.

What does Paul mean by "leaving" (Heb. 6:1) these first principles? Certainly he does not mean to leave behind "faith toward God" (Heb. 6:1), for he spends a whole chapter on its necessity later (Heb. 11). Since the manuscripts here do not vary, Paul may have intended to "leave off discussing them," or he might have loosely referred to going beyond and mastering further gospel lessons. In the latter case, the first principles could not be ignored any more than the alphabet is set aside in further study: "The first principles of Christian truth are basic to every stage of development and are no less essential at the end than they are at the beginning."[57] Joseph Smith agreed but preferred to revise an ambiguous meaning rather than to philosophize about it: " 'Leaving the principle of the doctrine of Christ.' If a man leave the principles of the doctrine of Christ, how can he be saved in the principles? A contradiction—I don't believe it. I will render it therefore, 'not leaving the principles of the doctrine of Christ, etc.' "[58]

Paul's "first principles" agree with Peter's preaching on the day of Pentecost. Peter preached the Messiahship and resurrection of

Jesus; to those who had faith to inquire, he answered, "Repent, and be baptized every one of you in the name of Jesus Christ for the remission of sins, and ye shall receive the gift of the Holy Ghost" (Acts 2:38). Paul's "first principles" so closely correspond to Peter's that one must define the other:

Peter on Pentecost	Paul in Hebrews
Jesus' Messiahship	"eternal judgment"
Jesus' resurrection	"resurrection of the dead"
Implied faith of converts	"faith toward God"
"repent"	"repentance from dead works"
"be baptized"	"the doctrine of baptisms"
"the gift of the Holy Ghost"	"laying on of hands"

The content about Christ is very similar in these accounts, though expressed in different words. In Acts and the letters, accepting Jesus as Messiah was accepting the forgiveness of sins through him, and his resurrection. His Messiahship also meant that he was mankind's judge, as shown in speeches of Jesus in the Gospels and of the apostles in Acts. These general professions of faith in Christ correlate. But the striking correlations in the above lists are what Latter-day Saints call the "first principles and ordinances of the gospel." Faith and repentance are obvious first steps, since without believing, one does not repent nor accept any ordinances at all. But on the two ordinances, commentators exhibit considerable confusion. "The doctrine of baptisms" comes out as "ablutions" (RSV) or "cleansing rites" (NEB). Fortunately, the rest of the recognized committee translations have the stability to retain "baptisms." The Greek *baptismós* here is not the normal New Testament word for baptism, and refers to Jewish washings in Mark 7, but several early manuscripts of Colossians 2:12 have no problem using it for Christian baptism. Though it refers to Jewish washings later in Hebrews 9:10, Josephus uses it of John's baptism.[59] All this merely shows that the word can be used of Christian baptism and Jewish cleansing rites. To think that Paul intended the latter in a list of basic Christian requirements is to scramble logic. On Pentecost, Peter insisted on baptism after repentance, which is clearly parallel to Paul's "doctrine of baptisms."[60]

Paul's second ordinance is the "laying on of hands," which has produced a spectrum of speculation among commentators. But comparison with Peter's Pentecostal preaching shows that the purpose of baptism was remission of sins to prepare the convert for the "gift of the Holy Ghost" (Acts 2:38). And as earlier discussed, Acts clearly identifies that gift with the laying on of hands in the cases of Peter (Acts 8:14-20) and Paul (Acts 19:1-6). Thus, the laying on of hands that followed baptism was not the ceremony for priesthood ordination or for healing the sick. Paul's sequencing of teachings "of the beginning" shows that the "laying on of hands" is what converts received after baptism, namely, for the gift of the Holy Ghost. Paul says right afterward that the end product of the "first principles" was to be made "partakers of the Holy Ghost" (Heb. 6:4). More commentators do not see this because Christian churches have not preserved this ceremony of the Early Church. In many Protestant churches, such a "confirmation" only inducts an older child into the church some years after his infant baptism, and receiving the Holy Ghost is not mentioned. Other Protestant churches omit such a laying on of hands altogether. And even Roman Catholic theology teaches that the Holy Ghost comes through all ordinances, thus diminishing the importance of confirmation; it teaches that although confirmation is obligatory on a practical level, it "is not strictly necessary for salvation."[61] Nevertheless Paul listed confirmation on the same level of importance with faith, repentance, and baptism.

These first principles are steps to the plateau bathed in the rays of God's inspiration. Through the Holy Ghost, those who walk there may taste "the good word of God, and the powers of the world to come" (Heb. 6:5). But with that special knowledge, they have special obligations. It is hard for commentators to envision how one so enlightened could rebel. But Satan is real and seeks to turn anyone back who is determined to rise out of his darkness. His tool is ego, for the gifts of God can be perverted for selfish purposes. Spiritual gifts must not be turned to gain "the things of this world" and the "honors of men" (D&C 121:35). One possessed by such goals might knowingly oppose God's work simply because of overriding personal ambition. Satan took that path of rebellion in the premortal life, and he seeks to infect the able with that spirit. So Paul says that if the fully enlightened fall, they risk not being able to return through repentance (Heb. 6:4-6). This is what John called the "sin unto death" (1 Jn. 5:16). It is "mysterious" to many scholars,[62] but modern revelation brings knowledge that those committing this sin allow themselves "through the power of the devil to be overcome, and to deny the truth and defy my power" (D&C 76:31). Like Satan, one has to rise high to fall below the power of forgiveness. Only one especially favored with spiritual certainty can rebel against God with knowledge of what he is doing. In Joseph Smith's words, "He has got to say that the sun does not shine while he sees it; he has got to deny Jesus Christ when the heavens are open to him."[63] This is the problem of the spiritually brilliant, but Paul reminds the Hebrews that most Saints have the problem of qualifying for full salvation through "diligence" (Heb. 6:11). The meaning of faith in Hebrews 11 is clearly forecast by the faithfulness of Abraham. Faith and revelation did not save him, for he "obtained the promise" only in living righteously (Heb. 6:15). And what was the key to his faithfulness? It was his "patience" (Heb. 6:12), the fact that he "patiently endured" (Heb. 6:15). These words are the noun and verb form of *long-suffering*. Full salvation does not come by pushing spiritual buttons, but through persistent and faithful gospel living.

Melchizedek Priesthood

Hebrews powerfully contrasts the "high priest taken from among men" (Heb. 5:1) with Christ as the "high priest" over the Church (Heb. 5:5). Commentaries extol the Lord as the only high priest, but that is contradictory on its face, since he is "called of God an high priest after the order of Melchisedec" (Heb. 5:10). This phrase comes from Psalm 110, and Paul applies "the order of Melchizedek" to Christ a half-dozen times in his discussion. If named after Melchizedek, this priesthood is obviously not unique to Christ—at least one mortal and one divine being held it. Many Protestants see priesthood as part of the Mosaic era, now superseded by the covenant of grace. But the "everlasting covenant" made with Abraham before Moses (Gen. 17:7-19) also contained "the covenant of an everlasting priesthood" (Num. 25:13; also Ex. 40:15). Although Moses referred to ancient Israel as a "kingdom of priests" (Ex. 19:6), Peter applied Moses' phrases to the Early Church: "a royal priesthood, an holy nation" (1 Pet. 2:9). And this was not a metaphor, for Christ's revelation to John speaks of the faithful as "priests of God and of Christ" in eternity (Rev. 20:6). Christ's true church had his priesthood.

Since Paul uses Jewish comparisons to reconvert the Hebrews, the Christian priesthood is not discussed directly. In Paul's day there was one Jewish high priest at a time, appointed by civil authority for a term or replaced at death (Heb. 7:23). Those released still had the name, though not the presiding office (Acts 4:6). Early Church sources sometimes use *priest* and *high priest* for Christian local and general authorities. Except in the book of Revelation, the New Testament does not use these terms of Christian priesthood. Whether or not the Early Church had the full range of priesthood offices, 1 Corinthians 12 and Ephesians 4 list more than are found in the traditional churches. The major source for priesthood ordination by the laying on of hands is quite naturally in the only detailed administrative letter of the New Testament. There Paul directs Timothy to appoint bishops and deacons but to "lay hands suddenly on no man" (1 Tim. 5:22). Obviously, he was to receive God's revelation before choosing, just as Hebrews indicates.

Paul introduces Christ's priesthood with the core principle of how true priesthood is obtained: no man takes "this honour unto himself, but he that is called of God, as was Aaron" (Heb. 5:4). That early time preceded the political domination of the high priest's office. Paul's bridge arches from Aaron to Christ, reinforced by the same method of delegation of authority. Modern revelation gives the proper name of the higher priesthood: "the Holy Priesthood, after the Order of the Son of God" (D&C

107:3). This means that Christ is the source of appointments; God gave his Son authority before the Creation. Aaron is a parallel for Christ, and Aaron is a specific model for priesthood delegation to men. Aaron was called by revelation, since God told Moses to appoint Aaron and his sons to the "priest's office" (Ex. 28:1); then Moses used the physical ceremony of consecration by anointing, which was anciently associated with the laying on of hands (Ex. 28:41), and Josephus added that the people "acquiesced in the divine selection."[64] This procedure was soon duplicated when Joshua succeeded Moses as the Prophet to Israel. God spoke to Moses, commanding the appointment of "Joshua the son of Nun, a man in whom is the spirit"; but to give authority Moses "laid his hands upon him," which was done "before all the congregation," strongly suggesting their approval (Num. 27: 18-23).

Since he used Aaron's example, Paul considered Moses' ordinations relevant to New Testament priesthood. One sees why, as the three steps of Moses were repeated by the apostles as they ordained others. Readers of Acts remember that the Twelve had a problem concerning fair distribution of daily food for the Greek widows of Jerusalem. Partly because sympathetic men were required for this task, the apostles delegated the nomination of welfare supervisors to "brethren," probably those of Gentile background. Yet the apostles retained supervision, for these seven assistants were brought to the Twelve, who "prayed and laid their hands upon them" (Acts 6:6, RSV, NEB, JB, NIV). Common consent also appears and is implied for the full proceedings: "The saying pleased the whole multitude" (Acts 6:5). Thus being "called of God, as was Aaron" (Heb. 5:4) was an operating reality in both testaments, despite the Protestant theory of "priesthood of the believers." Three steps are regularly discernible: the revealed call, group approval, and the laying on of hands.

What does Paul mean by "the priesthood being changed"? (Heb. 7:12.) Delegating authority was not changed. The methods of delegation were not changed. But a higher priesthood was given. Here Paul's purpose structured what he wrote. The

Hebrew converts were impressed by the Old Testament, so Paul talked of Christ's priesthood because that was prophetically documented: "Thou art a priest for ever after the order of Melchizedek" (Ps. 110:4). Since Acts and the letters mention many priesthood offices, priesthood is not solely possessed by Christ. But Paul's argument is simple—if the Levitical Priesthood is superseded by the Melchizedek Priesthood, the ceremonies of the Levitical Priesthood are also superseded (Heb. 7:11). But what is Melchizedek Priesthood? Hebrews poses problems that scholars admit cannot be answered without more information. And now a new Dead Sea Scroll fragment makes it harder to argue that Melchizedek Priesthood is limited to Christ, for Melchizedek appears as a prominent latter-day figure, Elijah-like, with a continuing role in ushering in the day of "good tidings . . . unto Zion" (Isa. 52:7). But he is not alone; Satan, called Belial (2 Cor. 6:15), will be opposed by him and those in "his lot": "the heritage of Melchizedek . . . who will restore them. . . . And he will proclaim release . . . for all sons of [light and] men [of the l]ot of Mel[chi]zedek . . . a year of good favor for Melchize[dek] . . . and the holy ones of God for a re[ig]n of judgment. . . . And Melchizedek shall exact the ven[ge]ance of the jud[g]ments of God [from the hand of Be]lial and from the hand(s) of all [the spirits of] his [lot]."[65]

Who was Melchizedek, and why was a priesthood named after him? His sole historical mention brings Abraham to pay tithes to him as one of greater status. Melchizedek is the "king of Salem . . . priest of the most high God" (Gen. 14:18). Philo, Paul's Jewish contemporary, called Melchizedek "the high priest (*mégas hiereús*) of the most high God."[66] These brief references in Genesis and Psalms 110 "are sufficient to indicate that he is a figure of unusual significance."[67] The growing literature about Melchizedek proves both his importance and the frustration of researchers on not knowing more. A recent study concluded after nearly two hundred pages: "We are no closer than when we began to knowing anything of real substance about a historical figure named Melchizedek."[68] So light can be shed only by new discovery or new revelation. And Latter-day Saints offer what no one else does—new information on the person and the priesthood of Melchizedek.

Joseph Smith added a major source in translating the Book of Mormon, which gave Jewish traditions on Melchizedek, who lived in a wicked generation but "exercised mighty faith" and "did preach repentance unto his people" (Alma 13:18). This is like Noah, who appears only as an inspired ark-builder in Genesis, but Peter knew enough about him to call him a "preacher of righteousness" (2 Pet. 2:5). Through his preaching Melchizedek "did establish peace in the land in his days" (Alma 13:18).[69] When Joseph Smith made his inspired review of Genesis, he added more striking information. Melchizedek showed his great faith "when a child" through miracles: "And thus, having been approved of God, he was ordained an high priest after the order of the covenant which God made with Enoch, it being after the order of the Son of God; which order came, not by man, nor the will of man; neither by father nor mother; neither by beginning of days nor end of years; but of God" (Gen. 14:27-28, JST). And the Joseph Smith Translation continues with the miraculous signs that followed this high ancient priesthood. Such revealed background explains the modern revelation on the name of the priesthood; Melchizedek substitutes for the name of the divine Christ "because Melchizedek was such a great high priest" (D&C 107:2). This was the priesthood of the favored patriarchs. Melchizedek "received it through the lineage of his fathers," going back to Abel, who "received the priesthood by the commandments of God, by the hand of his father Adam" (D&C 84:14, 16).

Was Melchizedek "without father, without mother, without descent, having neither beginning of days, nor end of life"? (Heb. 7:3.) In a variety of places Joseph Smith applies this phrase not to the person of Melchizedek, but to his priesthood: "For this Melchizedek was ordained a priest after the order of the Son of God, which order was without . . . descent" (Heb. 7:3, JST). The commentaries uniformly explain Hebrews' phrases as a mere symbolic argument from Genesis, where no antecedents or successors of Melchizedek are given. [70] But Paul's words are too striking to be set aside: like the Son of God, Melchizedek "remains a priest forever" (Heb. 7:3, NAB, NEB, JB). Of course, the point is to lead up to Christ's eternal priesthood, but what does the Melchizedek analogy mean? Hebrews speaks of an eternal priesthood for Melchizedek. The only sure definitions are descriptions of how they apply. Christ's eternal priesthood continued after death when he visited and preached to the spirits in prison (1 Pet. 3: 18-20). But the Early Church believed the same about its priesthood holders, as shown by the respected work from the brother of the Roman bishop mid-second century: "These apostles and teachers, who preached the name of the Son of God, having fallen asleep in the power and faith of the Son of God, preached also to those who had fallen asleep before them."[71] Christ's servants also had delegated authority to be used in eternity. Most discussions of Hebrews 7 are too abstract, for they do not start from the reality that the Early Church possessed offices that were not of the Levitical or Aaronic Priesthood. "The priesthood being changed" (Heb. 7:12) was a fact for Christ's Church as well as for Christ.

Since Latter-day Saints testify of the return of the lost Aaronic and Melchizedek Priesthoods, they will naturally draw fire from the religious establishment. Modern priesthood does not come from debatable scriptural interpretation, but from the physical appearances of John the Baptist, restoring the lesser Aaronic Priesthood, and then from Peter, James, and John, restoring the Melchizedek Priesthood. [72] Slashing tracts tell us that the Church cannot have Aaronic Priesthood because Paul said it had been "changed" (Heb. 7:12). But Paul's argument is based on the irrelevance of the sacrificial temple, as explained in Hebrews' following chapters. Aaronic sacrificial functions were changed, but in the Restoration, God assigned practical functions and basic ordinances to this priesthood—indeed changed, but continuing, fulfilling the "everlasting priesthood" promises to Aaron's house.

The attacking tracts also tell us that Latter-day Saints cannot have Melchizedek Priesthood because Paul speaks of the "unchangeable priesthood" of Christ (Heb. 7:24). With superficial learning, they claim that the adjective *aparábatos* here means "untransferrable." In this theory, Christ could not delegate to others. Thayer's very inadequate Greek lexicon did take that position in 1889. Yet the recent committee translations all give the idea of Christ holding a "permanent" or "perpetual," not "untransferrable," priesthood. The evidence solidly sustains this position. Ancient papyri provide "a very strong case against the rendering 'not transferable.'"[73] As far as ancient literature, Hebrews 7:24 is often "interpreted *without a successor*," but that meaning "is found nowhere else" and "rather has the sense *permanent, unchangeable*."[74] These are the clear views of the standard tools on word meanings, with no dissenting minority. Careful readers might have known that, since Paul is never far from his Psalms text that Christ is a "priest for ever" (Heb. 7:21), meaning that he will never lose his priesthood. Thus, "continually" (Heb. 7:3) and "forever" (Heb. 7:28, NKJB) give the same thought as the "unchangeable priesthood" (Heb. 7:24). Interpreters restrict Melchizedek Priesthood to Christ, but Paul does not. And Hebrews 7 fits the clear system in Acts and in Paul's letters describing priesthood authority transferred by the laying on of hands. The Bible is deeply consistent with a restored Melchizedek Priesthood.

Christ's Atonement

What does Hebrews add to Paul's preaching of the Atonement in early Romans and 2 Corinthians 5? The answer is dimension and depth, the same thing found in Book of Mormon and Doctrine and Covenants insights. Scriptural testimonies of the Atonement establish the main truth that sins are forgiven through Christ, but different prophets clarify why this is so. These explanations are spokes fixed to the revealed fact of the Atonement. An apt analogy is electricity—few can explain it fully, but all can operate the switches that give its benefits. From chapter 7:25 to chapter 10:21, Hebrews adds its witness to the necessity of Christ's power in man's quest for eternal success. Most seek earthly success, but many fail to seek salvation because they are ignorant of their need for it. Yet the light of mortal life will dim equally for those who seek salvation and for those who do not. The self-sufficient must sometime learn that eternal progress is not possible without the Savior and his servants.

Romans testified that Christ was "at the right hand of God" making "intercession for us" (Rom. 8:34; also v. 27). And Hebrews unfolds the Atonement with the same picture of the Lord "on the right hand of the throne of the Majesty in the heavens" (Heb. 8:1), living in eternity "to make intercession for them" (Heb. 7:25). Here is Christ the Advocate, one who walked un-scorched through mortal fires. The Advocate is literally the Father's Counselor, who from personal understanding petitions for mercy for mortals. The Petitioner asks not through mere pleading, but because he can boldly certify that he has paid the price of sin. The great truths of modern revelation show why Christ is an effective advocate, for he satisfied justice (Alma 42:14-15) and in trembling pain "suffered these things for all, that they might not suffer if they would repent" (D&C 19:16). God is playing celestial games if the Advocate is not a separate person from the Father, for the Romans-Hebrews verb for making inter-cession is an ancient legal term for appealing to another for aid. The same is true of the 1 Timothy-Hebrews noun "mediator." In both English and Greek the concept is "middleman," meaning a third person standing between two parties to bring them together. Paul said that the Law of Moses came through that ancient mediator (Gal. 3:19). And Hebrews speaks of the "Mediator"— greater because he is the "mediator of a better covenant" (Heb. 8:6; also 9:15 and 12:24). Thus, Christ literally intervenes be-tween the Father and mankind to produce harmony. He does more than seek peace and understanding—he pays the price nec-essary to bring forgiveness. He is the contributing Mediator, the effectual Savior.

Jeremiah foretold that God would make "a new covenant" with Israel (Jer. 31:31). As 2 Corinthians 3, Hebrews proclaims the fulfillment through Christ. Jeremiah used the clearest Hebrew word for "covenant," which Paul translated by the Greek *diath-*

ēkē—so that term should mean "covenant" in his letters. It does generally, though it is translated "covenant" only twenty times and "testament" thirteen times in the King James Version. In the latter case, the Joseph Smith Translation changed several cases of "testament" to "covenant" in Hebrews 9, including Paul's argument, "For where a testament is, there must also of necessity be the death of the testator" (Heb. 9:16). Scholars see Paul making use of the secular meaning of *diathēkē* here; although it was used in the Greek translation of the Old Testament to mean *covenant*, it nevertheless was the regular word for *will*. Perhaps stimulated by using "inheritance" just before (Heb. 9:15),[75] Paul made the human analogy that the testator, the maker of the will, had to die for the will or testament to be in force. This comment was based on the double usage. In Elder Bruce R. McConkie's words, "Paul uses both the legal and the gospel definition of terms and teaches that it is through Christ's death that gifts are willed to men."[76]

In his translation Joseph Smith stresses Christ as the offering for remission of sins. Hebrews' intense imagery features the prefiguring Old Testament sacrifices. There is the solemn Day of Atonement, when through offerings Israel became "clean from all . . . sins before the Lord" (Lev. 16:30). Paul stated the major principle of sacrificial forgiveness: there is "no remission" without "shedding of blood" (Heb. 9:22). When the "new covenant" would come, Jeremiah prophesied, God would "forgive their iniquity" and would "remember their sin no more" (Jer. 31:34). Paul quoted that promise (Heb. 10:17), explaining that Christ made this possible. God's people were first established through the sprinkling of "the blood of the covenant," symbolic of their obedience to God's laws and rites (Ex. 24:8). Paul quoted those historic words of Moses (Heb. 9:20). Jesus had also mirrored them for the meaning of his sacrifice: "For this is my blood of the new covenant [*diathēkē*], which is shed for many for the remission of sins" (Matt. 26:28, literal trans.).

Beyond analogy is Christ's agony, which gave forgiveness to all who join his covenant and its restoration in latter days. As the pure sacrificial offering, Christ was beyond sin; thus, he gave for sin what sin could not rightfully claim. As the perfect high priest, he gave himself as the perfect offering. He was "holy, innocent, spotless, set apart from sinners" (Heb. 7:26, literal trans.). He took on himself our blame, though "without spot"—or literally "blameless" (Heb. 9:14). Thus, his culminating sacrifice superseded the daily sacrifices. That is the point of Paul's long arguments—repeated altar slayings were no longer necessary, for Christ died "once" for sins to bring forgiveness to all. That thought and number is restated over a half-dozen times in about three chapters, revealing Paul's core message. Christ "offered one sacrifice for sins for ever" (Heb. 10:12). Roman Catholicism walks a tightrope here. Its theologians agree that the real Christ could be offered once, but the Mass outwardly perpetuates the Old Testament system of sacrifice:

> In this divine sacrifice which is celebrated in the Mass is contained and immolated in an unbloody manner the same Christ who once offered Himself in a bloody manner on the altar of the cross . . . . This is truly propitiatory and has this effect. . . . For, appeased by this sacrifice, the Lord grants the grace and gift of penitence and pardons even the gravest crimes and sins. For the victim is one and the same, the same now offering by the ministry of priests who then offered Himself on the cross, the manner alone of offering being different.[77]

Paul concludes his argument on forgiveness through Christ not with an exhortation to repeat his sacrifice, but with commands to be worthy of it. The bread and wine were taken in "remembrance," publicly showing commitment to him (1 Cor. 11:25-26). But the ceremonial reenactment of Christ's death is not documented in the Early Church. Instead, Paul challenges his readers to accept forgiveness through Christ and to retain it by progress in the righteous life. Paul preached "remission of sins" to the Jews in Pisidian Antioch on the first mission, but that came to the converts in Acts through baptism. Likewise, his letters of Romans, 1 Corinthians, Galatians, Ephesians, Colossians, and Titus all stress the righteous life based on the baptismal covenant. Hebrews did the same in asking for renewed faith, "having our hearts sprinkled from an evil conscience, and our bodies washed with pure water" (Heb. 10:22). The forepart of that instruction is a metaphor for the cleansing of all Israel, which came by sprinkling of blood to the whole people. It particularly used the prophetic image of sprinkling "clean water" to bring "a new heart . . . and a new spirit" (Ezek. 36:25-26). This figure from the Old Testament has nothing to do with Christian baptism. But "our bodies washed with pure water" is Christian baptism, since the above letters command the righteous life after referring to being clean through that ordinance. This is not Old Testament symbolism, since only the sacrificing priests washed in the giant basin before the temple, a comparison too restricted for general application. True to the format of Romans, Galatians, and other letters, Paul preached Christ first, mentioned baptism, and also preached the works that Christ requires.

Faith and Endurance

No group stresses the power of faith more than do the Latter-day Saints. Their publications from the beginning have asked why modern faith should not recreate the ancient miracles. Indeed, Hebrews 11 could be rewritten with great men and women of the Restoration who match Paul's summary of courageous trials and miraculous blessings. Hebrews 11 surveys great faith in action, and the chapter is a treasure to Latter-day Saints, who powerfully show the same fruits of faith. In Paul or modern revelation, salvation is not static but expanding. Salvation is growth toward God, the attaining of Christlike attributes. If eternal life involves progress, it must constantly involve faith to envision what may be. Thus, the first organized teaching materials of the Restoration were the "Lectures on Faith," which opened with faith as "the first principle in revealed religion, and the foundation of all righteousness"; "faith is . . . the principle of action in all intelligent beings."[78]

Theologians scorn the pragmatic approach to faith on the ground that divine faith is unique because it is "infused" by God. Protestants holding this basic position often add predestination as a companion because they feel that man's agency has little or nothing to do with faith. Latter-day Saints often say that faith is a gift from God but mean something far different. For instance, James E. Talmage stresses that "even faith is preceded by sincerity of disposition and humility of soul."⁷⁹ In other words, men and women must consciously choose to be worthy of every gift of God. The scriptures actually say little about faith as a gift of God, but they say much on the Holy Ghost as God's main gift. And in that case Peter tied receiving the Holy Ghost to worthiness, since it comes "to them that obey [God]" (Acts 5:32). Jesus always praised righteous acts and taught strict accountability for moral choices. This issue makes Latter-day Saints distinctive. They believe with other Christians that faith is at the center of receiving exaltation through Christ. But they do not believe that sacramental grace will bring righteousness apart from willpower, nor do they believe that the primary will to righteousness is from God. In a word, they fully accept individual agency and exaltation through cooperation with God. That view does not diminish the marvelous gifts of God, nor does it debase the human personality. Traditional Protestantism insists that "faith is God-given, and is itself the animating principle from which love and good works spontaneously spring"—otherwise one must taste the forbidden fruit of "man's contribution to his own salvation" or betray the Reformation by reviving "the doctrine of human merit."⁸⁰

The gospel of positive thinking falls far short of the gospel of Jesus Christ but nevertheless employs a true principle of faith as spiritual willpower. Jesus criticized those of little faith, and each person can do much to increase faith. In performing physical miracles, Christ never rewarded the doubter. And Paul says that no blessing will ever come from God without faith: "Without faith it is impossible to please him"—because one coming "to God must believe that he is, and that he is a *rewarder* of them that diligently seek him" (Heb. 11:6, italics added). The italicized word means literally "one who pays wages" and indeed pictures a God responding to the sincere motives and efforts of his children. The highest form of faith is that which seeks God, and saving faith is that with Christ as the object. These are gospel uses of the sweeping principle of faith, which Paul defines at the beginning of his survey of what faith has accomplished.

"Now faith is the substance of things hoped for, the evidence of things not seen" (Heb. 11:1). The main points from a shelf of commentaries are in the footnotes to the Latter-day Saint edition of the King James Bible. Translations favor "assurance" for "substance," because the Greek term means "foundation" or "reality."[81] Through faith one acts on realities that are not present. Paul's second idea parallels the first—faith operates like evidence to make one sure of things not seen. The Gentile apostle used the word *faith* forty times in Romans and thirty-two times in Hebrews, the two books in the New Testament that lead all others in using this term. Paul alone describes how faith works, and he gives occasional definitions; these, of course, throw light on his Hebrews' definition. In this earth we "walk by faith, not by sight" (2 Cor. 5:7) because the great realities are beyond this life. Faith perceives these "things which are not seen: for the things which are seen are temporal; but the things which are not seen are eternal" (2 Cor. 4:18). Since the gospel teaches how to prepare for eternity, faith points to the future. It is synonymous with hope: "For we are saved by hope: but hope that is seen is not hope. . . . But if we hope for that we see not, then do we with patience wait for it" (Rom. 8:24-25). The key to Paul's definition in Hebrews 12:1 is the confidence of faith plus what it looks to: "Things hoped for . . . things not seen."

But what is the difference between blind confidence and faith? That is one of the lessons each person was sent to earth to learn. What is the difference between a workable or fanciful plan in business or engineering? As it unfolds, there are indications and trends. In religious faith, the Holy Ghost is the source of spiritual confirmations, and the Savior promised finding by seeking (Matt. 7:7-8). Blind confidence in an untruth is shown by the Book of Mormon analogy of the infertile seed that no amount of good treatment can make grow (Alma 32:21-43). Operational faith is the focus of the scriptures—knowing the plan of salvation to prepare for an eternal future. Thus, faith is not primarily an intellectual but a creative process. Paul signals that at the outset of Hebrews 11 by an example of the divine use of faith: "Through faith we understand that the worlds were framed by the word of God, so that things which are seen were not made of things which do appear" (Heb. 11:3). A bridge or a building is drawn in detail before a beam or board is erected. Reality comes after the creative vision. So faith lies behind all actions, linking the inner image with working power to bring it about.

The divine act of creation leads Paul's long list of great results from faith. And it blends with the great sacrifices that faith inspired. Did faith make such deeds automatic? Is God-infused faith the basic principle from which "good works spontaneously spring"?[82] That phrasing contradicts profound human experience, for significant actions come from both planning and courageous follow-through. "Spontaneously" hardly describes the sustained spiritual choices that ignore persecution for the truth. Abraham was the model for faith in Romans and Galatians, and he is the central example of faith in Hebrews. He first appears in Hebrews 6 to show the double formula for salvation as Paul asks the Hebrews to become "followers of them who through faith and patience inherit the promises" (Heb. 6:12). "Patience" here is the spiritually sturdy word "endurance" (*hupomoné*), already discussed in connection with grace in Romans. Paul leaves no doubt about a second condition for God's approval; after Abraham's faith in God's "promise," Abraham "obtained the promise" only "after he had patiently endured" (Heb. 6:15). Here the last words are literally "after long-suffering."

When Hebrews 11 resumes this subject, the same testing of faith appears for Abraham. He was "called" by revelation but proved his faith because he "obeyed" (Heb. 11:8). Abraham's faith was "tried" in the case of Isaac (Heb. 11:17). Here Hebrews brings together Romans and James, something that Luther treated as impossible. In Romans Paul quoted the Genesis record that Abraham "believed in the Lord; and he counted it to him for righteousness" (Gen. 15:6). But this verse and Paul's explanation have an important context. The childless patriarch had just been told that his descendants would be as innumerable as the stars, and he had the faith to believe that revelation. In a general sense Paul denies that Abraham was "justified by works" (Rom. 4:2), as he speaks of the patriarch's trust in that particular revelation: though aged, he doubted not "the promise of God through unbelief, but was strong in faith" (Rom. 4:20). But did Paul think that God's blessings would continue if Abraham had disobeyed afterward? As just noted, Hebrews says that the "promise" was obtained by Abraham's "endurance" and "long-suffering," his works which followed faith. Whereas justification tends to be unitary in Protestant theology, it comes in two stages in Paul's thought, even in Romans. God's initial approval comes when a prophet or convert responds with undoubting faith, but final approval is strictly conditioned on the successful testing of that faith. The first approval of Abraham appears powerfully in Romans 4, whereas the testing of Abraham's faith appears in Hebrews 11. James speaks bluntly of this second stage in saying that Abraham was "justified by works, when he had offered Isaac his son upon the altar" (James 2:21). Hebrews uses the identical example of the test of faith (Heb. 11:17). Since Romans 4 talks strictly about Abraham's call before Isaac's birth, the beginning of Romans 5 fits Hebrews by teaching the testing of faith.

As seen in discussing Romans 5, that chapter begins with Paul's "ladder of salvation": after faith come trials; trials met successfully bring endurance; endurance results in a tested character. That major theme appeared early in Hebrews—Christ learned obedience through suffering and thus became "the author of eternal salvation unto all them that obey him" (Heb. 5:8-9). And stress on "endurance" introduces and concludes the great chapter on faith in Hebrews. Reviewing his early theme (Heb. 4:14), Paul insists that "confession" or "profession of our faith" is not enough (Heb. 10:23). It must mature into "love and to good works" (Heb. 10:24). Repeating the warning of Hebrews 6 against the unpardonable sin, Paul calls to mind the converts' early testing, when "you endured a great struggle with sufferings" (Heb. 10:32, NKJB). They indeed had faith, but they would not receive "the promise" without something else—"you have need of endurance" (Heb. 10:36, NKJB). Here again is the moral quality of persistence (*hupomonē*), usually translated "patience" in the King James Version. This quality enabled Jesus to face his detractors and the cross itself (Heb. 12:2-3); with his determination in mind, Paul exhorted, "Let us run with endurance the race that is set before us" (Heb. 12:1, NKJB). Thus, the great epistles of faith are also great epistles about endurance, for none will win the contest by faith alone.

Hebrews calls everyone to faithfulness who has sealed his faith and repentance through authorized baptism and received the Holy Ghost by the "laying on of hands" (Heb. 6:1-3). Without watchfulness the Saints could "fall short of the grace of God" (Heb. 12:15, NKJB), a warning so critical that it is repeated in modern revelation (D&C 20:32-34). Like most letters of Paul, Hebrews closes by asking for worthiness for salvation, not by a single act but by an active lifetime of keeping God's commandments. If good works spontaneously spring from faith, Paul would not command them again in every letter. Only determined faith in Christ will bring about good works; only the faith of sustained effort will bring salvation. Thus, Hebrews closes by stressing self-control and service to God and fellowmen. Sexual relations are honorable only in marriage (Heb. 13:4). Selfishness must be eliminated by avoiding covetousness (Heb. 13:5) and by showing the gospel love that all the apostles emphasized (Heb. 13:1). Twice Paul asks the Hebrews to obey their priesthood leaders (Heb. 13:7, 17), for Christ's words come through the apostles and those appointed by them. There was indeed a new priesthood in the new Israel of the Early Church. And like the summation of the Sermon on the Mount, the point of hearing is action, for Paul prays that God will "make you perfect in every good work to do his will" (Heb. 13:21).

Ancient Israel stood on holy ground near the mount of God's presence, and Paul's imagery speaks of present spiritual powers through the historical events of Exodus 19. Then God said of his people, "Israel is my son, even my firstborn" (Ex. 4:22). The "church of the firstborn" (Heb. 12:23) uses the plural in that last term, showing that the faithful Saints will be beloved in heaven just as is the Son, for whom *firstborn* is generally reserved in the New Testament.[83] Christ's favored status is exclusive, but not his sonship, for he told Mary that he ascended "unto my Father, and your Father" (John 20:17). Just as Romans and Galatians teach the fatherhood of God, so Hebrews shows the relationship of mankind to "the Father of spirits" (Heb. 12:9). He trains his children to spiritual maturity through challenges and difficulties. The restored gospel teaches the reality of Paul's testimony that men and women are God's "offspring" (Acts 17:28). Like Jesus, our heritage is in heaven, if we will learn in faith and live to be worthy of it.

NOTES

1. Samuel J. Mikolaski, "Galatians," in D. Guthrie et al., *New Bible Commentary, Revised* (Grand Rapids, Mich.: Eerdmans Publishing Co., 1970), p. 1092.

2. Paul saw Peter three years after Paul's conversion, and fourteen years later he went up to Jerusalem again (Gal. 1:18, 2:1). But Acts has a second visit to Jerusalem that is omitted; logically it should have been, since it was for the purpose of carrying welfare supplies (Acts 11:29-30) and had no bearing on the circumcision question that Paul was arguing in his highly spontaneous letter to the Galatians.

3. William F. Arndt et al., *Greek-English Lexicon of the New Testament*, 2d ed. (Chicago: University of Chicago Press, 1979), p. 62.

4. Mikolaski, p. 1091.

5. Arndt et al., p. 542.

6. G. Elson Ruff, "What Is a Lutheran?" in Leo Rosten, *Religions of America* (New York: Simon and Schuster, 1975), p. 161.

7. Milton V. Backman, Jr., *American Religions and the Rise of Mormonism* (Salt Lake City: Deseret Book Co., 1970), p. 480, citing a 1969 survey. Compare John S. Bonnell, "What Is a Presbyterian?" in Rosten, p. 203: "While baptism is urgently recommended in the Presbyterian Church, and while its omission is regarded as a grave fault, it is not held to be necessary for salvation."

8. Acts speaks of "remission" or "forgiveness" for sins. Both of these words translate the same Greek term. Peter declared remission of sins through Christ to the Sanhedrin (Acts 5:31), though a little earlier he had invited believers to be baptized "for the remission of sins" (Acts 2:38). Peter also declared to Cornelius, "Whosoever believeth in him shall receive remission of sins" (Acts 10:43), but he immediately afterward baptized him. This is very close to Paul's actions with the Philippian jailor, telling him first that salvation would come through belief in Christ, but baptizing him immediately after. Paul also preached remission of sins through belief in Christ in Pisidian Antioch (Acts 13:38). Luke is not contradictory in this double association of remission of sins with belief in Christ and also with baptism. Both conditions must be met to receive the benefit. Christ's atonement makes forgiveness possible, but he sets the conditions of receiving it, namely baptism and living up to the baptismal covenant. Thus, Galatians intimately fits into the practices of Peter and Paul in Acts—"putting on Christ" through the double process of faith and baptism (Gal. 3:26-27).

9. Mikolaski, p. 1089.

10. John H. Gerstner, "Good Works," in Everett F. Harrison et al., eds., *Baker's Dictionary of Theology* (Grand Rapids, Mich.: Baker Book House, 1960), p. 254.

11. This translation fairly accurately states Paul's Greek terms in present language, though I have made two changes: "anger" replaces "outbursts of wrath"; "factions" replaces "heresies," which can relate to ideas only.

12. R. A. Cole, *Epistle of Paul to the Galatians* (London: Tyndale Press, 1965), p. 164.

13. Ibid.

14. P. S. Watson, "Sanctification," in Alan Richardson, ed., *Dictionary of Christian Theology* (Philadelphia: Westminster Press, 1969), p. 303.

15. H. D. McDonald, "Justification by Faith," in Carl Henry, ed., *Basic Christian Doctrines* (New York: Holt, Rinehart and Winston, 1962), p. 214.

16. John Murray, "Sanctification," in ibid., p. 231.

17. *Emerging Trends*, vol. 4, no. 2 (March 1982), p. 1. (Published by Princeton Religious Research Center, Princeton, N.J.)

18. Ibid., p. 2.

19. Suetonius, *Augustus* 28:3 (Loeb Classical Library).

20. *Res Gestae Divi Augusti* (Loeb Classical Library), particularly the end summary but also references throughout.

21. Juvenal, *Satires* 3:62: "jampridem Syrus in Tiberium defluxit Orontes."

22. Suetonius, *Julius* 84:5.

23. Josephus, *Jewish Antiquities* 18:83-84 (Loeb Classical Library).

24. Suetonius, *Claudius* 25:4.

25. Dio Cassius, *Roman History* 60:6 (Loeb Classical Library).

26. See note 24 above.

27. Henry George Liddell and Robert Scott, *A Greek-English Lexicon*, rev. Henry Stuart Jones (Oxford: Clarendon Press, 1953), pp. 1978-79.

28. Quoted in Roland H. Bainton, *Here I Stand* (New York: Abingdon-Cokesbury Press, 1950), p. 65.

29. Martin Luther, Preface to the New Testament, cited in John Dillenberger, *Martin Luther: Selections from his Writings* (Garden City, New York: Anchor Books, 1961), p. 19.

30. William Temple, cited in McDonald, "Justification by Faith," p. 213.

31. Dietrich Bonhoeffer, *The Cost of Discipleship* (New York: Macmillan Co., 1963), p. 47.

32. "Candid Conversation with the Evangelist," *Christianity Today*, July 17, 1981, p. 19.

33. McDonald, "Justification by Faith," p. 217.

34. Roland Bainton, *The Reformation of the Sixteenth Century* (Boston: Beacon Press, 1952), p. 52.

35. Martin Luther, "Treatise on Christian Liberty," cited in Dillenberger, p. 69.

36. Andrew F. Ehat and Lyndon W. Cook, *The Words of Joseph Smith* (Provo, Utah: Religious Studies Center, Brigham Young University, 1980), p. 73.

37. John Calvin, *Institutes of the Christian Religion*, trans. Henry Beveridge (Grand Rapids, Mich.: Eerdmans Publishing Co., 1979) 3.21.5.

38. Ibid. 3.22.3.

39. Origen, *De Principiis* 2.10.7, translated by Frederick Crombie (Ante-Nicene Fathers).

40. Exodus twice says that God hardened Pharaoh's heart (Ex. 7:3; 9:12), but the Joseph Smith Translation makes Pharaoh responsible for his reaction, in accordance with his agency in the narrative. Compare Joseph Smith's comment (Ehat and Cook, p. 73): "Why did God say to Pharaoh, 'for this cause have I raised thee up?' Because Pharaoh was a fit instrument—a wicked man, and had committed acts of cruelty of the most atrocious nature."

41. Ehat and Cook, p. 3.

42. J. I. Packer, "Election," in J. D. Douglas et al., New Bible Dictionary, Second Edition (Leicester, England: Inter-varsity Press, 1982), p. 317.

43. T. H. L. Parker, "Grace," in Harrison et al., p. 258.

44. Charles Y. Glock and Rodney Stark, Religion and Society in Tension (Chicago: Rand, McNally & Co., 1965), p. 102.

45. Ibid., p. 106.

46. The Greek text gives greeting from "those from Italy," so some commentators argue that these are Saints from Italy visiting at some other place. That interpretation is forced, since Paul uses that preposition (apó) in the sense of "going out from" not "being away from." In this sense his message had gone out from Jerusalem (Rom. 15:19), and he had gone out from Macedonia (2 Cor. 1:16; Philip. 4:15). The natural idea is that "those from Italy" are going out through their greetings, not that they have already traveled out of Italy.

47. 1 Clement 36:2, trans. Kirsopp Lake, in The Apostolic Fathers (Loeb Classical Library).

48. Frederic G. Kenyon, The Chester Beatty Biblical Papyri, Fasciculus III Supplement: Pauline Epistles, Text (London: Emery Walker, Ltd., 1936), p. xi. The letters not in this collection are to persons and could have been gathered in a separate section.

49. For a technical discussion supporting Paul's authorship, see William Leonard, Authorship of the Epistle to the Hebrews (Rome: Vatican Polyglot Press, 1939).

50. Quoted in Eusebius, Ecclesiastical History 6:25.13-14 (Loeb Classical Library).

51. Ibid. 6:14.2-4. Clement may or may not have had historical knowledge that Luke translated Hebrews. Late manuscripts are the source of the note at the end of Hebrews in the King James Version; the note indicates that the writing was done by Timothy, which was apparently assumed from Timothy's mention in the epistle.

52. The last phrase comes from James Hope Moulton and George Milligan, The Vocabulary of the Greek Testament (Grand Rapids, Mich.: Eerdmans Publishing Co., 1930), p. 683.

53. 1 Clement 33:4, with Kirsopp Lake's translation of charaktér italicized, in The Apostolic Fathers (Loeb Classical Library).

54. F. F. Bruce, The Epistle to the Hebrews (Grand Rapids, Mich.: Eerdmans Publishing Co., 1964), p. 7. This opinion is typical; Bruce is highly respected by conservative scholars and by this writer.

55. Ibid.

56. Bruce R. McConkie, Doctrinal New Testament Commentary (Salt Lake City: Bookcraft, 1973) 3:157. The JST footnote says that "the 7th and 8th verses allude to Melchizedek, and not to Christ," though Heb. 5:9 clearly refers to Christ and has no JST comment. Joseph Smith clearly taught the progressive perfection of Christ (D&C 93:12-14); he also taught that the righteousness of Jesus was based on obedience. Thus, there is reason to doubt that the Prophet intended to make Hebrews 5:7-8 apply only to Melchizedek. Elder McConkie's point is that Hebrews makes Melchizedek "like unto the Son of God" (Heb. 7:3), so that a given statement about one would fit the other. To the quotation in the text, Elder McConkie adds that "the sermons of the early brethren of this dispensation," those who received the teaching of the Prophet, use Heb. 5:7-10 "as applying to our Lord."

57. Philip Edgcumbe Hughes, Commentary on the Epistle to the Hebrews (Grand Rapids, Mich.: Eerdmans Publishing Co., 1977), pp. 194-95.

58. Ehat and Cook, p. 256, with modification of punctuation and expanded abbreviations in the Willard Richards journal. Compare ibid., p. 72, where Joseph Smith again added "not" to the passage in a speech. Since Joseph Smith added the "not" to his translation of Heb. 6:1, the explanation quoted in the text is a valuable insight into his methods in making the translation.

59. Josephus, *Jewish Antiquities* 18:117.

60. Why did Paul list "baptisms" if he elsewhere preached "one baptism" (Eph. 4:5) and spoke of a single ordinance of coming into the "one body" (1 Cor. 12:13)? Commentators respond with terms like "puzzling." Since "baptisms" must be the ceremonies of the Early Church, one possibility is fascinating: the baptism for the living and the baptism for the dead (1 Cor. 15:29), two distinct types of baptism in Paul's day.

61. John A. Hardon, *Modern Catholic Dictionary* (Garden City, N.Y.: Doubleday & Co., 1980), p. 122.

62. Thomas Hewitt, *The Epistle to the Hebrews* (London: Tyndale Press, 1965), p. 108.

63. Ehat and Cook, p. 353, with abbreviations expanded.

64. Josephus, *Jewish Antiquities* 3:192.

65. Translation of Joseph A. Fitzmyer, with his brackets indicating breaks in the text, deletion symbols added, in his *Essays on the Semitic Background of the New Testament* (London: Geoffrey Chapman, 1971), pp. 249-50.

66. Philo, *On Abraham 235* (Loeb Classical Library).

67. Hughes, p. 237.

68. Fred L. Horton, Jr., *The Melchizedek Tradition* (Cambridge: Cambridge University Press, 1976), p. 172.

69. Hebrews 7:2 associates the Hebrew word for "peace" with ancient "Salem" in the title "king of peace." It also breaks "Melchizedek" into the two successive Hebrew ingredients of "king" and "righteousness."

70. See Hughes, p. 249: Genesis 14 "gives the impression of a continuous and uninterrupted priesthood." See also Myles M. Bourke, "The Epistle to the Hebrews," *The Jerome Biblical Commentary* (Englewood Cliffs, N.J.: Prentice-Hall, 1968) 2:392: The passage "concludes to his eternity" because the Old Testament "does not speak of Melchizedek's ancestors, birth or death. . . . This fanciful interpretation permits the author to emphasize . . . each has an eternal priesthood."

71. *The Shepherd of Hermas*, Sim. 9.16.5, (*The Apostolic Fathers*, Loeb Classical Library).

72. For convenient references to priesthood restoration, see Pearl of Great Price, Joseph Smith—History 1:68-74 and footnote; D&C 27:8-13; D&C 128:20. For a collection of sources, see Richard Lloyd Anderson, "The Second Witness of Priesthood Restoration," *Improvement Era* 71:18-26 (Aug. 1968).

73. Moulton and Milligan, p. 58.

74. Arndt et al., p. 80.

75. This is the perceptive suggestion of Bruce, p. 213.

76. McConkie, 3:183.

77. Council of Trent, 22d Session (1562), ch. 2, cited in John H. Leith, *Creeds of the Churches*, rev. ed. (Atlanta: John Knox Press, 1977) p. 439.

78. Joseph Smith, et al. (compilers), *Doctrine and Covenants of the Church of the Latter-day Saints* (Kirtland, Ohio: F. G. Williams and Co., 1835), p. 5. These "Lectures on Faith" are available in reprinted editions, including that of Wilford C. Wood.

79. James E. Talmage, *Articles of Faith* (Salt Lake City: The Church of Jesus Christ of Latter-day Saints, 1977), p. 107.

80. James I. Packer, "Faith," in Harrison, p. 211.

81. Compare Moulton and Milligan, p. 660: "These various uses are at first sight somewhat perplexing, but in all cases there is the same central idea of something that *underlies* visible conditions." The Greek *hupóstasis* parallels the Latin-derived "substance" in meaning "that which stands underneath."

82. See n. 80 above.

83. Consistent with general New Testament usage, in modern revelation Joseph Smith used "Church of the Firstborn" in the specific sense of "Church of Jesus Christ." The phrase is profoundly significant in both meanings.

7

Roman Imprisonment Letters

Paul's later letters fall into a basic order, with the close of Acts as a beginning point. The record of Paul's missions ended at Acts 20, with Paul's moving farewell to the Ephesian leaders. Then Paul was on his way to Jerusalem with the welfare contribution in 2 Corinthians and Romans, as briefly discussed at the end of chapter 3 of this book. Acts 13 through 20 furnish eight chapters of good detail on Paul's missionary message. But the final eight chapters of Acts cover Paul's arrest in Jerusalem and his four years in custody while waiting for release, so they include more events and less doctrine. They are surveyed here for background of Paul's going to Rome and the circumstances of his writing the first Roman imprisonment letters. Retelling the full Acts story here is unnecessary, since Acts does that so well. Yet it is important to review doctrinal highlights of the close of Acts, with an outline of how Paul came to Rome in order to understand the letters from Rome.

Acts and Romans highlight Paul's inspired worries about returning to Jerusalem. He was obligated to deliver the all-important collection from the Greek Saints, yet the voice of the Spirit told him of imprisonment ahead, and of what else he did not know. Agabus, who prophesied an earlier famine, met Paul after he landed at Caesarea. He bound himself with Paul's belt as a symbol that its owner would meet a similar fate, but Paul answered that he had considered that already: "I am ready not to be bound only, but also to die at Jerusalem for the name of the Lord

Jesus" (Acts 21:13). As Paul left Caesarea for the central hills, who would have expected him to return soon as a prisoner under military guard? In Jerusalem Paul met with James, the only apostle then there, and James counseled Paul to soften Jewish prejudice by accompanying some men in purification rituals in the temple. The principled Paul saw in this no basic conflict with his Christianity. As a Christian, he believed in the reality of God's past revelations to Israel, though he considered temple sacrifices not essential to salvation. Since Jews from Ephesus had seen Paul with a Gentile from their city, they angrily accused Paul in the temple of bringing a Gentile there. The inscription has been found that stood at the gates within the broad court of the Gentiles. Just as Josephus says, it forbids any Gentile to proceed past the separating wall of the inner enclosure: "Whoever is caught will have himself to blame for his death, which will follow."[1]

The shouts went up that Paul had "brought Greeks" into the temple and had "polluted this holy place" (Acts 21:28). In the menacing mob, whatever Paul said was unheard as he was pushed through the outer gate and given the first blows of an intended deadly beating. But the Roman garrison was trained to stop such riots before they spread, and they moved fast enough to save the apostle's life. Fortunately for Paul, he had been assaulted in the temple, for the Roman fortress Antonia loomed above the temple on the north with watchtowers high enough to see the first disturbance. The tribune in charge gathered a force and their centurions, who were named for commanding a hundred each. Rushing down in full battle gear on the crowd, they rescued Paul but chained him as their prisoner. Ascending the steps back into the fortress, Paul asked the tribune for the privilege of speaking. Impressed with Paul's assurance and skill at Greek, he allowed it, perhaps thinking the crowd had mistaken his identity. So the apostle in chains turned to address his countrymen in their own language.

What should Paul say? With a clever and conciliatory explanation, would he not be freed to continue to do the Lord's work? Yet Paul did not think of his safety but of his opportunity to explain the Lord's work. His goal was to move the Jewish crowd with the simple story of his divine call. "We saw" was Paul's basic claim when he had argued the Resurrection in 1 Corinthians 15, the same approach used by other apostles in their speeches and letters. Through the rest of Paul's imprisonment in Acts, he never defended himself without making divine revelation central to his argument. So on the temple steps he bore fervent testimony of his first vision (Acts 22:1-11). The next day he was called before the Sanhedrin, the council that condemned Christ and earlier threatened Peter and John. Paul neatly divided his accusers by insisting that he was a Pharisee and was accused for believing in the Resurrection (Acts 23:6). The Pharisees admitted that they should not "fight against God" if a supernatural being had appeared (Acts 23:9). Biographies commend Paul for a good tactic, but the strategy was incidental to his constant stress on the Resurrection and revelation as the core of his message. Since the more worldly Sadducees were skeptical of continuing revelation, Paul was defended just as Gamaliel once defended Peter and John. Though probably dead now, this teacher of Paul represented an open-minded point of view that shows that the apostle labored against Jewish prejudice, not against the inner nature of the Jewish religion.

The Roman commanding officer ordered Paul back to the fortress. At first he ordered him examined by the force of the whip, but Paul claimed his rights against this as a Roman citizen. Obligated to protect him, the tribune learned from Paul's nephew that forty men had sworn to kill Paul when the Sanhedrin assembled to hear him again. So senior officers were commanded to assemble seventy horsemen and four hundred foot soldiers, and they escorted Paul out of Jerusalem. Halfway the cavalry proceeded alone with Paul mounted among them; their leader carried the tribune's letter explaining why Paul was accused but under Roman law was not "worthy of death or of bonds" (Acts 23:29). The governor soon determined that for himself by hearing Paul and the Jewish leaders. Paul denied that he had violated law, but again he insisted that prejudice came from his belief in revelation and the Resurrection. The governor suspended decision. Although Luke suggests that he wanted a bribe, the political realities also forced a stalemate. He could not release Paul without enraging the leaders of the people he was governing; nor could he condemn Paul, since he had the rights of a Roman citizen. Two years Paul waited (Acts 24:27), with full visiting privileges (Acts 24:23). On one occasion he was heard by the governor and the governor's wife, who was of the Herodian line, and Paul shattered that official's self-composure by his plain words on righteousness and the day of judgment. A new governor arrived and wanted to take Paul to Jerusalem to settle the question of his guilt. But when first arrested, Paul received a vision of the Lord, who prophesied that Paul would testify of him in Rome (Acts 23:11). So when his life was threatened with the plan to go to Jerusalem, Paul appealed to Caesar (Acts 25:10-11).

Once King Aretas sought Paul's life in Damascus (2 Cor. 11:32), but now King Agrippa came to the governor's hearing and helped structure the report to the Roman emperor. The Lord's prophecy twenty-five years earlier was now being fulfilled, for he told Ananias that Paul would stand before kings (Acts 9:15). Thus, Paul's arrest gave him greater missionary opportunities. His appeal brought together subordinates of the governor Festus and of King Agrippa, and Paul was given a final chance to explain his position for the report that would accompany him to Rome. But Paul's defense shows that he was far more interested in testifying as an apostle than in proving his innocence. Roman administrators were notoriously practical, and all judges look at specific legal issues. So Festus could not contain himself as he heard the incredible story of Christ appearing and Paul's plain outline of the gospel: "Paul, you are mad; your great learning is turning you mad" (Acts 26:24, RSV). But Paul turned to the Herodian king, asking Agrippa if he did not know personally of the Christian church and if he did not believe in the prophets. Traditional interpretations here have King Agrippa confess near-belief, but most translations now see him squirming at the thought, trying to avoid Paul's directness: "In a short time you are persuading me to become a

Christian" (Acts 26:28, literal trans.). Paul's answer helps to determine whether Agrippa was serious or sarcastic, for Paul did not commend his faith but took his answer as ambiguous: "Both in a short time and a long one, I would pray God that not only you but all those hearing me today would become just as I am, except for these bonds" (Acts 26:29, literal trans.).[2]

In the eyes of God, Paul's judges were also on trial. And so are the readers of the record of Paul's testimony in Acts. Joseph Smith spoke strictly the doctrine of Christ and of Paul in saying, "Every word that proceedeth from the mouth of Jehovah has such an influence over the human mind, the logical mind, that it is convincing without other testimony—faith cometh by hearing."[3] Paul's testimony before Agrippa recapitulated the foundation doctrines of 1 Corinthians 15 and Hebrews 6: "That Christ should suffer, and that he should be the first that should rise from the dead" (Acts 26:23). Paul's speeches in Acts are as significant as his letters. He told Agrippa that Christ commanded him to preach the gospel—to bring "forgiveness of sins" to the Gentiles, that they have an inheritance with those "sanctified by faith that is in me" (Acts 26:18). At the same time, Paul taught that such blessings were only for believers who would "repent and turn to God, and do works worthy of their repentance" (Acts 26:20, literal trans.). One work of repentance in Acts is baptism—and post-baptismal duties are spelled out in Paul's letters.

The Lord's prophecy about going to Rome was about to be fulfilled. In the custody of Julius, an honorable centurion, Paul set sail by transport ships, a dangerously eventful journey of nearly two thousand miles. They left the massive harbor of Caesarea, which was artifically thrown out from a straight, sandy coast by means of massive foundation blocks, making sea walls and supporting the harbor installations.[4] They left late in the year, for the October Feast of Tabernacles was past and "sailing was now dangerous" (Acts 27:9). What follows equals any ancient literature in detail and adventure. Their transport was a "ship of Alexandria" (Acts 27:6), an authentic glimpse of the Alexandrian grainships, which were the supply line for Rome's bread. The "we" passages of Acts 27 and 28 show that Luke accompanied Paul to Rome, as did the fellow-missionary Aristarchus (Acts 27:2). Paul's warning not to risk the late season was ignored, and the ship ran uncontrolled before a deadly storm between Crete and Malta. Cresting waves and wet clouds were their main scenery for two weeks, but near the end Paul declared the assuring message that an angel had appeared to him to confirm that he would be "brought before Caesar" and that the company of the ship would be safe (Acts 27:24). That message probably saved Paul's life, for as the ship grounded the soldiers feared punishment if Paul escaped, and they intended to kill him. But the centurion Julius ordered him spared. The ship had been intentionally beached and broke up in the waves as its passengers and crew made way to shore, some on floating wreckage.

While waiting for the sailing season to resume, Paul took up a ministry in Malta for three months. It began with a dramatic sign of priesthood protection. Drying out after the shipwreck, the ever-active Paul was bitten by a poisonous snake while putting wood on the fire. But there was no harmful effect. That winter Paul performed miracles of healing, including curing the father of the prominent Publius of a feverish infection (Acts 28:8-9). Since Paul was still under arrest, it is not clear how much active preaching he did. In early spring the party of missionaries and escorting soldiers boarded another grain ship. They passed Sicily and in a few days reached Puteoli on the Bay of Naples. Paul would have seen a busy harbor; Seneca gave a first-century picture of Alexandrian mail boats arriving there, with nearly the whole city hurrying to the docks for news and excitement.[5] Paul's week-long stay with Saints at Puteoli enabled news of his arrival to precede him to Rome, so Roman "brethren" came some forty miles from the city to meet the apostle and accompany his party to Rome. They traveled up the Appian Way, looking at the tombs of the great and the wealthy on either side of the highway near the capital. The city swarmed as they entered the suburbs. Every man had his reason for coming to Rome, and for Paul it was not a political center but a collection of God's children needing the gospel of Jesus Christ.

Rome was the city of temples and tenements. Near Paul's time the encyclopedist Pliny boasted that "there has been no city in the whole world that could be compared to Rome in magnitude." He backed up his claim by the statistics of a dozen-mile circumference of the walls surrounding the seven hills and of some sixty miles of roadways within the city.[6] As appendix A indicates, Paul probably arrived in this world center in A.D. 61. Soon after his arrival, he called Jewish leaders to him to avoid misunderstanding; this led to a meeting where Paul preached the gospel. The length of his stay matched his Caesarean imprisonment: "He remained two whole years at his own expense and received all who came to him, preaching the kingdom of God and teaching the things concerning Jesus Christ, unhindered, with complete freedom" (Acts 28:30-31, literal trans.). Here Acts makes an important distinction between Paul's imprisonment in Caesarea, where his friends visited him (Acts 24:23), and the above custody in Rome, where he had unlimited opportunities to preach. These are his only known extended times in prison. Philippians has distinct Roman references and a description of the successful preaching of Paul there. The Roman evidence in Colossians and Philemon is not as clear, but a successful preaching ministry is alluded to in Colossians (Col. 4:2-4) that far better matches the Roman than the Caesarean imprisonment. Moreover, the slave mentioned in Philemon would more easily catch a ship to Rome, the center of commerce, than to out-of-the-way Caesarea, where a runaway would be more visible.

Paul's "bonds" are mentioned in the four letters written to Philemon, Colossians, Ephesians, and Philippians. The first three letters have an intimate relationship to each other, as a glance at the accompanying chart shows. These were carried by the same persons, and two contain greetings by the same persons—these three were written at the same time. Colossians and Ephesians blend with the fourth letter, Philippians, in teaching

Interrelationships of Paul's "Prison Letters"

Inter-relationships	Colossians	Philemon	Ephesians	Philippians
"Bonds"	Col. 4:18	Philem. 1:10, 13	Eph. 6:20	Philip. 1:7, 13-16; "The brethren which are with me" (4:21)
Persons sending greetings	Mark, Aristarchus, Jesus-Justus, Epaphras, Luke, Demas (4:10-14)	Mark, Aristarchus, Epaphras, Luke, Demas (1:23-24)		
Letter carriers	Tychicus, Onesimus (4:7, 9)	Onesimus (1:10-12)	Tychicus (6:21)	Epaphroditus (2:25—compare 4:18)
Local leader addressed	"To Archippus: Take heed to the ministry which you have received in the Lord" (4:17, NKJB)	"To . . . Archippus, our fellowsoldier, and to the church in your house" (1:2, NKJB)		
Roman references	Aristarchus and Luke send greeting—they traveled to Rome with Paul	Aristarchus and Luke send greeting—they traveled to Rome with Paul		"Caesar's household" (4:22)— "palace" (1:13) or "praetorian guard" (1:13, RSV)
Stylistic parallels	Christ the head of the body, the image of God, ruling all (1:13-18); Advice to husbands, wives, children, fathers, slaves, masters (3:18–4:1)		Christ the head of the body, ruling all (1:17-23); Advice to husbands, wives, children, fathers, slaves, masters (5:24–6:9)	Christ the form of God, ruling all (2:5-9)

the relationship of the Father and the Son as well as in fitting the circumstances of Roman preaching in Acts. The passages on Godhead, Christ's obedience, and imprisonment in Hebrews also make it a possible prison letter of this time. But 2 Timothy, the final prison letter, speaks a grimmer language and fits a later imprisonment. No matter what their place of origin, Ephesians and Colossians are clearly tied together in situation, and they integrate in message with Philippians. These three early prison letters stress doctrine, are moderate in length, and spend more time stating the positive gospel of Christ than in criticizing false doctrines. With Philemon, they give a picture of Paul at a mature stage of spirituality. Like Joseph Smith in Nauvoo, he is filled with love of the Saints and with insight on the majesty of God and the broad scope of God's work.

PHILEMON

Profile

Sent from:	Paul, probably at Rome, joined by Timothy.
Sent to:	Philemon, a wealthy Christian living in Colossae, in west central Asia Minor.
Date:	About A.D. 61.
Purpose:	To ask forgiveness for the runaway slave Onesimus.
Main theme:	Forgiveness and just relationships.

Background

Reason for Writing

The touching story of the slave Onesimus is contained in Paul's short letter to Philemon, his master, with further hints about them in the accompanying letter to Colossae. Paul honored the returning slave by naming him as the joint carrier of the letter to the Colossians, in which he called him "a faithful and beloved brother, who is one of you" (Col. 4:9). So the master Philemon lived at Colossae also. Being a slaveholder suggests that he was wealthy, as does the natural reading of "the church in your house" (Philem. 1:2, NKJB). Evidently Philemon had a home that could accommodate Church meetings, which is part of the picture of Philemon's "love and faith . . . toward the Lord Jesus and toward all the saints" (Philem. 1:5, NKJB). Paul commends Philemon's works, which have refreshed the Saints (Philem. 1:7). The King James Version translates "bowels" here from the Greek term referring to inner organs, so modern translations generally use the current idiom "heart" instead of that older English preference for inner emotions. The above glimpses complete what is known about Philemon, except that Paul converted him. This is clear from Philemon owing his "own self" to Paul (Philem. 1:19). Colossae was within the orbit of Paul's missionary influence and possible visits when "all they which dwelt in Asia" heard the word of the Lord from Ephesus (Acts 19:10). Although Paul says that he cared for those who had not seen him in that area (Col. 2:1), still others might have seen him.

Paul had also converted Onesimus, "whom I have begotten in my bonds" (Philem. 1:10). Such language is used only of his converts (1 Cor. 4:15). Onesimus had indeed wronged his master (Philem. 1:18) but providentially had "ministered unto [Paul] in the bonds of the gospel" (Philem. 1:13). If Philemon had lost for Paul's gain, now Paul was reluctantly returning Onesimus for restitution to Philemon. Paul plays on the name *Onesimus*, which means "profitable"; with another adjective Paul says Onesimus had not been useful to Philemon but now was useful to both his master and the Church leader (Philem. 1:11). Certainly he had run away. Some think he could not have made his way to Rome, but shipping was easily available to a worker or stowaway. Had he been frustrated by the huge and heartless city? Perhaps rebuffed and hungry, he sought out Christians, since he knew their brotherhood firsthand from the Christian household of Philemon. If he did not seek out Paul, possibly Christians learned his story and notified Paul. Paul clearly taught, converted, and fellowshipped. But Paul was legally obligated to send him back to Philemon. Like Timothy, Onesimus is called Paul's "son," probably an indication of his youth. Some fifty years later a senior bishop traveled through Asia and wrote to commend the Ephesians on their Bishop Onesimus, "a man of inexpressible love."[7] Whether or not this is the same person, Paul's letter stands for gospel outreach that breaks down worldly barriers.

Main Teachings

Forgiveness and Just Relationships

Sincere repentance certainly involves righting the wrong, giving satisfaction to the person sinned against. And when that is done, the major duty shifts to the person wronged. Revelation warns the person sinned against to overcome his resentment through forgiveness: "He that forgiveth not his brother his trespasses standeth condemned before the Lord; for there remaineth in him the greater sin" (D&C 64:9). This is the principle dramatized by Jesus in the parable of the unforgiving servant (Matt. 18:21-35), and Paul's letter calls on Philemon to forgive. Paul and Onesimus did their duty to return Philemon's "property." But Paul makes perfectly clear that the master legally owns only the slave's service, not his person. This tension between mortal law and God's higher morality makes this short letter a fascinating challenge to complacency. For it highlights the duty of every believer in God to respect every child of God, of whatever age, sex, race, or social or economic level. The letter to Philemon admits the wrongdoing of the runaway slave but guards against the further sin of the master in how he takes him back. In short, the letter is really about potential offenses to others from those who have been in the right.

Slavery was a reality in Paul's world. Cruel war had produced heartless enslavement of enemies, but Paul was on the high end of the social spectrum with the privilege of Roman citizenship. This meant that he was personally untouched by slavery and could have comfortably ignored it. But his Christian convictions did

not allow that, for several of his letters command righteous treatment of slaves. Nevertheless, the legal system supported slavery as
an institution. The population of larger cities may have been 33
percent slaves.[8] Their percentage empire-wide would have been
less, perhaps 20 percent. Their use would move up from the harsh
assignment to mines, to agriculture, to factories or business, to
domestic duty, and domestic slaves were often virtually family
members. Onesimus may have worked in the household or with
crops or flocks. The ancient ways of dealing with farm slaves are
shown in the *de Agricultura* of Cato the Elder, an incredibly un-
feeling manual explaining how to treat slaves as animals in order
to maximize profit. Fortunately Paul's century was more enlightened on the whole, for public opinion and the influence of
philosophy gave the slave dignity as a human being. Grave monu-
ments tell of slaves set free and marrying into patron families. So
there were human and economic trends toward tempering harsh
bondage, but Augustus's legislation restricted the number of
emancipations that could be made at a slave-owner's death. His
successors in the first and second centuries moved slowly but
surely to give slaves legal rights against cruel and unusual treatment.[9]

What were Philemon's options when Onesimus returned?
Merely probing them shows why Paul protected his new convert
with letters to Philemon and to the Colossian branch of the
Church. The Roman philosopher-statesman Seneca was Paul's
age and describes domestic slavery. He caricatures the aristocratic
glutton whose slaves must virtually stand at attention while he
eats, since their accidental coughs or sneezes merit beatings.[10]
Seneca has a higher standard, admitting that in treatment of
slaves "we Romans are exceptionally arrogant, harsh, and insult-
ing."[11] But Seneca's higher standard still fell far short of verbal
courtesy: "You are entirely right in not wishing to be feared by
your slaves, and in lashing them merely with the tongue."[12] And
these are glimpses of ordinary operations, not the punishment of a
returning fugitive. The fragments of preserved laws on the subject
show Paul's legal duty to send Onesimus back: "Anyone who has

hidden a runaway slave is guilty of theft." There were legal options to report to authorities or to return "to the owners." The process of formal return hints at how masters might treat returning slaves: "Carefully guarding them may even include chaining them up."[13] Second-century laws prevented owners from killing their slaves, but first-century masters seem to have been free to inflict almost anything to break a slave from deserting.

"Do not torment him," the senator Pliny wrote a friend, asking for leniency for an offending household servant. "Make some concession to his youth, his tears, and to your own kind heart."[14] Such an appeal is admirable but superficial when comparing that request for human decency with Paul's bold testimony of equality: "[Onesimus] departed for a while for this purpose, that you might receive him forever, no longer as a slave but more than a slave, as a beloved brother" (Philem. 1:15-16, NKJB). Such a request would not work unless Philemon really believed in eternal brotherhood. So Paul labors deftly but plainly for Philemon's conversion to that principle. He writes with the obvious goal of softening Philemon's heart, for the spirit of 1 Corinthians 13 is the spirit of this short letter. There, love leads out with faith and confidence in the right. So Paul simply tells Philemon that he knows that he will treat Onesimus fairly: "Although in Christ I have full freedom to command what is fitting, through love I prefer to encourage you" (Philem. 1:8-9, literal trans.). At this point the apostle with authority reverses the image by referring to himself as aged and in chains—setting aside for the moment any intimidation of Philemon and pointing out that he has converted both the slave and master and loves them equally in the Lord. Paul indeed put the burden of what to do on Philemon's conscience: "Trusting your obedience, I wrote you, knowing that you will do even more than I say" (Philem. 1:21, literal trans.). But what has Paul really asked of Philemon? Nothing directly. But without question he expects the runaway to be treated consistently with Christian brotherhood. And he approves the most liberal forgiveness that Philemon might consider—even to freeing the slave turned brother.

The realism of Paul's approach is as impressive as his recognition of Philemon's agency. Tyranny does not flourish in an atmosphere of honest counsel. By also addressing the letter to Philemon's associates, the apostle took a step to prevent a rash decision (Philem. 1:2). The woman Apphia is obviously Philemon's wife, and the "fellowsoldier" Archippus is the same one who has just received a "ministry . . . in the Lord" (Col. 4:17). So he has some official Church position—possibly he is Philemon's bishop. And accountability does not end until Paul's personal review. He will come and stay with Philemon upon his release from prison (Philem. 1:22) and will personally pay whatever the slave owes and cannot pay, a hint that Onesimus possibly stole money to aid his escape. The lawful master must himself decide on permissible options, though laws would not give such fearful power to individuals today. Through all this is the principle of answerable agency.

Paul's language in the accompanying Colossian letter is blunt on what the gospel requires: "Give unto your servants that which is just and equal," for there is a master of all "in heaven" (Col. 4:1). "Servant" in the King James Version is the same word translated "slave" in the modern translations of Philemon, clearly defined by Onesimus's status. In the scriptures all Saints are bond servants of God, with overtones of God as their rightful master. But a just relationship results from his laws, not from the whims of an arbitrary master. So "slave" is too harsh a translation for most New Testament passages. The apostles' teaching of this just relationship with God and fellowmen injected a powerful force for change into society. Christ, Peter, and Paul obeyed civil law but taught a higher morality. They were moral but not political revolutionaries, for the Early Church made every effort to support Jewish and Roman government while preparing men for the ultimate kingdom of God. In other words, they reformed the minds and souls of individuals instead of angrily demonstrating against unalterable policies. Church members today live under forms of government that permit change and under those that do not. Like Paul in the case of ancient slavery, they can afford to be patient while teaching eternal truth: "Christianity did not insist upon the actual liberation of the slave, but it did insist that he must no longer be regarded as a mere chattel. This in the long run meant the abolition of slavery."[15]

COLOSSIANS

Profile

Sent from: Paul, probably at Rome, joined by Timothy.

Sent to: Members at Colossae, in west central Asia Minor.

Date: About A.D. 61.

Purpose: To strengthen the branch on the return of Onesimus and to correct the false doctrine of "worshipping of angels."

Main themes: The Godhead; errors about Christ, days, and diet; developing celestial qualities.

Background

The City

Colossae lay in a high valley with mountain scenery resembling the arid west of the United States. A hundred miles east of Ephesus, it was mentioned on Xenophon's famous march from the coast and up the Meander River to the tributary basin of the Lycus River. Colossae was "prosperous and large," partly because it was on the east-west trade route.[16] Christianity later marched the hundred miles from the coast to Colossae, for Paul was at Ephesus and reached "all Asia" with the gospel message (Acts 19:26). The regional economy depended not only on trade but also on grazing lands that supported the wool industry in Colossae and in nearby Laodicea. The geographer Strabo reported of Paul's time, "The country around Laodicea produces sheep that are excellent, not only for the softness of their wool . . . but also for its raven-black color, so that the Laodiceans derive splendid revenue from it, as do the neighboring Colossians from the color [of wool] which bears the same name."[17]

Hierapolis and these two cities formed a triangle with sides about ten miles long. In writing to Colossae, Paul also named "them that are in Laodicea, and them in Hierapolis" (Col. 4:13). Substantial ruins of the latter city are spread out around its well-preserved stone theater. It was built adjacent to massive hot springs that attracted religious and recreational pilgrims. But Laodicea was the major city of the area in Paul's day. Just before Paul, Strabo wrote that Laodicea "grew large in our time and in that of our fathers." That geographer paid tribute to its "fertile territory" and the private wealth of some of its citizens.[18] Its ruins, including its theater, are badly deteriorated, but Laodicea's stone-strewn area is massive. Although Hierapolis is merely mentioned in Paul's Colossian letter, Laodicea is prominent, probably reflecting the size of the Church in that large city. Laodicea was possibly the regional center of Church administration. Three decades later John sent his letter to Laodicea as the most important branch of the Church in that area.

Reason for Writing

A letter to Colossae was certainly part of sending Onesimus back there, but another problem was serious enough to demand a separate letter of correction. How did Paul learn of this situation? Philemon's letter closes with a greeting from "Epaphras, my fellowprisoner in Christ Jesus" (Philem. 1:23). This is probably a way of honoring this man who was well known at Colossae; he was assisting Paul in prison, just as the returning Onesimus had done. Colossians also names Epaphras, "who is one of you, a servant of Christ" (Col. 4:12). The Colossians had "learned" the gospel from "Epaphras our dear fellowservant, who is for you a faithful minister of Christ" (Col. 1:7). Since he had "declared unto us your love in the Spirit" (Col. 1:8), Paul's knowledge of the current problems of that area came through this missionary with their interest at heart. And Paul apparently wanted them to know that negative information was relayed for their benefit, since Epaphras has a "great zeal for you, and them that are in Laodicea, and them in Hierapolis" (Col. 4:13). Only the letter to Colossians survives, but the lost Laodicean letter must have also included correction. That nearby branch probably had as many members as that at Colossae and was likely affected by the same false teaching.

What was the "Colossian heresy"? Biographies and commentaries discuss it but add little more than Colossians itself discloses. Some were debasing Christ's divinity and role in the Godhead, for chapter 2 refutes those who fail to hold Christ as "the Head" (Col. 2:19), whereas chapter 1 has Paul's most sustained testimony of the divinity and power of the Son. There is little contemporary religious information, but the writings of John went to the same locality some forty years later. They definitely show deviations from the gospel like those Paul criticized in his Colossian letter. The parallel with 1 Corinthians is striking, for Paul's inspired resurrection chapter answered their doubts on the Resurrection, just as Paul's powerful survey of Christ's mission corrected Colossian confusion. And Paul may have known more firsthand than is apparent. Some seven years earlier he had started his third mission by taking the land route from Antioch to Ephesus, visiting central Asia Minor (Acts 18:23) and going west from there through "the upper regions" (Acts 19:1, NKJB). This is clearly the east-west route through the Lycus River valley and the three cities under discussion. Paul expresses his intense concern for the Colossians "and for them at Laodicea, and for as many as have not seen my face in the flesh" (Col. 2:1). To some people that means that he had never seen the Colossians and Laodiceans, but his earlier journey through their area suggests the opposite—that he was worried about those from each city that he had met and also about those later coverted who had never seen him. Since Colossians 2:1 introduces Paul's refutation of the false teachings on Christ, it virtually identifies the heresy at both Colossae and Laodicea.

This last point is one strong reason for rejecting the insipid twenty apocryphal verses that pose as Paul's letter to the Laodiceans.[19] The real one existed once, for Paul obviously sent it with the messengers delivering letters to Philemon and Colossae: "When this epistle is read among you, cause that it be read also in the church of the Laodiceans; and that ye likewise read the epistle from Laodicea" (Col. 4:16). What truth is lost in this lost letter? The "Colossian heresy" was no doubt an area heresy, so both letters must have combined to correct it.[20] Colossians stresses the bodily reality of Christ. Was Laodiceans suppressed because it bluntly spoke of the physicalness of the Godhead? This doctrine of the Early Church soon disappeared in the verbiage of Christian councils that legislated God's nature. But the imitation letter of the Laodiceans corrects nothing and has no distinct message. Scholars consistently reject it because it is a "worthless patching together of Pauline passages and phrases, mainly from the Epistle to the Philippians."[21] But what if the real Laodiceans or the real 1 Corinthians someday came to light? Then creeds and Christians would be wrong in seeing the Bible as the whole revelation of God. And if the historical collection of apostles' letters is not complete, are there new revelations that God wishes to give today? Modern revelation testifies both to the truth of past revelation and also to its unfinished nature.

Main Teachings

The Godhead

Later philosophical ages produced the Christian creeds about God and Christ, but first was the age of the prophets. Peter, Paul, and John wrote and spoke the simpler language of experience; an example is Paul's moving testimony of the Father and Son opening Colossians. Yet orthodox Christians look more to councils than to scripture to explain what they worship. The first four legislative gatherings recognized as binding were called by emperors between the fourth and sixth centuries. And a major church historian summarizes their importance: "On account of their authority Pope Gregory the Great compared the first four councils to the four gospels, because they formulated the basic dogmas of the Church—the Trinity and the Incarnation."[22] Admittedly, the real source of the trinitarian doctrine is the Council of Nicaea, a gathering of some 318 bishops convened by Constantine. The narrow issue there was whether Christ was similar to or the same as the Father, and the latter option was decided and enforced.[23]

From a Latter-day Saint point of view, the Reformation did not fully reform, since major Protestant groups rely on councils instead of the plain testimonies of the apostles. An example of such a council decision is the basic Lutheran confession: "We unanimously hold and teach, in accordance with the decree of the Council of Nicaea, that there is one divine essence, which is called and which is truly God, and that there are three persons in this one divine essence, equal in power and alike eternal: God the Father, God the Son, God the Holy Spirit."[24] The English Reformation has the same theological continuity with Catholicism on the question of God. Indeed, the Methodist Church, which set out to reform the Church of England, adopted the first article of Anglican belief on God with minor verbal changes: "There is but one living and true God, everlasting, without body or parts. . . . And in the unity of this Godhead there are three persons, of one substance, power, and eternity—the Father, the Son, and the Holy Ghost."[25] Since Jews believe strictly in one God, they are monotheists, a term formed from Greek roots of "one only" (*mónos*) and "god" (*theós*). Are Christians monotheists? Orthodox creeds start to say so, and then modify their language by fitting in other Godhead members. Traditional Christianity is philosophically monotheistic, since "three" is combined with "unity" to make the blended concept of Trinity. On the other hand, Latter-day Saints are not really trinitarians but tritheists, for they bluntly hold to the individuality of each person of the Godhead. Joseph Smith saw the Father and the Son as "two Personages" in his First Vision (JS-H 1:17) and in the vision of the three degrees of glory (D&C 76:20-23). Just before his martyrdom Joseph Smith publicly reviewed the separate individuals in the Godhead and concluded, "These three constitute three distinct personages and three Gods."[26] Indeed, Joseph Smith severed any tie with traditional theology by announcing that Christ revealed at the outset that the "creeds were an abomination in his sight" (JS-H 1:19).

Paul consistently separates the Father and the Son verbally, as in the beginning of Colossians: "Grace be unto you, and peace, from God our Father and the Lord Jesus Christ" (Col. 1:2). This same phrase begins all the other letters of Paul except Hebrews, which opens with its own powerful summary of the distinct members of the Godhead. Colossians also gives thanks "to God and the Father of our Lord Jesus Christ" (1:3). In addition to such sharp distinction in wording, Paul divides the functions or operations of the Father and the Son. This is clear in Colossians 1:12-22, which is abstracted on the accompanying chart. Christ is God's "firstborn," a term that Colossians explains—Christ is above all earthly and heavenly beings in seniority and authority. Paul's message is that the Son has been given preeminence under the Father. He is also invested with authority as head of the Church (Col. 1:18); under the Father he brings redemption (Col. 1:14); under the Father he is the agent of creation (Col. 1:16); he is also the "firstborn from the dead" (Col. 1:18). So the Father participates with the Son on the level of supervision but not action; the above phrases represent unique activities of Christ's own mission. In Colossians Christ also sits "on the right hand of God" (3:1), just as he does in Hebrews (1:3) and in Romans (8:34). Paul's clear words about the Lord inspire confidence that they have no hidden meanings but are the face-value summaries of Christ's role in carrying out the Father's plans.

The true doctrines about Christ in Colossians 1 correct the false doctrines specifically refuted in Colossians 2. Christ's true position is twofold: his incomparable assignments from the Father, which have just been surveyed, and his material reality as divine Son of God. In John's Gospel the preexistent "Word," who made the world, "was made flesh, and dwelt among us" (John 1:14). Likewise Paul testifies that Jesus—walking in mortality or resurrected in eternity—is "the image of the invisible God" (Col. 1:15). Paul's Greek term for "image" (eikón) indicates a visible likeness and is used of Caesar's picture on coins (Matt. 22:20).

Paul's Testimonies of Christ and His Mission

Colossians 1:13-17

God has "translated us into the kingdom of the Son of his love" (NKJB)

"in whom we have redemption, . . . the forgiveness of sins"

"who is the image of the invisible God"

"the firstborn of every creature"

"for by him were all things created"

"and by him all things consist"

Hebrews 1:1-3, 6

God has "spoken unto us by his Son"

"who . . . by himself purged our sins"

"who being the brightness of his glory, and the express image of his person"

"appointed heir of all things . . . the firstborn" (NKJB)

"by whom also he made the worlds"

"upholding all things by the word of his power"

—Adapted from Francis W. Beare, "Colossians," The Interpreter's Bible (New York: Abingdon Press, 1955) 11:162

Thus, Paul is saying that the Father and the Son are physically distinct but have the same appearance. The same word appears in the Greek Genesis when God creates man "in his own image" (Gen. 1:27). In terms of authority and status, no human can begin to approach Christ, but in terms of outward form, there is no basic difference. The Father, his beloved Son, and the children of God on this earth all have the same "image." Theologians deliteralize plain words, assuring their readers that creation in "the image of God . . . relates to his moral nature."[27] But that sweeping assumption contradicts scriptures teaching that mortals do not yet have the moral image of God and that many will never attain it. But both Christ and human beings have the physical appearance of God, so the Father has form, shape, and a glorified body.

Catholic and Protestant theology vigorously denies this view. No church council legislated God out of material existence, but Christian philosophers early equated having a body with limiting God or humanizing his glory. Thus, in creeds or Christian explanations, "the Church teaches that God is an infinitely perfect spiritual being who has no body or spatial dimensions."[28] One contradicting this is seen as unsophisticated, holding an "anthropomorphic" view. This word combines the Greek for man (*ánthrōpos*) and form (*morphē*); it describes the belief that God has a manlike form. Christian thinkers close their minds to this possibility: "Anthropomorphism, unless it were poetic symbolism, would violate all the principles of theological propriety which have been established since the Middle Ages"; this because it would attribute "human nature" to God.[29] But God attributed human nature to himself by sending his Son to live with villagers who thought he was merely the carpenter's son. And when Philip asked Christ to let him see the Father, the Lord asked his apostle to look at him, not as a matter of identity but of similarity (John 14:6-9). That is the repeated theme of the Gospel of John from the beginning to the Last Supper. Paul declared the "unknown God" to the Athenians by teaching that he became known through Christ's resurrection (Acts 17:23, 31). In writing "the image of the invisible God" (Col. 1:15), Paul was not stressing "invisible" as much as he was Christ's "image"—the Father become visible through the Son. "Invisible" has English connotations of "not able to be seen," though it simply negates "seen" and would better be rendered "unseen." The Father is "unseen" by mortals now but is seen by those who dwell with him, and he was seen by chosen prophets to whom he has appeared.

Paul emphasizes that Christ as a divine person was physical. Paul drives the point home because of the false doctrines about Christ. Through "the body of his flesh" came the great atonement for sins and the means of the Saints' perfection (Col. 1:22). Now resurrected, Christ has "all fulness" dwelling in him (Col. 1:19). This statement is not philosophical, but anthropomorphic. Paul was certain that Christ existed in his resurrected form, since "God . . . raised him from the dead" (Col. 2:12) and since he was physically present "on the right hand of God" (Col. 3:1). Confirmed by 1 Corinthians 15 and Philippians 3, Paul's Colossian testimony is that Christ's mortal form was outwardly the same as his resurrected state—there is not a hint that he might have set aside that glorious body, which is the "image of the unseen God" (Col. 1:15, JB). Yet 84 percent of a Utah sampling of Protestant ministers agreed that "God is an immaterial Being without form or bodily parts."[30] This cannot be true if Christ revealed God. Nor can it be true if the physical, resurrected Christ is a part of the Godhead. By the authority of modern revelation, Joseph Smith solemnly declared, "That which is without body or parts is nothing. There is no other God in heaven but that God who has flesh and bones."[31]

Errors about Christ, Days, and Diet

Paul had given the Colossians the "more excellent way" (1 Cor. 12:31) before criticizing false views in Colossians 2. Here are some specifics of their revised doctrine, though their conceptions are not stated fully enough to bring agreement on what the "Colossian heresy" was. Yet there is a way through the maze of empty generalizations—the striking similarity of late New

Testament heresy with that criticized by Paul in Colossians. Their beliefs added Jewish ceremonialism to the gospel, in some way dethroned Christ, and also explained away the divinity of his physical person. This last point is hardly understood by the average writer on Colossians. Some thirty-five years later the apostle John wrote to the same area of Asia, warning seven branches of the Church of false teachers in their midst. Common errors had spread throughout western Asia Minor. Writing to Philadelphia, sixty miles from Colossae, John warned against those "which say they are Jews, and are not" (Rev. 3:9). Other churches received the same warning and also warnings against "idolatry" of Balaam and Jezebel, both of whom sought to lead Israel from worshipping the true God. Colossians 2 also combines Jewish heresy with concern for false teachings about Christ. Not long after Revelation, John wrote letters to this area, specifying what he meant by "idolatry." Only one confessing "that Jesus Christ is come in the flesh is of God" (1 Jn. 4:2), a caution repeated to reveal a major sickness in the Church (2 Jn. 1:7). This is a proved historical situation, for the letters of Ignatius were written soon after this and also show that some in every Asian area were denying the physicalness of Christ.[32]

Since the debate on Christ's flesh was raging in the area a few decades after Paul, it is not to be ignored in understanding his Colossian warning, particularly when 1 Timothy was soon sent to the area representative in Asia to warn against the same problems mentioned by John. Christian commentators do not face Colossians as rebuking those explaining away the physicalness of the second member of the Godhead. The tendency was there for the same reason that some Corinthians ridiculed the bodily resurrection. Since God surpasses the human moral and intellectual level, many seek to define his person as different from the human form. At the end of the first century, the Early Church was besieged by those teaching that Christ's divinity had not been contaminated by earthly elements. In Colossians Paul opposes this point of view. They are being robbed of their heritage: "Beware lest anyone take you captive through philosophy and empty deceit, according to the tradition of men, according to the basic principles of the world, and not according to Christ" (Col. 2:8, NKJB).[33] Right afterward Paul names the two misconceptions of Christ that he is correcting. The first: "For in Him dwells all the fullness of the Godhead *bodily*" (Col. 2:9, NKJB). Many commentators sidestep the italicized term by claiming that it can mean "essentially" or "really." But Paul used *sōmatikôs*, formed from *sôma*, the Greek word for "body," which Paul uses equally for man's earthly body and Christ's resurrected body. Thus, Paul testifies that Christ possesses godhood *physically*.

Paul adds his second correction: Christ "is the head of every authority and power" (Col. 2:10, literal trans.). Paul explains by building on his earlier testimony of Christ as the "head of the body, the church" (Col. 1:18). But false teachers added the "worshipping of angels," inventing things they had "not seen," which took away their true "head," Jesus Christ (Col. 2:18-19). Medieval Christianity added angels to intercede for mortals, whose lowly condition did not allow them to approach God. As will be seen in the next chapter, some first-century Christians taught the more radical doctrine that the physical creation was an inferior act of a lower divinity. And they added angels or divinities above the Old Testament creator. Paul fought such heresies at Colossae, for Christ's authority as the true creator was being challenged as well as his physical reality. Paul raised the standard of revealed Christianity—of believing in Christ as the only head and mediator under the Father—of believing in the physicalness of Christ, having the form of the Father.

Finally, the rituals of the Colossian heresy are a reminder that more extreme is not necessarily more religious. Little children graduate from the invariability of many rules to understand the principles behind those rules. That is why Paul warned the Galatians not to revert to the law that was "added because of transgressions" (Gal. 3:19). Just as some Colossians believed in additional holy beings, they also added Jewish dietary rules and rigid days of worship. The Early Church could obviously set its own day of rest without being tied to Jewish practices of the past. So the faithful were told to oppose legalism: "Therefore let no one judge you in food or in drink, or regarding a festival or a new moon or sabbaths" (Col. 2:16, NKJB). "Food" correctly changes the King James Version "meat," which was meant in the older English sense of any kind of food. This is obvious in the Hebrews warning against technical Jewish practices: "Meats and drinks, and divers washings, and carnal ordinances" (Heb. 9:10)—what is not drink is "meat," simply food in general in the Greek behind these English renderings.

Is such instruction relevant today? Proper diet is determined by common sense, nutritional science, and revelation in the case of the modern Word of Wisdom. But it is arrogance or ignorance to pursue hearsay theories and hobbies on what to eat and drink. Paul opposes overdone notions on this subject in a half-dozen epistles. Modern food fads frequently stem from religious fanaticism or desires for power over other people, certainly the motives behind the Colossian perversions of days and diet. But the gospel means renouncing mere theories of men, Paul reminded the Colossians, asking why they would subject themselves to "regulations—'Do not touch, do not taste, do not handle'" (Col. 2:20-21, NKJB). All major committee translations enclose these last phrases in quotation marks, since it is obvious that Paul here summarized the preaching of his opponents. Joseph Smith added words of explanation to make the same point of avoiding the "commandments of men, who teach you to touch not, taste not, handle not" (Col. 2:21, JST).

Developing Celestial Qualities

After correcting the unfaithful, Paul instructs the faithful: "Set your mind on things above, not on things on the earth" (Col. 3:2, NKJB). The goal is to live a celestial life, to prepare to be with God. This is not achieved by mere conversion or even baptism but is a process that builds on the foundation of the first principles. Just as clearly as Hebrews 6, Colossians calls the members to progress in their righteousness. The oldest members in their branch had been in the Church about seven years when Paul wrote his message of growth in the faith. His challenge came in the Romans metaphor of the death of the old life and creation of the new:

Therefore we were buried with him by baptism into death, that just as Christ was raised from the dead by the glory of the Father, even so we also should walk in newness of life (Rom. 6:4, NKJB).

Buried with him in baptism, in which you also were raised with him through faith in the working of God, who has raised him from the dead (Col. 2:12, NKJB).

This death-resurrection comparison continues throughout Romans and Colossians. "If ye then be risen with Christ, seek those things which are above" (Col. 3:1). Developing that theme, Paul commands, "Mortify therefore your members which are upon the earth" (Col. 3:5), the same message stated earlier as "mortify the deeds of the body" (Rom. 8:13). "Mortify" appears only these two times in the King James Version; it was formed from the Latin word for death (*mors*) and translates Greek that means "to put to death." So Paul is asking for the obliteration of earthly ways through repentance continuing after baptism. Through conversion these new members had taken the road to salvation, but years afterward they still needed instructions on replacing old qualities with new ones. Paul's letters to members were to help them qualify for salvation. Any other view demeans the time and attention he gave them. Romans 6 and Colossians 3 teach that the new person is created through baptism plus years of gospel growth afterward. If exaltation were automatic with conversion, there would be only letters of congratulation on salvation, not Paul's regular instructions on the higher life that God requires for his kingdom.

A number of Paul's letters list the most serious sins in God's sight, with plain warnings of risking the loss of salvation without firm repentance. But here the apostle tends to use the past tense, showing that active Saints were generally meeting these minimum gospel standards. Like the Corinthians (1 Cor. 6:11), the Colossians are told that they once lived worldly lives (Col. 3:7) but had "put off" the old, unspiritual personality (Col. 3:8-9). But post-baptismal reality emerges from comparing the death of the old and the birth of the new. The decision of faith may terminate evil acts in a dramatic way, but living the new ways of the kingdom presents the challenge of learning new habits. So Paul's clear goal for the Colossians is to be "fruitful in every good work, and increasing in the knowledge of God" (Col. 1:10). They will know God better not by a multitude of facts but in proportion to their good works. Just as faith can bring good works, good works open new vistas of faith.

A prominent psychologist claimed that it is easier to act oneself into a new way of thinking than to think oneself into a new way of acting. In reality, both thoughts and actions are tools to produce a new character, which is the overall purpose of Paul's instruction. Several letters stress "putting on" the new person, but in Colossians Paul emphasized the moral development of the new personality, "which is being renewed in knowledge after the image of its Creator" (Col. 3:10, RSV). Paul uses the Greek tense of repeated instead of single action. Thus nonliteral translations try to capture the idea of continued striving. The new person in Christ is "being constantly renewed" (NEB); "you have put on a new self which will progress toward true knowledge the more it is renewed in the image of its Creator" (JB). Here is the true teaching of the moral image, for Paul asks the Saints to use God's character as the model for their growth. They already have his physical image but have not yet reached the perfection of his personality. Earthly parents create the physical bodies of their children, but children's personalities emerge as a second stage of creation as they mature. The gospel similarly asks those created in the physical image of God to become Godlike, or Christlike, in character. This is Paul's teaching of the new person in Christ.

What positive qualities must the growing Saint develop? Colossians gives a pointed answer, a valuable statement of priority to accompany the more detailed answer of Ephesians to the same question. In Colossians Paul focuses on love as the main frontier of living after controlling anger, sexual drives, and dishonesty (Col. 3:5-9). Colossians' contribution is like that of 1 Corinthians 13; both value love as the highest Christian achievement but also go into detail on the qualities of pure love. First Corinthians 13 is virtually poetic in describing the characteristics of love, but Colossians 3 summarizes what a person does who possesses Christlike love: "Put on tender mercies,[34] kindness, humbleness of mind, meekness, longsuffering; bearing with one another, and forgiving one another, if anyone has a complaint against another; even as Christ forgave you, so you do also. And above all these things put on love (*agápē*), which is the bond of perfection" (Col. 3:12-14, NKJB).

The apostle is not here defining words but describing a loving attitude carried into life. One forgiven through Christ's gospel has received divine kindness that requires looking at others in a new light. Love is the end product, the one concept that can sum up all instructions on how to treat others. In 1 Corinthians 13 and Colossians 3:12-14, kindness, meekness, longsuffering, and the willingness to forgive are all aspects of love. In both places the King James translators preferred "charity," though the Greek *agápē* is generally translated "love" in that version (including its four other uses in Colossians) and should be correlated with the many other teachings of Paul and Christ using the same word.

Nothing in Christianity forbids the natural right of self-defense when life and safety are threatened. But exceptional actions to preserve life are wrong in daily affairs. Although outright force is generally absent from ordinary relationships, many constantly wage war with others by subtle social weapons of aggression, exploitation, and raw competition. One converted to the gospel knows that God's work is to "bring to pass the immortality and eternal life of man" (Moses 1:39). Whoever loves God will love his children, and whoever sees his fellow beings on earth through God's eyes will seek to build them up through encouragement. Thus, Paul's ideals of personal meekness and humility are not some form of self-abasement—his self-image was far from inadequate. He is asking confident people to rein in competitive reflexes and to build and encourage others. If the restored Church would apply these ideals of love, the result would not be suppressed personalities with false modesty. On the contrary, there would be vital people on fire with honest appreciation from those that they have personally recognized and encouraged. Just as Paul asks the Ephesians to put on the armor of virtuous qualities, he asks the Colossians to put on the clothing of righteous treatment of others. The "bond of perfection" is love (Col. 3:14, NKJB), "bond" meaning the uniting principle that ties all together, gathering kindness and forbearance and willingness to forgive into a consistent set of actions motivated by honest concern for the eternal welfare of others. And both Colossians and Ephesians place the family at the center of one's circle of concern.

EPHESIANS

Profile

Sent from: Paul, probably at Rome.
Sent to: Members at Ephesus, chief commercial city in the Roman province of Asia.
Date: About A.D. 61.
Purpose: To strengthen the Saints with a doctrinal review of the gospel.
Main themes: Pre-earth life and foreordination; the last dispensation; grace and works; church organization; "perfecting of the saints"; family life.

Background

The City

Paul's messengers from Rome evidently landed at Ephesus on their way up to the Colossian area with letters. The cities on the western coast of Asia Minor were heavily Greek because of earlier migrations across the Aegean, and they were wealthy both in money and in religious tradition. On his third mission Paul picked populous Ephesus as the hub for spreading the gospel through the province of Asia, discussed at the end of chapter 3. The geographer Strabo called Ephesus the greatest "emporium" or trade center of Roman Asia, which comprised the western third of Asia Minor.[35] Ephesus was a third-magnitude city, its population estimated at as large as a quarter of a million. Today it stretches in magnificent ruins from its silted-up harbor across flats and coastal hills. Acts 19 tells the story of Paul's mission there with geographical precision. The muddy Cayster River had moved the harbor miles away from the older city. In the first-century, Strabo commented on its "advantageous situation" for sea trade but ominously describes the river channel to the sea as dangerously shallow. There would be concern over the continued economic vitality of Ephesus, making the missionaries' inroads on pagan temple worship all the more threatening.

The riot in Acts 19 arose from the business loss of the image makers for the temple of Artemis or Diana. Mingling concern for profits with more noble civic pride, the silversmiths feared that the temple's "magnificence should be destroyed," since "all Asia and the world" worshipped Artemis (Acts 19:27). This shrine had long been famous and was generally listed as one of the seven wonders of the world. About the time Paul preached in Ephesus, Pliny the Elder described the massive sanctuary: "The length of the temple overall is 425 feet, and its breadth 225 feet. There are 127 columns . . . 60 feet in height."[36] Archaeology generally confirmed those dimensions for the base platform ascending to the temple proper. Those who defended their fertility goddess rushed to the great theater, which today rises in a colossal semicircle. It probably overflowed its 25,000 capacity as shouting citizens cried their loyalty to Artemis, who is pictured on their coins. Such opposition was vivid evidence of the great success of Paul's missionary administration in his three years of labor there.

Reason for Writing

Though Colossians suggests details of Paul's prison preaching, in Ephesians he asks supporting prayers to help him speak boldly, for he is a gospel "ambassador in bonds" (Eph. 6:19-20). Paul must have been in Rome; this was discussed at the beginning of this chapter. He was under close guard and chained at least part of the time, for the Greek word for "chain" is used in the above passage. Yet Paul regards his circumstances as a great opportunity to teach; he is providentially "the prisoner of the Lord" (Eph. 4:1; also 3:1). The chart at the beginning of this chapter shows that Ephesians went with the same messengers that carried the letters to the area of Colossae, and the phraseology in Colossians and Ephesians is remarkably similar. So these letters were clearly sent at the same time, with Ephesians delivered at the commercial capital of Asia before the missionaries started inland. In terms of circumstances of delivery, Ephesians was definitely sent to Roman Asia.

Why does Ephesians contain no personal greetings if the apostle wrote to the city that was headquarters for three years on his third journey? Paul chose to write a marvelously balanced doctrinal letter, letting the Ephesians know that Tychicus would bring full knowledge of "my affairs and how I am doing" (Eph. 6:21, NKJB). Nothing is known of Tychicus's conversion, but his faithfulness is clear; he was "a beloved brother, and a faithful minister and fellowservant in the Lord" (Col. 4:7; also Eph. 6:21). Furthermore, he was from Roman Asia (Acts 20:4) and was later sent to Ephesus to replace Timothy (2 Tim. 4:12). Tychicus clearly had the relationships in the Ephesian area to relay all the personal greetings that Paul wished to send there. Indeed, Luke's record of the third mission makes clear what a multitude was converted in Ephesus and Asia on Paul's third mission, as discussed at the end of chapter 3. It would have been self-defeating to begin to write greetings because of the many deep relationships that the apostle had in that area.

Ephesians pictures the converts there as heavily Gentile, which would be expected from the record of Acts. Possibly through the coming of Tychicus, Paul had "heard of your faith in the Lord Jesus, and love unto all the saints" (Eph. 1:15). His letter addressed no crisis. This does not mean that Paul perceived no problems there, for he left the area with the most intense prophecy of apostasy on his lips. Was the real issue lack of total conversion? Paul repreached the entire gospel to the Ephesians, showing them the relationships between salvation through Christ and the need of the Church, between the premortal heritage of the Saints and the strict duty of righteous works for salvation, including gospel living in the home. No New Testament letter so beautifully relates the parts of the gospel to the whole. In the words of a capable Protestant conservative, "Among Paul's epistles there is none more sublime and profound."[37] Is the obvious inspiration in spite of or because of Paul's imprisonment? Earthly difficulties may be the very means of refining souls and drawing them close to God, as Joseph Smith's later letters from Liberty Jail show.

The great relevance and richness of Ephesians makes to whom it was written somewhat beside the point. Yet some scholars doubt that it was sent there because "at Ephesus" (Eph. 1:1) disappears from the three oldest manuscripts. Yet the heading or footnote was generally unchanged; for instance, the Chester Beatty Papyri titles the letter "To the Ephesians," even though its first verse does not include that designation.[38] Since almost all Greek manuscripts carry "at Ephesus" in the first verse, accidental omission is possible, or even deliberate modification, based on the fact that the content is applicable far beyond that branch of the Church. The letter may have been intended for all the Asian churches, though written particularly to Ephesus. Was it copied and circulated in some branches without "at Ephesus" in its beginning? The existence of this scholarly debate underlines the superior value of Ephesians as a summary of the doctrines of the Early Church. A recent conservative evaluation makes that point: "It is generally conceded that Ephesians is the deepest book in the New Testament. Its vision of the purpose of God stretches from eternity to eternity."[39] Members of the restored Church will find in that letter a checklist of characteristics of Christ's true Church. Not tied to particular problems, Ephesians vividly challenges Latter-day Saints to be worthy of their high calling.

Main Teachings

Pre-earth Life and Foreordination

Predestination claims divine predetermination. This doctrine was favored by Reformation theology, especially by Calvinism, as was seen in our study of Romans 9. Though now disbelieved by many in these traditions, the doctrine is still vigorously defended. In this view God must have totally "free scope" in his "unsearchable counsels" of deciding who will be exalted: "grace is not measured by desert, but bestowed at the option of the donor. If I give all my goods to feed the poor or ransom a crew of galley-slaves, I have an undoubted right to select my beneficiaries as I think best."[40] In the King James Bible, God has "predestinated us unto the adoption of children by Jesus Christ" (Eph. 1:5; also 1:11). The word *predestination* appears only two other times (Rom. 8:29-30). But the Medieval and Reformation doctrine goes far beyond Paul's simple concept. His Greek word is *proorízō*, which combines the prefix meaning "beforehand" (*pró*) and the verb for marking off or determining (*horízō*). No scripture student can doubt that God planned this earth in advance—the question is whether man's agency is excluded. Restoration scripture insists that God sent man to earth with freedom and responsibility. So a better translation of Ephesians and Romans would be "fore-ordain," which avoids theological theories negating free agency.[41] Although some translations use that term, interpreters continue to grope for meaning in Ephesians 1 without modern revelation.

If mortals are created beings, then God's planning was done without consulting them or considering their development of qualifications for earth life. In Ephesians and Acts, Paul outlines a scheme of timing and assignment; before the creation God "determined allotted periods and the boundaries of their habitation" (Acts 17:26, RSV). Ephesians 1 gives the same message—that the Saints are deliberately sent to earth when the gospel is available. But on what basis was such planning made? Was leadership left to accident? God might foresee individual works and prophetically relate assignments to agency, but predestinarians quickly reject such a possibility. Thus, they teach a salvation superimposed on passive persons. But glorious light shines on these questions with the revealed knowledge that man existed in personal, spiritual form when the plans for earth life were made. The Father was dealing with known characteristics and capacities in planning for the next stage of the eternal venture of his children.

In declaring God's design for mortality, Paul told his most intelligent audience that Greek poets spoke correctly of man as God's "offspring" (Acts 17:28). Indeed, those who proclaim the restored gospel can also preach from English poets the divine heritage of the human race. For instance, Browning glimpsed the truth of stages of existence: "Ages past the soul existed/here an age 'tis resting merely/and hence fleets again for ages."[42] Christians know that this is true of the Savior, for on his last night on earth he said, "I came forth from the Father, and am come into the world: again, I leave the world, and go to the Father" (John 16:28). But why must Christian doctrine separate the other children of God from God's special Son, who referred to "my Father, and your Father" (John 20:17)? Hebrews preaches the special call of the physical Son of God but just as clearly speaks of the Father as "bringing many sons unto glory" (Heb. 2:10) because he is "the Father of spirits" (Heb. 12:9). Medieval theology invented the classification of uncreated and created. But as Paul said to Athenian philosophers, God's revelation places man in the image and family of God (Acts 17:28). Ephesians 1 is stunning in its applying to mankind a phrase clearly descriptive of Christ's premortal existence. In his intimate prayer of reunion with the Father, Christ said, "You loved me before the foundation of the world" (John 17:24, NKJB). And the Ephesian Saints had that same relationship with the Father: "He chose us in him before the foundation of the world" (Eph. 1:4, literal trans.). The same phrase that refers to Christ's premortal life must also refer to the premortal existence of the Saints.

The Greek of Ephesians 1 or Romans 8 contains a number of words that should refer to premortality. As already indicated, *pro* before a Greek verb adds the idea of "beforehand," a prefix in the borrowed word *prognosis*, which in current medical use refers to what is known beforehand about the future condition of the patient. The same Greek verb form is used of the Father's knowing Christ and men before mortality. This is best seen in the 1881 Revised Version that made the Greek *proginōskō* consistent in the following two passages. Peter taught the clear New Testament doctrine that Christ "was foreknown indeed before the foundation of the world" (1 Pet. 1:20, RV). But Paul taught the same doctrine concerning God and early Christians before birth: "For whom he foreknew, he also foreordained to be conformed to the image of his Son, that he might be the firstborn among many brethren; and whom he foreordained, them he also called" (Rom. 8:29-30, RV). The "calling" is conversion on earth, but there are two stages before that, God's foreknowledge and foreordination. In the case of Christ, Peter's language refers not merely to conceptualizing his future existence but to knowing him personally as a premortal spirit. Does Paul use "foreknow" of God's merely preconceiving the future existence of the "many brethren"? That switch of idea is arbitrary and unlikely. As surely as Peter spoke of Christ's preexistence, Paul spoke of those yet to become earthly Saints as personally alive and known by their Father when he made decisions about their foreordinations.[43]

The magnificent view of Christ's premortal life was reiterated in a powerful revelation to Joseph Smith. It restated Christ's glory "in the beginning, before the world was" (D&C 93:7) and added, "Man was also in the beginning with God. Intelligence, or the light of truth, was not created or made, neither indeed can be" (D&C 93:29). And by a sweeping reconstruction of Abraham's ancient vision, Joseph Smith gathered fragments scintillating throughout all scripture into the brilliant mosaic of the council that organized mortality and foreordained Christ and other leaders. Christ and "the noble and great ones" selected were of proven reliability, so their agency was perfectly consistent with the trust that God placed in them. All future mortals were there and were guaranteed freedom to succeed or to fail, a necessary condition of progress that is the complete opposite of predestination. The plan of salvation was predetermined, but the choice to come to earth and follow the plan was in the hands of each person. Their achievement of being ready for the next bold stage was recognized, with the promise if they were faithful of "glory added upon their heads for ever and ever" (Abr. 3:26). But critical to such success was the mission of the Son, who in great courage offered to come and die for man's eternal life (Abr. 3:27; Moses 4:1-2). Peter and John wrote of Satan's rebellion at this council, making it clearly possible that Paul referred to that occasion when the Saints received "all spiritual blessings in heavenly places in Christ" (Eph. 1:3).

Second-century Christianity still saw the beacon light of the premortal heritage and life's plan. About sixty years after Paul, Justin Martyr was converted to Christianity and not long afterward described the intense testimony of his first Christian contact, who taught that at death the "soul . . . goes back to the place from whence it was taken."[44] From about A.D. 150 has been preserved "the oldest Christian sermon extant,"[45] the so-called 2 Clement, which speaks confidently of the faithful belonging to "the first Church, the spiritual one which was created before the sun and moon." Such a church is obviously an organization of persons faithful to God; this has no meaning unless the Saints of the earthly Church were first organized in eternal relationships before coming to earth. And this doctrine came by apostolic authority: "And moreover the books and the apostles declare that the Church belongs not to the present but has existed from the beginning."[46] Other than Ephesians, what book of an apostle teaches the existence of the Church "before the foundation of the world"? Because of that opening of Ephesians, and because 2 Clement quotes Ephesians 6 on Christ and the Church, the simple Christian author of 2 Clement clearly saw Paul as the apostle teaching the premortal existence of the Saints as the Church.[47] This knowledge of how the Early Church interpreted Paul is an important path to Paul's intended meanings in Ephesians 1. The Shepherd of Hermas, another important second-century source, is even clearer on the premortal existence of the Church and of the Saints, but that will be discussed shortly in connection with the purpose of works in mortality.

The Last Dispensation

The day will come, Paul told the Philippians, when "at the name of Jesus every knee should bow, of those in heaven, and of those on earth, and of those under the earth" (Philip. 2:10, NKJB). Christ's name is rightfully on "every family in heaven and on earth" (Eph. 3:15, RSV). A short passage in Ephesians 1 surveys how this will come about; such a subject is a main theme, though but concisely stated. All will be gathered "in Christ, both which are in heaven and which are on earth" (Eph. 1:10, NKJB). Thus, salvation will be completed in the grand reconciliation of God and all his children. This great work of completion certainly did not take place in Paul's day, nor has it today, when nominal Christians are yet a global minority. In addition to Matthew 24 and the book of Revelation, one prophecy closely matches Paul's. Since they both talk of the final age of renewal, they are here placed together for comparison:

Having made known unto us the mystery of his will, according to his good pleasure which he purposed in him unto a dispensation of the fulness of the times, to sum up all things in Christ, the things in the heavens, and the things upon the earth (Eph. 1:9-10, Revised Version, 1881).

Times of refreshing shall come from the presence of the Lord. And he shall send you the appointed Jesus Christ, whom heaven must receive until times of restoration of all things, which God spoke through the mouth of all his holy prophets from the beginning (Acts 3:19-21, literal trans.).

Peter's "restoration of all things" is strikingly like Paul's concept of summing up or recapitulating "all things in Christ." The universal scope of Paul's "fulness of the times" is strikingly like Peter's "times of refreshing." In both prophecies Christ is central to the final scene of restoration reaching throughout heaven and earth. Commentators generally agree that Peter speaks of "the final era of salvation."[48] The striking correlation of Paul's prophecy shows that he is doing the same, as does a close examination of his words. His whole message emerges from the phrases that are its parts. For analysis the venerable Revised Version is used simply because it carefully mirrors Paul's Greek phraseology. Although the King James Version is usually remarkable in this respect, it is somewhat less literal here.

"The mystery of his will." As commentators note, Paul's "mystery" is not an eternal obscurity, something mystically beyond the

understanding of unquestioning believers. Paul does not proclaim
the mystery but "the revelation of a mystery kept secret for endless
ages" (Rom. 16:25, JB). The last phrase is "eternal times" (*chrónoi
aiốnioi*) and clearly places the origins of the gospel mystery prior to
the foundations of this earth. It was established then to be later
"made known to all nations for the obedience of faith" (Rom.
16:26). The best dictionary of New Testament Greek says of
"mystery": "Our literature uses it to mean the secret thoughts,
plans, and dispensations of God which are hidden from the
human reason . . . and hence must be revealed to those for whom
they are intended."[49] In Ephesians and Colossians Paul mingles
mystery and dispensation and revelation of salvation to the Gentile world. He is clearly talking of the premortal plan of salvation,
a mystery to the world during times of apostasy, but known and
proclaimed by the prophets in Paul's day.[50]

"*He purposed . . . unto . . . the fulness of the times.*" These
words may be the alpha and omega of God's plan of salvation, for
his purpose predates creation, whereas the fulness of times pre-
pares mankind to close mortal history. In his mind Paul may have
swept from premortality to the final era. Yet interpreters generally
see "unto" as a statement of purpose—that God planned in order
to bring about the dispensation of fulness of times. For many, this
is the beginning of the Christian era. After all, some contend, "in
these last days" God spoke by his Son (Heb. 1:2); he was sent
"when the fulness of the time was come" (Gal. 4:4). But this is a
superficial comparison, for in the Father's plan, events matured to
bring about the first coming of the Savior, and his second coming
was possible only after further long periods, referred to in the
plural by the "fulness of the times." Paul clearly looked to future
eras. Israel would not be ready to believe until "the fulness of the
Gentiles" had run its course (Rom. 11:25). Christ had come in
the "last" or "most recent" days from the point of view of one living then, but Paul still spoke of the "times and the seasons" in the
future that would bring about the Second Coming (1 Thes. 5:1).
There were still later days of trial and apostasy coming (1 Tim.
4:1; 2 Tim. 3:1). Paul did not claim to live in the final period, for

he told the Thessalonians that earth would see the coming of Satan's apostasy before Christ's time of perfecting all things. The *"dispensation of the fulness of the times."* What is a dispensation? This English word is a fair guide, for God's dispensing or giving out of authority establishes a dispensation. Paul used a Greek term of similar origin; *oikonomía* combined the word for *giving out* with *oîkos,* a household or material possessions. Thus *oikonomía* was assigned supervision in business or government. In Jesus' story of the scheming manager this word is translated "stewardship" (Luke 16:2-4). But in 1 Corinthians, Ephesians, and Colossians the same word is "dispensation." That comparison shows that Paul's "dispensation" is delegated authority. Classical Greek meanings are fundamentally "management" or "administration." For instance, Pharaoh's appointment of Moses over the king's grain supply is a "dispensation."[51] So translators are correct to render this concept in Ephesians 1:10 as "administration" or "commission." Although other translators miss this main idea, the following examples from Paul show that a dispensation involved delegated authority to earthly prophets.

Paul reminded the Ephesians of "the dispensation of the grace of God which was given to me for you" (Eph. 3:2, NKJB). At the same time he wrote the Colossians about his priesthood service "according to the dispensation of God which is given to me for you" (Col. 1:25). Through Paul's first vision and later temple vision, God had outlined his call not to Jews but to Gentiles. The first apostles sent him from Jerusalem to Tarsus-Antioch (Acts 9:27-30), after which Peter and his counselors gave Paul the "right hands of fellowship" and the commission to carry the gospel to the Gentiles (Gal. 2:9). So Paul's personal "dispensation" was agency under Christ to do his work. And no one has a right to change the apostle's definition in the case of the future dispensation.[52] Thus, the "dispensation of the fulness of the times" clearly means that God will again call trusted servants for his latter-day work, commissioning them to prepare the world for his coming.

"To sum up all things in Christ." For Peter, the final era was for restoration, which ties to the Old Testament vision that God

would gather his people from all lands before the end. Paul's Greek word plainly means to "sum up" in the sense of arguments being restated and summarized, or making a total from earlier entries. Modern committee translations all agree on this for Paul's other use of this term, where the Old Testament commandments were "summed up" by the Golden Rule (Rom. 13:9, NKJB). After naming the Mosaic laws there, Paul's point is that they are summarized by the law of loving one's neighbor. So he is using "sum up" in the sense of restatement, as did writers and speakers. The Roman rhetorician Quintilian gives that literary definition: "The repetition and grouping of the facts, which the Greeks call *anakephalaíōsis* and some of our own writers call the enumeration, serves both to refresh the memory of the judge and to place the whole of the case before his eyes."[53]

Thus, Quintilian explains that the sections of a speech must be concisely regrouped for "their cumulative effect." "Summing up" is a "final recapitulation" of the major strands of argument; "as the Greek term indicates, we must summarize the facts under the appropriate heads."[54] Understanding how Paul and his contemporaries used "summing up" is critical to understanding his message. His translators and commentators are simplistic, seeing the apostle as teaching once more that Christ will be acknowledged as the head. But Paul's "summing up" is talking of something else done through Christ's power, for the "things in the heavens and the things upon the earth" are "summed up." In other words, Paul's subject is not Christ, but how heavenly salvation will be brought to all through the process of "recapitulation" or "restoration." Thus, the King James "gather together" is Paul's basic idea—the strands of authority and truths of all the past will be reestablished at the final dispensation. This is in its nature pluralistic—the reintegration of God's prior revelations in the final time of preparing the earth for the judgment of Christ.

Joseph Smith has more logic here than have the interpreters, for he claimed the incredible authority of the great prophets returning past priesthood powers. Joseph Smith reviewed Paul succinctly: "The dispensation of the fulness of times will bring to light the things that have been revealed in all former dispensations, also other things that have not been before revealed. He shall send Elijah the prophet, etc., and restore all things in Christ."[55] The restoration of the full keys and their use was the burden of the Prophet's Nauvoo message: "Now the purpose . . . in the winding up scene of the last dispensation is, that all things pertaining to that dispensation should be conducted precisely in accordance with the preceding dispensations." He continued by explaining that eternal ordinances and authority must be revealed "from heaven to man or to send angels to reveal them."[56] As just quoted, Elijah would be one such messenger, fulfilling his latter-day mission to "turn the heart of the fathers to the children, and the heart of the children to their fathers" (Mal. 4:5-6).

Paul spoke of the unity of all the heavens and the earth; Peter said that the "living and the dead" must be prepared for judgment through the gospel "preached . . . to those who are dead" (1 Pet. 4:5-6, NKJB). This completes the circle of this discussion, which opened with Paul's insistence that every person who ever lived must acknowledge Christ in some degree. Latter-day Saints have the most comprehensive program ever known for preaching to the living and the dead and doing baptisms for the living and the dead. Joseph Smith was authorized by multiple mighty angels, "all declaring their dispensation, their rights, their keys . . . and the power of their priesthood" (D&C 128:21). The restoration of these powers is for the restoration of all of God's children to him through Christ, for the dead of all past times are to hear the gospel in the preaching begun by Christ (1 Pet. 3:18-20). And at the end, ordinances and sealings must unite all in heaven and earth, as Paul prophesied. The result is the marvelous "recapitulation" of Paul or "restoration" of Peter. The founding Prophet of this restoration sounded no uncertain trumpet on the inspired result: "For it is necessary in the ushering in of the dispensation of the fulness of times, which dispensation is now beginning to usher in, that a whole and complete and perfect union, and welding together of dispensations, and keys, and powers, and glories should take place, and be revealed from the days of Adam even to the present times" (D&C 128:18).

Grace and Works

"Not of works, lest any man should boast" (Eph. 2:9). So the tracts begin on salvation through Christ. Yet no one commanded works more firmly than did Christ, who closed his most urgent sermon with the warning that hearing without doing will bring destruction (Matt. 7:26-27). The true gospel is taught when all its parts are taught, not when one principle is isolated from the rest. Like the balance in Romans of initial grace and final works, the first three chapters of Ephesians emphasize grace while the last three emphasize the works that must follow grace for salvation. Besides a dozen times that grace and its synonyms appear in Ephesians, two dozen specific commandments are added to illustrate how the Saints must live for exaltation. In reality, Paul preached that neither faith alone nor works alone would result in salvation. In Ephesians both are blended and balanced. If seeking to please God through his commands is unchristian, Paul was unchristian.

Like Colossians, Ephesians declares the glory of Christ: king of kings (Eph. 1:20-21), head of the church (Eph. 1:22-23), and agent of the Father in creation (Eph. 3:9). But like Romans, Ephesians adds Paul's profound feeling for the Savior, whose love for his Saints is returned in everlasting love for him. Because Latter-day Saints show this love in action, they are targets of suspicion and even jealousy. The older Protestant tracts for them frequently closed with the invitation to believe in Christ "if you are a Mormon, or any other unsaved person."[57] Misguided missionaries to Latter-day Saints justify themselves by claiming that the Latter-day Saints believe in some other Jesus, which is simply an uninformed smear. As these words are written, tens of thousands of Latter-day Saint teachers are preparing Sunday lessons from the precious Gospels in a year when the five-million-member Church is studying the life of Christ. By the evangelical standard of salvation through accepting Christ, the Latter-day Saints are indeed saved. Their faith is written in the greatest scripture, the "book of life" that records faith as shown in "works" (Rev. 20:12). With Paul they worship "the Father of our Lord Jesus Christ" (Eph. 3:14), seeking to be "strengthened" daily by the Holy Ghost

(Eph. 3:16), and through solemn covenants "to know the love of Christ, which passes knowledge" (Eph. 3:19, NKJB). For they live for eternal glory with Christ, which will last "through all generations of time and of eternity" (Eph. 3:21, literal trans.).[58]

"For by grace are ye saved through faith" (Eph. 2:8). Grace here is no mysterious abstraction, but a relationship with God through Christ. This proof-text is a crescendo and recapitulation of the devotional language of the apostle in which prominent synonyms sparkle: "mercy" (Eph. 2:4); "his great love wherewith he loved us" (Eph. 2:4); "his kindness toward us through Christ Jesus" (Eph. 2:7). Nothing says that grace is an exclusive means to salvation. On the contrary, grace is God's initiative in showing his goodwill and presupposes a responsible answer. The timing is all-important if Paul's words are to be understood and are not to be mere fuel for debate. The apostle frequently uses "saved" in the future tense, but he does so in the past tense here. Saved from what? The Ephesian Saints were not told that they were saved in God's kingdom; as of then they were saved from past "lusts of our flesh" (Eph. 2:3). In other words, Christ's forgiveness came to blot out what they had done in their past ignorance of the gospel. God gave his grace freely to save them from their sins prior to their knowing the gospel. Thereafter they were to follow a higher standard, for Paul named the serious sins that must be put aside as a condition of "any inheritance in the kingdom of Christ and of God" (Eph. 5:5). Every important letter of Paul on grace also contains this strict list of moral conditions of maintaining the relationship in God's grace.

Thus "not of yourselves" (Eph. 2:8) and "not of works" (Eph. 2:9) have the particular context of conversion. The new convert can offer gratitude, not a record of high performance for the Lord. Yet at that point God trusts him with the priceless gift of forgiveness on condition that faith really leads to repentance and a holy life. Romans, Galatians, and Ephesians make the "gift" of forgiveness an immediate reality, with the two possibilities of perfecting title or losing possession. Indeed, one newly baptized has the position of a person who has signed a conditional sales contract for a desired physical object. Immediate possession and enjoyment is given, which is not disturbed as long as the required payments are met. Only in the event of careless or willful default does the property return to the seller. "Not of works" is accurate at the outset of discipleship but is plainly less true as one's responsibilities grow before the Lord. No amount of theorizing can explain away the required Christian works in the last three chapters of Ephesians.

"Not of works" is immediately followed by the challenge of works in the new Christian life: "For we are his workmanship, created in Christ Jesus unto good works" (Eph. 2:10). The creation here is the new member of the Church, the new life after baptism, "the new man, which after God is created in righteousness and true holiness" (Eph. 4:24). Thus, Paul's grace section agrees with his works section in insisting that righteous works are required of Church members in order for them to stay in God's favor. They have been baptized (Eph. 4:5) and have received "the holy Spirit of promise" (Eph. 1:13), the Holy Ghost that assures them of eternity. But they are warned, "grieve not the holy Spirit of God, whereby ye are sealed unto the day of redemption" (Eph. 4:30). How can they grieve the Holy Spirit, the Holy Ghost? This warning is among the commandments for a righteous life. As modern revelation also says, one must avoid sin in order to keep the Spirit (D&C 1:33). Grace and salvation follow the same principle, for they may be lost through sin.

Paul's passage also reminds the Saints that they were sent to earth to do good works. The full verse on post-conversion works reaches back to the reason for mortality: "For we are his workmanship, created in Christ Jesus for good works, which God has *prepared beforehand* that we should walk in them" (Eph. 2:10, NKJB, italics added). The italicized phrase is related to the premortal terminology of Ephesians 1; it is *proetoimázō*, which is also accurately rendered as "prepared in advance" (NIV).[59] That verb is followed by a Greek purpose clause indicating that God's premortal preparation had "good works" as its objective for earth life. Here is a case where many Christians see the life-giving water of grace without seeing the eternal snows that feed it. Ephesians teaches the great truth that God made this world as a place for men and women to achieve good works. Latter-day Saints immediately remember Abraham's revelation on the grand council, when the premortal Savior explained the purpose of mortality: "We will prove them herewith, to see if they will do all things whatsoever the Lord their God shall command them" (Abr. 3:25).

Thus, Paul's full teaching of grace and works leads back to Ephesians' testimony of the Saints' pre-existence. A source in Paul's shadow also blends the Saints' premortal life with their agreement to come to earth to learn to live God's commandments. This source is the Shepherd of Hermas, so named because the revealing angel came in shepherd's form to Hermas, a simple Christian unlikely to invent new doctrine. A source gives about A.D. 150 for this writing, since it refers to Hermas's brother as then bishop of Rome. [60] But the first part, in which the premortal existence appears, was written when Clement was bishop of Rome, at the end of the first century. [61] Hermas saw the Church in the form of an old woman because, as his messenger said, "She was created the first of all things." [62] Here is the second-century doctrine of the pre-existence of the Church strongly reiterated, for God created the world "for the sake of his Holy Church." [63] Straight logic requires some confrontations here, for there is no such thing as a church apart from the people that constitute it. And Hermas is not told that the Church was planned before the physical creation but that it was then organized, which means its members were in existence to have premortal relationships with one another. If creation was indeed for the sake of the Church, then those called to membership and leadership looked to earth as their next stage of progression. And this is what Hermas was told: "God . . . created the world . . . and by his own wisdom and forethought created his holy Church . . . and everything is becoming level for his elect in order that he might keep for them the promise which he made with great glory and joy, if they keep the commandments of God, which they received in great faith." [64]

Hermas here referred to an occasion of planning mortality when the heavens rejoiced and God's elect then "received" God's promises "in great faith." Such a group portrait has no meaning in terms of a scattered acceptance of the gospel on earth; the circumstances of hearing God's covenant are celestial and not mortal. Ephesians, Hermas, and the restored vision of Abraham all agree that men and women on earth must seek God's grace through the Atonement—and then give their lives thereafter to righteousness. All three sources also measure success by the condition given in Hermas's vision: "If they keep the commandments of God."

Church Organization

Christ taught that membership in his Church was necessary for eternal salvation. He charged the apostles to baptize all believers in all nations and then follow up by "teaching them to observe all things whatsoever I have commanded you" (Matt. 28:19-20). Conversion and baptism only begin the Lord's program of continued teaching. And no one has authority to alter his command to convert and teach by defining the first as essential to salvation without the second. The true gospel requires the decision for Christ and also the commitment to discipleship of Christ under his authorized servants. In other words, the true gospel requires the true church. And Ephesians joins with 1 Corinthians to indicate what divine organization the Church must have.

Protestants have long talked of the "invisible church," theorizing on a mystical unity that somehow overarches or overlooks the fragmentation of the visible churches. Paul's two leading epistles on Church organization stress unity and define it as harmony with Christ's living apostles. Nothing has produced more open pain among Christian leaders than this contradiction between the Christian constitution and the departure of Christianity from it. Thus, a devout commentator on Ephesians hopes that "its glorious picture of the true nature of the Church is God's message for a day marked by deep concern about the disunity of Christendom."[65] Such "deep concern" materialized in the ecumenical movement, which takes its name from the Greek word for the whole world, expressing the concept of a universal church.

The last decades have been characterized by Protestant and Catholic world councils and conferences on unity. With what success? Protestant interchurch unity is more verbal than real, though many bridges of understanding stand. Yet even supporters doubt the result: "It has become an axiom of the Ecumenical Movement that unity does not imply uniformity; diversity is essential for unity.[66]

Paul's standard was clearly otherwise. The Early Church exhibits personal tolerance and rich differences of personality but agreement in doctrine and allegiance to one set of leaders. Paul taught the necessity of patience with individuals, bearing with one another in love and long-suffering (Eph. 4:2). Yet there was but one Christian Church, and within it a "unity of the Spirit," to which Paul added seven doctrinal unities: "One body, and one Spirit . . . one hope of your calling . . . one Lord, one faith, one baptism, one God and Father of all" (Eph. 4:3-6). Here Paul gives the spirit and body image that is so powerful in 1 Corinthians 12. He had mentioned Christ's "church, which is his body" (Eph. 1:22-23). So "one body and one spirit" is in plain words one true Church inspired by the Holy Ghost. Organization without revelation is mechanical, but revelation without inspired supervision is chaos. This picture of one true Church arises in great part from Paul's desire in Ephesians to teach Gentile Saints their eternal calling to be united with Jewish Saints. Though these were historically apart, Christ had "broken down the middle wall of division between us" (Eph. 2:14, NKJB). Paul could scarcely have written this without thinking of the shoulder-high temple wall separating the Court of the Gentiles from the inner Israelite courts, for he nearly lost his life on the charge of bringing a Gentile across that barrier.[67] Gentiles are no longer outside, Paul says—Jew and non-Jew are "both one" (Eph. 2:14), "one new man" in the "one body" of the Church (Eph. 2:15-16).

Gentiles no longer are "strangers and foreigners" but belong to the same "household of God." Next, the Church becomes a beautifully framed building, and its members "are built upon the foundation of the apostles and prophets, Jesus Christ himself being the chief corner stone" (Eph. 2:19-20). Thus, apostles are hardly less important than Christ, because he appointed them to help bear the weight of the Church. Should the twelve apostles be considered as historical founders or as continued successors in present times? Christian theology chooses the former, seeing the papacy or preaching ministry as limited to proclaiming the apostolic revelation. The apostles' mission ended with "the task of foundation-laying."[68] In this view, any church founded on the Bible is using the apostles as a foundation. But how much of the apostles' teaching is in the Bible? What doctrines were in the lost letters to the Corinthians and the Laodiceans? And how much was never written in the first place? The Thessalonians were told that Paul had already clearly explained the apostasy and so was only reminding them of main points (2 Thes. 2:5). In the spirit of scolding for poor memory, Paul added, "Hold the traditions which ye have been taught, whether by word, or our epistle" (2 Thes. 2:15). Most of what Paul taught "by word" is not recorded at all.[69] And only minimal fragments are preserved from Peter, James, and John. Only the Early Church had the full foundation of living teachings. So traditional churches have an incomplete foundation, much of which disappeared when the apostles disappeared.

Memorials to dead apostles will never satisfy vital Christians. Paul insists that only living apostles can bring godliness to the Saints: "And [the Lord] himself gave some to be apostles, some prophets, some evangelists, and some pastors and teachers, for the perfecting of the saints for the work of ministry, for the edifying of the body of Christ, till we all come to the unity of the faith and the knowledge of the Son of God, to a perfect man, to the measure of the stature of the fullness of Christ" (Eph. 4:11-13, NKJB).

This is a remarkable statement on the goals of the Church—what Paul was working for in every speech and letter. This is Paul's version of Christ's commission to the apostles; the growth for salvation comes after baptism and through the member's faithfulness in Christ's church. Its members are collectively "the body of Christ," and they must be "edified," which in Greek means literally "built up." In Paul's comparison, their characters are in construction through instruction. In plain terms, Paul taught that only teaching directed by the living Twelve would bring the Saints to a "unity of the faith."

Christian churches have kept "pastors and teachers" but have left Christ's body without a head, for the "pastors and teachers" themselves cannot agree. Why the inconsistency of keeping some offices of Christ's church and ignoring the most important? Only a true apostolic government can command the respect of true Christians and lead them by true revelations. That is proved by what the Corinthians and Galatians did to the gospel when Paul was absent. Protestant leaders face the dilemma of knowing that disunity is wrong but fearing centralization. Those working for church union were branded as "ecumaniacs" some years ago by a prominent Methodist bishop. He felt that central administration would contradict the Protestant principle of free dissent. But that hard choice is essential. The religion of the apostles required believers to bridle their tongues, their appetites, and the human love for power and notoriety through pushing untested theories. "Unity of the faith" was the goal of the Early Church, and Paul said it could not be reached without the management of living apostles.

The embarrassment of believers intensifies in the situation of differing doctrines and multiple churches. A recent statement of conservative Bible teachers assesses a crisis: "We deplore the scandalous isolation and separation of Christians from one another. We believe such division is contrary to Christ's explicit desire for unity among his people and impedes the witness of the church in the world."[70] Here is proof of Paul's point, for he warned against the consequences without inspired general authorities: "That we be not children, thrown about and carried around by every wind of teaching through the deceit of men, through their evil designs of scheming and error" (Eph. 4:14, literal trans.). Paul makes apostles absolutely necessary to perform the function of keeping the Church together: one faith, one church, one set of leaders over it. He insisted that unity was brought about only by continuing apostles of the Lord. And Christian history proves his point.

The Early Church was an effective organization. Paul outlines the main structure of the Church in several major letters. Glimpses of the duties of different officers are found in his comments and also in the meaning of the names given these officers, as illustrated on the accompanying chart. The word *apostle* suggested special authority to the Greek-speaking branches; more important, Acts clearly describes how the Twelve exercised presiding authority over the Church. As earlier discussed, 1 Corinthians 12:28 places apostles "first" because all spiritual gifts are subordinate to priesthood authority. In Ephesians and 1 Corinthians 12, Paul names prophets next, using a word for one with spiritual discernment or a warning prediction, as shown in the cases of Agabus (Acts 11:27-29; 21:10-11) and the Corinthian testimony meetings (1 Cor. 14). In the New Testament, *prophet* indicates divine inspiration, and the word can be linked with any office of authority. When Paul said that the foundation of the Church was "apostles and prophets" (Eph. 2:20), he evidently used two words for the same calling—one for authority and the other for inspiration to lead. He reinforced that impression by referring to the mysteries of salvation revealed "unto his holy apostles and prophets" (Eph. 3:5).

"Prophets" are listed second because of their prominence in all Church leadership. Every administrative appointment should be carried out by the direction of the Spirit, which should make every Church officer a prophet in his appointed office. In 1 Corinthians 12, Paul names "teachers" as the third calling in the Church. Modern revelation has recognized the importance of person-to-person teaching by a grade of priesthood with the name of teacher, but there are many other appointments to teach throughout every Church level and jurisdiction. Perhaps Paul used "teacher" as a pervasive function rather than as a technical priesthood office. General authorities (2 Tim. 1:11) and local authorities (1 Tim. 3:2) are teachers, as well as are those they appoint to teach in special situations.

The Constitution of Christ's Church in Paul's Writings

Offices in Eph. 4:11:	apostle	prophet	evangelist	pastor	teacher
Greek term:	*apóstolos*	*prophḗēs*	*euangelistḗs*	*poimḗn*	*didáskalos*
Meaning:	"one sent," special messenger	"forthteller" or "foreteller"	bringer of good news	shepherd	teacher

Offices in 1 Cor. 12:28:	apostle	prophet	help	government	teacher
Greek term:	same as above	same as above	*antílēmpsis*	*kubérnēsis*	same as above
Meaning:	same as above	same as above	help or aid	director or administrator	

Specific local offices (1 Tim. 3; Titus 1; Acts 14:23; Philip. 1:1):	deacon	elder	bishop
Greek term:	*diákonos*	*presbúteros*	*epískopos*
Meaning:	servant	elder (a civic office)	overseer

What is a "pastor"? The accompanying chart shows that the "pastors" of Ephesians 4 are equivalent to the "helps and governments" of 1 Corinthians 12. The Greek word for *pastor* simply means shepherd, no doubt referring to the bishop with a local flock, for on both lists the first offices are general, with local offices afterward. Speaking to the presiding elders of Ephesus, Paul called them by the Greek word for *bishop* ("overseer") and charged them to watch over "all the flock" (Acts 20:28). But Paul evidently sent oral messages to bishops, who are not mentioned in the public letters except for Philippians, which was written with special relationships. More will be learned about early bishops from Paul's last letters.

And "some" are evangelists, Paul says in Ephesians 4. The historic fragments on this office remind one of the need for revelation about many details of the Lord's organization. The verb "evangelize" first meant to announce good news, and in the New Testament was used to refer to preaching the gospel. Thus, scholars naturally assume that an "evangelist" refers to a preacher of the gospel. If that is true, the restored Church well qualifies, with over twenty-five thousand missionary "evangelists" in all parts of the world as these words are written. But since the Early Church stressed missionary work intensely, it is strange that *evangelist* appears in the New Testament only three times, one of which is in the Ephesians list of Church offices. And Paul, the most successful missionary on record, never calls himself an evangelist. Joseph Smith defined the term as follows: "An evangelist is a patriarch. . . . Wherever the Church of Christ is established in the earth, there should be a patriarch for the benefit of the posterity of the saints, as it was with Jacob in giving his patriarchal blessing unto his sons."[71] If the missionary announces the good news of the gospel in public, the patriarch announces special messages of the Spirit on a sacred, private level. One ancient inscription calls a priest giving private oracles an "evangelist," showing the flexibility of the word. In the New Testament, Philip is called an evangelist many years after any of his known missionary journeys (Acts 21:8), and Timothy is told to do the work of an evangelist in the context of correcting and guiding the Saints who are in danger of apostasy, not of preaching to outsiders who do not have the truth (2 Tim. 4:2-5).

What is the core characteristic of Christ's organization? Seekers over centuries have concluded that the true church could not be on earth without authorized apostles and prophets. The medieval papacy was a centralized force for unity, but it differed strikingly in form and holiness from the apostolate of the Early Church. One mark of restored priesthood is the use of wise counselors at every level of Church government, for in management as well as in marriage, it is not good for man to be alone. As Hugh Nibley perceptively observed, divine Church leadership is not a chain with individual links able to split apart, but a twelve-strand cable in which joint strength prevents a break or bears the load if it happens. A committee of three apostles was central to Church government during Jesus' life and afterward (Matt. 17:1; Gal. 2:9). Thus, the corporate leadership of twelve, with committee direction within or in addition to that group, is the Lord's system in the New Testament. It is amazing that there have not been more attempts to duplicate it. One was made when Joseph Smith quietly reestablished the Quorum of the Twelve after being ordained by the ancient apostolic presidency of Peter, James, and John (D&C 27:12-13). In Britain Edward Irving had founded the Catholic Apostolic Church, and after his death in 1834 a modern council of the twelve was appointed. Four decades later most of them had died without replacements, but the striking claim caught the imagination of the leading Christian historian in the United States at the end of the century. Philip Schaff, who had carefully studied and written on the Early Church, noted the "astounding assumptions, which, if well founded, would require the submission of all Christendom to the authority of its inspired apostles."[72]

"Perfecting of the Saints"

The Church is a means to an end, not an end in itself. Devoted members seek to perfect the Church, but the Church exists to help members draw closer to God through faith, ordinances, and better lives. These measure the real work of the Church, not hours spent in meetings or numbers of buildings. Paul explained that the combination of general and local authorities would move the members from the level of "children" to "the measure of the stature of the fulness of Christ" (Eph. 4:13-14). This defines what he means by "perfecting" and "edifying" the Saints—their spiritual maturity is to grow to be like Christ. As in Romans and Colossians, the older, worldly person must disappear for the Christlike person to be formed. The old person walked in a worldly "conversation" (Eph. 4:22), an archaic term that translates a Greek word meaning "conduct." "Be renewed" (Eph. 4:23) is a program, an ongoing process that Ephesian members are vitally involved in long after their conversion.

The main New Testament name for Church members symbolizes their post-conversion growth. In every church Paul writes to the "saints"; the Greek term *(hágios)* is often translated simply as "holy" in the King James Version. Indeed, the English *saint* comes from the Latin *sanctus*, meaning "holy." So a saint is literally a holy person, though Paul's letters reveal a good deal of unsaintly conduct in those with that name. But God conferred the name "holy" on his people so they would know their true name and live up to it. They were in the process of becoming "sanctified," the verb form *(hagiázō)*. Thus, the goal of the Early Church is revealed by knowing that the "saints" were seeking "sanctification" or to become "sanctified." Christ gave himself for the Church, Paul said, "that he might sanctify and cleanse it with the washing of water by the word" (Eph. 5:26). Baptism did cleanse past sins for Church members, but Paul's letters show that the ideals of the kingdom were not yet fully realized. Dale Carnegie used to speak of reforming others by complimenting them on their best qualities, giving them a good reputation to live up to. Today human relations experts say the same thing in language of positive reinforcement. Growth comes to those who sincerely reach to higher goals in their own self-image. In the gospel, the past is set aside through baptism and repentance, and then comes the phase of proving worthy to be identified with Christ and the Saints. The covenant of perfection is the first step, and the second is becoming perfect under the guidance of the Spirit. There are certain things that those committed to Christ will always avoid, "as is fitting for saints" (Eph. 5:3, NKJB). Live up to your holy name and reputation, is Paul's command.

The "born-again Christian" may claim sudden reform or feel that God's grace makes his imperfections irrelevant. But New Testament salvation is deeply tied to character development, and a character is the sum total of one's moral habits. Moral growth follows the rule of life: practice makes perfect. Do the world's achievers have nothing to teach the Christian seeking eternal achievement? Voltaire's diligence is reflected in a saying attributed to him: "Perfection is attained by slow degrees; it requires the hand of time." Benjamin Franklin realized that principle early and listed the virtues he wanted to develop. His autobiography explains his successful strategy of improvement—he worked intensely on one quality at a time, and after upgrading one area of conduct, he concentrated on another. A basketball coach does the same thing by assigning a poor foul shooter to work intensely on that weakness; a musician does the same thing by repeating a difficult passage until he can play it flawlessly. Through Christ, the Saints have higher motivation and a model, and revelation teaches them eternal values. But mastering the elements of growth one at a time is the only practical way to grow. To seek to be generally good is not enough. What specific acts must cease, and what righteous attitudes and practices must arise in their place? Paul answers with Christian specifics.

Godliness is not achieved by prohibitions alone. So Ephesians identifies each evil practice and replaces it with the higher standard of the gospel. The bad habit of lying must cease and be replaced with the strict commitment to tell the truth to each other (Eph. 4:25). The worldly option is unrestrained anger, but Paul commands reconciliation quickly—before sunset (Eph. 4:26). To prevent stealing, Paul commands honest labor to be able to give instead of to take (Eph. 4:28). As in other letters, Paul reminds the Saints that sexual intercourse out of marriage may bar one from God's kingdom (Eph. 5:5). But how does one control sexual drives? Paul's answer is that one should be busy serving God and helping others. Then one thinks on the Lord and on righteous friendship and service; gratitude and goodwill are within, and joy is expressed in the music of the soul (Eph. 5:19-20). That person needs no drink or drugs to lift sagging spirits, for steady spiritual stimulation makes harmful stimulants a poor substitute (Eph. 5:18).

Living for eternity changes everyday relationships. Paul says a good deal about bad words springing from a bad attitude. He measures all speech by a golden rule of communication: "Do not let any unwholesome talk come out of your mouths, but only what is helpful for building others up according to their needs, that it may benefit those who listen" (Eph. 4:29, NIV). This means anything hurtful to another, including the barrage of bad names and lustful comments that permeate careless company. In a strong sexual context Paul forbids "foolish talk or flippant humor" (Eph. 5:4, literal trans.). What is wrong goes far beyond the words themselves. The King James Version says these are not "convenient," an archaic word for "fitting" or "appropriate" (Eph. 5:4). That is, profanity and sexual innuendo are simply inconsistent with the holiness that a true Saint is seeking. Instead, the apostle counsels, there should be "giving of thanks" (Eph. 5:4). This recurrent teaching in Ephesians pictures the true Saint with inner appreciation for God and all his children. The real sin of profanity and obscenity is the hostile feeling toward others that it reveals. Those who debase others in their minds produce blame, accusation, and insult in private comments. Saints who would be perfect have a clear choice between two ways of thinking, speaking, and acting:

Put away from you all bitterness and bad temper and anger and loud accusation and evil speaking, with every wrong (Eph. 4:31, literal trans.).

And be kind to one another, tenderhearted, forgiving each other, just as God also forgave you through Christ (Eph. 4:32, literal trans.).

Paul ends Ephesians with the call to war against Satan, the true enemy. His kingdom is as real as God's, and Satan's kingdom is governed by Satan's principles (Eph. 6:12). The object is to withstand him without adopting his methods. But God will protect his Saints in the struggle. Paul may have glanced up at his guard's armor as he wrote of battle gear, a theme also in earlier letters and scriptures. Faith and righteousness are the principles of protection, and the sure weapon is the "sword of the Spirit, which is the word of God" (Eph. 6:17). As described in the great Book of Mormon passage on the iron rod (1 Ne. 15:24), the word of God is a powerful means of success in life's struggle. The key to understanding it is Paul's identification of the Holy Ghost with the word of God. Personal revelation through prayer is the word of God; living prophets speaking by the Holy Ghost give the word of God; Christ and his prophets teach the word of God in scripture. All these give invincible strength to those seeking to be Saints in more than name only.

Scriptures sometimes associate sanctification with forgiveness through Christ, sometimes with the purifying influence of the Spirit—but more regularly with living Christ's laws, the means of obtaining both forgiveness and the constant guidance of the Holy Ghost. How these eternal realities of Ephesians apply today was summed up by Brigham Young: "Cast all bitterness out of your own hearts—all anger, wrath, strife, covetousness, and lust, and sanctify the Lord God in your hearts, that you may enjoy the Holy Ghost, and have that Spirit to be your constant companion day by day, to lead you into all truth, and then you will have good doctrine, good feelings, good wives, good children, a good community; and, finally, you will be Saints in the fullest sense of the word, but not yet. I believe we shall be Saints, through the grace of God."[73]

Family Life

"And walk in love, as Christ also has loved us and given himself for us" (Eph. 5:2, NKJB). Paul pictured the Church as those under covenant of righteous relations, following their Savior in uplifting all those around them. Husbands and wives receive special instructions in these principles; all the apostle said about concern for others is finally applied to the family. Indeed, Paul outlines a constitution of the family similar to the constitution of the Church in 1 Corinthians 12. This family structure is also defined in 1 Peter 3—these are the convictions of the Early Church. But constitutions define general relationships, leaving everyday living to be worked out within guidelines. This makes flexibility in different marriages inevitable as couples operate within general Christian roles.

Nothing written exceeds Ephesians 5 for its high view of married love. In our day of concern for women's rights, Paul's language about wives' "submitting" themselves to their husbands must be examined (Eph. 5:22). There are twin questions of what Paul meant and what application it has in gospel living today. By analogy, the modern world exists because of the principle of specialization; tasks are divided for better technology. So polarity between priesthood and motherhood is sound social engineering, making possible better-trained leaders in Church affairs and expert mothering in the crisis of a society losing its values. In this system neither sex is inferior (Gal. 3:28), and Latter-day Saints believe that God gave preexistent callings to serve in given sexual roles.[74] Paul's "submit" has the literal meaning of "subordinate" in both Greek and Latin. This refers to placement in order, and is frequently a military term of arranging forces near each other and sometimes an anatomical term of the relationship of parts of the body. Thus, men and women fit into the orderly arrangement of Church and family with equal dignity and importance before God.

One avoids the emotional booby trap of "subordination" by asking specifically what it means in action: "Wives, submit yourselves unto your husbands, as unto the Lord" (Eph. 5:22; also Col. 3:18). The first step in understanding is to see the many relationships of submission that Paul teaches. "Submitting yourselves one to another in the fear of God" (Eph. 5:21) had just been given as a general principle for all Saints. This also meant subordination of all to lawful government on the local and national levels (Rom. 13:1, 5; Titus 3:1). Men and women also shared "submission" to appointed local leaders in the Church (1 Cor. 14:32; 16:16). "Obey them that have the rule over you, and submit yourselves: for they watch for your souls" (Heb. 13:17); these branch leaders "labour among you, and are over you in the Lord, and admonish you" (1 Thes. 5:12). In what does the bishop admonish his members? He deals with questions of spiritual health and physical well-being, not with choice of menu, colors of dress, or the thousand personal decisions that express individuality. With proper counsel, the bishop plans and carries out group activities of worship, assistance, and recreation. In Paul's specific comparison, the husband is head to the wife "even as Christ is the head of the church"; but this analogy suggests strongly that Christ taught all things necessary for salvation and certainly did not dictate in the ordinary choices of everyday life (Eph. 5:23-24).

It is critical for husbands who imagine they have a mandate to think for their wives to understand what family presidency really is. Christ is the model for priesthood leadership in the home because he taught gospel truths, because he was a perfect example of living the truths that he taught, and because in the end he gave his life for the disciples that he loved. Paul gives husbands the duty of following Christ as the model leader; this is not a blank check for dominance. The word of the Lord is equally available to husbands and wives, and spiritual matters are questions of conscience for which both must answer to God directly. Just as the husband ought to have the providing role in a childbearing marriage, he is also assigned to lead in providing regular times of prayer, family teaching, church participation, and companionship and communication with wife and children. Because of common commitment, the wife is told to respect and support her husband's religious leadership. And the husband with a knowledge of good leadership will respect the principle of consultation before decision. As Paul says, Christ led with his only goal the salvation and eternal fulfillment of his disciples. On that analogy every caring husband will sacrifice time and money to see that his wife continues to have opportunities to develop her talents and interests in and out of the home.

Leadership always includes two opposing problems—lack of use, and abuse. And Paul warns fathers not to overdirect. The apostle commands, "Husbands, love your wives, and be not bitter against them" (Col. 3:19). But children also face the danger of leadership without love: "Fathers, provoke not your children to anger, lest they be discouraged" (Col. 3:21). Ephesians repeats that instruction with the substitution of a positive program: "Bring them up in the training and admonition of the Lord" (Eph. 6:4, NKJB). Wives and husbands normally share the education and moral training of their children, but many women today stand at the head of single-parent households. So President Spencer W. Kimball's words on male leadership have great insight for mothers also. After using Paul's metaphor of Christ's sacrificing all for the Church, he added:

> When the husband is ready to treat his household in that manner, not only his wife but also his children will respond to his loving and exemplary leadership. It will be automatic. He won't need to demand it; it will come because they will want to do what they understand to be necessary and right. Certainly if fathers are to be respected, they must merit respect. If they are to be loved, they must be consistent, lovable, understanding, and kind—and they must honor their priesthood. They must see themselves as fortunate trustees of precious spirit-children whom God has entrusted to their care. [75]

PHILIPPIANS

Profile

Sent from: Paul, at Rome, joined by Timothy.
Sent to: Members at Philippi, in northern Greece, "with the bishops and deacons."
Date: About A.D. 62.
Purpose: To thank the Philippians for help and to encourage them to perfect their lives.
Main themes: Christ and obedience; progressive salvation.

Background

The City

Philippi was named for its refounder Philip, the father of Alexander the Great, the world conqueror. But a different world conqueror came when Paul arrived with his small missionary group in obedience to the vision of the pleading man of Macedonia (Acts 16:9). They landed at Neapolis (modern Kaválla) and made their way over the coastal range to the interior plains flanked by spectacular mountains. From the high acropolis above the theater, one views Paul's city below, with the wide circumference of the periphery wall and small stream beyond, and a sea of fertile fields on the outside. The remodeled second-century city lies in crumbled splendor, with walls and gates and forum located where Paul walked earlier. Besides the road from the coast, the main east-west road ran through Philippi, which increased its economic and intellectual vitality. Communication and help to the apostle went out on these routes.

As one of the first missionaries, Luke sketched the place of first European preaching: "Philippi, a city of the first rank in that district of Macedonia, and a Roman colony" (Acts 16:12, NEB). Anthony and Augustus had defeated Julius Caesar's assassins at the battle of Philippi; afterward that "small settlement" was "enlarged" by immigration of rewarded veterans.[76] Later, Augustus eliminated Anthony, and many who lost their Italian lands were permitted to resettle in Philippi and other eastern cities.[77] This explains the social overtones when Paul was beaten for teaching "customs which are not lawful for us to receive, neither to observe, being Romans" (Acts 16:21). "Colony" was a technical term for Romans settled outside Rome. That Philippi was a colony implies that it had civic rights of Rome and the honor of modeling its local government after that of the mother city. The old Roman virtues were loyalty and reliability. These qualities certainly summarize the remarkable faithfulness of the Philippian Christians.

Church Members

Trusting in the Troas vision, Paul entered Philippi and found the devout women meeting at the place of prayer on the edge of the city. One of their number was a vital personality—Lydia, whom the Greek calls a "dealer in purple" (Acts 16:14, NEB), was from Roman Asia and probably had import contacts. She had a large enough house for four missionaries and the means to insist that they stay with her (Acts 16:15). She may be one source of assistance that Paul received from Philippi soon after and long after leaving. The other convert named in Acts is the Philippian jailor, baptized after the humility of despair when the earthquake deprived him of his prisoners. But this literal act of God was discerned by this man of faith, whose household joined the Church with him (Acts 16:33-34). The same was true of Lydia's household (Acts 16:15). Paul met with these members and others before leaving Philippi after his first visit (Acts 16:40).

When Paul wrote a dozen years later, the Philippian church was directed by the "bishops and deacons" (Philip. 1:1), suggesting that its growth had resulted in several household churches. Moreover, the quality of the members there rises above that of all other known branches. Paul's warm feelings are expressed at the beginning of the final chapter, where he calls the Philippians "my joy and crown" (Philip. 4:1), terms not used elsewhere. Appreciation to the strong women of that branch is evident as he asks for harmony between Euodia and Syntychē and mentions "those women which laboured with me in the gospel" (Philip. 4:3). They were to be assisted by Paul's "true yokefellow," who Clement of Alexandria thought was Paul's wife, temporarily staying in a trusted branch of the Church.[78] Another intriguing name follows, Clement, a trusted "fellowlaborer." Yet others merit that title, "and their names" are "in the book of life."[79] Here is another unique compliment to the Philippians. In fact, they are told that they "have always obeyed, not as in my presence only, but now much more in my absence" (Philip. 2:12). What other letter to a church made such a statement? Paul could not say anything like that to the Corinthians or Galatians, so the Philippians stand at the high end of the spectrum of faithfulness. What Paul would teach them is most revealing on the subject of how exaltation is obtained.

Reason for Writing

Paul and Silas left Philippi with the formal apology of the city fathers and fresh scars of their public beating. But Saints eternally blessed by the missionaries would not ignore their practical needs. Paul and his companions went seventy-five miles west to Thessalonica, where ugly opposition was stirring, and the Philippians filled Paul's needs there once and then sent help again (Philip. 4:16). After a riot in that place, persecution soon forced Paul to the new field of labor in southern Greece. He left three branches of the Church in northern Greece, which explains another compliment to the Philippians: "In the beginning of the gospel, when I departed from Macedonia, no church shared with me concerning giving and receiving but you only" (Philip. 4:15, NKJB). In this time Paul was at Corinth, laboring intensely at missionary work and earning bread by his trade. He preached the gospel to the Corinthians "freely"; "other churches" paid the cost of Corinthian service, for "that which was lacking to me the brethren which came from Macedonia supplied" (2 Cor. 11:7-9).

These references of aid at Corinth show that the Philippians were able to send messengers three hundred miles. They did the same thing when Paul was more than twice that distance in Rome. Of the prison epistles, Philippians has the clearest references to imprisonment at the empire's capital. Since it is fashionable to doubt that location, the two Philippians' references to Rome must be surveyed. First, the Saints "of Caesar's household" sent greetings (Philip. 4:22). Commentaries create a wrong impression by assuring readers that the imperial household extended throughout the empire. Any reigning Caesar directed a huge official staff, a civil service handling finances and resources. Outside Rome, the imperial establishment did not staff provincial political centers but collected some taxes and managed scattered business operations.[80] Greetings from provincial staff on a state property or from minor tax collectors would be vague and puzzling to the Philippians. Moreover, Philippians 1 makes the point that Paul's imprisonment had extended the gospel to prominent places. Since the imperial bureaucracy concentrated in Rome, a simple "Caesar's household" implies the center of the empire. In Josephus, for instance, Herod's son Antipater used the slave of Augustus' wife in a plot and was accused of "having corrupted the household of Caesar"—at Rome.[81] Again Philo tells how Herod's grandson Agrippa was made king and en route to Palestine visited Alexandria; there Agrippa was considered worthy of honor partly because he was "a member of Caesar's household."[82] This supposedly shows how "Caesar's household" could be used outside of Rome, but it proves the opposite, for Agrippa had just come from Rome, where he was fostered by the new emperor. In these first-century examples, Rome is strongly indicated when "Caesar's household" is used without modification.

The other Roman reference in Philippians is Paul's indication that his "bonds in Christ" were becoming known "in the whole *praetorium*" (Philip. 1:13, literal trans.). This Latin term was written in Greek form, which the apostle obviously expected to be clear without explanation. The King James Version uses "palace" because the New Testament uses the term of Pilate's headquarters and of the building in Caesarea where Paul was brought after the Jerusalem arrest. But as discussed at the beginning of this chapter, Acts describes no general missionary work during Paul's Palestinian arrest—perhaps he felt restrained because of Jewish hostility while imprisoned. So vitally expanding conversions do not fit the Palestinian buildings or situations. But custody at Rome was another mission, Luke says, for Paul taught the gospel "with complete freedom" (Acts 28:31, JB). That is the situation in Philippians 1, which fits the Roman imprisonment. Thus, "praetorium" in that setting could be the military barracks or more probably the praetorian guard stationed there. That is the common meaning of *praetorium* in historical writings and inscriptions of Paul's century.[83] So the gospel that Paul preached to visitors was heard by his Roman guards and began to spread through the ranks as it had also through Caesar's staff. Some Bible-bound scholars say that Paul could be imprisoned elsewhere than Rome because the praetorian troops were stationed in other major cities. But special personal missions aside, the imperial guard was stationed only at Rome to guard the emperor.[84]

Paul wrote to the Philippians near the end of his two-year imprisonment (Acts 28:30), for he had a specific expectation of release instead of general faith that it would happen: with the Lord's blessing he would "come shortly" (Philip. 2:24). This fits the time necessary for communications to go back and forth between Paul and the Philippians. After all their prior help, they had sent Epaphroditus to Rome with things to support the chained apostle (Philip. 4:18). Paul was grateful and recounted their relationship of more than a decade by sending thanks "for your fellowship in the gospel from the first day until now" (Philip. 1:5). Support for a messenger on the long journey to Rome probably took some organizing, which is evidently reflected in the opening recognition of the bishops and deacons, unprecedented in the other letters that have survived. With the letter Paul was sending back the messenger. Epaphroditus was appreciated as a "brother and fellow-laborer" (Philip. 2:25, literal trans.). This man had longed for his Philippian friends; he was discouraged at being sick but was also discouraged because word came back from Philippi that they knew he "had been sick" (Philip. 2:26). In fact, Epaphroditus had been critically ill, for Paul makes the point that this messenger risked his life to help Paul—"for the work of Christ he came close to death" (Philip. 2:30, NKJB). The devotion of Epaphroditus is a symbol of the solid faith and works of the Philippians. Far on the road of progression, they received a letter underlining how much diligence is required for the prize of exaltation with God.

Main Teachings

Christ and Obedience

The most faithful branch of the Early Church was not exempt from the warning of conditional salvation. They were commended and challenged, which is the key to the apostle's preaching of eternal exaltation. Whether discussed in Galatians, Hebrews, or Philippians, continued righteous living is required. Paul's theme verse has been dulled by the traditional "conversation," but literally reads: "Only let your conduct be worthy of the gospel of Christ, so that whether I come and see you or am absent, I may hear of your affairs, that you stand fast in one spirit, with one mind striving together for the faith of the gospel" (Philip. 1:27, NKJB). The watchwords to the faithful are the same as to those in danger of apostasy: "stand fast"—"live worthily." In the Sermon on the Mount, the Savior had given the same conditions for personal salvation, and Paul repeats several of those teachings. Jesus required bearing fruit (Matt. 7:15-20), which Paul explains as "the fruits of righteousness" (Philip. 1:11). Jesus gave a crucial comparison in opening his sermon: "Ye are the light of the world" (Matt. 5:14), which Paul applies to the Philippians, who "shine as lights in the world" (Philip. 2:15). Meaning what? Paul's compliment is based on Jesus' commandment: "Let your light so shine before men, that they may see your good works, and glorify your Father which is in heaven" (Matt. 5:16).

Religious people generally feel that good works are important. But those teaching a theology of grace see them as the natural result of grace and minimize the personal moral struggle. Yet what could be plainer than Paul's core message to these accomplished Saints? "Work out your salvation with fear and trembling" (Philip. 2:12). Philippians has several capsule sermons on grace and works, and this is one. Because human effort can be only partial, "fear and trembling" is trusting the Father's leadership and Christ's atonement in the midst of the confusing pressures of life. But because grace is also partial, the command is to do good works. Some vigorously deny this by quoting Paul's qualifying verse: "For it is God who works in you both to will and to do for his good pleasure" (Philip. 2:13, NKJB). Does this mean that God controls the righteous like robots, or does it mean that he powerfully motivates the humble? On this subject there is more wisdom in the following story than in many theological abstractions. A minister walked by a perspiring man pulling weeds; the minister commented, "That is a lovely garden that you and the Lord have." The gardener answered, "Yes, but you should have seen it when the Lord had it alone." This story is really an analogy of Paul's missionary work, of the Philippians' help to Paul, or of a modern Saint's faithfulness. God has given his marvelous physical and spiritual resources, but they lie dormant without man's positive actions. Christ would not have commanded works, nor would Paul have exhorted the Philippians to work out their salvation, unless these were central obligations with specific rewards attached to them.[85] Philippians teaches works for salvation. God has done his part through Christ, and individuals are expected to do their part.

Paul associated "working out" salvation with the fact that the Philippians had "always obeyed" (Philip. 2:12). Although believing in Christ is a form of obedience, Paul is asking seasoned believers to obey, which clearly refers to the high moral life commanded in every epistle he wrote. Paul is less specific in his letter to the Philippians than he is elsewhere because their lives show no glaring problems. He bluntly refutes false teachers and Judaizers, but in warning, not in correction (Philip. 3:1-3).[86] So the nature of obedience is clearer from an epistle like Romans. There the subject is righteous living after baptism; Paul commands not to "obey" sin (Rom. 6:12) and demands a choice between following "sin unto death, or of obedience unto righteousness" (Rom. 6:16). In Philippians, one of Paul's major teachings is to face trial and evil as courageously as Christ did. In Hebrews Paul also presents the Son of God as first perfected through obedience and then offering "eternal salvation unto all them that obey him" (Heb. 5:8-9). That is exactly Philippians' reasoning on the premortal and mortal Christ. Coming to earth among men, he was "obedient unto death, even the death of the cross" (Philip. 2:8). Then Paul follows that powerful picture with the command to continue in obedience like the Savior and work out salvation (Philip. 2:12). The disciple is to gain salvation just as his Savior brought about salvation. Jesus had grace and revelation, but he also had the responsibility of free choice, an independent power to act for good. If he was not a passive instrument, neither are those who follow him. For Paul makes him the strict model of obedience in his sacrifice, suffering, and consistent courage in facing every evil.

Thus, Paul taught that salvation is won only through sacrifice. In teaching that, he added a panorama of Christ and his mission—equaled only in Colossians 1 and Hebrews 1. In the premortal existence Christ was "in the form of God" (Philip 2:6). Yet service, not status, was his goal. Modern revelation throws precious light on Christ's attitude then. Satan remodeled the Father's plan for mortality and sought God's power, but Jesus offered to die as a Savior for mankind, saying, "Father, thy will be done, and the glory be thine forever" (Moses 4:1-3). This fits Paul's theme, for just before picturing Christ, the apostle stressed humility and true concern for others, asking an end to "strife or vainglory" (Philip. 2:3), the latter word literally meaning "empty honor." Satan sought this, but Paul teaches that Christ did not compete for reputation but sought to serve in humility. Thus, he literally "emptied himself" (Philip. 2:7, NKJB) or nullified his former status by coming to earth "in the likeness of men" (Philip. 2:7). Here is the magnificent picture of the Savior "made flesh" (John 1:14)—his glory was set aside and restored, but he had obtained his physical body.

Christ is still in the "form of God" (Philip 2:6) and the "form" and "likeness of men" (Philip. 2:7). Though he has returned to glory, mortals will be physically raised in his likeness. For a time after death, men and women will leave behind "the flesh" (Philip. 1:22-23). But at his coming the Lord "will transform our lowly body that it may be conformed to his glorious body, according to the working by which he is able even to subdue all things to himself" (Philip. 3:21, NKJB). Jesus once stood before stunned apostles and extended his arms and proved his physical existence by eating with them. He was observably in the form of men after his resurrection. And this resurrected body is the model for the resurrection of each individual. Since Christians believe that Christ is God, one of the members of the Godhead has a physical body. To avoid this fact, many ministers will claim that Christ took up his resurrected body to show his reality and then set it aside. And some will even deny the physicalness of his resurrection in spite of the apostles' sensory experiences. But Paul plainly teaches that Christ will come with "his glorious body" (Philip. 3:21), which means that Christ still has physical form, and that his physical form is like the Father's is shown in Philippians 2, Colossians 1, and Hebrews 1. Joseph Smith was not ashamed of the restored knowledge that man has God's outward form and his divine potential. Joseph Smith's visions clarify Paul's testimony of the physical image shared by the Father, Christ, and man. "If men do not comprehend the character of God they do not comprehend themselves"[87] was the modern prophet's challenge. He added with authority, "God himself who sits enthroned in yonder heavens is a man like unto one of yourselves."[88]

Progressive Salvation

"And this I pray, that your love may abound still more and more in knowledge and in all discernment, that you may approve the things that are excellent, that you may be sincere and without offense till the day of Christ" (Philip. 1:9-10, NKJB). Philippians has the same opening and closing subject—growth in the gospel. Already complimented on moral living, these Saints are told to improve in understanding and moral excellence. This was the gospel to the members, as written to Thessalonica a decade earlier (1 Thes. 3:12; 4:1). The purpose of the Church was clearly to build character, and the preaching of the gospel was to bring salvation (Rom. 1:16). Then are not character and salvation intimately related? This does not mean a gospel of perfectionism and guilt at slow growth. Philippians is a book of joy (Philip. 3:1; 4:4), encouraging faith to pray and to "not be anxious about anything" (Philip. 4:6, NIV). Yet confidence is not complacency here. Philippians does not know static salvation but continual development.

Salvation is the constant subject of Christian preaching, but traditional explanations of salvation are strangely sterile. Negative definitions are common because all people experience personal weakness, sin, and resulting self-doubt. One thoughtful Christian definition of salvation is "The gracious act of God whereby man is delivered from his sinful selfhood into newness and fullness of life."[89] Protestant and Catholic theology harmonize though differing on the means of sacraments as well as on belief. But the above definition is earth-bound, promising a better life but with great vagueness on its nature. And the definition is flawed on another serious issue—"the gracious act of God" implies a moment of forgiveness rather than the process that Paul preached. Joseph Smith also defined what a person was saved from, but in a setting of eternal progression: "Salvation means a man's being placed beyond the powers of all his enemies";[90] "When we have power to put all enemies under our feet in this world and a knowledge to triumph over all evil spirits in the world to come, then we are saved."[91] Many Christians claim to have salvation now. Have they victory over death? That is promised in the future. Is sin really overcome in their lives? If not, they have verbal salvation only.

Since Philippians teaches progressive salvation, one must also ask, "Progression to what?" Christian theology has stressed the passive enjoyment of God by those who are saved. Catholic theologians speak of the "beatific vision." Some talk of enjoying loved ones but declare that "happiness consists essentially in the immediate vision and love of God."[92] This picture of heaven does not include personal activity, only watching God's activity. And the traditional Protestant view emphasizes "blessed rest" and "blissful enjoyment of the Lord."[93] If that is the Christian future, there is no personal preparation to make. A simple believer here can be an intelligent spectator there. But the restored gospel adds that humans will share God's glory, power, and activity in eternity. Without displacing the Father or Christ, faithful Saints will share divine creation and leadership that traditional theology restricts to God. That potential future activity demands that training in integrity and leadership must start now.

Latter-day Saint theology teaches preparation here for competence hereafter in the same sense that a professional school teaches skills for helping others after graduation. Many a Christian has been dissatisfied with the traditional static view of heaven. One such was the vigorous Hebrew scholar who became president of the expanding University of Chicago. President William Rainey Harper spoke bluntly in a graduation exercise attended by Joseph F. Merrill, a Latter-day Saint scientist later called to the apostleship. Elder Merrill later said, "President Harper remarked that he did not want to go to the heaven pictured by some Christians, where he would sit with a crown on his head around the throne of grace. . . . 'I want to go,' he said, 'where I can continue my studies and my work.' To myself I said, 'Brother, you want to go to the Mormon heaven'—the one indicated by the doctrine of eternal progress."[94] Although Philippians says little about the activities of heaven, it requires a character achievement from the Saints that is far more profound than the view of "believe now and praise hereafter."

Paul compares gaining salvation to winning a race, one of his most revealing analogies. He uses an athletic theme in five letters and in one speech,[95] so its teaching of the importance of effort before the reward cannot be ignored. Outside of Philippians, the best example is the Corinthian challenge: "Do you not know that all those running a race run to get the prize? So run to take it. Each one competing uses self-control in everything—they indeed to get a perishable crown, but we an imperishable one. And so I now run, not aimlessly, and so I box, not as flailing the air. But I press my body and force it to serve, lest after preaching to others, I should be rejected" (1 Cor. 9:24-27, literal trans.).

Important Greek cities in which Paul preached held athletic contests. The Corinthians, for instance, were familiar with their great games at nearby Isthmia, which rivaled the games of Olympia and Delphi. The crowns at these panhellenic contests were of olive, laurel, pine, or wild celery.[96] So Paul stresses the necessary labor for a temporary honor that will dry and crumble. How much more valuable is exertion for an eternal reward? Does that come without effort? No, Paul answers. The athlete sacrifices comfort for the hard training before the race and then gives total energy during it. The analogy is clear—God furnishes the prize, but men and women must give their all to obtain it.

Philippians matches Paul's Corinthian challenge thought for thought. For the main subject is the necessary struggle for the Saints, whether epitomized in the phrase "work out your own salvation" or in the vivid comparison of running to obtain the crown. There is no honor in mere belief or in mere belonging. The apostle bares his soul as a totally dedicated person, achieving not because of faith alone but because of a divine partnership: "I can do all things through Christ, who gives me power" (Philip. 4:13, literal trans.). Sharing his feelings, Paul tells how grace operated in him. Looking back on his Jewish self-sufficiency (Philip. 3:5-6), he emphasizes that his own righteousness was not enough without "the righteousness which is of God by faith" (Philip. 3:9). This summarizes but does not explain Christian salvation. Cooperation between divine initiative and human agency is evenly balanced in the intense picture of Paul's race for exaltation: "Not as though I had already attained, either were already perfect: but I follow after, if that I may apprehend that for which also I am apprehended of Christ Jesus. Brethren, I count not myself to have apprehended: but this one thing I do, forgetting those things which are behind, and reaching forth unto those things which are before, I press toward the mark for the prize of the high calling of God in Christ Jesus" (Philip. 3:12-14.)

This is the personal version of the Corinthian challenge—the same comparison, the same striking word agreements, and the same straining for salvation. And salvation was not yet acquired by Paul. As Paul told the Corinthians, if he did not carefully control his life, he would not qualify for God's kingdom (1 Cor. 9:27). Though the apostle is charged with "the perfecting of the saints" (Eph. 4:12), he says bluntly that he is not yet perfect and that his salvation is not won. As in a race, the test is not in starting but in finishing. Eternal salvation is not obtained until the efforts for Christ are finished. And the required output is great, for who ever watched a leisurely race? "Race" in Paul's Corinthian challenge is *stádion*, the 200-yard contest of the length of the "stadium," sometimes doubled to 400. Such short distances demand a fast pace. An ancient observer, Lucian of Samosata, gives the image: "The good runner, from the moment the barrier falls, simply makes the best of his way; his thoughts are on the finish line, his hopes of victory in his feet; he leaves his neighbor alone and does not concern himself at all with his competitors."[97] Paul might have written this, for Corinthians and Philippians carry the message of competition with self, of reaching all-out for the real goal of life, exaltation in God's kingdom.

Saved by grace? Yes, but only if the disciple gives as much for Christ as Christ gave for him. The great result takes the total cooperation of the Lord and of his son or daughter. In the above King James translation, "apprehend" describes this partnership not of grace alone or works alone. "Apprehend" means to grasp or to lay hold of, translating the same Greek word used for taking the prize in 1 Corinthians 9:24. In Philippians, Paul is dashing at full speed to reach salvation, the purpose for which Christ reached to him: "I press on to take hold of that for which Christ Jesus took hold of me" (Philip. 3:12, NIV). Here is Paul's insight on the relationship of his first belief to his life afterward. This mature passage focuses on the sequence of grace, which came first, with the response of a lifetime of activity. Grace is not even discussed in Philippians. Paul did not teach "push-button salvation," getting glory in one move. Even Paul was pursuing perfection, so grace is a call to grow. If the offer of that opportunity is not met by growth, grace is robbed of its result. Every Saint has the choice to respond in daily life, the agency of action.

And what does God expect after sincere belief and baptism? The roots of Philippians are in the Sermon on the Mount and its searching questions are on the full frontiers of sexual morality, honesty, worship of God, and love of his children. After Joseph Smith outlined Latter-day Saint beliefs in twelve of the Articles of Faith, he reached to Philippians for the open-ended challenge of maturing in Christlike qualities. Paul asked the Philippians to consider deeply whatever things are "true, . . . honest, . . . just, . . . pure, . . . lovely, . . . of good report"—to seek "virtue" and whatever merits "praise" (Philip. 4:8). Such qualities glow in those committed to Christ in thought, word, act, habit, and character. These character ideals in Philippians are best explained by the voice of conscience. The King James translation of these traits is accurate, with only two words needing comment, "honest" and "virtue."

"Honest" in the King James Version has an obsolete meaning that still had some use in the time of Joseph Smith. The dictionary of his period gives one meaning as "decent, honorable, or suitable."[98] That is the meaning of Paul's adjective—to seek the conduct that moral people recognize as admirable and worth praising. What is true and pure and lovely includes the beautiful in art, music, and literature. But Paul stressed what is true and pure and lovely in personal conduct and human interrelationships. And this leads to "virtue," a word of unrecognized depth. Paul's "virtue" is the Greek *areté*; in early literature it referred to prowess on the battlefield. A word of skill in living, it refers to merit in the personal sense or, as in modern translations, to moral "excellence" (RSV, NIV). Paul is not talking of abstractions but of the devoted life that he had led for the Lord (Philip. 4:9). Joseph Smith underlined this truth by adding this thought to Paul's ideals: Latter-day Saints seek to be "benevolent" and to do "good to all men" (A of F 13). This kind of virtue is forged in fires of inspiration from God, producing self-control like pure steel, and a radiant awareness of others. Such virtue is both individual and social, for its product is service, not solitude.

Paul's final church letter closes with the evidence of the nearness of God. Jesus left the Twelve with the promise of a peace above anything that the world could offer (John 14:27). From his own experience the seasoned apostle promised the same: "the peace of God, which surpasses all understanding, will guard your hearts and minds through Christ Jesus" (Philip. 4:7, NKJB). This word for peace appears nearly a hundred times in the New Testament, about half of these times in Paul's writings. Not many lives had such conflicts as did Paul's; Paul knew few comforts, and eventually his life was taken. But peace was his constant companion, for it was one sure "fruit of the Spirit" (Gal. 5:22). Through the Holy Ghost, Paul consistently knew the rightness of his course and God's love for him. Paul found this peace by repentance, accepting the true Church and its ordinances, and using every opportunity thereafter to do what God commanded him. His words and his life combine to teach progressive salvation.

NOTES

1. For the language on two stones found and a photograph of one, see Jack Finegan, *The Archaeology of the New Testament: The Life of Jesus and the Beginning of the Early Church* (Princeton: Princeton University Press, 1969), pp. 119-20.

2. The King James "almost" of Acts 26:28-29 is a simple adjective used in a typical Greek prepositional phrase: *en olígō*. It means "short" or "small" and implies a noun: "in a short [time]." The standard lexicons give regular uses like this in the New Testament and in works of New Testament times.

3. Andrew F. Ehat and Lyndon W. Cook, *The Words of Joseph Smith* (Provo, Utah: Religious Studies Center, Brigham Young University, 1980), p. 237.

4. See Josephus, *Jewish War* 1:408-16; *Jewish Antiquities* 15:331-41 (Loeb Classical Library).

5. Seneca, *Epistles* 77:1-3 (Loeb Classical Library).

6. Pliny the Elder, *Natural History* 3.5.66-67 (Loeb Classical Library).

7. Ignatius, Ephesians 1:3 (*Apostolic Fathers*, Loeb Classical Library).

8. M. I. Finley, "Slavery," *The Oxford Classical Dictionary*, 2d ed. (Oxford: Clarendon Press, 1970), p. 995.

9. Imperial edicts from the first and second centuries are cited in Naphtali Lewis and Meyer Reinhold, *Roman Civilization* (New York: Columbia University Press, 1955) 2:268-70.

10. Seneca, *Epistles* 47:3.

11. Ibid. 47:11 (Robin Campbell trans.).

12. Ibid. 47:20 (Loeb Classical Library).

13. Ulpian, *On the Edict 1*, cited in Justinian, *Digest* 11.4.1, cited in Thomas Wiedemann, *Greek and Roman Slavery* (Baltimore: Johns Hopkins University Press, 1981), p. 190.

14. Pliny the Younger, *Letters* 9:21 (Betty Radice trans.). The runaway in this case was a freed slave with a continuing relationship with his old master.

15. John Edwin Sandys, *Companion to Latin Studies*, 3d ed. (New York: Hafner Publishing Co., 1968), p. 365.

16. Xenophon, *Persian Anabasis* 1.2.6 (Loeb Classical Library). Compare the earlier Herodotus, *Persian Wars* 7.30, which comments on the size of Colossae and its situation on the Lycus River.

17. Strabo, *Geography* 12.8.16 (Loeb Classical Library).

18. Ibid.

19. For a translation from existing Latin copies, see Edgar Hennecke, *New Testament Apocrypha*, ed. Wilhelm Schneemelcher, trans. R. McL. Wilson (Philadelphia: Westminster Press, 1965) 2:131-32.

20. Some have thought that Ephesians was this letter under a different name, but the burning issue of false doctrine about Christ is not discussed directly there. The letters to the Corin-

thians and Galatians show that Paul wrote specific refutations to the problems in specific locations.

21. Knopf-Krüger, cited in New Testament Apocrypha, p. 129. Compare the opinion of Erasmus: "No argument against a Pauline authorship can be stronger than the epistle itself." Cited in D. Edmond Hiebert, Introduction to the New Testament (Chicago: Moody Press, 1977) 2:230.

22. Hubert Jedin, Ecumenical Councils of the Catholic Church, trans. Ernest Graf (Freiburg: Herder, 1960), p. 13.

23. For the original creed of the Nicene Council, different from the later "Nicene Creed," see Henry R. Percival, The Seven Ecumenical Councils, Select Library of Nicene and Post-Nicene Fathers (Grand Rapids, Mich.: Eerdmans Publishing Co., n.d.) 14:3. The Father and Son were defined as the "same" in "reality," or "being," or "essence" (homooúsion)—this is normally translated "of one substance."

24. John H. Leith, Creeds of the Churches (Atlanta: John Knox Press, 1973), p. 67.

25. Ibid., p. 354. For the similar Church of England model, see ibid., pp. 266-67.

26. Ehat and Cook, p. 378, abbreviations expanded.

27. Donald Guthrie, "Colossians," in D. Guthrie et al., The New Bible Commentary, Revised (Grand Rapids, Mich.: Eerdmans Publishing Co., 1970), p. 1143.

28. John A. Hardon, Modern Catholic Dictionary (Garden City, N.Y.: Doubleday, 1980), p. 29 ("Anthropomorphism").

29. Alan Richardson, Dictionary of Christian Theology (Philadelphia: Westminster Press, 1969), p. 11 ("Anthropomorphism").

30. Milton V. Backman, Jr., American Religions and the Rise of Mormonism (Salt Lake City: Deseret Book Co., 1970), p. 479.

31. Ehat and Cook, p. 60.

32. See Richard Lloyd Anderson, "Clement, Ignatius, and Polycarp," Ensign (Aug. 1976), p. 53.

33. Several translators have used "elemental spirits" instead of "basic principles" in this passage. In Hebrews 5:12 the latter meaning is clear, and the former meaning is purely speculative in Paul's writing. The Greek term means "elemental spirits" in mystic and astrological writings, which Paul's writings are not.

34. "Tender mercies" is literally "inner feelings of mercy." The King James Version's obsolete use of "bowels" is discussed under the background of Philemon.

35. Strabo, Geography 12.8.15.

36. Pliny the Elder, Natural History 36.95

37. Henry Clarence Thiessen, Introduction to the New Testament (Grand Rapids, Mich.: Eerdmans Publishing Co., 1954), p. 239.

38. Frederick G. Kenyon, ed., Chester Beatty Biblical Papyri, Fasciculus III Supplement, Pauline Epistles, Plates (London: Emery Walker, Ltd., 1937), f. 75. r. (Ephesians 1:1-11).

39. D. Edmond Hiebert, An Introduction to the New Testament, vol. 2, The Pauline Epistles (Chicago: Moody Press, 1977), p. 267.

40. E. K. Simpson in E. K. Simpson and F. F. Bruce, Commentary on the Epistles to the Ephesians and the Colossians (Grand Rapids, Mich.: Eerdmans Publishing Co., 1965), p. 25.

41. Since "predestination" is used heavily as a Calvinistic term, "foreordination" is theologically more neutral. Even though the two terms are similarly constructed and used interchangeably in dictionaries, eternal planning with conditional agency is meant when Latter-day Saints use the term "foreordination."

42. Robert Browning, "Cristina," in Bells and Pomegranates, The Complete Poetic and Dramatic Works of Robert Browning (Cambridge, Mass.: Houghton Mifflin Co., 1895), p. 170.

43. One powerful term in Ephesians 1:12 has not been discussed, *prohelpízō*, which means "first trusted," its usual translation, or "trusted beforehand," which would be a far more consistent rendering in the context of several other terms of the premortal existence. Paul talks of a stage of original hope (Eph. 1:12) and a following stage of conversion (Eph. 1:13). If both stages belong to the same persons, this repeats the Romans 8:29-30 sequence of being foreknown, then foreordained, and then converted. Most interpreters and translators avoid this by making those converted different from those who first hoped. Thus, they assume that Old Testament Judaism or New Testament Jewish converts first hoped and that then Gentiles were also converted. But that is not the argument of Ephesians 1, which starts with the sweeping statement that all Christians were chosen "before the foundation of the world"; thus, the "we" first trusting in Christ is all-inclusive (Eph. 1:12), of which the "you," the Ephesians converts, are a part (Eph. 1:13). Thus, the Ephesian converts trusted in their salvation before this earth and then came to the earth to accept the gospel.

44. Justin Martyr, *Dialogue with Trypho* (Ante-Nicene Fathers) 1:198 (ch. 6).

45. Johannes Quasten, *Patrology* (Westminster, Md.: Newman Press, 1962) 1:53.

46. 2 Clement 14:1-2 (*Apostolic Fathers*, Loeb Classical Library).

47. See Quasten, 1:56 on the passage just quoted: "The author shows here that he was greatly influenced by St. Paul's line of thought, particularly by the latter's Epistle to the Ephesians (1, 4, 22; 5, 23, 32), for he calls the Church the mystical body of Christ and represents her as his bride."

48. I. Howard Marshall, *The Acts of the Apostles* (Grand Rapids, Mich.: Eerdmans Publishing Co., 1980), p. 93.

49. William F. Arndt et al., *Greek-English Lexicon of the New Testament*, 2d ed. (Chicago: University of Chicago Press, 1979), p. 530.

50. Many studies of the Dead Sea Scrolls show a strikingly similar use there: "In the Qumran texts the 'mysteries' are particularly those of creation and God's eschatological time-table." Karl Georg Kuhn, "The Epistle to the Ephesians in the Light of the Qumran Texts," in Jerome Murphy-O'Connor, *Paul and Qumran* (Chicago: Priory Press, 1968), p. 119.

51. Josephus, *Jewish Antiquities* 2:89. Thackery translates *oikonomiá* as "the administration of this office."

52. Recent translators have relied on "arrangement" as a business term in papyri, but they have failed to relate it to the basic concept of authorization, from which it came. The key passages for Paul's usage are the two just discussed plus 1 Cor. 9:17. Here Paul's "dispensation" is personally given to him, which is the root concept of delegation of the word. Some modern versions produce the strange result of translating *oikonomía* as "management" and "stewardship" in Luke 16:2-4, as "administration," "commission," "stewardship," and "divine office" in Paul's letters generally, but arbitrarily selecting "plan" for Eph. 1:9-10 alone.

53. Quintilian 6.1.1 (Loeb Classical Library). The Greek word in the quotation is the noun of Paul's Greek term. It is the exact equivalent of the Latin form "recapitulation," the prefix (*aná*) meaning "back" or "again" and the balance of the word meaning "summary," coming from the Greek "head."

54. Ibid., 6.1.2

55. Ehat and Cook, p. 79.

56. Ibid., p. 39.

57. Without any attempt at collection, this author has a dozen tracts in his possession that all end with the quoted sentence.

58. A few translations approach literalness here: "Throughout all generations, forever and ever" (NIV). The Greek reads, *eis pásas tàs geneàs toû aiōnos tôn aiōnōn*.

59. This verb appears one other time in the New Testament, as Paul stresses the premortal calling of the faithful: "That he might make known the riches of his glory on the vessels of mercy,

which he had prepared beforehand for glory" (Rom. 9:23, NKJB). Traditional interpretation here favors God selecting the elect before their existence, but Paul does not say that God prepared for the elect, but that he prepared them, which strictly assumes their existence. Modern revelation strongly teaches that worthiness is the basis of either premortal or mortal selection for blessings.

60. See the Muratorian Canon, second century in origin: "But Hermas composed the Shepherd quite recently in our times in the city of Rome, while his brother, Pius, the bishop, occupied the seat of the city of Rome." Cited in Daniel J. Theron, *Evidence of Tradition* (Grand Rapids, Mich.: Baker Book House, 1958), p. 113. Pius's death is estimated to have been about A.D. 150.

61. At the end of vision 2, Hermas mentions Clement—probably Clement, bishop of Rome, whose letter in the Apostolic Fathers collection is dated about A.D. 96. This means that at least the earlier portions of Hermas were written at that time.

62. The Shepherd of Hermas, vision 2.4.1 (*Apostolic Fathers*, Loeb Classical Library).

63. Ibid., vision 1.1.6. Compare vision 2.4.2., speaking of the Church: "For her sake was the world established."

64. Ibid., vision 1.3.4. Kirsopp Lake's Loeb edition is the source for the literal "forethought" (*prónoia*) of the translation; in all significant parts Lake agrees with the quoted translation, which is followed for its exactness. Graydon F. Snyder, *The Shepherd of Hermas, The Apostolic Fathers,* ed. Robert M. Grant (Camden, N.J.: Thomas Nelson and Sons, 1968) 6:33.

65. Hiebert, p. 269.

66. R. M. C. Jeffery, "Ecumenical, Ecumenical Movement, Ecumenism," in Richardson, p. 107.

67. The Acts episode and Josephus's description of the wall appear in the opening pages of this chapter.

68. E. K. Simpson in Simpson and Bruce, p. 94. The traditional position of prophecy limited to the past is verbally modified by many liberalizing writers, but there is a difference between those anciently called by actual revelation and those enthusiastic leaders only rhetorically referred to as prophets or apostles.

69. Paul also refers to the large amount of unwritten instruction in other letters. After brief corrections on the sacrament of the Lord's Supper, Paul adds, "The rest will I set in order when I come" (1 Cor. 11:34), which supplements other references of what Paul had already taught that was not written (1 Cor. 11:2; 15:1-2). Paul did not need to repeat to Timothy the "words which you have heard from me" (2 Tim. 1:13, NKJB: Compare 2:2).

70. "The Chicago Call: An Appeal to Evangelicals," issued by forty Christian opinion leaders, mostly midwest theological schoolteachers, in *Christianity Today,* June 17, 1977, p. 29.

71. Ehat and Cook, p. 6.

72. Philip Schaff, *The Creeds of Christendom* (New York: Harper and Brothers, 1919) 1:908.

73. *Journal of Discourses* 8:33 (1860 speech).

74. Joseph Smith taught that leading priesthood assignments were given in the premortal existence, which logically also involves leading female assignments (Ehat and Cook, p. 367). See President Spencer W. Kimball, Women's Fireside Address, Sept. 15, 1979, *Ensign,* Nov. 1979, p. 102: "Remember, in the world before we came here, faithful women were given certain assignments while faithful men were foreordained to certain priesthood tasks. While we do not now remember the particulars, this does not alter the glorious reality of what we once agreed to. You are accountable for those things which long ago were expected of you just as are those we sustain as prophets and apostles."

75. President Spencer W. Kimball, *Men of Example* (Salt Lake City: Church Educational System, 1976), pp. 9-10.

76. Strabo, *Geography* 7:41.

77. Dio Cassius, *Roman History* 51.4.6.

78. Cited above, ch. 5, n. 5.

79. For background, see "Book of Life" in the Bible Dictionary of the Latter-day Saint edition of the King James Version of the Bible (Salt Lake City: The Church of Jesus Christ of Latter-day Saints, 1979).

80. For a survey of operations of the imperial staff of slaves and freedmen, see P. R. C. Weaver, *Familia Caesaris* (Cambridge: University Press, 1972), pp. 6-8.

81. Josephus, *Jewish Antiquities* 17:142.

82. Philo, *Against Flaccus* 35 (Loeb Classical Library). Compare ibid. 23 for mention of the "Augustan House" in the sense of the Julio-Claudian emperors at Rome.

83. See Charlton T. Lewis and Charles Short, *A Latin Dictionary* (Oxford: Clarendon Press, 1955), p. 1436, "praetorium," meaning II. Compare the inscriptions under *praitōrion* in Moulton and Milligan, p. 533, and in Hugh J. Mason, *Greek Terms for Roman Institutions, American Studies in Papyrology* (Toronto: Hakkert, 1974) 13:78.

84. The Roman origin of Philippians is established by "Caesar's household" (Phil. 4:22) and the Acts-Philippians agreements in Paul's preaching. Then the meaning of *praetorium* becomes clear (Phil. 1:13). But there is a trend among current writers to surrender to the rhetoric of a supposed Ephesian imprisonment on the third journey, during which Paul penned Philippians. But such an imprisonment is a theory, not founded on a single historical reference in Acts or in the letters. Paul's use of *praetorium* goes heavily against that theory: if it means "praetorian guard," that was stationed at Rome, as discussed; if it means "governor's residence," it has not been proved that the governor sat at Ephesus, which was apparently the economic center of the province, not necessarily the political capital.

85. This issue is verbally sidestepped by the claim of some scholars that "salvation" here means that the Philippians were to work to make their church healthy or sound. But Paul never uses "salvation" of an earthly condition in the twenty-one times that it appears in his letters.

86. In identifying the Judaizers Paul uses a play on words. The faithful are the true circumcision, a term meaning literally to be "cut around" (*peritomē*) But those perverting the gospel are the "concision," an obscure English word adapting the Greek *katatomē*) meaning a cutting downward, an incision, sarcastically suggesting mutilation.

87. Ehat and Cook, p. 340.

88. Ehat and Cook, p. 349.

89. Roger Hazelton, "Salvation," in Marvin Halvertson and Arthur A. Cohen, *Handbook of Christian Theology* (Cleveland: World Publishing Co., 1966), p. 336.

90. Ehat and Cook, p. 202.

91. Ehat and Cook, p. 200.

92. Hardon, p. 244.

93. J. A. Motyer, "The Final State: Heaven and Hell," in Carl F. H. Henry, *Basic Christian Doctrines* (New York: Holt, Rinehart and Winston, 1962), p. 295.

94. Joseph F. Merrill, *The Truth Seeker and Mormonism; A Series of Radio Addresses* (Independence, Mo.: Zion's Printing and Publishing Co., 1946), p. 51.

95. See Gal. 2:2; Eph. 6:12; 1 Tim. 6:12; 2 Tim. 2:5; 2 Tim. 4:7; Heb. 12:1; Acts 20:24.

96. Pausanias, *Description of Greece* 8.48.2 (Loeb Classical Library). This second-century traveler added, "At most games, however, is given a crown of palm, and at all a palm is placed in the right hand of the victor." Compare Paul's contemporary Vitruvius, *On Architecture* 91, who pictures the victors at the national festivals, including Isthmia, as standing "with palm and crown."

97. Lucian, *Slander* 12, in H. W. Fowler and F. G. Fowler, *The Works of Lucian of Samosata* (Oxford: Clarendon Press, 1905), p. 6. That translation is modified by replacing "winning post" with "finish line" for *térma*.

98. Noah Webster, *An American Dictionary of the English Language* (New York: S. Converse, 1828), "honest."

8

Letters to Leaders

Paul's last known letters were sent to his trusted assistants Timothy and Titus. They blend in speaking about common problems in the Church and in Church leadership. They are normally called the Pastoral Letters because Timothy and Titus are often pictured as bishops. As discussed with Ephesians 4, *pastor* means *shepherd* and strongly suggests the bishop, the direct leader of a flock. Although Bible annotations ending 2 Timothy and Titus call these men bishops, unknown scribes gave these opinions long after the apostolic age. Timothy and Titus were not bishops because Paul left them to choose bishops and to direct Church affairs in a region. But bishops of the Early Church supervised cities and towns. So Timothy and Titus stood between general and local authorities. They might be what Latter-day Saints have called assistants to the Twelve, regional representatives, stake presidents, or mission presidents. The Pastoral Letters are like Philippians in the sense that Paul felt confident in the faith of those to whom he wrote. But the Pastorals go beyond any public letter to reveal personal convictions and counsel of the great apostle.

The end of Acts is the close of a consecutive narrative in Paul's life. But Luke abruptly stops without a hint that Paul's work was then finished. Earlier, Festus heard Paul and sent him to Rome with no charge of legal wrongdoing (Acts 26:31-32). Then the Pastoral Letters mention Paul's visits to Asia Minor, Greece, and Crete that are clearly late in his life. They show that he was released and had some Mediterranean ministry before the final

grim imprisonment described in 2 Timothy. So these letters continue the book of Acts. The introduction of 2 Timothy will discuss how Paul died as a result of the fire of Rome and of Nero's accusation of the Christians afterward. The fire was the summer of
A.D. 64, and waves of investigation and execution followed. The
earliest sources say simply that Paul died under Nero, which could
be as late as A.D. 68. Appendix A shows that Paul's imprisonment
in Acts ended about the spring of A.D. 63, which gives from one
to five years for the events mentioned in the Pastoral Letters.

Thus, the closing years of Paul's life are illuminated in these
letters, though many scholars disbelieve what they see. Some
claim that the administrative regularity in the Pastorals must
come from a later age. But does the evolution of administration take decades? The Latter-day Saints began in 1830 with a
handful of members governed by two presiding elders and a few
unassigned elders and members of the lesser priesthood. But only
a dozen years later a sophisticated organization met the needs of
thousands of members in many lands. Bishops, elders, and
deacons are mentioned in the Pastoral Letters, officers clearly present long before that, as indicated in the chart accompanying the
discussion of Ephesians 4. Paul left his first Gentile converts with
presiding elders on the first mission (Acts 14:23). Should scholars'
preconceptions modify the Pastoral documents? Good history
arises when documents correct preconceptions. The Pastorals
give details about local organization not found in Paul's letters to
branches, for Timothy and Titus were assigned local supervision.

A related issue divides Pastoral students along the same lines.
These final letters refer to false teachers who are strikingly like the
Gnostics of the second century. These pseudo-Christians quite
generally sought salvation by mystic knowledge of the ultimate divinities behind the Old Testament Creator. Many detested the
Creation because it formed matter, and many sought to explain
away the Resurrection for the same anti-physical biases. Because
the Pastoral false teachers resemble second-century Gnostics,
some scholars insist on post-Pauline dating. But this is unnecessary. As already seen, Colossians (about A.D. 61) refutes a heresy

like Gnosticism. And John's letters (about A.D. 100) do the same (1 Jn. 4:1-3). History is the study of causation and sequence, and many a "first" is later outflanked by the discovery of the same thing earlier. Those who denied the physicalness of Christ were strong when John wrote after A.D. 96. A similar philosophy could have existed when Paul wrote thirty years earlier, particularly in light of the early "Colossian heresy."

The Pastoral Letters are vigorously challenged on the basis of vocabulary and style. But the greater the man, the greater his possibilities of creative expression. One example will illustrate the objections and answers. The Pastorals have about 175 words not used elsewhere in the New Testament. But that figure will be deflated by looking at this list, which includes many common Greek words that Paul would inevitably use in discussing religious and moral issues.[1] Moreover, many of these 175 unique words are simply different forms of words already used by the apostle. For instance, Paul regularly uses "otherwise" and also the common word "to teach"; 1 Tim. 6:3 combines these forms into a verb "to teach otherwise." Should that really be considered a unique word in the Pastorals? Subtraction of such related words lowers the percentage of variance to be more in line with other letters. Yet one would expect the general letters to the churches to differ from those to priesthood leaders. Style generally follows content, time of writing, and the moods and needs of both writer and reader. In the Pastorals we see Paul writing in his maturity, with details about the special subjects of apostasy and Church government, without the urgency of reconverting or correcting members, and more openly sharing his personal thoughts with associates. A varied vocabulary would naturally follow such different circumstances.

Some scholars prefer to build skyscrapers on stylistic sand. By subjective judgment they define what Paul could have written, break letters into supposed originals, identify interpolations, and demote documents to anonymity in spite of ancient inclusion in the works of an identified author. Before the knife of such "knowledge" is applied to the Pastorals, consistency demands that they be judged by the standard applied to other books. The debate on style can exist only because Paul's authentic letters are identified by early information. Paul's unchallenged letters are validated by examining the quotations from the second century and by examining the manuscript collections and references thereafter. And the Pastorals pass this test. Since Paul's first letter to Timothy was written to Ephesus, its first certain quotation comes appropriately from the neighboring bishop of Smyrna about A.D. 110.[2] Writing to the Philippians, he deliberately features quotations from Paul in order to motivate them to follow their founder.

Polycarp himself describes his method near the beginning of his letter, an early glimpse of "standard works": "Paul . . . wrote letters to you, from the study of which you will be able to build yourselves up into the faith given you."[3] A phrase from Galatians immediately follows, and the two next quotations are from 1 Timothy:

But the beginning of all iniquities is love of money (Polycarp 4:1, literal trans.).	For the root of all evils is the love of money (1 Tim. 6:10, literal trans.).
We brought nothing into the world, but we do not have anything to take away (Polycarp 4:1, literal trans.).	For we brought nothing into the world, and it is certain that we are not able to take anything away (1 Tim. 6:7, literal trans.).

Because Polycarp surveys Paul through short snippets, the above use of 1 Timothy is clear. Other Pastoral references are probable, though shorter. As a young man, this early bishop of Smyrna had personally known John, but nevertheless emphasized Paul's teachings because of the apostle's relationship with the Philippians.

The most important early document about New Testament books dates about sixty years after Polycarp. It is a list of scriptures accepted by the second-century Church, written in rough Latin. Called after its discoverer, the Muratorian Fragment begins in the middle of a discussion of the Gospels and afterward names Paul's authentic letters, separating them into the categories of those

written to churches and those written to individuals: "One to
Philemon and one to Titus, but two to Timothy for the sake of affection and love."[4] Thus, the external evidence for the Pastorals is
basically the same as that for Romans and Galatians.[5] Indeed, the
argument of style could be made against those books for departing
from the norm of the Corinthian letters by overemphasizing
grace. But within the treasure of Paul's letters there is much variety of mood and of emphasis. The strength of these letters to leaders is their special insight into Christian living and practical
Church government, as well as their intense themes of authority
against the threat of false teachers. Their pages are bright leaves
from the autumn of the Church, which stood full before the imminent winter of apostasy.

1 TIMOTHY

Profile

Sent from: Paul, possibly in or near Greece.
Sent to: Timothy, directing the Church in the area of
Ephesus.
Date: Probably between A.D. 63 and 66.
Purpose: To instruct Timothy in appointing bishops
and supervising his region of the Church.
Main themes: False teachers; priesthood offices; earthly and
eternal welfare.

Background

Timothy

Timothy may have been about eighteen when Paul revisited
the Galatian churches and added him to the missionary group on
its way west to Greek lands. Perhaps Paul earlier converted his
family on the first mission as he visited Lystra, Timothy's home
(Acts 16:1). Did they help after Paul's stoning? Did they ignore

threats when Paul revisited their branch and preached about the test of opposition? (Acts 14:22.) Whenever he was baptized, Timothy was well respected by the priesthood leaders in the area when Paul added him to the second mission (Acts 16:2). Nothing is known of Timothy's father beyond his being Greek. But Paul remembered Timothy's first "sincere faith" (2 Tim. 1:5, RSV), which he received from his grandmother Lois and his mother Eunice (2 Tim. 1:5). His mother was Jewish and an early convert (Acts 16:1). Thus, Paul protected him against Jewish hostility by having him circumcised (Acts 16:3). "Honoring God" is a free translation of Timothy's name, which no doubt expressed the devotion of his parents. He clearly grew through spiritual as well as physical nourishment. The King James "from a child" is probably not strong enough; Paul says literally, "From infancy you have known the holy scriptures" (2 Tim. 3:15, NIV).

So the fire of faith passed through Jewish generations to the young man who would serve under an apostle called to declare the Messiah to the Gentiles. Paul could not do his work without delegation and assignment. And no one was more constantly used and trusted than Timothy, whom he called his "true child in the faith" (1 Tim. 1:2, RSV) or his "beloved child" (2 Tim. 1:2, RSV). Paul also used these affectionate phrases earlier when he sent his trusted Timothy to settle troubles at Corinth: "I sent to you Timothy, my beloved and faithful child in the Lord, to remind you of my ways in Christ, as I teach them everywhere in every church" (1 Cor. 4:17, RSV). Paul warned the Corinthians not to despise Timothy, but this is less an evidence of Timothy's tentativeness than of their strong opposition to all priesthood authority (1 Cor. 16:10-11). Timothy's worth is proved by his continued labors with Paul, for Timothy's history is virtually the history of Paul's missions. Paul added Timothy's name to the opening of seven letters and mentioned his trustworthiness in two others. Paul had many powerful companions, but not one continued to be closer to him.

Timothy had served in missionary work and in building the branches over a dozen years when Paul sent him to Ephesus to preside over that region (1 Tim. 1:3). Then he was probably in his early thirties, and Paul counseled him to speak with authority: "Let no one despise your youth" (1 Tim. 4:12, NKJB). The issue here is not some supposed bashfulness of this experienced associate, whose vigor is written in thousands of missionary miles. He was assigned by an apostle called directly by God. The problem was that rebellious teachers openly challenged the true priesthood, beginning the era of evil that 2 Thessalonians 2 describes. But Paul told Timothy that he had the power and ability to fill his calling—that if he would not fail, the Lord would not fail him. In the Pastoral Letters, Paul twice refers to Timothy's blessings by the laying on of hands. Perhaps Paul had also set him apart to the regional authority over Asia Minor, for he referred to the inspired promises that Timothy could depend upon: "I set this commandment before you, child Timothy, according to the earlier prophecies upon you, so that through them you might carry on the good warfare" (1 Tim. 1:18, literal trans.).

Reason for Writing

Paul had arrived in Rome in the spring and was imprisoned two years, with a probable release at the beginning of the travel season of A.D. 63 (Acts 28:30-31). The angel's prophecy said he would stand "before Caesar" (Acts 27:24), which he apparently did before leaving Rome. Why didn't Luke write the rest of the story? The best explanation for breaking off writing is that he was too busy making history to write it. This missionary-recorder must have been involved in the labors of the final years. After joining in greetings at the end of Colossians and Philemon, Luke does not appear again until the painful notice that he is the only one present to support Paul in his final crisis (2 Tim. 4:11). Christians high and low were then being executed. If Luke did record the last years, his work probably perished with him in the brutal events surrounding 2 Timothy. So the Pastoral Letters stand alone in this closing era.

What came of Paul's intent to visit Spain? He told the Roman Saints that he would see them "whenever I travel to Spain" (Rom.

15:24, literal trans.). But during his intervening imprisonment he planned to visit Philemon (Philem. 1:22) and also the Philippians. In the latter case, events would permit him to see them "shortly" (Philip. 2:24) and even before that to send Timothy "shortly unto you" (Philip. 2:19). These plans just before an intended release would logically be carried out before any visit to Spain. So 1 Timothy and Titus could come from an Aegean visit right after release or from a later visit after traveling to Spain. If the latter happened, it would have been a major mission, filling considerable time before the final arrest documented in 2 Timothy. Writing about A.D. 96, Clement of Rome said that Paul had reached the "boundaries" or "limits of the west," a phrase far more appropriate for Spain than for Rome.[6] The early Muratorian Fragment also says that Paul visited Spain, though its source of information is debated.[7] There is no certain evidence, though the fourth-century historian Eusebius hints at early sources beyond the Roman imprisonment of Acts: "Having, therefore, made his defence at that time, it is recorded that the apostle again journeyed on the ministry of preaching, and, having set foot for the second time in the same city, was perfected in his martyrdom."[8]

Paul's concern for reliable bishops suggests his purpose in writing. The earliest post-apostolic letters picture the bishop as the critical leader in the fight against apostasy. Paul said that he had excommunicated two who apparently spoke against the constituted authorities, "whom I have delivered unto Satan, that they may learn not to blaspheme" (1 Tim. 1:20). Paul told Timothy to remain at Ephesus; the apostle was on his way to Macedonia, perhaps to visit the Philippian branch again (1 Tim. 1:3).[9] He had assigned Timothy "so you may command certain people not to teach different doctrines" (1 Tim. 1:3, literal trans.). Thus, true priesthood is linked with true doctrine. In these critical needs Paul not only instructed but planned to return "shortly" to throw his strength into the battle (1 Tim. 3:14). There is an urgency in 1 Timothy from the opening warning about rebuking false teachers to the closing language of command. "O Timothy, guard what has been entrusted to you" (1 Tim. 6:20, RSV) is spoken in sober warning against those reforming the revealed gospel.

Main Teachings

False Teachers

Paul does not dignify the counterfeit leaders with detailed refutation. His labels build a significant picture, however, with certain criticisms throwing a solid shadow of the false beliefs. At first glance, Paul's criticisms seem directed at scattered untruths, but the errors link into an integrated philosophy that choked the Christian Church at the close of the apostolic era. The opening and closing of 1 Timothy use the same word for those who have literally "missed the goal" or "swerved from" the faith (1 Tim. 1:6; 6:21). They are opposing the gospel with what the King James Version calls "science falsely so called" (6:20). But this "science" is the only time the King James Version translates the Greek *gnôsis* as anything but "knowledge" in over two dozen appearances. Although "science" means "knowledge" in Latin, the translation is unfortunate. Here and in related passages Paul speaks of false religious knowledge rather than of any science-religion conflict, for there is little evidence of such a conflict elsewhere in the New Testament.

Paul's phrase is "falsely-named knowledge," an early slogan in the fight against apostasy. The first post-apostolic historian was Hegesippus, a second-century Jewish Christian who wrote five books on the Church and on heresies. Significant extracts from his books exist in the fourth-century history of Eusebius. Hegesippus reported a whirlwind of false teachers when the apostles' deaths created a vacuum in leadership, a parallel to the Book of Mormon picture of no further apostles because of the wickedness of the people (4 Ne.; Morm. 1). Hegesippus said that these false teachers preached a substitute gospel, which he called "falsely-named knowledge," the identical phrase of 1 Timothy 6:20.[10] As a whole, the second-century heretics are called "Gnostics," from *gnôsis,* the Greek term meaning "knowledge." Their ancient critics described many sects, with endless theories and strange galaxies of divine beings. Like many sects that have broken from the Church today, the Gnostics generally claimed secret doctrines to add to the Church's public message. With recent discovery of Gnostic books, intense debate centers on when Gnosticism came into existence.

Paul accuses the false teachers of speculating about Judaism and of lacking logic. And Hegesippus describes the earliest Gnostics as Samaritans and Jews, significant because he had concentrated his investigations on early events in Palestine.[11] Two careful scholars commented on such Gnostic origins: "It is remarkable that Gnostic heresy entered Christian circles in Palestine through Jewish channels."[12] One of Hegesippus's Gnostic sects came from Simon Magus, the scheming convert of Samaria who opposed Peter in Acts 8. Simon and his first imitators were contemporaries of Peter and Paul. Moreover, another source supplements Hegesippus—Justin Martyr, born in Samaria at the beginning of the second century, had special local knowledge about Simon. He detailed the Samaritan background of Simon Magus, indicating that Simon's mistress was "the first 'thought' generated by him."[13] This concept marks Simon's theories as Gnostic, for most sects had elaborate systems of sub-divinities springing from the true God, their method of reducing the Old Testament Creator to a junior divinity who made a physical world by mistake.[14]

The Christian champion against Gnosticism in the late second century was Irenaeus, and his description of the system of Simon Magus may be based on an earlier lost work of the Samaritan Justin Martyr.[15] So Irenaeus must be taken seriously when he outlines Simon's blasphemous teachings:

1. Simon Magus was the true creator, who first generated "thought," supposedly incarnate in his mistress.

2. "Thought" migrated to lower space "and generated angels and powers, by whom . . . this world was formed."

3. Simon came to redeem the imprisoned, transmigrating "thought" and "conferred salvation upon men, by making himself known to them." He appeared in the form of Jesus but was not a man; he appeared "to have suffered in Judea, when he had not suffered."

4. Since the prophets were inspired by lower divinities, the

enlightened can ignore them, and "being free, live as they please; for men are saved through his grace, and not on account of their own righteous actions."[16]

Simon's system was strong from his time to the mid–second century, when Justin said that it had captured "almost all the Samaritans, and a few even of other nations."[17] Earlier Simon was a successful religious impostor when confronted by Peter in Samaria about A.D. 35, so the peak of his influence was during the closing years of Peter and Paul. All of this does not prove that Paul argued directly against Simonism in the Pastoral Letters, but the first Christian records prove that such ideas were clearly taught within Paul's lifetime.

Today's anti-Mormon literature proclaims against genealogical work by quoting Paul: "Neither give heed to fables and endless genealogies" (1 Tim. 1:4). But that was not the interpretation of Paul and the New Testament writers, for Matthew begins with Jesus' genealogy to Abraham, and Luke 3 takes it back to Adam, just as endless as an earthly genealogy can be. Paul preached that Christ descended from David (Rom. 1:3), and the apostle knew his own descent from Benjamin (Rom. 11:1). Indeed, the Gentile convert Luke records the lineage of the prophetess Anna from the tribe of Asher (Luke 2:36) and notes that Barnabas came from the tribe of Levi (Acts 4:36). In short, true genealogy, a serious Latter-day Saint goal, is sustained by the practice of the Early Church. Paul's phrases, however, show that he condemns only false genealogies. Paul's term never appears alone, but as part of a pattern, which is translated literally in its two appearances as follows: "Myths and endless genealogies . . . questions . . . empty talk" (1 Tim. 1:4); "Foolish questions and genealogies and strifes, and warring about the law" (Titus 3:9). Similar Pastoral phrases crop up regularly to characterize the false teachings as unsubstantial, untrue, filled with "unholy and blabbering myths" (1 Tim. 4:7, literal trans.) or "unholy and empty talk" (1 Tim. 6:20, literal trans.). Paul is clearly condemning irresponsible theories and invented stories, the meaning of the Greek *mûthos* of the above passages. The "genealogies" condemned by Paul are clearly those that are debatable and fictitious.

Each is free to envision what false genealogies Paul had in mind. Several good scholars are confident that the apostle refuted false explanations of the ancestry of the Creator. Paul's problem was not Jewish attitudes but Christian heresy of Jewish origin. Paul's criticisms are not Romans-like, against Jewish pride; they are against inventing anti-physical doctrines on resurrection and marriage. So the early Gnostic genealogies of the misguided creator fit this picture. In their view, the material world was a mistake, so from Simon on, their lower creator-divinity was elaborately descended from their highest god. The scheme was Jewish because it gave a counterexplanation of Genesis. Thus, it fits Paul's warning not to be seduced by "Jewish myths" (Titus 1:14, literal trans.).

The teachers of false genealogies had once known the truth but had "turned aside" to their "foolish reasoning" (1 Tim. 1:6, literal trans.). Gnostic myths generally aimed at saving the true God from contaminating himself with physical things, so their ultimate god would have nothing to do with creation, crucifixion, or resurrection. Creation of human bodies was a related problem for them, as were foods. And Paul prophesied that false teachers would be found "forbidding to marry, and commanding to abstain from foods which God has created to be received with thanksgiving" (1 Tim. 4:3, NKJB). The prophecy logically refers to a false revulsion toward the body both in marrying and in eating (the King James "meats" was written in 1611 as a general term for food). Paul also speaks of the "latter" or "later" times; the adjective is neutral, not suggesting how far in the future he means (1 Tim. 4:1).

Paul's prophecy on marriage soon began to be fulfilled. Some Gnostic sects treated morality and eating with indifference on the theory that the soul was not affected by the flesh, but others taught that sexual relations and eating flesh contaminated the soul. Among the latter was the group founded by Saturninus, close successor of Simon Magus: "They declare also that marriage and generation are from Satan. Many of those too, who belong to his school, abstain from animal food, and draw away multitudes by a feigned temperance of this kind."[18] Medieval Christianity inherited its ascetic practices from ancient attitudes that produced such thinking. Although not forbidding marriage for the normal person, it defined marriage as a lower way of life. The danger of Gnosticism was in its anti-materialistic premises. Christian theologians know that Gnosticism was defeated as a movement in the second century. But the overall conflict between God and matter was never really defeated. True, the Fathers of the Church vigorously upheld the scriptural accounts of the Creation and of the Resurrection. Yet the strange result is that they taught that Christ is physically resurrected but that his Father is eternally a non-physical being. This discrepancy puts great pressure on Christian ministers to spiritualize the Resurrection or to explain it away as a temporary sign.

The real answer to false doctrine is the truth. Paul regards debate as pointless but powerfully stresses Christ as the true revelation of God and the only means of salvation. The relationship of the Father and of Christ is shown throughout 1 Timothy. One careful analyst notes that the "favorite titles" for divinity in 1 Timothy are *Lord* and *Savior:* "The remarkable feature of these two titles is that the author uses them interchangeably for God and Christ."[19] Christ is also "God." "He therefore leaves himself open to the charge of virtual Ditheism."[20] This last word means belief in two Gods and comes in an unusual comment for a Christian scholar. Paul does verbally separate Christ and the Father here and elsewhere in his letters. One distinctive concept taught in 1 Timothy is that Christ is between the Father and his children: "For there is one God, and one mediator between God and men, the man Christ Jesus" (1 Tim. 2:5). Here the Greek *mesítēs* has the same meaning as the English "mediator." Thus, Christ stands as a third party with the Father and mankind—he is the literal "go-between," the arbitrator assigned to overcome alienation and bring peace among the parties. Before the merging of the Father and Son by the Nicene Council, Arius had claimed that the Son was subordinate and was thus a distinct person himself. And one capable Christian, while doubting that the Pastoral author intended this doctrine, feels that the above language severs the persons of the Trinity: "An Arian Christ is the logical conclusion of the mediator-christology which we have here."[21] In everyday English, Paul's "mediator" is separate from the Father; this is also the testimony of the restored Church.

Paul's testimonies of Christ in 1 Timothy are now seen as bits of creeds or hymns, an intriguing but unprovable line of inquiry. In the letter they are spontaneous gems of personal testimony, artfully composed but probably Paul's core thoughts on the Savior repeated in some form over and over during his life. One sentence captures the essence: Christ was "manifested in the flesh" (1 Tim. 3:16, NKJB). Pungent phrases follow on the Savior's mission, perhaps with chronological intent, for he was "seen by angels" at the Resurrection and Ascension and was finally "taken up in glory" with the same physical body that a moment before had stood before the awestruck apostles (Acts 1:9-11). This summarizes the "mystery of godliness," which here, as in Ephesians, is the plan to be openly revealed through Jesus Christ. The Christian mystery is never one permanently hidden from mortals, but is one to be shown fully as soon as God's children are able to understand.

This principle applies also to the Father, who is called invisible" in virtually every translation of 1 Timothy 1:17. As pointed out in Colossians 1, the same Greek word is simply "unseen" and has no connotations of some eternally nebulous God. As the logical A. T. Hanson says, "This is the only passage in the entire New Testament in which God is described as invisible without the accompanying assertion that he has made himself known in Christ or in his works of creation."[22] In other words, the implied thought behind not seeing the Father is always that the Son reveals him—the visual equivalence of Christ as "the image of the unseen God" (Col. 1:15, JB). Paul's strongest statement on the veiling of the Father is in the present tense: the Father is "dwelling in unapproachable light, whom no man has seen or can see" (1 Tim. 6:16, NKJB). Here Joseph Smith used a leading doctrine of the New Testament to override the impression of isolated words—for the Saint with "the light and the hope of immortality dwelling in him" will live to see God (1 Tim. 6:16, JST). That is the message of Jesus' beatitude: "Blessed are the pure in heart: for they shall see God" (Matt. 5:8).

Did the apostle who watched Stephen seeing the Father and the Son deny that man had ever seen God? Probably he meant that ordinary men never see God unless called as prophets or sustained by God's Spirit. Possibly Paul also denied that the real Father had been seen by Christian apostates with their invented schemes of the being higher than the Creator. Certainly Paul stressed that the unseen Father was sending the Son in the mighty drama of "the appearing of the Lord Jesus Christ," which once more is the New Testament message that the Father is revealed through the Son (1 Tim. 6:14). The full beliefs of the Early Church were well understood and were referred to only in part in such letters. John, who also called the Father unseen (John 1:18), portrayed the thrones of the Father and the Son in the presence of the Saints in the glorified city (Rev. 22:3; compare 3:21). And Paul's most powerful passage on Christ revealing the person of the Father (2 Cor. 4:4-6) promises that the faithful will see eternal realities (2 Cor. 4:14) that are temporarily unseen in this life (2 Cor. 4:18). That is how the Early Church understood this language, for soon after Paul the martyr-bishop Ignatius spoke of Christ as "invisible, who for our sakes became visible."[23] Likewise the Father is unseen for the period of mortality, after which the righteous will see him.

Priesthood Offices

To become a minister today one certifies through college training and then is generally hired by a local church. In the Early Church no prior training was required but only a call from Christ or his servants. Priesthood is a necessary concept in any organized church, though the word itself may be avoided. Who has the right to baptize and administer the sacrament of the Lord's Supper? Roman Catholics have a regularly ordained priesthood for the ordinances, but Protestants also have orderly procedures of appointment. Priesthood is the right to perform ordinances and to lead, which means that Church management is a type of priesthood. The source of authority may be the "call" of a Church, as mentioned in the survey of Protestant ministers in Utah, 45 percent of which agreed that "the ministerial office is or should be conferred upon incumbents through the congregations."[24] But should authority be given by ordination? The same group was asked this question, and 71 percent of these ministers denied that "authority is conveyed by the laying on of hands by those who have received the authority in this manner."[25]

Joseph Smith spoke of delegated priesthood by quoting Paul's instruction not to neglect the "gift" given "by prophecy, with the laying on of the hands of the presbytery" (1 Tim. 4:14). This is not confirmation after baptism, for prophecy rarely precedes that ordinance. But the opposite is true of a priesthood call. In other words, all baptized converts freely receive the laying on of hands for the gift of the Holy Ghost. But priesthood comes on a selective basis, making the inspired call a prerequisite. This double stage of inspiration plus ordination appears in several situations of Paul's life. At Antioch before the first mission, "the Holy Ghost said, Separate me Barnabas and Paul," after which they were set apart by the laying on of hands (Acts 13:1-3). And Paul summoned "the elders of the church" from the Ephesian area and told them that "the Holy Ghost made you overseers" (Acts 20:28, literal trans.). So local officers were not given the right to act without prior designation by revelation. The inspired call and the laying on of hands are the first two steps of divine authority already discussed in connection with Hebrews 7.

That discussion also gave biblical evidence for a third proper step, approval of the group over which the officer will preside. This also appears in the letter of Clement, bishop of Rome, written about the time that John was imprisoned at Patmos. He was shocked that the Corinthians had perverted their right of approval by dismissing their leaders, who were installed by the apostles: "We consider therefore that it is not just to remove from their ministry those who were appointed by them, or later on by other eminent men, with the consent of the whole church."[26] The survey near the beginning of this discussion indicates that a sizable number of Protestant leaders are called by their congregations, but that group had neither the right to call nor to dismiss in the procedures of the Early Church. Appointment came through supervising priesthood leaders, with the group's right to accept or reject those so appointed. The rationale would be that they had the right to show their own willingness to be directed, a check and balance on inspired leadership but not a substitute for it. This was the pattern when Paul and Barnabas organized their first converts. The pronouns of Acts clearly indicate that the apostles placed the elders over the members, which justifies the slight liberty of the first translation following as compared with the literalism of the second: "Paul and Barnabas appointed elders for them in each church" (Acts 14:23, NIV); "They had appointed elders for them in every church" (Acts 14:23, RSV).

Timothy was told that after prophecy came "the laying on of the hands of the presbytery" (1 Tim. 4:14), meaning the body of elders. Joseph Smith explained the principle: "A man must be called of God, by prophecy, and by the laying on of hands by those who are in authority, to preach the Gospel and administer in the ordinances thereof" (A of F 5). This requires a visible chain of authority, each link being a valid ordination by one having authority. That is just what Paul required in individual ordinations, for Timothy was told, "Lay hands suddenly on no man" (1 Tim. 5:22). Once more, the selective procedure clearly indicates priesthood ordination. This is the letter that spells out what qualifications bishops and deacons must have, cautioning Timothy to weigh and consider before appointing bishops and deacons. Timothy's ordination (1 Tim. 4:14) is one link in the chain of authority, and his ordination of others (1 Tim. 5:22) is a second link. How many more would appear if there were fourteen letters on priesthood appointment instead of two? Yet ordination clearly appears where it should appear in the letters and in Acts. Self-appointed and congregationally appointed leaders are ruled out in the procedures of the Early Church, which had a regular line of authority from Christ and his apostles.

The Master summarized the "top-down" priesthood appointment of the Twelve: "You have not chosen me, but I have chosen you, and appointed you" (John 15:16, NKJB). And the apostles followed that pattern in local appointment by the higher authorities. Selection and ordination were the responsibility of Timothy and Titus as regional officers appointed by the apostle Paul. The old Protestant view was a church patched together out of cooperating sectional elements, but the Early Church expanded through the central leadership of the apostles. Clement of Rome, who looked back on the Neronian persecution and the martyrdom of Peter and Paul, defined the true Church as that organization with local authorities appointed under the direction of the apostles: "They appointed their first converts, testing them by the Spirit, to be bishops and deacons of the future believers."[27] The true Church would continue while the true gospel was preached by a priesthood linked by a chain of authority to the founding apostles. Few churches even talk about tracing the laying on of hands as it is outlined in 1 Timothy. Those with traditional orientation may speak of a general succession without any records to sustain the validity of early ordinations. But Latter-day Saint priesthood holders can trace their lines of ordination back to the glorious restoration of the priesthood to Joseph Smith and Oliver Cowdery by John the Baptist and the ancient presiding apostles.

Paul's instructions on appointing bishops make a final point about priesthood calls by revelation. The Holy Ghost speaks to the calling officer in quiet assurance more than in overpowering force, though apostles today have experienced the force of the Spirit as an inner burning or even as a spiritual shock. Yet Paul talks about practical investigation together with the stage of revelation. The bishop must have specific qualities of worthiness, as is shown in the choice of an apostle to replace Judas, where the requirements were outlined by Peter and met by two men, with the Lord's will then sought (Acts 1:15-26). So Paul required Timothy and Titus to do their best thinking as a part of the process of inspiration. Latter-day Saints are well aware that the Lord commanded Oliver Cowdery to "study it out in your mind; then you must ask me if it be right" (D&C 9:8). Thus, thoughtful analysis is a part of the process of revelation. This insight into priesthood callings has tremendous relevance to the operation of the restored Church, though members do not always understand as well as do those called to ward and stake leadership. This author's assignment in the latter situation in the last three years has been an overwhelming personal experience, for the revelations of the Spirit are profound realities in the calling of bishops and of other Church officers today.

Paul's list of bishop's qualifications is really much more than that. The Early Church was not divided into a relatively few especially holy Saints contrasted with the great mass of members. Leaders and members were both expected to live up to the same standards. Thus, 1 Timothy 3 and Titus 1 contain a practical profile of the ideal life for anyone who aspires to serve God. These two sources are nearly identical in their picture of the effective leader. And what dedicated disciple can ignore leadership? The Church of Jesus Christ is a divine system of service and support. Every member should be a teacher and an example to someone else—all perform the functions of the bishop on some level. Every serious parent leads the family as the bishop leads his flock. Thus, Paul's standards for the bishop become a moral measurement.

The good leader has tested integrity and skill in serving. Paul summarizes in saying that the bishop should not be a "novice" (1 Tim. 3:6), in literal Greek "newly planted" or "newly converted." Jesus challenged the baptized to live that people "may see your good works, and glorify your Father which is in heaven" (Matt. 5:16). Righteousness neither parades itself nor hides its reality. So Paul notes that one living the gospel will have a "good report" among honorable outsiders (1 Tim. 3:7). If slander occasionally misrepresents, reliable honesty is reflected in credit reports and in one's reputation for keeping personal and financial promises. Directing others starts with directing oneself. That means controlling temper, turning down liquor, and curbing greed for material possessions. These areas of self-control are summed up in a powerful word translated "sober" (1 Tim. 3:2; Titus 1:8). In Greek *sōphrōn* is an intense cultural ideal, controlling one's life with a sound mind, making desires serve intelligent moral convictions. So the faithful leader is indeed what the translations here call "sober-minded" (NKJB) or "self-controlled" (NAB, NIV).

The bishop must be "the husband of one wife"? (1 Tim. 3:2; Titus 1:6.) Marriage is assumed, but the emphasis is not on "a wife" but on "one wife." So some commentators have seen a prohibition against polygamy, which was not a marriage custom in Timothy's Greek world. Others have seen a prohibition of remarriage in case of death of the first wife. But this runs counter to Paul's instructions for younger widows to remarry and live productive family lives (1 Tim. 5:14). Moreover, that woman following Paul's rule could be widowed again. Would she then be ineligible for welfare help, which required her to be the "wife of one man"? (1 Tim. 5:9.) Consistency demands the interpretation of moral faithfulness in marriage here; welfare eligibility of the second-time widow would be judged not by her number of marriages but by her morality in each marriage. So "husband of one wife" must mean sexual loyalty to the lawful spouse. Common sense dictates that Paul is talking about fundamental morality here, just as he talks about fundamental honesty and goodwill to others. Translators have no right to confuse the issue by the rendition "married only once," since the Greek of the above verses is literally "man of one woman" or "woman of one man." Perhaps these phrases have the right connotation by translating "one woman's husband" and "one man's wife." Sexual relations must be restricted to marriage.

A bishop must also be a successful family leader. But from the early middle ages the Catholic bishop was not married, on the theory that single clergy would have more time for the Lord. But

Paul looks to the quality of such time, for an unmarried man lacks the social experience to lead a small flock effectively. Reaching out to his own children was a prerequisite to being trusted with a group of the Lord's children. "Children in subjection" (1 Tim. 3:4) or "faithful children" (Titus 1:6) is the result of two wills— the well-motivated parent and also the well-motivated child. Paul does not demand perfect success but encourages a righteous approach to parenting. The bishop is a person who is careful with human feelings, who is not violent and quick tempered. In modern terms, he does not abuse his wife or children physically or emotionally. And he is a good teacher of the gospel—in the home before he is called to teach in the Church. And he reaches with warm "hospitality"—in the home before he is called to do the same in the Church. Whether one is called to Church leadership depends on the Lord's needs, but every parent should be able to upgrade family leadership with Paul's insights here.

Ephesians 4 gave "the perfecting of the saints" as the purpose of priesthood offices, both general and local. The name for each office throws light on its goal. "Bishop" evolved from the Greek *episcopos,* literally an "overseer." In Paul's farewell address to leaders at Ephesus, he reminded them how revelation had made them "overseers," which probably means "bishops" (Acts 20:28). They were to care for the flock, suggesting their image as pastors, or shepherds, as discussed in Ephesians 4. The bishop leads a flock by "looking after" its welfare. Scholars spend time debating whether there was corporate leadership or sole leadership of the bishop within the New Testament churches. But in the restored Church, bishops act with counselors, which probably explains why bishops merge with elders in some early sources.[28] Because history is so often evolution, historians can be misled by superficially assuming evolution. The New Testament documents the existence of bishops, but only in fragments. But the earliest post-apostolic literature shows bishops with centralized authority. The same thing was no doubt true earlier—the evolution is in the quality of the sources, not in the bishop's office.

Paul's instructions to Timothy and Titus indicate strong centralized leadership—such high qualifications naturally pertain to one specially selected, for joint appointment of many in one small branch would exhaust leadership quickly and make these qualifications meaningless. Paul tells Titus that the bishop is "the steward of God" (Titus 1:7). In Greek that term is "household manager," given in one translation as "representative" (JB), because the bishop holds the delegated management of his unit, what Paul termed a "dispensation," as discussed in connection with Ephesians 1. The first well-documented bishop is Ignatius of Antioch, who about A.D. 110 was arrested and escorted to Rome via Asia Minor. Before leaving that area he wrote to six churches, and his message to each was that apostasy could be stayed only by following the bishop. "Let no one do any of the things pertaining to the Church without the bishop"—that meant that no administration of the sacrament of the Lord's Supper was valid without him or the one "whom he appoints"; nor was any baptism or meeting to be held without his authorization.[29] The bishop, then, was a local officer, for there is a bishop in each church addressed. Ignatius gives wise practical advice to Bishop Polycarp of Smyrna, encouraging inspiration for individual needs: "Not all wounds are healed by the same plaster."[30]

Ignatius continually names elders and deacons after the bishop, the elders being compared to the Council of the Twelve, which suggests their role as counselors.[31] Indeed, the name of *elder* arose from the senior councils that governed Greek communities, so elders were like a board of advisors under executive direction. In A.D. 96 the bishop of Rome complained that the Corinthians had rejected their presiding elders; with references to the bishop intermingled, this could mean the bishop and his assistants.[32] But that letter does not discuss offices in detail. Since the unity of the Church is strongly stressed in the letters of Ignatius and Clement, any apparent differences probably relate to our lack of full information. In addition to administrative functions, early Christian elders had the personal assignments that Latter-day Saint home teachers have today. That is strongly suggested in the New Testament as James encourages the sick to call for the elders for blessings. And Polycarp later describes how elders helped the bishop watch over the Church: "Let the elders also be compassionate, merciful to all, bringing back those that have wandered, caring for all the weak, neglecting neither widow, nor orphan nor poor."[33] Polycarp is clearly a sole bishop but joins "the elders with him" in writing the letter, indicating that they are senior priesthood leaders of that church.[34] In addition to the strong bishop of 1 Timothy 3, there are "the elders that rule well, . . . especially they who labor in the word and teaching" (1 Tim. 5:17, literal trans.). Some elders appear to have been called to special positions of leading or assisting out of the pool of those regularly serving the Saints.

The last priesthood office in the above sources is the deacon. In Philippians 1:1 deacons are named after the bishops, and the same is true in 1 Timothy 3. Again, their name profiles their function, for the common verb of serving or helping furnishes the noun *diákonos.* "Helper" has a more general use in the New Testament, with Paul using the term frequently of himself (generally translated "minister"), with application even to Phebe of the port near Corinth (Rom. 16:1). But this woman's reference is followed up by no job description as a priesthood office. The same lack of application dooms the attempt to make deacons' wives into officials; they are charged with the responsibility to support their husbands (1 Tim. 3:11). Like bishops, deacons go through the two stages of proving worthiness and then being called (1 Tim. 3:10). Named right after the bishop, they meet similar standards, though personal competence in teaching and social skills are not stressed.

So here is an important distinction—the deacons are successful family heads like the bishops, but unlike the bishop they do not preside. Deacons are not told that they cannot care for the Church without successfully caring for a family first (1 Tim. 3:5). Their married status is related to the Jewish background that required Levitical priests to be thirty years old, a general pattern that the Savior honored before beginning his ministry. Yet his ability at age twelve in the temple shows youth's potential for early priesthood service. The restored Church began with older deacons and lowered the age when the Church became stable with regular supervision from experienced priesthood leaders. Those in the Old Testament ordained to serve God were from the tribe of Levi only and restricted their work to the temple. But by revelation the comparable New Testament office of deacon was given to any Israelite or Gentile member who qualified. Since God's work grows, there is flexibility in who receives priesthood, when it is received, and assignments in it. But the authority remains the same, and the continuity of Early Church and the Restoration is illustrated by Justin Martyr's written defense to the emperor about A.D. 150 explaining what happens after the symbols are blessed in sacrament meeting: "Those who are called by us deacons give to each of those present to partake of the bread and wine mixed with water . . . and to those who are absent they carry away a portion."[35]

Since many priesthood offices have disappeared or lain idle, thoughtful people must ask whether the priesthood disappeared after Christ and the apostles. The deacon's office is missing in many churches, though there is a dynamic movement in both Catholic and Protestant faiths to "restore" its early vitality.[36] The medieval church added many priesthood offices that have no basis in early Church government. On the other hand, many Protestant churches hardly have a skeleton of the organization in Paul's day. But modern revelation has restored all the offices found in the New Testament and in the earliest Christian sources. The offices of teacher, priest, and high priest appear in early sources, but only by incidental mention, preventing a full understanding of what is meant.[37] For that matter, the final dispensation should have the offices of the Primitive Church and more if God so commands. But the New Testament and earliest bishops completely support Joseph Smith's claim of restoring "the same organization that existed in the Primitive Church" (A of F 6).

Theologians classify different churches in terms of their basic framework or "polity." Emphasis on governing boards of elders is called Presbyterian, and emphasis on the supreme authority of bishops is called Episcopalian polity. Yet the Early Church was both of these and more, for it had the government of apostles directing all offices of the priesthood. Regional and world bishops are known in Eastern Orthodox, Roman Catholic, and some Protestant churches. But archbishops, metropolitan bishops, national bishops, or a worldwide bishop are all substitutes for the traveling and supervising council of apostles. First- and second-century bishops supervised in a given city. Polycarp writes to the Philippians with the apologetic opening, "Not at my own instance, but because you first invited me," and explains that he cannot take the place of the apostle Paul.[38] Under imperial arrest, Ignatius writes to Asian churches and to Rome itself to share testimony but not to govern: "I do not order you as did Peter and Paul—they were apostles."[39] A dozen years earlier, Clement had written from Rome, but in the most circumspect terms, not as a presiding priesthood officer, but as the "Church of God which sojourns in Rome to the Church of God which sojourns in Corinth."[40] In facing the ultimate Corinthian sin of dismissing its priesthood officers, he complains but does not discipline.

In a lesser crisis Paul warned the Corinthians of his coming and promised excommunications. In the process of shaming but not directing, Clement recalls how the authorized "bishops and deacons" were first appointed by the apostles, who "preached from district to district, and from city to city."[41] No bishop had this apostolic jurisdiction between cities, but apostles were set over the entire Church. The Early Church was a balanced system of general and local authorities, with the legitimacy of the latter dependent on the former. The Pastoral Letters show the power of bishops, elders, and deacons in upgrading lives; these offices were by nature person to person and were not concerned with the administration of a region or of the whole Church. Regional bishops later evolved, but apostles or their special assistants are in this position in the Pastoral Letters. Great medieval bishops developed as unauthorized expansions of local offices. And councils of hundreds of bishops usurped the apostolic function of revealing doctrine, which is clearly described in Acts and in 1 Corinthians

12. Through priesthood restoration, the missing general authorities have now been reestablished in their proper position in Christ's Church.

Earthly and Eternal Welfare

Superficial religion relaxes in heaven before its time. Impractical churches have treated symptoms of poverty without going to causes of the disease. Modern national materialism arose in reaction to the failure of religion to be practical. But a church speaking only of distant salvation is not the successor to the religion of the New Testament, for the first six chapters of Acts give equal weight to saving souls and to meeting the practical needs of the converted. The author of Christian welfare principles was Christ, who defined love as service and explained service as the range of others' physical, social, and emotional needs. He outlined the question on the day of judgment—whether others have been helped (Matt. 25:31-46). Have they been fed and clothed? Have they been welcomed when strangers? Have they been visited and fellowshipped when isolated from society? The Early Church addressed these needs, but through principles more profound than only easy handouts and occasional visits.

Behind 1 Timothy 5 is the commitment to productive labor, exemplified by Paul's regular tent-making and requiring industry as a condition of full fellowship in 2 Thessalonians 3. Greek philosophy idealized the contemplative life, but for Paul one is serving God when producing goods or serving God and neighbors. Paul is prayerful and thoughtful, and is a scholar of the scriptures. But where is Paul's advice to withdraw to meditative cloisters? The principle of activity is applied to widows in 1 Timothy. Not until age sixty are they to be "enrolled" (1 Tim. 5:9, literal trans.). Some unnecessarily imagine a formal order of women devoted to prayer and charitable works. But the issue here is only Church obligation, not organization. And the rule was to not give support while a woman was able-bodied. People who lived to age sixty were about as vigorous as moderns before wonder drugs. Younger widows were encouraged to remarry, raise families, and dre

211111

"manage the house" (1 Tim. 5:14, NKJB). But Paul vigorously attacked idleness, for an aimless life is more than a wasted life, as his contrast between Christian widows and worldly widows shows. Evil is avoided by filling life with righteous activities.

So Paul insisted on productive work from those able to work, with the warning that anything less invited Satan's temptations. The exceptions seem to be the welfare collection at Antioch before a coming famine and the welfare collection that Paul brought to Jerusalem from the Gentile branches, discussed in connection with 2 Corinthians 8 and 9. Though no one knows how these resources were distributed, their collection was for special circumstances of Jerusalem poverty, with the high percentage of widows indicated in Acts 6. So Paul's teachings in 2 Thessalonians and 1 Timothy harmonize with giving help freely for special needs but in normal times requiring the able to be self-reliant. There is no evidence that Latter-day Saint leaders studied these two letters of Paul in their economic leadership after the 1929 American depression. Yet their inspiration agreed wholly with Paul's welfare principles as they sought to aid the jobless and still preserve "independence, industry, thrift, and self respect"—"the aim of the Church is to help the people to help themselves."[42] Decades earlier, Brigham Young's inspired reflections on his "experience" had led him to the same truth: "It is never any benefit to give out and out to man or woman, money, food, clothing, or anything else, if they are able bodied and can work . . . when there is anything for them to do."[43]

Thus, the Early Church handled welfare by rules of self-help and emergency assistance, but like Latter-day Saints, they insisted on one further essential. The Pastoral Letters show the family as the basic teaching unit of the Church, indicated by the idea that a bishop must be one who has successfully taught his children. The economic analogy is clear. Teaching in the Church backs up family teaching but does not replace it; likewise, Church welfare support will be available only when family resources have failed. The rule is simply that believing "men and women" who run households must help widows related to them—"Let not the

Church be burdened, that it may assist those who are really widows" (1 Tim. 5:16, literal trans.). And the family relationship is not defined narrowly, for the commandment of Moses to honor father and mother is extended to honoring grandmother. This elderly matriarch is to be "reverenced" (1 Tim. 5:4, literal trans.). Paul explains this duty of respect along with the duty of support: "Let them first learn to reverence their own household and to return what they owe to their progenitors" (1 Tim. 5:4, literal trans.). In the King James Version this privilege of repayment belongs to the "children or nephews," but "nephews" is used in the obsolete sense of "grandchildren" or "descendants," the exact meaning of the Greek term. And lest anyone mistake his plain words, Paul underlines the religious obligation: "But if anyone does not provide for his own, and especially for those of his household, he has denied the faith and is worse than an unbeliever" (1 Tim. 5:8, NKJB).

Self-respect is related to the respect of others, especially in critical youth and old age. Christ's atonement showed that every individual is worth the suffering of the Son of God. And the rule of family support says to every individual that lifelong labors for children are seeds sown for an autumn harvest. Grandmothers are stressed in 1 Timothy mainly because they lived longer than their husbands. As long as anyone survives, the comfort of eternity is sweeter through the comfort of loved ones this side of it. Ancient and restored churches unite in assuring the aged of care when self-support and family support are exhausted. This inspired system gives the elderly unquestioning acceptance, and the senior knows seniority in love and understanding. The elderly can still give generous affection. Paul profiles the worthiness of widows for help, and this stands as a model for the lifetime service of married and unmarried: "If she brought up children, if she showed hospitality, if she washed the Saints' feet, if she assisted the afflicted, if she pursued every good work" (1 Tim. 5:10, literal trans.).

Is worthiness for earthly welfare unrelated to worthiness for eternal welfare? Since Paul teaches good works as the basis for the full respect of the Church, are good works unrelated to the full salvation of God? Writing to the regional leaders, Paul's overall message was worthiness—of bishops and deacons, of women for welfare, of Timothy in his calling, of the Saints for eternity. Salvation is not a distant condition unrelated to practical life, but the outgrowth of how a person lives. Joseph Smith taught such continuity to Brigham Young, who explained it in many spontaneous sermons: "I am decidedly in favor of practical religion—of everyday useful life" was his theme. This meant preparing for the great things of eternity by daily responsibilities here: "But I would not be prepared for that sphere of action, unless I could manage the things that are now within my reach."[44] This is exactly what Paul required of the prospective bishop—proven skill on a small scale before managing a greater responsibility. And the Church helped its needy on the same basis that God grants exaltation—meeting full needs after a member had made all possible efforts at self-help. Brigham Young saw that principle as permeating every relationship with the Lord here and in eternity: "You know that it is one peculiarity of our faith and religion never to ask the Lord to do a thing without being willing to help him all that we are able, and then the Lord will do the rest."[45]

Living worthily requires living with eternal values. Paul first contrasted the superficial and the eternal in women's lives. He pictured the philosophy of dress to impress, and he asked female Saints to ask the more profound question of what kind of person was within the clothes: "I desire . . . that women dress themselves with clothing well designed in modesty and good taste, not with braiding or gold or pearls or expensive apparel—but using what fits women committed to godliness, good works" (1 Tim. 2:9-10, literal trans.). It helps to know that Paul lived two years in Rome before he wrote these words. He would have nothing against the elegantly natural braids that have always cascaded over women's shoulders. But in Nero's last years Roman society erupted with gross exaggerations. Surviving statues of aristocratic women have a high layering that must come from hairpieces. And the Roman rich unwittingly bequeathed innumerable gold rings and bracelets to the museums. The Romans themselves laughed at the extremes of the time of 1 Timothy; the elder Pliny was incredulous at pearls hanging from finger pieces, in clusters on earrings, or even worse: "They even use them on their feet, and fix them not only to the laces of their sandals but all over their slippers."[46] Today's fads are equally ridiculous, but as Paul emphasized, the woman cultivating "good works" is putting on eternal beauty.

Paul also exposed the superficial in the ancient male world of muscles and money. The women's challenge to seek godliness was repeated in Timothy's terms: "Train yourself in godliness; for while bodily training is of some value, godliness is of value in every way, as it holds promise for the present life and also for the life to come" (1 Tim. 4:7-8, RSV). There is some sarcasm here for the Greek culture that heaped praise on its professional athletes. Yet Paul must have been in superb physical shape from many travels, and he does not deny value in the careful training of the athlete, which he knew well enough to mention regularly. But far more important is regular spiritual exercise. Paul could look upon modern streets and be mildly pleased with joggers and striders caring for their bodies. And then he could open family-room doors for the strange sight of men dedicating days to television sports while going out of physical and spiritual shape from inactivity. And how does one become spiritually fit? Through practice in spiritual things—in prayer, worship, and scripture reading, and in teaching and serving family, the larger Church family, and friends beyond that fellowship (1 Tim. 4:13). As a leader, Timothy must be what he preaches, and Paul's checklist of qualities reminds every Saint not to break training "in word, in conduct, in love, in spirit, in faith, in purity" (1 Tim. 4:12, NKJB).

Paul continues his athletic language in closing with personal advice to Timothy: "Fight the good fight of faith, lay hold on eternal life" (1 Tim. 6:12). These are words for competition in many events of the Greek games, so Timothy will get the reward through valiant effort, as discussed in Philippians. So will the rich Saints if they are "rich in good works" (1 Tim. 6:18-19). This same message came to grasping men and overdressed women. Only eternal things are worth having, for all else will pass away. Selfishness comes in many forms, but most obviously in the greed for things. Paul does not condemn owning possessions but praises the man of wealth who is "ready to distribute, willing to communicate" (1 Tim. 6:18). This last word simply repeats the first thought, for the King James "communicate" usually translates the Greek word meaning "to share." So the fault with many of the rich is not their wealth but their poverty of spirit, a fault also shared by masses of men and women without wealth. Thus, *money* is not "the root of all evil" but the "*love* of money," in Greek *philarguría,* which is used in the general sense of "avarice" and "greed." As President Spencer W. Kimball is fond of saying, the sin behind all sin is selfishness. And greed for material things is epidemic. As Paul says, we will not carry wealth out of this world. So what is permanent and eternal?

The answer is positive qualities of character. Not only are all bank accounts left here at death, but also left are real estate, houses, automobiles, drugs and alchohol, elaborate clothes, false power, and empty status—the list can easily be expanded. What men and women take to eternity is themselves. The real joy of the gospel is not the promise of possessions in the hereafter. Without the right inner qualities, one could have celestial mansions and be as dissatisfied there as here. But true gospel riches bring the present possession of the Holy Ghost, who communicates the love and nearness of God, virtually an immediate reward for moral choices here. Happiness is not what one owns, but what one is. Untold individual acts forge each of the qualities here that are transferable to eternity: "righteousness, godliness, faith, love, patience, meekness" (1 Tim. 6:11). In the King James Version these words are all accurate except "patience," the strong Greek word (*hupomonē*) meaning "endurance," which is the required completion of faith in Romans 5:3 and in the verses before Hebrews 11. Paul's main message to Timothy is woven through his prior letters; hold fast and "continue," for by that effort "you will save both yourself and those who hear you" (1 Tim. 4:16, NKJB). Paul's sunset letters are understandably conscious of his years of faithfulness and the requirement of faithfulness for future rewards. The Pastoral Letters weld worthiness to salvation.

TITUS

Profile

Sent from:	Paul, possibly in or near Greece.
Sent to:	Titus, directing the Church in Crete.
Date:	Probably between A.D. 63 and 66.
Purpose:	To instruct Titus in appointing bishops and supervising his region of the Church.
Main themes:	The premortal promise; qualifications for bishops; ideals for men and women; grace and saving works.

Background

Titus

Titus was an early convert from the Greek world who became a trusted associate in Paul's missionary work and direction of the Church. With slightly less intimacy than to Timothy, Paul calls Titus his "true child in the common faith" (Titus 1:4, literal trans.). Other subtle contrasts establish Titus' individuality. "Let no one despise your youth" (1 Tim. 4:12, NKJB) was Timothy's charge, expressed to Titus as, "Let no one despise you" (Titus 2:15, NKJB). This suggests that Titus was older than Timothy, though the common name of "son" would indicate that they were both younger than Paul. Titus was possibly converted earlier than Timothy, for he went to the Jerusalem Council before Timothy was called as a missionary. That council took place right after the first mission, when Paul assigned strong converts to stay with their branches (Acts 14:23). So Titus was probably not a first mission convert, but being "a Greek" (Gal. 2:3) he would likely come from earlier Gentile areas, from Paul's work with Barnabas at Antioch before the first mission, or from Paul's little-known labors at Tarsus just before that.

Out of many inevitable conflicts over the gospel, Titus's trial at the Jerusalem Council stood out. Jewish brethren teaching circumcision insisted that Titus become a full Jewish proselyte in addition to becoming a Christian. But Paul would not even consider such a compromise for a Gentile (Gal. 2:5), and Titus was not "compelled to be circumcised" (Gal. 2:3). Further presiding or missionary assignments surely followed, though there is no record of such service. But Titus emerges as a seasoned assistant in disciplining the Corinthian branch of the Church. The story is found here and there in 2 Corinthians. Paul had expected to meet Titus to hear his report in Asia Minor (2 Cor. 2:12-13) but crossed to Northern Greece, where his fears were replaced with the comforting news that the branch as a whole had repented (2 Cor. 7:7). Titus obviously had done his work with courage and capacity, but Paul goes further to show another critical ingredient in his success—his love for the people that he sought to help. "And his heart goes out all the more to you, as he remembers the obedience of you all, and the fear and trembling with which you received him" (2 Cor. 7:15, RSV). Paul says literally that Titus was not covetous toward the Corinthians—that he sincerely worked for their interests and not his own (2 Cor. 12:18).

How many times did Titus do the same thing in several different branches of the Early Church? After many years of Titus's proving and growing, Paul assigned him to direct the work in the branches on the large island of Crete. His choice obviously rested on Titus's faithful experience but no less on the "earnest care" for the Saints that continued in "the heart of Titus" (2 Cor. 8:16, RSV). The opening chapter of Titus shows that confused conditions in Crete demanded strong leadership and that Paul had complete confidence that Titus would measure up to the task. Some five years earlier, Titus had well earned Paul's solid description of him as "my partner and fellow worker" (2 Cor. 8:23, NKJB).

Reason for Writing

On his Roman voyage Paul inched around the eastern point of
Crete and sailed slowly past the high cliffs of the southern side of
that long island (Acts 27:7-8). While debating about whether to
winter there, he no doubt learned more about Crete and its
people. The decision was made to put in to a harbor in Crete protected from winter gales, but sudden winds overruled and forcibly
sped the apostle west to shipwreck at Malta (Acts 27:12-15). But
after Roman release, he evidently revisited Crete. He "left" Titus
in Crete "that you might straighten out what was left unfinished"
(Titus 1:5, NIV), which opens a clear possibility that Paul first labored with Titus there and built up Church membership but not
the full Church organization. Missionary work there would resemble that in Greece, inasmuch as early migrations to Crete had
established cities with the same proud traditions of the mainland.
Moreover, there were Jewish groups in the major centers of the
island, for Cretans were among the pilgrims at Pentecost (Acts
2:8-11). The first seeds, if not the first conversions, were laid
when Peter preached so powerfully by the Holy Ghost on that historic day in Jerusalem.

Crete was a picturesque theater for the drama of the spread of
the gospel. Lying like a sleek Greek warship, it stretches 160 miles
east to west with a trim average girth of 25 miles. Its size exceeds
the combined states of Delaware and Rhode Island. Crete is the
largest and nearly the southernmost of the island extensions
thrown south and east from the Greek mainland. Divided by
rocky ridges and high mountains, the island was described by
Strabo as "thickly wooded" but punctuated by "fertile hollows."[47]
Crete nourished its inhabitants with grain and olive and grape, all
mentioned in prehistoric sources and no doubt still the backbone
of the economy in Paul's time.[48] Homer spoke of Crete as the
island of a hundred cities, and in Paul's day Pliny the Elder listed
forty as still vital.[49] Island society had strong traditions of landed
and subordinated classes, with Spartan-like military organization
and an accompanying pattern of homosexuality found elsewhere

in Greek culture.[50] Roman occupation had changed much politically, for Crete was organized as a province with the nearby section of Northern Africa.[51]

When Titus was assigned to "set in order" or "straighten out" Church affairs, a great part of his job was to choose strong bishops or presiding elders: "Appoint elders in every city as I commanded you" (Titus 1:5, NKJB). The Church had been in Crete long enough to have branches in many cities, but it was under attack of the "gainsayers," an archaic King James term meaning literally those "speaking against" or "opposing." They were so combative that Paul said not to continue to debate with them—"after the first and second admonition" they were to be ignored (Titus 3:10). In this verse the opposer is a "heretic," which word ties to the "heresies" Paul opposed in the Corinthian and Galatian branches (1 Cor. 11:19; Gal. 5:20). All these words adapt the Greek for "divisions," and Paul used "heretic" in that exact sense of a believer causing factions within the faith. At the end of Paul's life these reorganized Christians were everywhere. In Crete there were "many unruly" (Titus 1:10) or "many insubordinate" (Titus 1:10, NKJB), the latter translation exactly mirroring the Greek. The apostates would not stay in the ranks or submit to authority. In 1 Timothy such conditions were rampant around Ephesus as Paul directed Timothy to take vigorous measures to defend the faith. An island might be thought to be immune to such trends, but identical conditions in both places show that apostasy was the major problem everywhere at the end of Paul's life. So he wrote Titus not merely to have bishops appointed but to ensure that men would be called who would face the cross fire of the most dangerous enemies of the apostles—the rebels against their teaching and authority.

Priesthood organization is clearly behind the letter to Titus, though not as obviously as in 1 Timothy. Direction by the general authority is evident in Paul's assignment of Titus to Crete, and regional authority is evident in Titus's appointment of the elders to direct congregations as bishops. Paul does not need to explain ordination to the experienced Titus; he mentioned laying on of hands to Timothy in the personal reminders of their close relationship. The letter to Titus adds other intriguing glimpses into Paul's delegation of authority. He perhaps planned to open a new mission field, telling Titus to come immediately to Nicopolis when Paul would send Artemas or Tychicus. The former is unknown, but Tychicus had shown his reliability in accompanying Paul to Jerusalem with the welfare collection, and he had earlier carried the letters to Ephesus and Colossae. Much like Titus in experience, Tychicus was the kind of man whom Paul would consider as the new regional supervisor in Crete. Paul planned to transfer Titus to Nicopolis in view of wintering there (Titus 3:12), which no doubt meant Paul would do missionary work in that city, where Titus's assistance would be invaluable. "Nicopolis" means "city of victory," a name given to several cities in gratitude for winning a battle. But this last known field of Paul would symbolize many victories over error in teaching Christ's gospel.

Since 1 Timothy and Titus pertain to labors around Greece, the proper Nicopolis would be in this region—on the west coast of Greece opposite the boot of Italy. Augustus won sole power there and commemorated this earthly glory by uniting the local populations into a new city, which a generation before Paul was said to be "populous" and growing.[52] With typical showmanship, Augustus set up international games there, and with typical flattery, Herod the Great had "helped construct the greater part of their public buildings."[53] Apparently Paul labored here in his last known winter, probably with Titus at his side. The King James footnote to Titus says that Paul wrote this letter from Nicopolis, but that is a late manuscript addition with no historical value, apparently added because of the mention of Nicopolis in the letter. However, the letter itself mentions the probable messengers carrying it: "Zenas the lawyer," a fascinating reference to one otherwise unknown, and Apollos, the talented and dynamic fellow laborer so prominent at the end of Acts 18 and throughout 1 Corinthians. He was still faithful and working under Paul's direction. The apostle instructs Titus to send them on their way and to supply their needs (Titus 3:13). Were they going to deliver

1 Timothy at Ephesus after seeing Titus? Or were they en route to a regional assignment like that of Timothy and Titus? Either case is a reminder of the constant apostolic supervision over the Early Church found in New Testament letters.

Teachings

The Premortal Promise

Paul writes "in hope of eternal life, which God, that cannot lie, promised before the world began" (Titus 1:2). This sentence sums up the first half of Ephesians 1. Thus, careful treatment is demanded of the gospel's central invitation—when it came, and to whom. This doctrine is woven throughout Paul's writings (Rom. 16:25). It is undeveloped except in the first two chapters of Ephesians; yet that book and the early Christian sources in the previous discussion of it show that the premortal existence of mankind was assumed in discussing the premortal promise of salvation. Understanding the importance of the doctrine and its present Christian neglect requires some background on the meaning of "promised before the world began" (Titus 1:2), the equivalent of God having "chosen us in him before the foundation of the world" (Eph. 1:4).

The discussion of Ephesians pointed out that apostles had used such phraseology of Christ, with his premortal glory specifically in mind. And the doctrine of Saints being preknown and prechosen must be judged by the meanings that Paul applied to the Lord. The same words applied to Christ and the Saints indicate that they both experienced the same type of premortal life. The Lord proved his physical parallel with mankind by totally sharing physical and emotional mortality before returning to God. Will not men and women share his kingdom and resurrection in the future? Then what revelation ever denied that they shared Christ's premortal existence of the past? When the consistent and spiritually sensitive Gandhi tried to understand Christianity, he was puzzled by this divided thinking. Why should he believe that "Jesus was the only incarnate son of God"? He explained a logic that is near blasphemy to all but Latter-day Saints: "If God could have sons, all of us were his sons. If Jesus was like God, or God himself, then all men were like God and could be God himself."[54] The issue here is what Paul meant by God's pre-earthly promise, but that question cannot be divorced from the biblical and logical association of mankind with Christ in the premortal existence.

Paul's "promise" is a bold word in describing the premortal plan of salvation. He might have said that God made an "inner resolution," but he did not. Whether in English or Greek, a promise is normally made to *someone*; unless the self is specifically mentioned, promising is a social act. Paul's word (*epaggéllo*) is related to the English "angel"—both come from the root for giving news to another. Earlier Paul's term meant to announce, with the idea of promise coming from proclaiming an intention. Such acts require a receiver or an audience, just as discussed in latter-day revelations about the great council in heaven, where the plan of salvation was decided and announced to the spirits coming to earth (Abr. 3:22-28). Christian theology has difficulty with the idea of souls living before the creation of earth and of their bodies. Yet many scholars agree that God's "promise" of salvation suggests a hearer, so they alter the time when it was made: "Since there is reference to a promise, the phrase refers not to God's eternal design . . . but to the promise of salvation made at the beginning of human history and frequently repeated."[55]

But that is a most inconsistent position. In the words of the King James Version, God's promise of salvation was made "before the world began" (Titus 1:2). The Greek phrase is *prò chrónōn aiōníōn,* literally "before the eternal times." The adjective appears seventy-one times in the King James New Testament and is always translated as "eternal," "everlasting," or the equivalent. And "before" indicates that God's promise was made prior to measuring ages and times. This is not God's revelation of salvation to Noah or Abraham, as some commentaries weakly contend, but God's announcement prior to all earthly eras. Most translations give that idea: "Before the beginning of time" (NIV) or "Before time began" (NKJB). Their accuracy is proved by Paul's identical words concerning Christ's appointment "before the world began" (2 Tim. 1:9). Here the phrase must refer to God's precreation plan, as commentators agree. But what is clear about Christ's premortal appointment should also be clear of the premortal assurance to mankind. Some translations contradict themselves here, for they have Christ chosen "from all eternity" (2 Tim. 1:9, NEB) or "before the beginning of time" (2 Tim. 1:9, JB). But with the same Greek phrase the same translations make God's promise of salvation "long ages ago" (Titus 1:2, NEB) or "so long ago" (Titus 1:2, JB). Yet Paul gave the same eternal perspective to Timothy and to Titus. God could promise salvation to mankind only by selecting a Savior for them—both of these events took place at the same time before the Creation.

Such confusion comes from modern Christian assumptions that differ from Paul's. Jewish commentators look at these scriptures with far more empathy for the idea of mankind sharing a pre-earth life with Jesus because rabbinical and Jewish apocryphal writings contain many references to premortality.[56] The prevalence of this idea in Paul's culture demands a more open-minded look at Paul's allusions to it. An idea never mentioned is an idea probably not believed, but an idea incidentally mentioned is often an idea so well accepted that an author had no reason to explain it. This is the case with Paul's indications of a human pre-earth life. Paul disagreed with some Jewish concepts and refuted them, but others he accepted. His mention of the premortal life puts it in the latter category. Josephus says that the most devout Jewish sect, the Essenes, believed that souls were immortal before birth, were placed "in the prison-house of the body," and finally left "as though liberated from a long servitude."[57] And their writings in the Dead Sea Scrolls are greatly illuminated by this understanding, as Hugh Nibley has explained at length.[58] Other references to the earlier life of souls are in pre-Christian writings well accepted by first-century Pharisees. A little before Paul's birth, the writer of the Wisdom of Solomon reflected, "As a child I was by nature well-endowed, and a good soul fell to my lot; or rather, being good, I entered an undefiled body."[59] And from the century before, there is the profound writing of Jesus Ben Sirach, a Jewish scribe who represented the intelligent pre-Phariseeism of his day. He wrote of the Creation in terms of God choosing Israel and mankind's testing period. And he spoke of a Creation covenant, which is different from that later given to Moses, for then Israel saw the cloud but not God, and heard Moses' voice but not God's: "He established with them an eternal covenant and showed them his judgments. Their eyes saw his glorious majesty, and their ears heard the glory of his voice. And he said to them, 'beware of all unrighteousness.' And he gave commandment to each of them concerning his neighbor."[60]

These glimpses before the Gospels explain a Jewish view shown when Jesus' "disciples" asked whether a disadvantaged man had sinned, or his parents, since "he was born blind" (John 9:2). Scholars too quickly explain the question by legalistic discussions of the rabbis. But the highly educated did not ask it, only ordinary Israelites. The question assumes a premortal life because it raises the issue of premortal sin. And Jesus negated the latter without criticizing the former. Representative writings are the sampling techniques available to understand ancient history, and they show a widespread Jewish belief in intelligent life for each soul before birth. Paul agreed, as shown in his opening remarks to Titus about the premortal promise. Indeed, such language refers to God's precreation covenant, which is found in the traditional Jewish materials of Jesus Ben Sirach and in the early Christian traditions of the Shepherd of Hermas, discussed in connection with Ephesians 2. And Titus 1:2 is the key that unlocks Romans 8 and Ephesians 1, for God's earthly callings of Israel and of the Gentiles played out the script prefashioned in the heavenly council. The full gospel teaches that before birth God's children were present to see God's covenant made and that here they carry that knowledge in their inner souls as well as learn of it through the prophets. This is why poetic inspiration reaches for the same truth, no thanks to self-centered earth:

> The homely nurse doth all she can
> To make her foster-child, her inmate Man,
> Forget the glories he hath known,
> And that imperial palace whence he came.[61]

Qualifications for Bishops

See the earlier section on "Priesthood Offices" under 1 Timothy.

Ideals for Men and Women

Few subjects in world literature have attracted such outdated comments as the subject of the feminine role. Yet woman's image in the Early Church has vital meaning because her dignity in the family was recognized and because her personal potential was made equal to man's. Paul has the reputation of not agreeing with this picture, but his negative comments have a Corinthian context, as has been seen, and in the Pastoral Letters seem to be defensive because of false teachings. On the other hand, there is the inspiring harmony of the marriage roles discussed in Ephesians. And taken as a whole, the women's teachings in 1 Timothy and Titus equate the personal qualities of men and women, which has important implications for the challenges faced by married and single females in modern society. This subject is not a dry historical topic, but a dynamic set of issues demanding relevant application. In suggesting some interpretations, it is critical to see that the Early Church worked with certain revealed principles; for the same reason that they must not be compromised, neither must they be exaggerated and overdone.

The Pastoral Letters' main contribution here is their vision of how many moral qualities Saints of both sexes ought to share. The sexual double standard is unfortunately alive and well in many religious countries, but men and women are equally responsible before the Lord for avoiding intimate relations outside of marriage. As has been seen, the Early Church met this problem with excommunication, not with tactful sermons. Both sexes must also be judged by the same rule for honesty and by all other commands of righteousness. As Paul said in Romans 1, moral laws are written in the hearts of both men and women (Rom. 1:26-27). That is why there is a great deal of overlap in Greek and Roman ideals and the apostles' standards for Christian living. For instance, Aristotle divides sex roles into male courage for the defense of the state and female homemaking for the life of the state. Yet in his view both sexes should strive for the same personal quality, *sōphrosúnē*, the control of one's life by intelligent wisdom.[62] The adjective for this same quality is *sōphrōn,* translated in the King James Version as "sober" and already discussed as one of Paul's prerequisites for a good bishop (1 Tim. 3:2; Titus 1:8). And this adjective of self-discipline leads off Paul's list of character achievements for mature men (Titus 2:2) and young women (Titus 2:4), reinforced by the same quality required in young men (Titus 2:6). If assignments of the sexes diverge, the gospel still expects them to face the same process of developing moral skills.

Paul lists women's personal standards in outlining the female ideal (1 Tim. 2:9-15), requirements for deacons' wives (1 Tim. 3:11), values for elder women (Titus 2:3), and values for young women (Titus 2:4-5). A dozen qualities on these lists equal or are similar to men's standards. The few unique feminine qualities pertain to dress, homemaking, and mothering. Thus, the gospel establishes an area of special female competence but defines the majority of personal values as shared by both genders. Scripture knows no artificial stereotypes like the helpless female or the combative male. One would expect the apostles' letters to be true to Jesus, whose courage no one doubts, but who blended assertiveness with tenderness and sensitivity. And did Paul deny this range of qualities to women? As discussed in connection with 1 Corinthians 14, Paul's docile woman is a wrong impression based on his criticism of some women interrupting public worship. And the

Pastoral rule must be read in a similar context: "And I do not permit a woman to teach or to have authority over a man, but to be in silence" (1 Tim. 2:12, NKJB). But the background is the severe apostasy that hangs like a cloud over the Pastoral Letters.

Timothy and Titus are both told not to allow their authority to be challenged (1 Tim. 4:12; Titus 2:15). And the woman "in silence" follows Paul's command that leaders pray "without anger or quarreling" (1 Tim. 2:8, RSV). The King James "doubting" for this last word (*dialogismós*) makes no sense with "anger," an act of social aggression, so committee translations favor the view that here "the thought of outward disputing and discussion is uppermost."[63] Thus, Paul asks priesthood officers to seek harmony in worship just before asking women to respect authority, two sides of the same coin. The woman's "silence" is respect for those presiding as the Church gathered, the exact situation of Corinthian women told not to take over the meetings, though they participated in them (1 Cor. 11:5). It is even doubtful whether "silence" is the right translation for the Pastoral caution, for there is another obvious alternative. Paul uses *hēsuchía,* which in classical Greek meant a state of rest and contentment.[64] Paul clearly uses that sense in asking Thessalonian men to avoid idleness, to work "with quietness . . . and eat their own bread" (2 Thes. 3:12). "Silence" is not what Paul had in mind there; he was referring to being at peace with one's work, a message extended to all the Thessalonian converts (1 Thes. 4:11). On this evidence Paul was not stressing "silence" to women as much as he was peaceful support of their leaders.

The same basic issue is behind the other apparent limitations for women: they are to learn "with all subjection" (1 Tim. 2:11); to be "obedient to their own husbands" (Titus 2:5); in earlier letters, to "submit" to their husbands (Eph. 5:22; Col. 3:18). There are some important steps in understanding Paul here. First, the above terms translate forms of *hupotássō,* which means to put under the organizational leadership of another. Second, every person in the Early Church, including Christ himself, was placed in such a relationship, as discussed in connection with Ephesians 5.

An example is the duty of all men and women "to be subject to" civil authorities (Titus 3:1). This suggests what such terms meant in practice. No wife is commanded to be blindly "obedient" (Titus 2:5), a most unfortunate translation if it suggests to some husbands that they are in charge of their wives' personal decisions. But since all are commanded to be subject to Church and governmental leaders, "submit" means to support the one assigned to plan for the group. Civil leaders seek the security and welfare of the state and have authority to request resources or personal help for those purposes. Family members are likewise "subject" to the family leader in the sense of accepting assignments for the common good of the family.

"Submit" is probably offensive today but remains significant in stating leadership relationships. Instead of being emotionally unnerved by a word, thinking people will ask what concept is being taught. "Cooperate" is a loose translation, but that is the working concept that Paul asks of all Saints—cooperation with Church and civil leaders, and cooperation of wives with the family leadership of their husbands. The Early Church and the restored Church also make the husband responsible for cooperation with his wife—supporting her financially, responding to her emotionally, and helping with their common tasks. Since Eve is an essential role model, Paul's comment on her should be seen as incidental reasoning, not revelation, for Paul's subject was not Eve but the importance of following priesthood leadership (1 Tim. 2: 12-14). Modern revelation teaches that the Fall was as much preplanned as was the Atonement. And just as Christ used his agency to carry out his part of that plan, so did the original parents of mankind, who were given the consequences of their actions and the right of choice. (Moses 4:8-9; also 4:17). So Latter-day Saints have viewed the fall in eternal perspective: "This was a transgression of the law, but not a sin in the strict sense, for it was something that Adam and Eve had to do."[65] These words of Joseph Fielding Smith rephrase what was said many times by Brigham Young: "We should never blame Mother Eve, not the least."[66] Rather than downgrading Eve for her initiative, Latter-day Saint doctrine opens the opposite possibility of her superior insight in taking the first step to create the mortal condition for our testing.[67]

Husbands well know areas where wives' skills and awareness exceed their own. This is not so much a matter of sexuality as it is a matter of individuality, for business, government, and Church councils exist because decisions are usually better made by a group than by an individual. Married couples need the best thinking of each partner to reach their maximum potential. The husband's assignment as provider drains much of his time and thought away from the home, while the wife probably uses a greater range of skills in the home. This is illustrated by the timeless pattern written as a Roman epitaph just before Paul: "She loved her husband in her heart; she bore two sons, one of whom she left on earth, the other beneath it; she was pleasant to talk with, and she walked with grace; she kept the house and worked in wool."[68] A successful wife is companion, psychologist, teacher, nurse, nutritionist, economist, interior decorator, custodian, craftsman, and seamstress. Those handling that many areas in the business world are on the executive level. Paul gives moral goals rather than exact roles, but his picture of the woman's world includes critical teaching and managing. But today's woman manages and teaches in a world shaken by technological explosions and in societies weakened by loss of values.

Today's greatest problems and their solutions are in the home. Paul's values for men and women stress example, teaching, and discipline in the home. This is the business of the parental partnership. The greatest problem in our society is the abandonment of children through the abandonment of parental leadership. Mass media and profit-motivated entertainment are falsely educating young people everywhere. For over a century Latterday Saint leaders have stressed the home as the leading unit to counterattack the forces threatening the young. In recent decades, they have seen the home as the main teaching arm of the Church. "Every member a missionary" is now supplemented by "Every parent a teacher." The gospel must be taught in discussions at the dinner table, in private conversations, in scheduled scripture reading, in the sincerest pleadings of family prayer, in family home evening lessons, and in family church attendance. The greatest success will come to parents who know the gospel, who know their children, and who know the world that they all live in. In short, gospel education and broad education for life are critical skills for parenting.

Women have historically suffered from double standards of morality and economics. And from Paul's day to the nineteenth century, discrimination and economic necessity emphasized schooling for men far more than for women, as men were trained to make a living. Now women face the same economic reality prior to marriage, sometimes during marriage, and again during widowhood. But a nonworking mother certainly needs knowledge for effective homemaking and the training of her children, and any woman should seek knowledge for its own sake. President Spencer W. Kimball's profile of women has been inspiring. The Latter-day Saint woman may be single or married, a mother or childless; she is service oriented and measures priorities by the values of the restored gospel. She is not at the mercy of others' opinions, for she studies scripture herself;[69] her mind is developed: "Good women are articulate as well as affectionate."[70] Her goals may be personal improvement or service to family, Church, or community, but in her own way and without compulsion she seeks to meet President Kimball's challenge: "Sharpen the skills you have been given."[71] President Kimball has emphasized, "We do not desire the women of the Church to be uninformed or ineffective."[72]

Grace and Saving Works

Hundreds of tracts and sermons on being saved reiterate a few basic propositions: the sinfulness of mankind, the threat of punishment, and the acceptance of God's grace through Christ to prevent the punishment. Good works have no significant place in such a scheme because of the fallen nature of human beings and because of God's total power of initiative. As one Protestant writer puts it, "Faith wrought by the grace of the spirit lays aside trust in self, denies all self-confidence, renounces any thought of merit even in our faith; and entrusts the believer as a helpless, undeserving, ill-deserving, hell-deserving sinner wholly to the goodness, mercy, love, kindness, and grace of God revealed in Jesus Christ."[73] There are more subtle presentations of basic Protestantism, but none more forthright. Popular presentations stress the total guilt and spiritual incompetence of men and women.

The young Gandhi was exposed to such Christianity after deeply feeling that "morality is the basis of things, and that truth is the substance of all morality."[74] Therefore he recoiled from this religion that altered the punishment without changing the person. When he was taught that the Atonement was superimposed on the sinner and that "all good works were useless," he replied, "If this be the Christianity acknowledged by all Christians, I cannot accept it. I do not seek redemption from the consequences of my sin. I seek to be redeemed from sin itself, or rather from the very thought of sin."[75] In other words, he judged the Protestant premise to be morally shallow, feeling in his heart that true religion would result in gradually ridding one's life of the sins that caused alienation from God. But a religion rewarding works contradicts the traditional Christian principle that men and women are created to be noncontributing beings. Calvin emphasized their degradation before God:

> Observe that the righteousness of God is not sufficiently displayed, unless he alone is held to be righteous, and freely communicates righteousness to the undeserving. . . . For so long as man has anything, however small, to say in his own defense, so long he deducts something from the glory of God. To this purpose, indeed, Paul . . . says, that all the parts of our salvation are treasured up with Christ, that we may glory only in the Lord (1 Cor. 1:29). For he intimates that whosoever imagines he has anything of his own, rebels against God, and obscures his glory. Thus . . . we never truly glory in him until we have utterly discarded our own glory.[76]

Here, works ride on a religious teeter-totter. Only by abasing mankind and their righteous acts can God's majesty rise. But such traditional views developed because medieval Christianity lost its knowledge of man's eternal heritage. Modern revelation does not picture man as a groveling creature: "Man was also in the beginning with God" (D&C 93:29). God's basic relationship with men and women did not arise after Adam sinned, but when Christ stood before Adam and all his future descendants prior to creation. Critics have barked at the heels of the most spectacular source for our knowledge of the premortal council, the Book of Abraham, revealed to Joseph Smith as an inspired translation or reconstruction. Hugh Nibley recently published the striking parallels of the Apocalypse of Abraham, a book dated at about Paul's time, in which God speaks of those who first existed "in the light . . . and then afterwards I gave commandment to them through my word."[77] Commentators are puzzled by Paul's reference to God as the "Father of spirits" (Heb. 12:9). But Joseph Smith bluntly taught that mankind is of the race of the Gods: "Spirits are eternal. At the first organization in heaven we were all present and saw the Savior chosen and appointed, and the plan of salvation made, and we sanctioned it."[78] Titus, the book stressing the importance of people's works for salvation, starts with the importance of people—God's promise of eternal life to them "before the world began" (Titus 1:2).

Far from being Calvin's low objects of grace, men and women are the literal children of God, and the world was framed for their advancement. God's children have come knowing the risk of venturing to earth, trusting in the premortal promise that the Savior would come to atone for their sins, but with their responsibility for discerning the light and for walking in it. They are independent agents in God's universe; under him they are creators within their own spheres of assignment. This is the earthly completion of salvation that began as a divine assurance prior to mortality: "God . . . saved us and called us with an holy calling, not according to our works, but according to his own purpose and grace, which was given us in Christ Jesus before the world began" (2 Tim. 1:9). Full salvation was then a promise before any opportunity to do works, so it did not originate by works. Yet the

Pastoral Letters contain a dozen forthright commands to good works. So mortal works fulfill the plan of the premortal promise. If grace is stressed and works also are stressed, the simple answer is that both are important to salvation.

Sensitive men and women are grateful for the Atonement. But God's unlimited mercy should elevate their self-confidence, not erase it. God's power and man's significance blend, just as the related issues of his grace and man's works blend. Paul plainly teaches that Christ's goal was not merely to cancel past sins but to lead mankind to a life above sin. Greek has a very specific purpose clause, introduced by the preposition *hína*, translated literally "in order that." And Paul strikingly expresses the purpose of the Atonement by using this construction twice to reinforce his point. "The grace of God" is manifest "in order that" we may avoid "worldly lusts" and "live with righteousness and godliness in this world" (Titus 2:12, literal trans.). And the point is driven home as he restates the doctrine: "Jesus Christ . . . gave himself for us in order that he might redeem us from all iniquity and purify a people special to himself, zealous of good works" (Titus 2:13-14, literal trans.). Paul clearly considers the Atonement incomplete without individual actions. The main point of Titus is to stress the good works necessary to retain Christ's grace.

Yet some give the proof-text "Not by works of righteousness which we have done, but according to his mercy he saved us" (Titus 3:5). But quoting that alone perverts Paul's message, for here Paul refers to salvation from the evil works mentioned just before (Titus 3:3)—and salvation comes not through mercy alone but "by the washing of regeneration, and renewing of the Holy Ghost" (Titus 3:5). In English or Greek, "regeneration" is literally rebirth, the same act of baptism that Jesus challenged Nicodemus to accept (John 3:5). So saving grace came to the early Saints through their agency in accepting the ordinances. Paul's point is not to subtract righteous works from salvation, but to show that the Lord mercifully offered salvation when only wicked works were in view. "Not by works of righteousness" really indicates the need of such works in the future, as God had to send his Son to compensate for their lack in the past. The apostle's message here is that in spite of unrighteous works, God allowed forgiveness through Christ and its acceptance through baptism. After that ordinance, the momentum of a continuing righteous life is required for exaltation.

That is also the thought of the grace-works message of Ephesians 2, for Paul there teaches salvation "when we were dead in sins" (Eph. 2:5)—grace came by repentance to people formerly undeserving of grace. And Titus emphasizes that the purpose of the forgiveness is to reach a higher life; in Ephesians grace is also followed by the command that one reborn in Christ must be "created . . . unto good works" (Eph. 2:10). Paul concluded the grace passage of Titus 3:5 with the doctrine that baptized members have the duty "to maintain good works" (Titus 3:8). Those who think that Paul downgraded works are in for a shock if they will open a complete Bible concordance. Paul used *érgon* eighty-two times; it is translated as "work" and sometimes "deed," mostly in the positive sense of asking the Saints to produce good works. Those books confronting the Judaizers are the exception and use "works" negatively in a limited context. Hebrews is an example, contrasting the "dead works" of the superseded temple (Heb. 9:14; also 6:1) with the "good works" expected of every true Saint (Heb. 10:24; also 13:21). Excluding the nondoctrinal note to Philemon, every other letter of Paul expects the performance of "good works" from the baptized members. Paul's letters were generally written to reinforce faith in God's grace and to command the actions consistent with it. And his last letters state vividly this double formula for salvation.

These Pastoral Letters stress good works for salvation because they oppose false Christians teaching the irrelevance of works. Simon the Samaritan, whom Peter rebuked, was discussed in connection with the false teachers of 1 Timothy. Early Christian sources make Simon Magus the pioneer of Gnostic systems that grew more elaborate in the second century. He had already taught a central heresy imitated by later Gnostics—the scheme of imagined "angels and powers, by whom also he declared this world was formed."[79] As noted, these false generations of gods correlate with Paul's condemnation of "genealogies," which are false and debatable deviations (Titus 3:9). And Simon's strange "theology" was matched by a new morality, for he taught that standards of virtue came from inferior gods "to bring men into bondage . . . and that those who are his should be freed from the rule of them who made the world." The result is the striking opposition of apostolic truth by a justification through faith: "Those who place their trust in him . . . are saved through his grace, and not on account of their own righteous actions."[80] Irenaeus, the second-century bishop reporting these views, knew in his day that Simon's successors "lead profligate lives," and earlier information showed that Simon's first followers were "free" and could "live as they please."[81]

Peter's last known letter confirms that teachings like Simon's permeated the Church: "While they promise them liberty, they themselves are slaves of corruption" (2 Pet. 2:19, NKJB). In the immediate decades afterward, Jude and John wrote letters revealing the same lawless piety. All of this greatly illuminates the false teachers opposed by Paul in writing to Titus and Timothy. The struggle was critical, "for there are many rebellious people" (Titus 1:10, NIV). They were literally "insubordinate" (Titus 1:10, RSV) in the sense of not following their appointed leaders. One causing division was to be warned only a few times, for he had "turned away" from the faith (Titus 3:11, literal trans.). Paul wrote again that apostates "turn away from the truth" (Titus 1:14, literal trans.); this striking phraseology appears also in Paul's last letter of 2 Timothy. Thus, Paul wrote, "It is necessary to silence those who are overturning whole households, for shameful gain teaching things they ought not to teach" (Titus 1:11, literal trans.). Their "Jewish myths" (Titus 1:14, RSV) must not be taken merely as Judaism, for Paul accepted the Old Testament. These were perversions of Judaism itself—a reinterpretation of the Old Testament that Simon and later Gnostics were guilty of. "Unto the pure all things are pure" (Titus 1:15). This applies to overdone dietary restrictions of religious or health faddists. Paul may well have had in mind early Gnostic prohibitions of eating flesh, as discussed in connection with 1 Timothy. Since he spoke against intoxicating drink, his principle does not apply to harmful substances opposed by the prophets.

In a striking parallel to the close of 1 Timothy, Paul ridiculed the special knowledge claimed by these counter-Christians. The Lord himself had given the test of action to his apostles: "If ye love me, keep my commandments" (John 14:15). And for Paul, belief in Christ without doing Christ's works is false teaching: "They confess that they know God, but in works they deny him" (Titus 1:16, literal trans.). Thus, a religion failing to make disciples' deeds a condition of full salvation is just as wrong as is a religion failing to teach forgiveness through Christ. Grace and works both save because both contribute to salvation in the celestial kingdom, as modern revelation makes clear (D&C 76: 50-53, 69). Faithful Protestants are moral people, displaying more profound religion than the Reformation slogans—faith alone and grace alone. That reduced formula is presumptuous, for no one can go to Paul's letters and weight the exact proportions of grace, faith, and faithful works required for exaltation. Wisdom is found in the common saying "Pray as though everything depends on the Lord, and work as though everything depends on you."

Just as in modern revelation (D&C 130:20-21), Paul teaches that blessings come by obedience to God's laws, including the ultimate blessing of being with God in eternity. The Greek word for law is *nómos*, and theologians use "antinomian" to describe Simon-like people who consider moral rules irrelevant to salvation. Protestantism is admittedly close to the brink here: "Yet the antinomians have a point. The gospel itself, as Wesley saw, is 'within an hair's breadth' of antinomianism."[82] But Paul's last word should settle this subject: "The law is good if one uses it lawfully" (1 Tim. 1:8, NKJB)—that is, the law is good if one uses Paul's blending of grace and obedience, faith followed by works. Protestant theory permanently shatters man's ability to perform: "The best the law can do for us is to bring home to us our sinfulness . . . and so prepare us for the remedy offered in the gospel. . . . Hence the gospel calls us, not to do, but to believe."[83]

On the contrary, Paul taught that the new person in Christ would put sinfulness behind and learn to live a higher life. This progress is the eternal purpose of Christ's restored gospel.

2 TIMOTHY

Profile

Sent from: Paul, in prison at Rome.

Sent to: Timothy, supervising the Church in the Ephesian region.

Date: About A.D. 66.

Purpose: To request Timothy's coming before Paul's execution and to share Paul's final testimony and prophecies about the Church.

Main themes: Apostasy of the Church; enduring to the end.

Background

Paul's Martyrdom

"At Rome Nero was the first who stained with blood the rising faith," Tertullian wrote around A.D. 200, naming Peter and Paul as Nero's victims there.[84] Tertullian was a converted lawyer, expert in Roman affairs and Roman history; he was also passionate about truth and information from the Early Church. Thus, his details about Paul's death must be respected, even though their origins are not clear. Tertullian had no doubt that Paul was "beheaded," a death "suited to Roman citizenship," since it spared him the agony of suffering.[85] Elsewhere Tertullian lists the cities where the apostles founded churches, including Rome, "where Paul wins his crown in a death like John's," a reference to the similar beheading of John the Baptist.[86] The later historian Eusebius accepted this story, writing of Nero, "It is related that in his time Paul was beheaded in Rome itself." [87] The source of this information was apparently Origen, a careful scholar of the early third century, who also wrote that Paul "was martyred in Rome under Nero."[88] Much earlier, there is unmistakable reference to this death of Paul from Clement, bishop at Rome before the end of the first century. But to understand it, one must first understand Paul's involvement with Nero's persecution of the Christians.

In July, A.D. 64, summer heat lay upon the center of the empire, where news of Nero's scandals would periodically infect the city. Fire broke out in the huddled shops near the great circus. A fateful wind projected the flames down the length of the circus, through narrow streets, and over the hills, sparing nothing and no one. Fleeing refugees stared at escape routes cut off by sudden fiery walls. The only defense was to destroy lines of buildings that otherwise would have been bridges for the blaze. After five days of chaos, only four of the city's fourteen districts were untouched: "Three were levelled to the ground, while in the other seven were left only a few shattered, half-burnt relics of houses."[89] The astute and aristocratic Tacitus is the best surviving source of information about the fire; he hated Nero but gives no reason to believe rumors of his complicity. But public outrage made Nero the scapegoat; then he proved his innocence by blaming the strange sect of the Christians. Although Tacitus considered Christianity a "destructive superstition," he reported that his sources were sorry for Christian sufferings, since they were not "for the public good, but to glut one man's cruelty."[90]

Any true disciple, Jesus said, must be prepared to "take up his cross, and follow me" (Matt. 16:24). Many first-century Christians did this literally:

> Nero fastened the guilt and inflicted the most exquisite tortures on a class hated for their abominations, called Christians by the populace. Christus, from whom the name had its origin, suffered the extreme penalty during the reign of Tiberius at the hands of the procurator Pontius Pilate. And the destructive superstition, thus checked for the moment, again broke out not only in Judaea, the source of the evil, but even in Rome, where all things hideous and shameful are collected from the world and become popular. First, therefore, those who confessed were arrested. Then upon their information an immense multitude was convicted, not so much for the crime of arson as for the hatred of mankind.

And mockery was added to their deaths. They were covered with the skins of beasts, torn by dogs, and perished; many were fastened to crosses or were burned with fire; and after daylight others were burned as torches in the night.[91]

This judicial assault at Rome apparently left the Christians of the rest of the empire relatively safe. Though public prejudice permitted the persecutions, Tacitus writes as though the technical charge was "the crime of arson." Christian belief itself was never illegal by any evidence during Paul's life. As discussed, he had probably been released a year before Nero's fire, at which time he would have been in Spain or in the general area around Greece. He would have continued his labors. From Rome there may have been expanding waves of judicial inquiry, finally reaching the leaders. Or more likely, enemies cried treason to try to implicate Christian leaders and outlaw the religion. The martyrdom of Paul and Peter was under Nero, for no Christian source suggests their death date after A.D. 68. As mentioned in appendix A, the historian Eusebius dates their deaths as A.D. 67, perhaps on the basis of information that they outlived the Roman fire by some years. Some scholars mechanically place their deaths right after the fire of A.D. 64, but without certainty.

When the Roman bishop Clement wrote the Corinthians thirty years later, he linked the apostles' courage and the Neronian persecution. The opening of his letter suggests that he wrote about A.D. 96; some tact was demanded during the last part of the reign of Domitian, another Nero. In these circumstances Clement referred to "the greatest and most righteous pillars," who were "persecuted and contended unto death."[92] With this unmistakable but careful reference to martyrdom, he surveyed the lives of Peter and Paul and added his clear reference to the "immense multitude" of martyrs that Tacitus had described: "To these men with their holy lives was gathered a great multitude of the elect, who were the victims of jealousy and offered among us the fairest example in their endurance under many indignities and tortures."[93] Since no other major persecution is known in the first century, Clement of Rome plainly ties the deaths of Paul and

Peter to the Roman events of Nero's last years, a general association without any strict chronology. He notes their martyrdom only three decades after the death of Paul, who faced execution for the faith in the Christian trials between A.D. 64 and 68.

Reason for Writing

"The time of my departure is at hand" (2 Tim. 4:6). This tells how serious Paul's feelings were as he wrote his last letter to Timothy, and also how seriously anyone ought to read his convictions written in the shadow of eternity. He had suffered in many prisons and had faced death many times. Now the Spirit whispered that his mission was finished, and he wrote with the realization that Nero had made Christian blood cheap. Indeed, what could he expect but to walk to Calvary with the Master, who promised nothing less to his apostles? But, like the Lord, on the eve of his death he continued to pour out precious counsel to those about him. He asked for some help but repaid it by giving the strength of his mind and spirit, not complaining but building up others to the end. Paul's final example of courage is as precious as are the words of his letter. His faith glows so strongly that it is easy to read 2 Timothy without realizing the grim conditions under which it was written. These are barely sketched by Paul's strong words of appreciation to Onesiphorus, who "arrived in Rome" and made considerable effort to find out where Paul was imprisoned (2 Tim. 1:17, NKJB): "He often refreshed me, and was not ashamed of my chain" (2 Tim. 1:16, NKJB). Perhaps the same thing could be said of the Roman Saints that sent greetings, including Linus and the woman Claudia (2 Tim. 4:21).[94]

Did Timothy send Onesiphorus to Rome to find Paul and deliver a message and assistance? Here was a man who evidently could afford the journey, for Paul mentions "how many things" he furnished Paul earlier at Ephesus (2 Tim. 1:18). Paul's care to mention his household is perhaps gratitude for everybody's risk in allowing Onesiphorus to come to Rome. Perhaps this brother was now returning with Tychicus, whom Paul was sending "to Ephesus" (2 Tim. 4:12). Such greetings to an Ephesian family combine with Timothy's concern for what is happening "in Asia" (2 Tim. 1:15); also, the apostate Hymenaeus (2 Tim. 2:17) was at Ephesus (1 Tim. 1:20; also 1:3). Thus, 2 Timothy was addressed to Paul's trusted understudy, probably still presiding over the Church in the Roman province of Asia and its metropolis of Ephesus. His ministry was surveyed in the background material of 1 Timothy. This second letter updates his work and reveals the spiritual power of this young assistant to Paul. The letter is Timothy's transfer: "Be diligent to come to me quickly" (2 Tim. 4:9, NKJB). Why, then, did Paul write much advice on Timothy's personal life and on the use of his presiding authority? The obvious answer is that Paul could not be sure whether he would be alive when Timothy arrived. Thus, 2 Timothy contains precious personal advice on how to live the gospel and serve when called.

Paul had probably been visiting Timothy shortly before his arrest. This seems connected with Paul's warning: "Alexander the coppersmith did me much evil" (2 Tim. 4:14). Though the name is common, this man is probably the same man excommunicated at Ephesus by Paul earlier (1 Tim. 1:20). Timothy must guard against him in that area, for he "greatly withstood our words" (2 Tim. 4:15). Probably this former Church member accused Paul before the authorities with lies and distortions, making Paul's defense futile. Paul was probably sent to Rome automatically, inasmuch as Christian leaders would be of special concern to Nero. Perhaps they sailed from nearby Miletus, where a companion Trophimus had to be left because of sickness (2 Tim. 4:20). Paul had left personal things in the more northern city of Troas (2 Tim. 4:13); he may have been arrested there or he may have visited Troas on the way to Ephesus or in custody on the way to Rome.

Now Paul wanted his books and his cloak (2 Tim. 4:13), for circumstances had turned against him. He had received an initial hearing and was apparently awaiting final trial; he was obviously held as probably guilty. "At my first defense no one stood with me, but all forsook me. . . . But the Lord . . . strengthened me. . . .

And I was delivered out of the mouth of the lion" (2 Tim. 4: 16-17, NKJB). None of this fits his Acts imprisonment, for the letters of that time looked forward to a release, whereas in 2 Timothy Paul looks only to final condemnation. With time on his hands, he wanted the books. He needed Timothy immediately, urgently asking a second time that he come "before winter" (2 Tim. 4:21). With the cold season coming on, the thick cloak would be necessary in his stone prison.[95]

No known document describes Paul's final trial. When he sent 2 Timothy, visitors were still allowed, and the literate Luke was still with him (2 Tim. 4:11). Timothy was coming and was instructed to bring Mark. Years after being considered unfit for a Gentile mission, Mark had now proved his worth as being "useful to me for ministry" (2 Tim. 4:11, NKJB). Is this a hint that Mark was needed at Paul's trial? He could testify of Paul's earliest missionary work, as Timothy could testify of all thereafter. Mark could also report the earliest preaching of the Jerusalem apostles—perhaps even something of Jesus himself. By then both Mark and Luke had probably written their Gospels and were the historians of the faith. It could not yet have been a crime to be a Christian—Paul would not have asked Timothy and Mark to march into certain death. The hundreds of their brothers and sisters condemned after the fire were apparently accused of starting it. The issue now was surely different. Was Paul risking the brightest minds of the Church to prevent a decision that Christian belief was unlawful? Accused in some form of being a traitor to the state, Paul wrote for help in facing his trial. Yet he did not expect anything less than execution. Because of this, Paul shared his inner convictions with his son in the gospel, affording a matchless perspective on Paul's life and his knowledge of the future of the Early Church.

Main Teachings

Apostasy of the Church

The classic Latter-day Saint study distinguishes between "apostasy *from* the Church" and "the apostasy *of* the Church."[96]

All scholars agree that the former topic permeates the Pastorals. Yet Christian scholars do not look for evidence of complete apostasy and therefore miss the big picture in the Pastorals. But the theme of 2 Timothy cannot be seen by looking in gopher holes—one has to stand up and view the landscape. The danger to the Church is signaled by the unusual act of Paul naming six people in 2 Timothy who have turned from the faith.[97] Moreover, the time of writing is all important—first in comparison with the other later writings of the New Testament. Paul's last letter is his most pessimistic, and so is Peter's. Writing in the next decades, Jude and John have a siege mentality. For instance, John notes the many false teachers and bluntly says, "It is the last hour" (1 Jn. 2:18, NKJB), with clear reference to apostasy and not the Second Coming. None of these apostles, least of all Paul, prophesies that the Early Church would continue in favor with God. Under these circumstances, the total divine rejection of the Church is a critical issue.

By any analysis, 2 Timothy was written after the Neronian persecution started. As discussed in introducing this letter, both pagan and Christian historians stressed the "huge crowd" of Christians then slain for the faith. Can one overestimate how many deserted the faith everywhere after that event? True, massive execution was confined to the city of Rome, but obviously there was fear of its repetition in other centers of the empire. Indeed, Paul was arrested outside of Rome, probably in the province of Asia, present western Turkey. Timothy received Paul's last letter there and was reminded about conditions known to him in his region: "This you know, that all those in Asia have turned away from me" (2 Tim. 1:15, NKJB). But the commentators here show mass apathy. Paul wrote only three years after the greatest shock the Early Church had experienced, and scholars' opinions show only that these watchmen are not on the walls. They speak of Paul overstating conditions because of depression or frustration—or complaining of those who failed to defend him at his arrest in Asia, or of those from Asia in Rome who failed to come to his aid.

This last is the worst possibility, since Paul appealed to Timothy's knowledge, which pertained to Asia but not to Rome.

Paul's following mention of Onesimus' help is supposed to prove that "all . . . Asia" was a reference only to those failing to help. But the key here is the preceding verses, not the afterthought. Reference to Timothy's knowledge—"this you know"— shows that common concerns of Paul and Timothy were the subject of "all . . . Asia." Just before that, Paul told Timothy to follow the "sound words" that Paul taught him (2 Tim. 1:13)— and to "guard the truth that has been entrusted" to him (2 Tim. 1:14, RSV). [98] When "all . . . Asia" appears in the next sentence, it is simply to say that this section has now "turned away" from both "sound words" and the truth entrusted to Timothy. And Paul's key verb is one of gospel rebellion, for he earlier warned Titus of those "that turn from the truth." The real context of "all . . . Asia" is doctrinal disbelief.

A whole province lost to the true gospel? The only knowledgeable commentator is the historian of the conversion of that province. Luke's epic of massive conversions was followed by the prophecy of apostasy in Asia, reviewed toward the end of chapter 3 of this book. Scholars have noted the close ties of 2 Timothy 4 with Paul's farewell speech at Ephesus, recorded by Luke in Acts 20. But Paul's reference to the turning away of "all . . . Asia" in 2 Timothy 1 has the same close ties to Acts 19, where Luke went out of his way to note membership "throughout all Asia" (Acts 19:26), prefaced by the "all" in Asia who heard the gospel (Acts 19:10). Luke probably wrote Acts just a few years before 2 Timothy, and with phrasing based on mutual missionary rejoicing. So "all Asia" was already Christian vocabulary for the entire province. The larger point is that Luke's theme for the third mission is the Church's rise and fall in Asia. After vividly showing the conversion of hundreds and even thousands, he closes the story with the apostle's pathetic prophecy that Asia would be choked by apostasy "after my departing" (Acts 20:29). As the accompanying chart shows, ten years before writing 2 Timothy,

The Asian Apostasy During the Apostles' Lives

Event	Date (A.D.)	Reference	Scripture
Widespread conversion in Asia	54	Acts 19:10	"All they which dwelt in Asia heard the word of the Lord"
		Acts 19:26	"Almost throughout all Asia" Paul converted people from worship of Pagan deities
Warning to Ephesus	58	Acts 20:29-30	"After my departing shall grievous wolves enter in among you, not sparing the flock. Also of your own selves shall men arise, speaking perverse things, to draw away disciples after them"
Widespread Asian apostasy	66	2 Tim. 1:15	"All those in Asia have turned away from me" (NKJB)
Prophecies of total apostasy	66	2 Tim. 3:13	"But evil men and impostors will grow worse and worse, deceiving and being deceived" (NKJB)
		2 Tim. 4:3-4	"For the time will come when they will not endure sound doctrine, but according to their own desires, because they have itching ears, they will heap up for themselves teachers; and they will turn their ears away from the truth, and be turned aside to fables" (NKJB)
		2 Tim. 3:1-5	"But know this, that in the last days there shall come difficult times. For men shall be lovers of themselves, lovers of money . . . lovers of pleasure rather than lovers of God, having a form of godliness, but denying its power" (literal trans.)
Final Warning at Ephesus	96	Rev. 2:5	"Remember therefore from what you have fallen; repent and do the first works, or else I will come to you quickly and remove your lampstand from its place—unless you repent" (NKJB)

Paul stood before the Ephesian leaders. At that time he wept in warning that the wolves would lacerate the Asian flock. Later, he faced departure from life, still preoccupied with the same apostasy of "all . . . Asia"—and beyond.

Luke and Timothy were present when Paul warned the Ephesian elders about the coming apostasy, and Luke chose to end his record of the final mission of Paul on that pessimistic note, just as Paul wrote his last letter in the same mood. It should not tax the imagination that so many deserted in Asia. Paul was writing from Rome, where Nero still lived and the threat of death surely turned lukewarm believers into apostates. After all, at Paul's first hearing "no man stood with me" (2 Tim. 4:16), which comes perilously close to saying, "All those in Rome have turned away from me." If the fever was raging in these major locations of the Early Church, the whole patient was critically ill. As mentioned, the problems in 1 Timothy are the same in Titus, which shows that serious dissent had spread throughout the branches. This picture is validated by the Lord's messages to the Asian churches in the later book of Revelation. There a typical branch has "a few names" that are still faithful (Rev. 3:4), and all are given stern warnings to repent while there is still time.

The terms closing 1 Timothy are repeated in 2 Timothy as Paul warns of specific false teachers "who have fallen from the truth, saying that the resurrection has already come" (2 Tim. 2:18, literal trans.). This same thinking tenaciously prevailed three decades later when John identified the "antichrists" as teaching that Christ did not "come in the flesh" (1 Jn. 4:3). As discussed, the Gnostics were characterized by their antimaterialistic bias from their first-century roots. Their complex mythologies and grotesque doctrines generally had the inner logic of saving their god and his worshippers from contact with physical things. Orthodox Christian councils and scholars have also adopted this antimaterialistic premise for the Father's person— most Gnostics did the same for the Father's creation, the person of the Son, and the resurrection of the human race. For to them, nothing material was truly eternal, so the Resurrection must be explained away. Specific first-century evidence comes from a primitive Gnostic named Menander.[99] Samaritan Justin Martyr said that Menander was a Samaritan and a "disciple" of Simon the Sorcerer.[100] Menander taught his followers "that they should never die," and his reasoning was that "they obtain the resurrection by being baptized into him."[101] So the Resurrection was spiritualized and thus denied. This illustrates the similar false teachings that Paul opposed in 2 Timothy.

In this letter and in the writings of John, the priesthood organization of the Early Church was shown under attack. There is one clear casualty. Demas was earlier mentioned as a fellow-laborer with Luke (Col. 4:14; Philem. l:24). But at the end he has "forsaken me, having loved this present world, and is departed unto Thessalonica" (2 Tim. 4:10). Paul afterward says that he sent Tychicus to Ephesus, and others named after Demas were probably away from Rome on assignment. No less than nine men seem to be fellow-laborers sent by Paul to different areas as his life closed. Tychicus must be typical; he was from Asia and was sent there to replace Timothy, who was now coming to Rome to be with Paul. Both "beloved" and "faithful" (Col. 4:7), Tychicus is obviously another regional representative, directing bishops in a major area. Forces of rebellion probably consumed the main attention of these leaders, for the Pastoral Letters mainly guide regional leaders to direct members and to keep them from deception. To accomplish this, area supervisors had to appoint leaders and train them, the real meaning of Paul's reminder to teach "faithful men" (the bishops) so they could "teach others" (their flocks). This verse (2 Tim. 2:2) has nothing to do with handing the Christian faith down through the centuries.

The absence of missionary orientation contradicts the normal understanding of Timothy's charge to "do the work of an evangelist" (2 Tim. 4:5). Though the thought might be to convert non-Christians, the reality is otherwise, for this immediately follows Timothy's duty to save the members from turning away to false teachers. Indeed, this calling is the same one assigned in 1 Timothy, where he was told to be "an example of the believers"

(1 Tim. 4:12). An example from the believers for outsiders, or "an example *to* the believers"? Some variation of the latter is preferred by scholars and current committee translations, partly because Titus was to be an example to Church members (Titus 2:7), and Paul held himself up as the example of gospel living (Philip. 3:17, 2 Thes. 3:9). What did Timothy do? In 1 Timothy, he selected leaders, taught the members of the Church, guided the welfare program, and opposed all who taught false doctrine. This goes far to vindicate Joseph Smith's view that an evangelist in the Early Church blessed the members, as discussed in connection with Ephesians 4. No evidence in the Pastoral Letters shows Timothy laboring with nonmembers. Did the Neronian persecution cause the Church to be cautious about doing missionary work in Paul's final years? Or did the spreading apostasy demand that leaders give their whole time to protecting the flock? Right after 2 Timothy, Paul and the many regional leaders under his direction simply disappear. Were these associates also martyred after the trials of the presiding apostles?

Paul's last letter underlines the coming transition at the deaths of the apostles, and so does the Savior's prophecy on the Mount of Olives. Because the latter is detailed, it is a guide to Paul's similar language. The easy comparison shows that Paul clearly knew Jesus' words and explained the future of the Church in those terms. It is both faith promoting and instructive to see how both sets of prophecies validate and illuminate the other. The following basic questions will help get at the main issues through comparisons:

1. *What times are Jesus and Paul speaking about?* Jesus was asked about Jerusalem's destruction and the end of the world (Matt. 24:1-3). His answer was long and involved, showing that many events would intervene between the Crucifixion and the Second Coming. Like Christ and like other apostles, Paul knew of "the times and the seasons" (1 Thes. 5:1), showing his understanding of the complexities of future religious history. Occasionally Paul mentioned that Christ had come in the latter days of the world, meaning the later dispensations. As discussed in 2 Thessalonians 2,

Paul expected the reign of Satan on earth before the reign of Christ could come. Some conditions of apostasy were in the near future, as when Paul's Greek reads "following times" (1 Tim. 4:1, literal trans.), suggesting immediate later days instead of latter days. So like Jesus, Paul wrote of events from his time up to the extreme wickedness of "the last days" (2 Tim. 3:1).

2. *Can latter-day events be separated from those of the immediate future?* Jesus mentioned two points of departure, the persecution and deaths of the apostles and the destruction of Jerusalem. After each of these events Jesus outlined the era of false teachers and wickedness, giving an overview first (Matt. 24:9-12) and then reviewing the same period after describing Jerusalem's fall (Matt. 24:23-26). He twice refers to this trying period as the time of "false prophets" (Matt. 24:11, 24), and it clearly takes place right after the above events of the first century. Paul is also preoccupied with the coming era of false teachers. Writing almost forty years after Jesus' prophecy, Paul is in the midst of transition from true to false teachers. They surround him. That is why his latter-day prophecy (2 Tim. 3:1-5) abruptly stops on a present note—"from such turn away" (2 Tim. 3:5).

3. *What conditions are in the latter-day world?* There is a verbal correlation between Paul and Christ here. Paul says, "In the last days perilous times shall come" (2 Tim. 3:1). But the Greek reads literally "harsh times," rendered as "difficult times" (JB) or "times of stress" (RSV). Thus, Paul's basic idea is exactly that of Jesus, who speaks of Jerusalem's fall and the following "great tribulation" (Matt. 24:21). This is often translated "affliction" in the King James Version and "distress" in modern translations. Thus, Paul and Christ speak of an age of great difficulty when the world is to be dominated by Satan. Paul gives more details about human degradation and pictures mankind as turning from the love of God to the love of self, money, and pleasure (2 Tim. 3:2, 4). Jesus is less specific but makes the same observation: "Because iniquity will increase, the love of many will grow cool" (Matt. 24:12, literal trans.).

4. *Where is the Church in the age of wickedness?* Christ's

prophecy gives a long period of tribulation before the faithful are gathered out from the world to prepare for his Second Coming. As discussed in connection with Ephesians 1:9-10, Paul also looked forward to a restoration era, but that is not his subject in 2 Timothy. Yet clear parallels with Jesus in his treatment of apostasy show that Paul also expected the latter-day gathering referred to in Matthew 24. Neither Jesus nor Paul give any hint that the true Church will exist in the age of wickedness. As stated, the Savior's formula is clear because he repeated it twice: after Jerusalem's fall come "false Christs and false prophets" to "deceive the very elect" (Matt. 24:24); this restates what he said would occur right after the apostles' martyrdoms: "Many false prophets shall rise, and shall deceive many" (Matt. 24:11). As Paul wrote, many had indeed been deceived; he mourned with Timothy that "all Asia" had deserted Paul and the truth he taught. And with those severe conditions present, Paul added, "Evil men and impostors will grow worse and worse, deceiving and being deceived" (2 Tim. 3:13, NKJB). "Impostors" here is the unanimous choice of current committee translations instead of the King James "seducers." Since Greek-speaking Jews used that term in the sense of false prophets, Paul matched Jesus' "false prophets" with a synonym.[102] Paul also used Jesus' exact word for "deceiving and being deceived." One province was then spoiled—"worse and worse" must mean the loss of others and finally all. Paul's total pessimism can be explained only by his conviction of total apostasy, which he earlier had expressed in 2 Thessalonians 2 in saying that the temple of God, meaning the Church of God, would be possessed by Satan.

In 2 Timothy the final result is "having a form of godliness; but denying the power thereof" (2 Tim. 3:5). This remarkable headline summarizes latter-day conditions and also characterizes the false teachers facing Timothy.[103] So here is the bridge between Paul's day and the future, implying a long absence of the truth. The implications are stunning in "having a form of godliness; but denying the power thereof" (2 Tim. 3:5). This could be said only of religions that have the name but not the reality. "Power" in

Paul is not to be taken lightly, for in the plural it is the word for revelations and miracles. Christian churches today claim the Bible for their guide but on the whole make prophets and the full gifts of the Spirit a matter of history. One commentator writes that after the first century "the gift of prophecy itself, in spite of occasional revivals, gradually fell into disuse and in some measure into disrepute."[104] The charismatic movement has spread across traditional churches in their attempts to revitalize old organizations, a demonstration that much has been lost. And a reader of Paul cannot forget that the gospel itself is power—the "power of God unto salvation" (Rom. 1:16; 1 Cor. 1:18). If the form is without the power, the preaching is without salvation.

Like Jesus, Paul repeats his prophecy of the coming deceptive apostasy: "The time will come when they will not endure sound doctrine. . . . And they shall turn away their ears from the truth, and shall be turned unto fables" (2 Tim. 4:3-4). And who will turn away? Obviously the prophecy fits only Church members; those outside the faith could not lose the truth, for they did not have it. Timothy's commission was to teach "good doctrine" to "the brethren" (1 Tim. 4:6). As discussed, his ministry was to Church members; just before the above prophecy Paul reminded Timothy to strive to keep the members in the faith. But the point of the prophecy is that Timothy is not promised success.

The prophecy on losing sound doctrine also tells how the members will transform the faith: "After their own lusts shall they heap to themselves teachers, having itching ears" (2 Tim. 4:3). But these last three words should appear with "they" and not after "teachers." For translations now follow the clear meaning of the Greek, which makes "having itching ears" apply to Church members: "Because they have itching ears, they will heap up for themselves teachers" (2 Tim. 4:3, NKJB).[105] Thus, the real threat to the Church was not opposition but inner corrosion. Here Paul's last prophecy on the Church fits his last recorded speech on the subject, Acts 20. Both carry the same pessimism about the Church's future and the same mechanism for its failure. What made Paul's Ephesian farewell heartrending to him was not his leaving but his realizing that the great flock he had gathered would be divided and spoiled. There would be successors to the apostles, but not true successors, for after Paul left would come "savage wolves . . . not sparing the flock" (Acts 20:29, NKJB). Again, the real threat to the Church was not opposition but disintegration: "Of your own selves shall men arise, speaking perverse things, to draw away disciples after them" (Acts 20:30). The first known subapostolic writing deals with this very issue; as might be expected, the Corinthians had dismissed their authorized leaders. But the most significant point here is that Clement of Rome wrote and quoted the Lord as prophesying of inner division: "Our apostles also knew through our Lord Jesus Christ that there would be strife for the title of bishop."[106]

Thus, Paul's last words on the Church are words of warning—about counterfeit leaders and a substitute gospel. Christians who recognize the apostasy of Judaism from Jehovah must examine their own roots in the long perspective of Old Testament cycles. Time and again the Lord raised up new prophets with Jeremiah's message: "The prophets prophesy falsely . . . and my people love to have it so" (Jer. 5:31). So the theme of imitation prophets is an old one, simply because it is too easy for inquiring faith to degenerate into self-serving smugness. Paul's career is a reminder that professionals may miss God's message while they are mightily engaged in religious minutiae. Paul told Timothy that the truth would be turned into "fables," literally "myths" in his language (2 Tim. 4:4); and he told the Ephesian elders that future Christian leaders would teach things that were "perverse" (Acts 20:30), meaning in Greek and Latin "turned around," twisted or distorted. Who but God could cut through two millennia of theological complications and reestablish the powerful and understandable set of truths preached by Paul and the early apostles? Latter-day Saints testify of this reality through modern revelations as powerful as Paul's. Their claim cries to be considered with increased seriousness, for there has never been a day of more obvious religious floundering, where leaders were less sure of what Christ's Church is or where to look for it. As a case in point, the following comes from the draft of a "contemporary statement of faith" of a major Christian church: "The body of Christ is one, but its oneness is hidden and distorted by the struggles and enmities that persist in the church as they do in the world. . . . Nonetheless the church is one body in a unity yet to be disclosed."[107]

Enduring to the End

The outer Paul is shown in his missionary history in Acts, but the inner Paul is glimpsed from time to time in his writings, and nowhere more intensely than in his last letter, which is less pastoral than personal. Overall it is well summarized as "an epistle of mingled gloom and glory,"[108] for, in the words of a careful scholar, "humanly speaking, the Church was trembling on the brink of annihilation."[109] We have just seen that statement to be accurate. Thus, Paul's gloom is for the future of the Church, the painful loss of those lost, and the crumbling work of a lifetime. But the glory was his own certainty that he had filled his calling well. He had written powerfully on enduring to the end (Heb. 3:6, 14). But he preached what he also sought to achieve, telling priesthood leaders that neither inconvenience nor persecution could alter his purpose: "That I might finish my course with joy, and the ministry, which I have received of the Lord Jesus, to testify [to] the gospel of the grace of God" (Acts 20:24). Paul was pressing "toward the mark for the prize of the high calling of God in Christ Jesus" (Philip. 3:14). Virtually his last recorded words express satisfaction that the race was won and the crown gained.

Paul's life is a study in priority. Life is not long enough to reach many goals, and Paul reached his because he devoted his life to it. That goal was not comfort, recognition, or possession. He had renounced the world, but not to seek the same false values in more subtle ways in Christ's church. Paul exchanged comfort for thousands of missionary miles; he forfeited the respect of devoted Jews in and out of the Church for the principle that God's will must be done for the Gentiles; at the end he sent for his total personal possessions not on his body—a cloak and parchments (2 Tim. 4:13). Paul's sacrifices were not calculated but grew naturally from his choice to serve the Lord. One following his path of discipleship may not be called to make the same sacrifices, but he or she will be called to place service above self. Paul finally followed his Master to martyrdom, but this was only the last scene of a life drama of making the Master's cause first. Paul's dying for the faith is impressive because he consistently lived for the faith. Paul's convictions that led him to this are the most intriguing parts of 2 Timothy. The book deserves careful reading for gospel advice to Paul's young understudy—this is concentrated in chapter 2 and sprinkled elsewhere. But this closing letter mainly offers priceless insight into why Paul became such a great servant of the Lord. Understanding these personal dimensions of Paul may give direction for equally great service to the Lord today.

Paul's advice to Timothy reveals what was finally important to Paul. Converted on the Damascus road, Paul stayed converted to death, above all giving love and respect for "Jesus Christ . . . raised from the dead according to my gospel" (2 Tim. 2:8). The apostle sought to be worthy of his relationship with the Lord in the gospel. "Flee . . . youthful lusts" was the advice of a mature man who had learned to channel his desires according to righteousness and selfless love (2 Tim. 2:22). This love is rendered "charity" in the King James Version, but the Greek term is Paul's regular word for love (*agápē*), explained so eloquently in 1 Corinthians 13. The older man shared another aspect of self-control with the younger. Paul was always ready to defend the revealed truth—no other example is necessary beyond the Corinthian correspondence. But he cautions Timothy to know the difference between teaching and mere debating: "And the servant of the Lord must not strive" (2 Tim. 2:24). Paul obviously speaks of the striving that is strife, for his word is Greek for doing battle physically or verbally. Teaching others requires patience and humility, Paul explains (2 Tim. 2:24-26)—one can learn this also from his sustained relationships with the Corinthian and Galatian Saints.

Paul's letters prove that he searched the scriptures; the parchments he wanted were probably copies of them (2 Tim. 4:13). And he told Timothy to read the scriptures, though one verse that seemingly says this really doesn't: "Study to shew thyself approved unto God" (2 Tim. 2:15). This sentence uses a Greek word for giving total attention: *"Be diligent* to present yourself approved to God" (2 Tim. 2:15, NKJB, italics added). But Paul writes a moving passage on the power of scripture that shows how years of scripture study moved him: "All scripture" is literally "inspired of God" (literal trans.); it is given "for doctrine, for reproof, for correction, for instruction in righteousness" (2 Tim. 3:16). In other words, scripture is the measuring rod, containing those revealed principles for guiding the thoughts and lives of the Saints. Did "all scripture" mean the New Testament as well as the Old? Timothy was told that he had known the scriptures literally "from infancy" and that they could make him "wise unto salvation," a phrase quoted alone with misleading impact (2 Tim. 3:15). Protestantism, which raised the Bible high in judgment over the medieval church, has justly stressed but wrongly exaggerated this verse. Protestants sometimes tell Latter-day Saints that God would give no more revelation because the Bible was enough to make Timothy "wise unto salvation." But Timothy had only the Old Testament, which by itself did as much to prevent as to promote the salvation of the Jews of that time.

But Paul's full words on scripture suggest the full truth. The prophecies and inspired moral teachings of the Old Testament made Timothy "wise unto salvation through faith which is in Christ Jesus" (2 Tim. 3:15). More is taught here than the principle of believing in Christ—living prophets had to update older scriptures before they had relevance for Timothy. And Paul closes by saying that scripture may make a person "perfect, throughly furnished unto all good works" (2 Tim. 3:17). Ephesians 4:11-12 teaches that this perfection is achieved through apostles and other priesthood leaders. So scripture from past prophets must be supplemented by present and future prophets. Together they make up "all scripture." Stated another way, past scripture is incomplete without the true Church led by prophets. Utah Protestant ministers were asked whether "affiliation with a church is necessary for salvation"; 81 percent answered no, with another 3 percent undecided. [110] But Paul's gospel was larger, for salvation came in Acts as the scriptures led honest people to the true Church for the saving ordinances and inspired guidance to perfection afterward. As discussed in chapter 3, this issue is raised by Acts 15: scripture alone does not make the true Church, but the true Church with authorized prophets makes new scripture.

It is hard to spend time with Paul's writings without loving his commitment to Christ and admiring his talented discipleship. He thought deeply and wrote with the solid themes and brilliant variations of an inspired symphony. His spirit was attuned to heaven, and his mind was continually at work. His language is alternately elevating and practical; it uses precise logic and knows the traps of logic; it is filled with the peace of spirituality and with sarcasm against lethargy and wickedness. Christ's gospel is impressive for satisfying such a mind and giving it lifelong answers. Paul writes with great knowledge but without sham—that he described personal visions makes their existence certain. What believer in the gospel does not admire Paul's power in the gospel? Eulogy is easy but somehow inappropriate for the man who wrote his eulogy in deeds. Because he wrote at the end to his son in the faith, we have his list of achievements important to him. In intimate sharing, Paul notes that Timothy has literally "followed along" with him and knows "my doctrine, manner of life, purpose, faith, long-suffering, charity, patience" (2 Tim. 3:10). These attributes are great stepping-stones that Paul used to cross the stream of life. They speak for themselves, with comment needed only for the last two. That comment has already been given for "charity," Paul's powerful "love" of 1 Corinthians 13.

But "patience" needs probing. Some was done in showing its place on Paul's ladder of salvation at the beginning of Romans 5 and in showing the setting of "endurance" for Hebrews 11, Paul's great chapter on faith. When Timothy was reminded of the apostle's "patience," the word Paul used is *hupomoné*, a noun usually translated "patience" in the King James Version. But the verb form (*hupoméno*) is normally translated "to endure." Simply because "patience" is now considered passive, "endure" is a better translation. These words literally refer to "holding up" (*ménō*) "under" (*hupó*) life's difficulties and pressures. Paul uses this term for "undergoing" chaining and imprisonment: for the sake of offering the gospel to the world "I endure all things" (2 Tim. 2:10). He soon repeats the same word for the price of being with Christ: "If we endure, we shall also reign with him" (2 Tim. 2:12, NKJB). That is the core message to Timothy: "All that will live godly in Christ Jesus shall suffer persecution" (2 Tim. 3:12). That was historical truth, for Timothy had just been reminded that Paul had suffered "at Iconium," where Paul was threatened, and "at Lystra," Timothy's city, where Paul was stoned and left for dead (2 Tim. 3:11; Acts 14). Timothy knows also of Paul's persecutions and sufferings "at Antioch" (2 Tim. 3:11); here Acts is silent, but Paul's list of sufferings suggests possible imprisonment and synagogue whippings (2 Cor. 11:23-27).

Thus, enduring to the end has a double component. Believing the gospel may require facing physical or emotional abuse. But it regularly requires the courage to avoid cheap pleasures and the easy "success" of evil. As Jesus said, "Strait is the gate, and narrow is the way" (Matt. 7:14). Resisting temptation is no more easy than exercising muscles that are out of practice. Both moral and physical effort bring initial pain but also bring the reward of great joy in the strength developed. Paul's teachings open the path of repentance, baptism, finding the true Church, and being faithful in it—living God's laws of righteousness and love. Paul's example shows the difficult but exhilarating way of sharing, forgiving, encouraging, and in all things setting the example. Paul in Rome or Joseph Smith in Liberty Jail prove that great troubles may be opportunities for great spirituality. These servants of the Lord rose above self-pity to seek the Lord's strength, which in the night is as sure as the coming sunrise. The joy of life is not in creature comfort but in doing well what one was sent to earth to do. As Socrates said, the state respected him for staying at his assigned post in battle, and heaven would value him only as he stayed at his assigned moral post in life.[111] That is the message of the life of the

apostle to the Gentiles, as he explained its meaning on the brink
of giving his life:

> For I am now being sacrificed.
> And the time of my departure has come.
> I have run the good race,
> I have finished the course,
> I have kept the faith.
> Thus there is laid up for me
> the crown of righteousness,
> which the Lord, the righteous judge,
> shall award me on that day.
> And not only to me,
> but to all who have loved his appearance.
> (2 Tim. 4:6-8, literal trans.)

No comment deserves to supersede Paul's self-portrait. But
there is an epitaph. This is not found in the pointless search for
his grave or his relics; it is found in the evaluation of the Roman
bishop three decades after Paul's death. No one knows whether
this Clement was the fellow laborer greeted in Philippians 4:3.
But he wrote with probable early knowledge of what Paul had
done and with the convictions of the Early Church on the meaning of Paul's life. That life is surpassed only by that of the Savior in
its message of enduring to the end: "Through jealousy and strife
Paul showed the way to the prize of endurance. Seven times he
was in bonds; he was exiled; he was stoned. He was a herald both
in the east and in the west; he gained the noble fame of his faith;
he taught righteousness to all the world. And when he had
reached the limits of the west he gave his testimony before the rulers, and thus passed from the world and was taken up into the holy
place—the greatest example of endurance."[112]

NOTES

1. A convenient list of the Greek terms appears in Joseph Henry Thayer, *A Greek-English Lexicon
of the New Testament* (New York: American Book Co., 1889), pp. 706-7. Thayer's count was
168 unique words. Note his following list (pp. 707-8) of 53 words found only in the Pastorals
and other letters of Paul, excluding Hebrews.

2. A later dating of Polycarp is sometimes assumed on the basis of his Philippians 7:1, which quotes John 4:1-3 on not confessing that Christ has come in the flesh; Polycarp then adds, "This man is the firstborn of Satan." Irenaeus later reports an anecdote of Polycarp applying this phrase to Marcion about A.D. 140 (*Against Heresies* 3.3.4). But like John, Polycarp apparently had favorite phrases, which could be used generally in the epistle and applied specifically later, the explanation that Kirsopp Lake gives in footnoting this passage in the Loeb Classical Library edition. The close of Polycarp's epistle mentions collecting the letters of Ignatius shortly after he had left, so about A.D. 110 is a necessary date if one assumes the unity of the letter, and there is no objective basis on which to question that.

3. Polycarp to the Philippians 3:2 (*Apostolic Fathers*, Loeb Classical Library). In his marginal notes translator Kirsopp Lake finds phrases from eleven of Paul's fourteen letters. Ones with no traces are 1 Thessalonians, Philemon, and Titus.

4. Daniel J. Theron, *Evidence of Tradition* (Grand Rapids, Mich.: Baker Book House, 1958), p. 111. The fragment is named for the discoverer, L. A. Muratori, and comes from an eighth-century copy, dated by reference to the recent times of Pius, Roman bishop in the mid–second century. For background see Johannes Quasten, *Patrology* (Westminster, Md.: Newman Press, 1964) 2:207-9.

5. Some argue against authenticity from the absence of the Pastorals in the Chester Beatty Papyri, of the same date as the Muratorian Fragment and discussed under the authorship evaluation at the beginning of Hebrews. But the end of the Chester Beatty manuscript is destroyed; the scribe could have included the Pastoral Letters by writing smaller or adding supplementary pages. There is another valid possibility: since the Muratorian Fragment lists Paul's Church letters separately from Paul's personal letters, that arrangement might also have been followed by the Chester Beatty Papyri scribes.

6. 1 Clement 5:7 (*Apostolic Fathers*, Loeb Classical Library).

7. Theron, p. 109: "Paul's departure from the city as he was proceeding to Spain."

8. Eusebius, *Ecclesiastical History* 2.22.2, trans. Hugh Jackson Lawlor and John Ernest Leonard Oulton, *Eusebius* (London: S.P.C.K., 1954), p. 55.

9. As mentioned earlier, the annotations at the end of Paul's letters have no value as evidence because they are later scribal entries.

10. Eusebius, *Ecclesiastical History* 3.32.7.

11. Ibid. 4.22.4-7. This quotation from Hegessipus indicates the infiltration of Gnostic teachings in the Church at Judea after A.D. 62.

12. Lawlor and Oulton 2:143.

13. Justin Martyr, *First Apology* 26 (*Ante-Nicene Fathers*). This translation is changed by substituting "thought" for "idea," translating the Greek *énnoia*.

14. Gnostic systems taught "endless genealogies" of beings springing from other beings, "endless" in the sense that such speculations seemed never to cease, and also "endless" in the quantitative sense. Before the middle of the second century Basilidès had complex groups springing from the ultimate God, arranged in a subordinated system of 365 heavens, obviously taken from the number of days in the year. Irenaeus, *Against Heresies* 1.24.3-4.

15. See Justin Martyr, *First Apology* 26: "But I have a treatise against all the heresies that have existed already composed, which, if you wish to read it, I will give you." Justin's conversion was in the early second century. As just discussed in the text, he had special access to Samaritan sources on Simon.

16. Irenaeus, *Against Heresies* 1.23.2-3 (*Ante-Nicene Fathers*). Scholarly skepticism against Irenaeus's details on Simon is not justified. Second-century Gnosticism is far more elaborate, and there is no reason to doubt that Simon taught the basic ideas in the first century, as Justin outlines and Irenaeus details. Indeed, Peter's harsh condemnation of Simon in Acts 8 is hardly justified without knowing his fraudulent career before and after his conversion. Even before his conversion he was saluted as "the great power of God" (Acts 8:10). Competent historians

have trusted the informational link from Irenaeus to Justin Martyr. Compare Louis Duchesne, *Early History of the Christian Church,* 4th ed. trans. (London: John Murray, 1947) 1:114-16.

17. Justin Martyr, *First Apology* 26.

18. Irenaeus, *Against Heresies* 1.24.2. Saturninus is early second century.

19. A. T. Hanson, *The Pastoral Letters* (Grand Rapids, Mich.: Eerdmans Publishing Co., 1982), p. 39. In this and following quotations, it is evident that Hanson, like many scholars, does not accept Paul as the Pastoral author.

20. Ibid., p. 40. Hanson is forthright enough to note that 1 Timothy diverges from Christian orthodoxy here, though he backs away from his conclusion by a strange faith that the author must not have intended to say what he did: "We may be quite sure that any such doctrine was far from his conscious mind."

21. Ibid., p. 69.

22. Ibid., p. 62.

23. Ignatius, *To Polycarp* 3.2 (*Apostolic Fathers,* Loeb Classical Library). Compare 2:2: "But pray that the invisible things may be revealed to you."

24. Milton V. Backman, Jr., *American Religions and the Rise of Mormonism* (Salt Lake City: Deseret Book Co., 1979), p. 481.

25. Ibid.

26. 1 Clement 44. "Other eminent men" no doubt refers to the appointment of bishops by apostolic assistants such as Timothy and Titus after the first missionary work.

27. Ibid. 42. Compare the quotation and comment at note 26 above.

28. Standards for the "bishop" (Titus 1:7) are preceded by Paul's instructions to "ordain elders in every city" (Titus 1:5). While scholars see the two titles as synonymous, it is certainly possible that Titus ordained elders in each city and appointed one bishop also. The same possibility exists for other early sources mentioning elders and bishops.

29. Ignatius, *Smyrnaeans* 8.

30. Ignatius, *To Polycarp* 2:1.

31. Ignatius, *Trallians* 3:1 and elsewhere.

32. 1 Clement 44, 57.

33. Polycarp 6:1 (*Apostolic Fathers,* Loeb Classical Library).

34. Polycarp, preface.

35. Justin Martyr, *First Apology* 65.

36. See James M. Barnett, *The Diaconate: A Full and Equal Order* (New York: Seabury Press, 1981), ch. 9.

37. Compare Hermas, *The Shepherd,* vision 3.5.1 (*Apostolic Fathers,* Loeb Classical Library), which lists key Church offices as "apostles and bishops and teachers and deacons" and then repeats "bishops and teachers and deacons." Compare the Book of Mormon offices of elders, priests, and teachers (Moro. 3:1-4).

38. Polycarp 3:1-2.

39. Ignatius, *Romans* 4:3. Compare *Trallians* 3:3: "I did not think myself competent, as a convict, to give you orders like an apostle."

40. 1 Clement, preface.

41. 1 Clement 42.

42. First Presidency Statement, Oct. 2, 1936, cited in James E. Clark, *Messages of the First Presidency of The Church of Jesus Christ of Latter-day Saints* (Salt Lake City: Bookcraft, 1975) 6:19.

43. *Journal of Discourses* 11:297, cited in John A. Widtsoe, ed., *Discourses of Brigham Young* (Salt Lake City: Deseret Book Co., 1925), p. 274.

44. *Journal of Discourses* 5:3-4, cited in Widtsoe, p. 11.

45. *Journal of Discourses* 5:293, cited in Widtsoe, p. 43.

46. Pliny the Elder, *Natural History* 9.56.114 (Loeb Classical Library).

47. Strabo, *Geography* 10.4.4 (Loeb Classical Library). The second phrase is retranslated.

48. See John Chadwick, *The Decipherment of Linear B* (Cambridge: University Press, 1958), p. 120, which summarizes the goods inventoried in the Palace tablets during the second millennium before Christ. Of course, animals are also mentioned, as are cheese and figs. Compare p. 126.

49. Pliny 4.12.58-59.

50. See, for example, Strabo 10.4.17-22, dependent on the early Ephorus.

51. Ibid. 17.3.35.

52. Ibid. 7.7.6.

53. Josephus, *Jewish Antiquities* 16.147 (Loeb Classical Library).

54. Mohandas K. Gandhi, *An Autobiography* (Boston: Beacon Press, 1957), p. 136.

55. George A. Denzer, "The Pastoral Letters," in Raymond E. Brown et al., *The Jerome Biblical Commentary* (Englewood Cliffs, N.J.: Prentice-Hall, 1968) 2:360.

56. Ludwig Blau, "Preexistence," *Jewish Encyclopedia* (New York: Funk and Wagnalls, 1905) 10:182-83.

57. Josephus, *Jewish War* 2:154-55 (Loeb Classical Library).

58. See Hugh W. Nibley, "The Expanding Gospel," in *Nibley on the Timely and the Timeless* (Provo, Utah: Religious Studies Center, Brigham Young University, 1978), pp. 21-47.

59. Wisdom of Solomon 8:19-20, Revised Standard Version, Old Testament Apocrypha.

60. Ecclesiasticus, or the Wisdom of Jesus the Son of Sirach 17:12-14, Revised Standard Version, Old Testament Apocrypha.

61. William Wordsworth, "Ode: Intimations of Immortality from Recollections of Early Childhood," cited in Arthur Quiller-Couch, *The Oxford Book of English Verse, 1250-1918* (New York: Oxford University Press, 1940), p. 629.

62. Aristotle, *The "Art" of Rhetoric* 1.5.6 (Loeb Classical Library).

63. James Hope Moulton and George Milligan, *The Vocabulary of the Greek Testament* (Grand Rapids, Mich.: Eerdmans Publishing Co., 1980), p. 151.

64. Josephus, *Jewish Antiquities* 18.245, uses this word of the satisfaction of Herod the Tetrarch with his kingdom—Feldman's translation in the Loeb series is "tranquillity."

65. Joseph Fielding Smith, *Doctrines of Salvation*, ed. Bruce R. McConkie (Salt Lake City: Bookcraft, 1954) 1:115.

66. *Journal of Discourses* 13:145, also cited in Widtsoe, p. 103.

67. Brigham Young insisted that Eve accepted a truth when she believed Satan's explanation that anyone eating of the fruit would "see as the Gods see." *Journal of Discourses* 12:70, also cited in Widtsoe, p. 103.

68. Mary R. Lefkowitz and Maureen B. Fant, *Women's Life in Greece and Rome* (Baltimore: Johns Hopkins University Press, 1982), p. 133.

69. Edward L. Kimball, ed., *The Teachings of Spencer W. Kimball* (Salt Lake City: Bookcraft, p. 321.

70. Ibid.

71. Spencer W. Kimball, "The Role of Righteous Women," *Ensign*, Nov. 1979, p. 103.

72. Ibid.

73. William Childs Robinson, "Predestination," in Carl F. H. Henry, ed., *Basic Christian Doctrines* (New York: Holt, Rinehart, and Winston, 1962), p. 55.

74. Gandhi, *An Autobiography*, p. 34.

75. Ibid., p. 124.

76. John Calvin, *Institutes of the Christian Religion*, trans. Henry Beveridge (Grand Rapids, Mich: Eerdmans Publishing Co., 1979) 2:68-69 (3.13.1-2).

77. G. H. Box, trans., *The Apocalypse of Abraham* (New York: Society for the Promotion of Christian Knowledge, 1918), p. 68 (sect. 22). Box's translation of the manuscript reading "in the light" is followed, though he favors the Bonwetsch emendation of "in the (divine) world-counsel." See also Hugh W. Nibley, *Abraham in Egypt* (Salt Lake City: Deseret Book Co., 1981), pp. 17, 19.

78. Andrew F. Ehat and Lyndon W. Cook, *The Words of Joseph Smith* (Provo, Utah: Religious Studies Center, Brigham Young University), p. 60.

79. Irenaeus, *Against Heresies* l.23.2.

80. Ibid. 1.23.3.

81. Ibid.

82. S. Watson, "Antinomianism," in Alan Richardson, ed., *A Dictionary of Christian Theology* (Philadelphia: Westminster Press, 1969), p. 11.

83. S. Watson, "Law," in Richardson, pp. 190-91.

84. Tertullian, *Scorpiace* 15 (Ante-Nicene Fathers).

85. Ibid.

86. Tertullian, *On Prescription against Heretics* 36 (Ante-Nicene Fathers).

87. Eusebius, *Ecclesiastical History* 2.25.5.

88. Ibid. 3.1.3, followed by: "This is stated exactly by Origen in the third volume of his commentary on Genesis." The work has been lost.

89. Tacitus, *Annals* 15:40 (Church and Brodribb Translation).

90. Ibid. 15.44.

91. Ibid., with translation condensed by more literally following the Latin text. These persecutions did not take place in the Colosseum, which was finished a dozen years after Paul's death.

92. 1 Clement 5:2.

93. Ibid. 6:1, with "elect" replacing Lake's "chosen."

94. A century later Irenaeus claimed that Linus was the first Roman bishop. *Against Heresies* 3.3.3. Compare the much later view of Eusebius that Linus was bishop for a dozen years following A.D. 67. He apparently held the puzzling view that the first Roman bishop was appointed at the time of the martyrdom of Peter and Paul. Caution is required, however, because of Tertullian's statement about "the church of Rome, which makes Clement to have been ordained . . . by Peter." *On Prescription against Heretics* 32. This would eliminate earlier bishops or move their appointments back in time. There are many theories about Claudia, a common name in Roman society.

95. The "cloak" of 2 Tim. 4:13 is a Greek term for the Latin *paenula*, which is "a woolen outer garment covering the whole body, a kind of cloak or mantle, worn on journeys, and also in the city in rainy weather." Charlton T. Lewis and Charles Short, *A Latin Dictionary* (Oxford: Clarendon Press, 1955), p. 1289.

96. James E. Talmage, *The Great Apostasy* (Salt Lake City: The Church of Jesus Christ of Latter-day Saints, 1968), p. 23.

97. Except for two named in 1 Timothy, Paul did not earlier single out individuals past repentance in his letters. The polarization of those fighting against the Church is not pronounced until the Pastoral Letters.

98. This translation of the Revised Standard Version is accurate in meaning, though not literal. The Greek term is *parathēkē*, meaning something entrusted or deposited. "The good thing entrusted" in this verse is identical with the "good doctrine" (1 Tim. 4:6), "sound doctrine," or "sound words" that appear many times in the Pastoral Letters.

99. Menander flourished right after Simon the Sorcerer, who perhaps died before Peter. Compare Lawlor and Oulton 2:97.

100. Justin Martyr, *First Apology* 26.

101. Justin Martyr, *First Apology* 26, is the source of the first quotation here, and the second is from Irenaeus, *Against Heresies* 1.23.5. Clear evidence exists of second-century Gnostic sects that continued this teaching, as well as the following direct reasoning from "a late second century Christian Gnostic": "Therefore, do not think in part, O Rheginos, nor live in conformity with this flesh for the sake of unanimity, but flee from the divisions and the fetters, and already you have the resurrection . . . Why not consider yourself as risen and (already) brought to this? . . . It is fitting for each one to practice in a number of ways, and he shall be released from this Element that he may not be misled but shall himself receive again what at first was." *The Treatise on Resurrection* 49, in James M. Robinson, ed., *The Nag Hammadi Library in English* (San Francisco: Harper and Row, 1977) p. 53. See p. 50 for the quoted opinion on the date.

102. The "seducers" of 2 Tim. 3:13 is a fairly rare Greek word, *góēs*, which early meant "sorcerer" but is used in Josephus and Philo in the specific sense of "religious impostor" or "false prophet." See the valuable note on the word in L. G. Feldman, Josephus, *Jewish Antiquities*, books 18-20 (Cambridge, Mass.: Harvard University Press, 1965), p. 440 (Loeb Classical Library).

103. Paul reminds Timothy that Moses was opposed by counterfeit leaders, naming "Jannes and Jambres," which were forms of names for the Egyptian sorcerers of Exodus 7:11. Paul's contemporary Pliny the Elder names Jannes in commenting on Jews and magic (*Natural History* 30.2.11). Compare the Zadokite document 5:17-18, an Essene work of the same period: "When, in antiquity, Israel was first delivered, Moses and Aaron still continued in their charge . . . even though Belial in his cunning had set up Jannes and his brother in opposition to them." Cited in Theodor H. Gaster, trans., *The Dead Sea Scriptures*, 3rd ed. (Garden City, N.Y.: Anchor Books, 1976), p. 72.

104. E. E. Ellis, "Prophecy in the Early Church," *Interpreter's Dictionary of the Bible* (Nashville: Abingdon, 1976), supp. vol., p. 701.

105. King James translators tended to follow Greek word order, where "having itching ears" follows "teachers." But in Greek, "having" has the subject or nominative ending, leaving no doubt that it ties to "they," the subject of the sentence.

106. 1 Clement 44. This section is often used to argue for Christian continuity, since Clement says that the apostles commanded that if they should die, "other approved men should succeed to the ministry." That may be true on a short-term basis. But since Clement begins the section with the Lord's prophecy of strife over the bishopric, his concept is on its face limited by knowledge of the impending apostasy that would interrupt both priesthood succession and gospel tradition. This fact similarly limits similar but weaker language of 1 Clement 42:4.

107. "Presbyterians Draft New Confession," *Christianity Today*, Oct. 23, 1964, pp. 38-39. The final version was a weak defense of divided organizations: "The institutions of the people of God change and vary as their mission requires in different times and places. The unity of the church is compatible with a wide variety of forms, but it is hidden and distorted when variant

forms are allowed to harden into sectarian divisions, exclusive denominations, and rival factions." "The Confession of 1967," sec. 2, *The Constitution of the United Presbyterian Church in the United States of America, Part 1, Book of Confessions,* 2d ed. (New York: Office of the General Assembly, 1970) 9:34.

108. Henry Clarence Thiessen, *Introduction to the New Testament* (Grand Rapids, Mich.: Eerdmans Publishing Co., 1954), p. 267.

109. D. Edmond Hiebert, *New Testament, The Pauline Epistles* (Chicago: Moody Press, 1981) 2:352.

110. Backman, p. 480.

111. Plato, *Apology* 28 E ff. (17).

112. 1 Clement 5.

Appendix A

Chronology of Paul's Life

The book of Acts generally gives some measurement for each of Paul's assignments after he was called to Antioch by Barnabas. But Acts gives only bare details on Paul's life for the years after his conversion. Yet these years are described in the opening of Galatians, where Paul reviews his work up to the Jerusalem Council. Thus, it is possible to determine the chronology of many events in Paul's life by studying Acts and Galatians. But a reader must correlate these events with the calendar. Since the New Testament mentions public events and personalities, secular dates should furnish a frame of reference for Paul's life as described in Galatians and Acts. This is especially true for the closing years of Paul's life, as dates are known for the fire of Rome and the death of Nero. For understanding the period covered by Galatians and Acts, the most useful secular dates are those of the death of Herod Agrippa, which occurred when Paul visited Jerusalem from Antioch, and the governorship of Gallio at Corinth, during which Paul was on his second missionary journey. This last event ties specifically into the missionary labors in Acts. It requires some thought to understand the time of Gallio's coming to Corinth, but the fairly exact result makes the effort worthwhile.

Fragments of a stone at Delphi contain a letter to that city from Claudius, emperor between A.D. 41 and 54. It was inscribed for public display because it pertained to the rights of the city. In it, the head of the empire mentioned Gallio, "my friend and proconsul," using the official title of the governor of southern

Greece.[1] Gallio's arbitrary character in Acts is supported by Roman sources that portray an opinionated aristocrat; he commented that the climate of Achaia (the technical name of his province) made him sick.[2] The Delphi inscription dates Gallio's term as governor because the emperor dates his letter in the period when he had been voted the honor of *imperator* for the twenty-sixth time.[3] This self-centered reckoning was standard procedure for the Roman executive, and other similar inscriptions establish cutoff points. One inscription names the twenty-seventh time Claudius was honored as *imperator;* this is dated no later than August 1, A.D. 52.[4] Going backward, this honor for military victory was given for the twenty-fourth time within a period beginning January 25, A.D. 51.[5] So the Gallio inscription with the twenty-sixth imperatorship must fall between January 25, A.D. 51, and August 1, A.D. 52.

Roman procedures add further light, for governors at this time were required to leave the capital in late spring and take office about July.[6] Furthermore, their term was normally for one year.[7] So it is quite clear that Gallio entered his governorship the summer of either A.D. 51 or A.D. 52. Probability comes into play here. As noted above, an inscription simply says that Claudius had already received his twenty-seventh acclamation as *imperator* by August 1, A.D. 52. Because this honor came before that time, and the twenty-sixth acclamation came before that, the date of the latter is likely before the change of provincial administration of the summer of A.D. 52.[8] That means that Gallio, who was governor while Claudius was *imperator* for the twenty-sixth time, very probably began his term of office in the summer of A.D. 51. A number of careful scholars have reached this conclusion.[9]

The narrative in Acts 18 applies this chronological scheme to Paul. The Lord promised protection to the apostle as he first arrived in Corinth (v. 10). Then Paul preached there for a year and a half (v. 11), after which the Jewish community accused Paul "when Gallio was proconsul of Achaia" (v. 12, NKJB). This attempt to stop Paul's preaching would be made when the new governor arrived. There had been Jewish hostility from the beginning, but Paul's enemies now saw a new chance to discredit him. So Paul had been preaching a year and a half when Gallio arrived on the above date, the summer of A.D. 51. Thus the apostle probably arrived at Corinth about the beginning of A.D. 50. Further discoveries could modify that date, but only within narrow limits.

In addition to the entries on the chart below, short explanations are necessary on Paul's birth and also on his review of his early period in the Church. Paul was probably born at the beginning of the Christian Era, though there is no way to set an exact year. Stephen's stoning came after the crucifixion, both events of the early thirties, when Paul is called a "young man" (Acts 7:58). Note 12 of chapter 2 indicates that "young man" is appropriate in ancient literature up to about age forty. And Jewish patriarchal society required the age of thirty for priesthood participation in temple service. So Paul would fit this general picture if born shortly after Christ. He would also fit the "aged" description he applied to himself when writing Philemon about A.D. 61 (Philem. 1:9). But Paul's birth is a free-floating problem compared with the more precise times that he gives for two Jerusalem visits after his conversion.

This information comes in the opening two chapters of Galatians as Paul argues that the gospel was early revealed to him apart from his later relationships with the first apostles. He did not see them, he recounts, until three years after his conversion (Gal. 1:15-18) and "then after fourteen years I went up again to Jerusalem" (Gal. 2:1, NKJB).[10] Both English and Greek here are quite equivalent—the natural reading is that Paul's visit with Barnabas and Titus about circumcision came fourteen years after his first Jerusalem visit, not fourteen years after his conversion. Thus, the time of conversion plus three years plus fourteen years is the time of the Jerusalem Council, which was shown in the Galatians discussion to be the same meeting referred to in Galatians 2. Paul left that council, spent about a year at Antioch, revisited Galatian branches, labored in Northern Greece, and finally came to Corinth. As seen above, his arrival in Corinth was about A.D. 50. Thus, fifty minus one minus seventeen should closely approximate the year of Paul's conversion. Perhaps these figures should be compressed somewhat in order to account for portions of years and approximate estimations of Paul. But the figures should give a nearly correct result. Some Latter-day Saints may wish to place the crucifixion later than this conversion date of about A.D. 33. But the time of Jesus' birth may need to be set back somewhat—at least careful Latter-day Saint scholars have left that question open.[11]

All history is based on working assumptions. So alternative dates for Paul's life are often possible, as shown on the following chart. The chart is meant to be general, sometimes leaving out evidence for times of the year. It has the advantage of giving an approximate scheme, but the events themselves are far more important than anyone's estimate of when they happened. Yet from a historical viewpoint, the close approximations of years are quite remarkable. After Paul's early years, dates cannot be adjusted more than a few years on any assumption. That is partly because Paul's first biographer was Luke, a man of precision of thought and accuracy in his references to places and people. Enough care was given to the record to be able to make a good chronology, one that fits ancient realities much better than can be shown in the following outline. Thus, the framework of early Christian history is an additional testimony to the truth of the great spiritual events in the life of Paul.

Chronology of Paul's Life

Event	Date (A.D.)	Source	Comment
Birth	1	Inference from Acts 7:58 and Philem. 1:9	All further dates are clearly A.D.
Conversion	33	Gal. 1:18 and 2:1 give seventeen years prior to the Jerusalem Council of 49	See above material for details
Mission in the Damascus area	33-36	Gal. 1:18: Jerusalem visit "after three years"	See ch. 2 for preaching data

CHRONOLOGY OF PAUL'S LIFE

Event	Date (A.D.)	Source	Comment
First Jerusalem visit	36	Gal. 1:18; Acts 9:26-29	See also Acts 22:17-21
Mission in the Tarsus area	37-42	Acts 9:30: "The brethren . . . sent him . . . to Tarsus"	Paul labored in Cilicia, the region around Tarsus (Gal. 1:21)
(Claudius made emperor)	41	Agreement of Roman sources	
Mission in the Antioch area	43	Acts 11:19-26: Barnabas is sent to Antioch and calls Paul from Tarsus	Acts 11:26: labors of one year relate to next date
Second Jerusalem visit	44	Acts 11:27-30; 12:23-25 give Paul's return after Herod's death	Josephus gives Herod's death after Claudius reigned three years[12]
First Gentile mission	45-47	Acts 13 and 14	Time is estimated. Compare Acts 14:3 for one city
Labors in Antioch	48	Acts 14:26-28	They remained a "long time"
Jerusalem Council	49	Acts 15	Date obtained by deducting travel time to Corinth
Second Gentile mission begins	49	Acts 15:36-41; Acts 16-17	Time in Antioch, Galatia, northern Greece, and Athens
Arrival in Corinth	Early 50	Acts 18:11-12: a year and a half before Gallio came	Date of Gallio's coming is discussed beginning appendix A

Event	Date (A.D.)	Source	Comment
1 Thessalonians	50	See ch. 4	Written soon after coming to Corinth
2 Thessalonians	50	See ch. 4	Written soon after 1 Thessalonians
Second Gentile mission ends	Early 52	Acts 18:18-21: Paul continued "many days" (RSV)	Coming feast of Acts 18:21—probably Passover (springtime)
Jerusalem visit	52	Acts 18:21-22	"Going up" refers to the Jerusalem hills
Labors in Antioch and Galatia	52-53	Acts 18:23: "some time" in Antioch	Additional time in the Galatian branches
Third Gentile mission begins	54	Acts 19:1	Perhaps arrival after winter
(Nero made emperor)	54	Agreement of Roman sources	
1 Corinthians	57	See ch. 5	Written in spring (1 Cor. 16:8)
Third Gentile mission ends	57	Acts 20:1. See Acts 19:8-9; 20:31	Overall about a three-year mission
2 Corinthians	57	See ch. 5	Written in northern Greece
Farewell visit in Greece	57-58	Acts 20:2-3	Three months spent there: 1 Cor. 16:6 suggests the winter
Galatians	58?	See ch. 6	Cannot visit Galatians?
Romans	58	See ch. 6	Written near Corinth

Event	Date (A.D.)	Source	Comment
Jerusalem visit	58	Acts 21:17	Acts 20:6 suggests late spring
Imprisonment at Caesarea	58-60	Acts 24:27	Two years under one governor plus negotiations with another for appeal
Journey to Rome	60-61	Acts 27:9; 28:11	Sailing was October or later; they wintered on Malta
Roman imprisonment	61-63	Acts 28:30	"Two whole years" would mean spring release
Philemon Colossians Ephesians	61?	See ch. 7	These letters sent in a group
Philippians	62	See ch. 7	Written near release: Philip. 2:24
Hebrews	62?	See ch. 6	Written near release: Hebrews 13:23
Mediterranean ministry	63-64— perhaps to 66	1 Tim. and Titus	Spain is possible; Pastoral Letters identify Asia Minor, Greece, and Crete
Roman fire and persecutions	64	Tacitus, *Annals* 15:44	Tacitus identified consuls for the year 64
1 Timothy	65?	See ch. 8	Acts is silent on closing years
Titus	65?	See ch. 8	Acts is silent on closing years

Event	Date (A.D.)	Source	Comment
Final arrest	66?	2 Tim. 1:16-18; 4:14-17	Paul has had a first hearing and expects death (2 Tim. 4:6)
2 Timothy	66?	See ch. 8	Paul asks Timothy to come before winter and bring his cloak (2 Tim. 4:13, 21)
Martyrdom	67?	See ch. 8—background of 2 Tim.	Clement of Rome (A.D. 96) associates Paul's death with Nero's martyrs
(Nero commits suicide)	68	Agreement of Roman sources	

NOTES

1. For a picture, see Adolf Deissmann, *Paul: A Study in Social and Religious History*, 2d ed. (New York: Harper and Brothers, 1957), plate 1, with transcriptions on pp. 272-73. Although the text is fragmentary, many missing words are filled in from parts and from other imperial communications that use standardized titles and dates. For a translation, see George Ogg, *The Chronology of the Life of Paul* (London: Epworth Press, 1968), p. 107.

2. Seneca, *Epistles* 104:1. Seneca, chief executive assistant to Nero, was Gallio's brother.

3. The Greek numerical system adapted the alphabet, writing "26" as "KS." The sigma is written in the style of "C" on the inscription, visible on the Deissmann photograph on fragment 3, line 2.

4. See Ogg, p. 109, for the inscription from the Claudian Aqueduct mentioning the twenty-seventh acclamation. This inscription has a specific terminal date because Frontinus, a Roman with political and engineering credentials, wrote a history of aqueducts at the end of the first century, naming August 1, A.D. 52, for the completion of the Claudian system. *De Aquis* 1:13.

5. See Ogg, p. 109, for the text of the twenty-fourth acclamation. Dating is possible because of the double entry on most of these public notices. The formal vote of honor as *imperator* was given anytime some victory seemed to merit it. Yet inscriptions frequently add the year of the emperor's tribunician power, a constitutional authority renewed annually on the anniversary of his inauguration—in the case of Claudius from January 25 of each year. But a given count for the honor of *imperator* may have been in effect months prior to any tribunician year. Ogg, p. 108, gives the twenty-second acclamation as *imperator* in an inscription also naming the eleventh year of tribunician power, a period beginning January 25, A.D. 51. This twenty-second acclamation was still in effect at that date and might have preceded it. But any further acclamations naming the eleventh year would come after January 25, A.D. 51. This is because the twenty-second acclamation covered the period from an undetermined date to at least Jan-

uary 25, A.D. 51. So the twenty-fourth acclamation as *imperator*, mentioned in the text and citation beginning this note, must follow January 25, A.D. 51, since it also names the eleventh tribunician year. Thus, the Gallio inscription, naming the twenty-sixth imperatorship, must be no earlier than January, A.D. 51. For further explanation, see Jack Finegan, *Handbook of Biblical Chronology* (Princeton: Princeton University Press, 1964), p. 98.

6. A decade before Paul came to Corinth, Claudius had been troubled with new governors who "had been in the habit of tarrying a long time in the city." So he first decreed April 1 as their time of departure and then in A.D. 43 required leaving before mid-April. Dio Cassius, *Roman History* 60.11.6; 60.17.3.

7. The rule under Claudius is stated by mentioning its occasional exception: "He allowed some of them to govern for two years." Ibid. 60.25.6.

8. Whereas the tribunician year is absent from the twenty-sixth acclamation mentioned on the Gallio stone, another inscription (Ogg, p. 108) associates the twenty-sixth imperatorship with the twelfth tribunician year. This means that the twenty-sixth imperatorship lasted into the year beginning January 24, A.D. 52. Since the twenty-sixth award could have been a little earlier, this number on the Gallio stone indicates the governor was ruling between winter of 51 and about late spring of 52. This would fit his arrival date just discussed in the text.

9. For the most concise and accurate presentation, see Ogg, pp. 104-11. See also Deissmann, pp. 261-84.

10. Some wish to make this Galatians 2:1 visit the same as the "famine visit" of Paul and Barnabas in Acts 11:27-30, mainly on the ground that Paul is narrating his first two visits to Jerusalem in Galatians. But that is not Paul's point. He denies contact with the Twelve until three years after his conversion. Then after Paul mentions his first visit to Peter, his subject changes to the agreement of the "pillars" with his program of going to the Gentiles. That is the subject of the letter, not biography, so there is a logical but not chronological progression of ideas.

11. See J. Reuben Clark, Jr., *Our Lord of the Gospels* (Salt Lake City: Deseret Book Co., 1962), pp. vi-viii; see also Bruce R. McConkie, *The Mortal Messiah* (Salt Lake City: Deseret Book Co., 1979) 1:349.

12. Josephus, *Jewish Antiquities* 19:351. Compare Finegan, pp. 302-3.

Appendix B
Two Descriptions of Paul

There is a striking ancient word portrait of Paul, and a modern one even more striking. The first is in the work known as the Acts of Paul and Thecla. Thecla is presented as a virgin martyr, the center of this apocryphal work that includes her supposed conversion at Iconium. Scholars now consider this work part of a much larger production, the Acts of Paul, a complex and unrewarding piece of fiction.[1] Tertullian knew that this work was a pious forgery invented shortly before he wrote at the close of the second century. He scorned those who argued from "Thecla's example" that women should baptize; he stressed that these materials "wrongly go under Paul's name," adding that "in Asia the presbyter who composed that writing, as if he were augmenting Paul's fame from his own store, after being convicted, and confessing that he had done it from love of Paul, was removed from his office."[2] This superstitious novel gives a description of Paul, which some have speculated might be an earlier nugget of information incorporated in the Thecla story.[3] That remains a possibility, but there is not yet any earlier evidence for the word portrait. Pious art cannot wait for such debates to end; the Thecla profile has "set the type for this apostle's portraits from an early time."[4]

This ancient description may well have been read by Joseph Smith, since it was printed in 1820 in a fascinating collection of the authentic Apostolic Fathers plus a fair sampling of imaginative apocrypha of the New Testament. William Hone wrote a preface critical of traditional Christianity and prefaced his selection with a typical title of the time: "The Apocryphal New Testament, being All Gospels, Epistles, and Other Pieces Now Extant, Attributed in the First Four Centuries to Jesus Christ, His Apostles, and Their Companions, and Not Included in the New Testament by Its Compilers." One can argue that Joseph Smith might have read the "Acts of Paul and Thecla." The Nauvoo Library and Literary Institute was organized in early 1844, and minutes list titles of books donated by individuals, including Joseph Smith, who among other titles gave the "Apocryphal Testament."[5] This does not prove that Joseph Smith picked up the book, turned to page 100, and read the early sketch. That evidence would have to come from a diary that no one now knows about or from inference from a parallel quotation also unknown. But the Hone publication is quoted here because it would have been the most likely for Joseph Smith to have seen:

> At length they saw a man coming (namely Paul), of a low stature, bald (or shaved) on the head, crooked thighs, handsome legs, hollow eyed; had a crooked nose; full of grace. For sometimes he appeared as a man; sometimes he had the countenance of an angel.[6]

This ancient picture is not quoted by Joseph Smith in any known source, but he gave a more detailed one of his own. It appears in the private notes of William Clayton, one of the three most significant recorders of the Prophet's private and public teaching. The introducing notation reads, "By Joseph, Jany. 5th 1841, at the organization of a school of instruction."[7] The verbal portrait reads:

> Description of Paul—He is about 5 foot high; very dark hair; dark complexion, dark skin; large Roman nose; sharp face; small black eyes, penetrating as eternity; round shoulders; a whining voice, except when elevated and then it almost resembles the roaring of a lion. He was a good orator.[8]

There are nine characteristics of Paul in the Thecla description, and twelve in Joseph Smith's. But the profiles overlap in only two respects: the ancient "crooked nose" compares to Joseph Smith's "large Roman nose," and the ancient "low stature" compares to Joseph Smith's "about 5 foot high."

These two points of resemblance are important, for Joseph Smith adds a specific detail to each. Much apocryphal literature is boring because it narrates in generalities. Granted, a creative historical forger might give particulars; but in real life, vagueness generally reflects lack of firsthand observation, and pictorial sharpness comes from having been personally on the scene. Joseph Smith's description of Paul is stunning for that reason — it includes exact measurements, complexion, shapes, even sounds. The modern Prophet comments with the precision of one who has seen and heard. Joseph Smith was sometimes stimulated by an idea to inquire of the Lord for himself. So he might be dependent on the Thecla sketch purely as a point of inquiry. Or he might never have seen it. Joseph Smith might also have been stimulated by biblical inquiry from (1) Barnabas being called the head god Jupiter, possibly because he was more imposing than Paul (Acts 14:12); (2) Paul's admission that his appearance was not imposing (2 Cor. 10:1, 10); (3) the possibility that Paul's Gentile name had literal significance, since the Latin adjective *paulus* means "little" or "small." One or more of these points might have stimulated the Thecla description. But Joseph Smith went far beyond any of this.

After giving Paul's profile, the Prophet sought no publicity from it, leaving it as a private description given a small study group. But then, he named a dozen historic prophets who appeared to him and gave detail on only a few when there were special points to be made about the heavenly personages. There is no reason to sensationalize Joseph's description of Paul when he gave it without comment. But many who respect this great modern prophet feel that his description of these twelve specific features could have come only through some form of revelation. The significance is that the prophet of the last dispensation knew so well the great apostle to the Gentiles. Thus, Paul is likely one that Joseph Smith had in mind when he wrote that "divers angels" from Adam to the "present time" had come, each with keys and information (D&C 128:21).

NOTES

1. For a full survey of background, see Edgar Hennecke, *New Testament Apocrypha*, ed. Wilhelm Schneemelcher, trans. R. McL. Wilson (Philadelphia: Westminster Press, 1965) 2:322 ff.

2. Tertullian, *On Baptism* 17 (Ante-Nicene Fathers).

3. Although Henneke-Schneemelcher are hostile to that particular idea, thinking this is a typical Jewish description (p. 333), nevertheless they think the author a "compiler . . . of legends which were current" (p. 329).

4. Johannes Quasten, *Patrology* (Westminster, Md.: Newman Press, 1962), 1:131.

5. Kenneth W. Godfrey, "A Note on the Nauvoo Library and Literary Institute," *Brigham Young University Studies* 14:386-87 (Spring 1974).

6. William Hone, ed., *The Apocryphal New Testament* (London: Ludgate Hill, 1820), p. 100.

7. Andrew F. Ehat and Lyndon W. Cook, *The Words of Joseph Smith* (Provo, Utah: Religious Studies Center, Brigham Young University, 1980), p. 59.

8. Ibid.

Appendix C
Baptism for the Dead

Else what shall they do which are baptized for the dead, if the dead rise not at all? why are they then baptized for the dead? (1 Cor. 15:29.)

The gospel has more than its share of stumbling blocks, as Jesus and Paul both noted. Mortals do not easily understand God's reasons and his full programs. It is hard for non-Christians to understand why a Savior must suffer in the place of men and women—to do something for them that they cannot do for themselves. But once that nourishing truth is known, it is one step further to learn that faithful Saints on earth might perform baptisms for the righteous dead who did not have the opportunity to be baptized. The principle of serving others permeates the gospel. Much opposition to baptism for the dead boils down to skepticism about baptism. Large numbers of Christians of all persuasions do not really think that God requires water baptism, so baptism for the dead is often considered superstitious on its face. But what if Jesus' words to Nicodemus are strictly and eternally true? The Lord made no exception: "Unless one is born of water and the Spirit, he cannot enter the kingdom of God" (John 3:5, NKJB). Paul used the same image of rebirth, saying that God saves through his mercy and "the washing of regeneration" (Titus 3:5). And his concise epistle of grace makes baptism the required expression of faith: "As many of you as have been baptized into Christ have put on Christ" (Gal. 3:27). If, as Peter said, remission of sins comes only by adding baptism to faith (Acts 2:38), then neither the living or the dead are exempt from baptism. Christians cannot consider baptism for the dead seriously until they take baptism as seriously as the Lord and his apostles intended it.

There is a strange ambivalence in the various commentaries on 1 Corinthians 15:29. Surveying the current ones leaves the overall impression that they try to explain away the verse rather than to explain it. There is a fair sprinkling of loaded phrases like "strange practice," "unusual baptism," or "abnormal baptismal rite." Yet with all the motivation to minimize, scholar after scholar admits that the Corinthians were baptizing for their dead. Outside of responsible commentaries, many cheap explanations circulate: baptism for the dead meant baptism in order to be joined to the faithful dead, baptism to avoid dead sins, or even baptism over the graves of the dead. But though puzzled by the practice, the best scholars today are convinced that substitute baptism existed. One calls baptism for the dead "a notorious difficulty"; nevertheless, "the most natural meaning of the expression is that some early believers got themselves baptized on behalf of friends of theirs who had died without receiving that sacrament."[1] A top historian-linguist puzzles over how vicarious baptism was used but thinks the concept is clear: "The *prima facie* meaning of these words points to a practice of baptism by proxy."[2] Today's Christian scholars sharply counteract any easy allegorizing here:

> Close inspection of the language of the reference makes all attempts to soften or eliminate its literal meaning unsuccessful. An endeavor to understand *the dead* as persons who are "dead in sin" does not really help; for the condition offered, *if the dead are not being raised at all*, makes it clear that the apostle is writing about persons who are physically dead. It appears that under the pressure of concern for the eternal destiny of dead relatives or friends some people in the church were undergoing baptism on their behalf in the belief that this would enable the dead to receive the benefits of Christ's salvation.[3]

These views show the current understanding of Paul's words. Truth is not made by majorities, but informed people can show the reasonable positions on a problem. While not understanding the practice, the best Greek scholars overwhelmingly support vicarious baptism as the only correct translation of Paul's challenge. Many translators continue to follow the "for the dead" of the King James Version. But of the six committee translations most used in this book, four have the phrasing of the Revised Standard Version: "Otherwise, what do people mean by being baptized on behalf of the dead? If the dead are not raised at all, why are people baptized on their behalf?" This is also the trend of competent private translators, such as Moffatt and Goodspeed in the last generation. Some, such as J. B. Phillips, vary the English to "being baptized for the dead by proxy." Two technical reasons are persuasive to scholars. The preposition behind the King James "for" is *hupér*, followed by the noun in a possessive form. The meaning can be physically "over" or "beyond," but it is regularly the concept of representation of one person for another. For instance, in the business documents on papyrus this construction regularly describes agency, the power of attorney of one to represent another; this is basically the "substitutionary sense, as when one man writes a letter for another, seeing that he is unable to write it himself."[4] A second consideration is usage in the New Testament, where this same construction appears over a hundred times to describe Christ's vicarious sacrifice "for us" (1 Cor. 5:7; 11:24; 15:3). Since baptism for the dead is mentioned in the same wording as the Atonement, it is hard to argue that the latter is vicarious but not the former. Just as Christ in suffering represented others, the Saints were empowered to be agents for their loved ones in baptism.

The practice of baptism for the dead is less disputed now, though its ancient application is debated.[5] Its importance is minimized by some because it appears a single time in the scriptures, but it was a doctrine for believers and would rarely be discussed publicly— several practices of the believers appear only in the candid discussions of problems in 1 Corinthians. Others say with false learning that Paul disapproved the practice, but putting words into his mouth is highly dangerous in a chapter where he insists time after time that he is telling God's solemn truth. Paul was most sensitive to blasphemy and false ceremonialism—of all people he would not have argued for the foundation truth of the Resurrection with a questionable example. He obviously did not feel that the principle was disharmonious with the gospel. But scholars generally will not accept Paul's approval of baptism for the dead, so the trend is to claim that Paul simply referred to a local custom for the sake of argument.[6]

Such speculation is inconsistent. If the Corinthians invented proxy baptism out of concern for their loved ones, why limit such concern to that branch of the Church? Similar concern is seen in 1 Thessalonians 4. This deep desire for family salvation was everywhere. Here writers on 1 Corinthians are seeing only a root of one tree, not the trunks towering above. The issue of God reaching the entire human race is an intense issue in the New Testament and in Christian sources immediately afterward. In plain terms, can one talk of baptism for the dead without the parallel doctrine of preaching to the dead? Christ is the first source here, for he told the thief on the cross that he would be in paradise "to day" (Luke 23:43), and Peter says that immediately after death Christ went not to heaven but to the spirit world to continue his preaching (1 Pet. 3:18–21).

The preaching in the spirit world competes with baptism for the dead for the prize of the "most difficult" scripture in the New Testament—different scholars apply this language to both doctrines. There is no doubt of the preaching to the spirits in prison, and there are inevitable questions of consistency. Since the Church taught that the righteous dead heard the gospel, the issue of their baptism is inescapable. Can preaching to the dead be isolated from baptism for the dead? Christ's mission to the pre-Christian dead must start with Peter's teaching, which vividly says that Jesus was crucified but "quickened"—in Greek literally "made alive"—in the spirit and "went and preached unto the spirits in prison; which sometime were disobedient, when once the longsuffering of God waited in the days of Noah" (1 Pet. 3:18–20). Christ's visit to the dead is a frequent theme in the next generations after Peter. Justin Martyr quoted an earlier prophecy that was also a Christian article of faith: "The Lord God of Israel remembered his dead sleeping in the earthly grave, and he descended to them to preach the gospel of his salvation to them."[7]

Early references to this subject are plentiful, as Hugh Nibley showed years ago.[8] Christians were very concerned with pre-Christians from the beginning. So if baptism for the dead is rare, the overall problem is most visible. What was the purpose of Christ's preaching to the dead? An early answer comes from Irenaeus, who had youthful contact with Polycarp, who knew John. Perhaps with that link in mind, Irenaeus starts an indirect quotation, "As I have heard from a certain elder, who had heard from those who had seen the apostles."[9] Irenaeus develops the idea of the mercy of God for those called in the Old Testament; then he resumes the quotation to say, "The Lord descended to the parts under the earth, announcing to them also the good news of his coming, there being remission of sins for such as believe on him."[10] In Acts, remission of sins was the result of faith plus baptism. Irenaeus has a simplistic view of Old Testament forgiveness but preserves the above understanding that Christ's preaching to the dead had the same goal as his historical preaching to the living — the perfection of the person to prepare him to meet God. Peter also says this in his verse following his description of Christ's preaching in the spirit world; all must appear before the judge of "the living and the dead" (1 Pet. 4:5, NKJB): "For this reason the gospel was preached also to those who are dead" (1 Pet. 4:6, NKJB).

Some scholars are too cautious to link 1 Peter 3:19 on Christ preaching in the spirit prison with 1 Peter 4:6 on the general preaching to the dead. But the key words for preaching in those verses are *kērússō* and *euangelízō*, the only two words in the New Testament that are consistently used of the missionary proclamation of the gospel.[11] These synonyms show that Peter is talking of similar events. God cannot reach all his children without sending messengers to the worlds of the living and of the dead. And the two Greek words just mentioned constantly refer to teaching baptism as well as faith. For instance, nearly every baptism mentioned in Acts is preceded by one of these words, generally translated "preach" or "preach the gospel." Christ's commission to the Twelve at the end of Matthew and Mark commands baptism as the immediate result of the preaching. Thus, Peter virtually suggests Paul's baptism for the dead in his verbs for preaching to the dead, the same verbs that are found in the above early Christian references on Christ's visit to the spirit world. In turn, Paul virtually suggests Peter's concern for the living and the dead in the context of baptism for the dead in 1 Corinthians 15:29, as already discussed in the chapter treating that letter. And the two interrelated doctrines come together in the document known as the Shepherd of Hermas, which derives its name from a series of visions and teachings from an angel as a shepherd. In the second century the Muratorian Canon gives the date as midcentury: "But Hermas composed the Shepherd quite recently in our times in the city of Rome, while his brother, Pius, the bishop, occupied the chair of the city of Rome."[12]

The Shepherd of Hermas is not a source for new doctrine, for its main theme is preserving the faith. Its author is dutiful and conservative, seeking to hold to what he had been taught in a Christian career going back to the turn of the century and Clement of Rome, whom he mentions. Quasten sizes up the author as "an earnest, pious, and conscientious man, one who had proven himself steadfast in time of persecution."[13] Thus, he is a source for the common doctrines and practices of the Christian Church. And he welds preaching to the dead to baptism for the dead. These doctrines come in the allegory of building the tower, which the angel defines as the Church. The three lower courses of stones represent the foundation generations of the righteous men of the Old Testament, with the last and largest number of 40 representing the "prophets and teachers of the preaching of the Son of God." These have the seal, clearly defined as baptism by (1) the requirement "to come up through the water that they might be made alive"; (2) the quotation of John 3:5, referring to water as the way to "enter into the kingdom of God"; and (3) the summary, "the seal, then, is the water."[14] As the following passage begins, Hermas's messenger is explaining that the pre-Christian dead — "who had fallen asleep" — were also baptized; this is followed by the explanation that the New Testament priesthood bearers had been baptized again to make this possible:

"So these also who had fallen asleep received the seal of the Son of God and 'entered into the kingdom of God'. . . . This seal, then, was preached to them also, and they made use of it 'to enter into the kingdom of God.' "

"Why, Sir," said I, "did the 40 stones also come up with them from the deep, although they had received the seal already?"

"Because," said he, "these apostles and teachers who preached the name of the Son of God, having fallen asleep in the power and faith of the Son of God, preached also to those who had fallen asleep before them, and themselves gave to them the seal of the preaching. They went down therefore with them into the water and came up again, but the latter went down alive and came up alive, while the former, who had fallen asleep before, went down dead but came up alive. Through them, therefore, they were made alive, and received the knowledge of the name of the Son of God. . . . For they had fallen asleep in righteousness and in great purity, only they had not received this seal. You have then the explanation of these things also."[15]

Some parts of the above message are obvious, and others are clear in the light of Hermas's purpose in writing. Since the above words explain the vision-parable or allegory, they relate to Christian doctrine and practice. The plainest point is that after death the "apostles and teachers" continued their missionary labors in the spirit world, adding the dimension that preaching to the dead continued after Christ. The consequences of that doctrine are revolutionary. Thus, the spirits do not merely receive an announcement of Christ's victory; continued preaching assumes individual growth there and acceptance of gospel principles beyond simple belief. Thus, the emphasis on baptism for the pre-Christian righteous logically fits the scheme. But what kind of baptism? The normal understanding overestimates the author: "Thus Hermas is so thoroughly convinced that baptism is absolutely necessary for salvation that he teaches that the apostles and teachers descended into limbo after death . . . to baptize the righteous departed of pre-Christian times."[16]

The above conclusion lacks common sense. Hermas's book proves that he is a Christian traditionalist, and the spirit-world passage underlines the point by three repetitions of the words of John 3:5 on entering the kingdom of God through water. He is so bound by scripture that he cannot imagine salvation without baptism, and he obviously writes with consciousness of Peter's words on preaching in the spirit world. Thus, Hermas also writes with awareness of Paul's reference to baptisms of the living for the dead. Those "fallen asleep" in his passage are, of course, the dead, and his subject closes with plain words about the righteous who had died without baptism. So Hermas is discussing what Christians believe about baptism for the dead; so this "pious and conscientious" author certainly refers to the known baptism for the dead and not the unknown. That explains his question to the angel, for he found it contradictory that the New Testament priesthood leaders went into the deep again, the symbol of their personal baptisms. If they would merely baptize others, there could be no puzzle. So Hermas's question was really about rebaptism of those already baptized. The explanation was that both groups go into the water, but the effect of remission of sins is only for those dying without baptism. This cooperative baptism is proxy baptism, the only type mentioned by the "apostles and teachers" that he refers to. The joint immersion in water is part of the symbolism not expressly interpreted, referring to the earthly baptisms that were a shared experience of the living and the dead.

Latter-day Saints have that clear understanding through the sweeping vision received by their twentieth-century prophet Joseph F. Smith. His great message was the continuing preaching to the dead after Christ, the instruction necessary to benefit from proxy baptism—for only "the dead who repent will be redeemed" (D&C 138:58). Latter-day Saints well know that the founding prophet Joseph Smith instituted baptism for the dead and planned the first latter-day ordinance temple before his martyrdom. But how much Joseph Smith said about the preaching to the dead needs to be stressed—for in no sense was proxy baptism ever cheapened into mechanical salvation without the faith and repentance of the one for whom baptism was done. Joseph Smith taught the fair opportunity to be baptized if a person lived when the true gospel and its authority was not on earth. But he also taught the fair opportunity to hear the gospel, whether on earth or in the spirit existence after death: "All who have not had an opportunity of hearing the gospel, and being administered to by an inspired man in the flesh, must have it hereafter, before they can be finally judged."[17] This statement is two years earlier than Joseph Smith's first sermon on baptism for the dead and has overtones of 1 Peter 4:5–6, where all are readied for judgment by hearing the gospel, whether alive or dead. Indeed, Joseph Smith's early thinking is clear, for he completed his New Testament corrections on February 2, 1833. Coming to 1 Peter 4:6, he read, "For thus was the gospel preached also to them that are dead" and changed the verb to "is," indicating his knowledge that the preparation of the spirits for the blessings of the gospel is continuous.[18]

The Prophet had in mind the personal welfare of those who had died without the gospel as he contemplated leaving Missouri for Illinois. The great work of restoration was moving to "a time to come in the which nothing shall be withheld" (D&C 121:28). And the work would involve the dead in the spirit world, for their eyes were on the coming revelations, "which our forefathers have awaited with anxious expectation to be revealed in the last times" (D&C 121:27). In 1840 the Prophet announced and authorized baptism for the dead, generally restricting the work to near relatives and commanding that careful records be kept of it, "lest we should run too far." The principle balanced what was taught in the spirit world with what could be done only on earth. Even after death, "there is never a time when the spirit is too old to approach God." But God's plan and not wishful thinking must govern the procedures of salvation: "There is a way to release the spirit of the dead; that is, by the power and authority of the priesthood, by binding and loosing on earth."[20] But the earthly work is always dependent on repentance and the agency of the individuals themselves: "Now all those [who] die in the faith go to the prison of spirits to preach to the dead in body, but they are alive in the spirit, and those spirits preach to the spirits that they may live according to God in the spirit. And men do minister for them in the flesh, and angels bear the glad tidings to the spirits, and they are made happy by these means."[21]

The cable of salvation for the dead has many strands in past scriptures; yet it was produced from the fresh steel of revelation. Joseph Smith explained baptism for the dead to the Church with this observation: "The only way to obtain truth and wisdom, is not to ask it from books, but to go to God in prayer and obtain divine teaching."[22] At this time the Twelve were in England, and the Prophet notified them of the new teaching by mentioning 1 Corinthians 15:29 but indicating further knowledge "independent of the Bible."[23] Nowhere is the point more powerful than in Joseph Smith's two formal letters to the Church on the subject, using the language of revelation. "Verily, thus saith the Lord" is the authority for the practice and its procedures (D&C 127:6). History is implied in reestablishing any principle, but divine reconstruction is not dependent on fragmentary sources: "For I am about to restore many things to the earth, pertaining to the priesthood, saith the Lord of Hosts" (D&C 127:8). This appendix started with the views of scholars narrowly analyzing the single verse of 1 Corinthians 15:29. Joseph Smith was far from anti-intellectual, but he employed a method beyond scholarship. In writing to the Church on baptism for the dead, he gave an inspired synthesis, a revealed correlation of important scriptures that throw great light on the practice (D&C 128), not to mention the passages from 1 Peter 3 and 4 cited throughout his discourses. The Prophet had a synoptic view of his subject, not an isolated interpretation of 1 Corinthians 15:29. He eloquently pictured God's concern with the salvation of all his children.

The candid and universal spirit in Joseph Smith remarkably mirrors these same qualities in Paul, who expressed deep admiration for the faithful martyrs of the past and a harmony with them in God's great work: "They without us should not be made perfect" (Heb. 11:40). Joseph Smith used no scripture more often in explaining work for the dead, for it indicates the unity of the family of God in all ages and suggests salvation through interdependence, just as the turning of the children to their fathers does at the end of Malachi. One with the truth is obligated to share the gospel with the living, and Joseph Smith insists on the same horizon for the dead, "for their salvation is necessary and essential to our salvation" (D&C 128:15). Joseph Smith admitted that vicarious baptism was indeed a "bold doctrine," yet one he rightfully declared because he held "a dispensation of the priesthood . . . by actual revelation" (D&C 128:9).

This appendix stresses the main points that baptism was an ancient practice and that it could be reestablished only by divine instruction to latter-day prophets. It will close with a scholar's views on both of these issues. Here is one of the off-the-record conversations with experts that goes behind their more formal lectures and publications. It comes through my friend and Brigham Young University colleague Paul R. Cheesman, who took the trouble to outline his visit with Edgar Goodspeed on the subject of baptism for the dead. Goodspeed was best known for his popular and precise "American Translation" of the New Testament, where 1 Corinthians 15:29 begins, "Otherwise, what do people mean by having themselves baptized on behalf of the dead?" Professionally, he was a world expert in the Christian documents of the first two centuries and the everyday language of the papyri that reveal so much about New Testament words. So his testimony is impressive, captured in its main points by Professor Cheesman's reconstruction:

> Interview between Dr. Edgar J. Goodspeed and Paul R. Cheesman, held in Dr. Goodspeed's office on the campus of the University of California at Los Angeles during the summer of 1945.

> Cheesman: Is the scripture found in 1 Corinthians 15:29 translated properly as found in the King James Translation?
> Goodspeed: Basically, yes.
> Cheesman: Do you believe that baptism for the dead was practiced in Paul's time?
> Goodspeed: Definitely, yes.
> Cheesman: Does the church to which you belong practice it today?
> Goodspeed: No.
> Cheesman: Do you think it should be practiced today?
> Goodspeed: This is the reason why we do not practice it today. We do not know enough about it. If we did, we would practice it.
> Cheesman: May I quote you as a result of this interview?
> Goodspeed: Yes.[24]

NOTES

1. Leon Morris, *The First Epistle of Paul to the Corinthians* (London: Tyndale Press, 1964), p. 218.

2. F. F. Bruce, *The New Century Bible Commentary: 1 and 2 Corinthians* (Grand Rapids, Mich.: Eerdmans Publishing Co., 1971), p. 148.

3. William F. Orr and James Arthur Walther, *1 Corinthians* (Garden City, N.Y.: Doubleday, 1981), p. 337.

4. James Hope Moulton and George Milligan, *The Vocabulary of the Greek Testament* (Grand Rapids Mich.: Eerdmans Publishing Co., 1980), p. 651.

5. B. M. Foschini is the most vigorous spokesman for the minority view that Paul's words translate into something other than proxy baptism. He has appeared to be near those claiming that many past interpretations make no interpretation possible, but his unusual solution is to modify the normal understanding of the preposition and the punctuation, one that finds little support by Greek scholars. See "Baptism for the Dead," *New Catholic Encyclopedia* (New York: McGraw-Hill, 1967), p. 68.

6. Compare Foschini's feeling for the inconsistency of those who claim that Paul argued from a practice with which he did not agree: "We cannot, however, conceive how a man like St. Paul could leave uncensured such a superstitious rite, had it existed." (Ibid.) But if the ceremony did exist, the apostle's tolerance, so apparently strange, is a clue to deeper views than most biographers realize.

7. Justin Martyr, *Dialogue with Trypho the Jew* 72:4, literal translation from the text of Edgar J. Goodspeed, *Die ältesten Apologeten* (Göttingen: Vandenhoeck and Ruprecht, 1914). The translation in the Ante-Nicene Fathers reads: "The Lord God remembered his dead people of Israel who lay in the graves, and he descended to preach to them his own salvation." Justin claimed this a deleted passage from Jeremiah. Irenaeus's use clearly shows that second-century Christians considered it an accurate summary of Christ's visit to the spirit prison. See *Against Heresies* 3.20.4 and 4.22.1—the Latin reading has influenced my translation of "the Lord God of Israel."

8. Hugh W. Nibley, "Baptism for the Dead in Ancient Times," *Improvement Era*, Dec. 1948 through April 1949.

9. Irenaeus, *Against Heresies* 4.27.1. The version here and in the next quotation is that of J. B. Lightfoot, *The Apostolic Fathers* (Grand Rapids, Mich.: Baker Book House, 1962), pp. 277-78, a translation carefully following the Latin.

10. Ibid.

11. Compare Richard L. Anderson, *Euangelion—A Study in New Testament Context* (Brigham Young University, M.A. Thesis, 1957).

12. Daniel J. Theron, trans., *Evidence of Tradition* (Grand Rapids, Mich.: Baker Book House, 1958), p. 113, with "chair" substituted for "seat."

13. Quasten 1:93.

14. *The Shepherd of Hermas,* similitude 9.16.2-4 (Loeb Classical Library, Kirsopp Lake trans.).

15. Ibid., 9.16.3-7.

16. Quasten 1:101.

17. *The Elders Journal* 1:43 (July 1838), also cited in Joseph Smith, *Teachings of the Prophet Joseph Smith,* selected by Joseph Fielding Smith (Salt Lake City: Deseret Book Co., 1938), p. 121.

18. For the date of completion of the manuscript, see Robert J. Matthews, *"A Plainer Translation": Joseph Smith's Translation of the Bible* (Provo, Utah: Brigham Young University Press, 1975), pp. 36-37, 96. Dean Matthews courteously took the time to share his transcribed notes of the manuscript of the Joseph Smith Translation, which show that the verses on preaching to the dead in 1 Peter 3 and 4 are singled out by being handwritten, with no evidence of corrections

after first being written. Thus, that the correction was made by 1833 is quite clear. Dean Matthews also noted characteristic misspellings of Sidney Rigdon in the handscript of the letters of Peter (compare his book, p. 89). Historian Dean Jesse knows of no document showing Sidney Rigdon as the Prophet's scribe after leaving Kirtland.

19. Ehat and Cook, p. 268.

20. Ibid., p. 77.

21. Ibid., p. 370, with my bracketed word and punctuation.

22. Ibid., p. 77.

23. Joseph Smith to the Twelve, October 1840, cited in Joseph Smith, *History of The Church of Jesus Christ of Latter-day Saints*, 2d ed. rev., edited by B. H. Roberts (Salt Lake City: The Church of Jesus Christ of Latter-day Saints, 1932-51) 4:231.

24. Interview reconstruction written by Paul R. Cheesman in 1964 and given to Richard L. Anderson June 16, 1964. Professor Goodspeed had a distinguished career at the University of Chicago before retiring and coming to Los Angeles, where he died in 1962.

Appendix D

Glossary of Ancient Sources

Paul's physical world and the world of thought surrounding him have been illustrated in this book through the best available sources of his time. This short dictionary gives dates generally estimated or reconstructed for persons, plus a concise identification to estimate the value of each source. None of these sources have been quoted for insight into Paul's life and thought unless they are nearly contemporary with him, though information about his cities must often come from a wider time spectrum. Further information is easily available from standard reference works, such as the *Oxford Classical Dictionary* or the *Oxford Dictionary of the Christian Church*. Additional ancient sources used in the appendixes are identified there.

Apocalypse of Abraham Considered to have been written at the end of the first century. A Jewish-Christian book describing Abraham's conversion from idolatry and his visions of the preexistence and the Creation. See chapter 8, note 77, for Hugh Nibley's evaluation.

Apostolic Fathers A.D. 96–150. A standard collection of the earliest Christian writings after the apostles, the most significant of which are the letters from the bishops Clement of Rome, Ignatius, and Polycarp, as well as the long Shepherd of Hermas.

Aristotle 384–322 B.C. The Greek philosopher who began as a pupil of Plato and learned enough to write on the whole range of science and humanities known to the ancient world.

Augustus 63 B.C.–A.D. 14. The first emperor, a leader who brought peace and a new constitution to Rome just before the Christian era.

Catullus 84–54 B.C. A Roman poet who illustrates the changing values of Italian society prior to Paul.

Chester Beatty Papyri A.D. 175. The oldest nearly complete New Testament manuscripts, discovered and collected in the 1930s.

Cicero 106–43 B.C. A prominent Roman statesman whose writings reveal political and geographical conditions of his time.

Clement, First See Clement of Rome.

Clement, Second Probably first half of first century. Early Christian letter or sermon found in the collection known as the Apostolic Fathers.

Clement of Alexandria A.D. 150–215. A competent Alexandrian Christian scholar who had access to second-century information on the earlier Church from teachers and writings.

Clement of Rome Prominent about A.D. 96. The first bishop after the apostles whose writings have survived. At the end of the first century he directed a letter from Rome to Corinth, criticizing the Corinthian Saints for dismissing their priesthood leaders, who had been lawfully appointed. This letter is known as 1 Clement.

Dio Cassius Prominent at the beginning of the third century. A senator and Roman historian who capably used earlier sources.

Ecclesiasticus Written about 180 B.C. A book of the traditional Apocrypha that contains the wisdom of the orthodox scribe Jesus, son of Sirach.

Epicurus 341–270 B.C. The founder of one of the most influential schools of thought after Plato and Aristotle.

Eusebius A.D. 260–340. Prominent Christian bishop whose scholarship was recognized by Constantine. His *Ecclesiastical History* is invaluable for its quotation of early sources now lost.

Hegesippus Prominent in the mid–second century. A historian of early Palestinian Christianity, fragments of whose writings survive in the history of Eusebius.

Hermas See Shepherd of Hermas.

Ignatius A.D. 35–107. Bishop of Antioch who was arrested and martyred in the early second century. On his way to Rome he wrote seven letters that describe chaotic conditions in the Asian churches. These are found in the collection known as the Apostolic Fathers.

Irenaeus A.D. 130–200. Bishop of Lyons, France, at the height of the threat of the Gnostics, whose views he reports from contemporary and earlier information.

Jesus, the Son of Sirach See Ecclesiasticus.

Josephus A.D. 37–100. Jewish political and military leader who was taken to Rome after Jerusalem's fall of A.D. 70. His detailed histories are a prime source of first-century Jewish information.

Justin Martyr A.D. 100–165. A philosopher converted to Christianity, whose debate with Trypho the Jew dates from A.D. 135 and who also described second-century worship in a defense to the emperor.

Juvenal Prominent in the early second century. A poet whose biting satire gives insight into Roman society shortly after Paul.

Lucian Prominent after the mid–second century. A Greek philosopher-satirist who describes ancient life while exposing its inconsistencies.

Mishnah Compiled about A.D. 200. The earliest written version of the Pharisees' laws. Easily available in the translation of Herbert Danby, it is a mine of information on ancient Judaism, much of it dating back to great Rabbis of Paul's time.

Muratorian Fragment A.D. 175. A partially preserved list of New Testament books accepted as authentic by the Christian churches in the second century. Traditional background is included for some books and for the end of Paul's life.

Origen A.D. 185–253. A brilliant and prolific Alexandrian scholar who was well informed on what the Christian church of his day knew about its origins.

Pausanias Prominent about A.D. 150. A traveler who left detailed descriptions of his tours through the mainland Greek cities.

Philo 20 B.C.–A.D. 50. A Jewish scholar of Alexandria who blended Hebrew traditions with the Greek education of his day.

Plato 429–347 B.C. An Athenian deeply influenced by his teacher Socrates. In addition to writing many other probing dialogues, Plato reconstructed Socrates' defense, given before Socrates was sentenced to death.

Pliny the Elder A.D. 24–79. A member of the Roman middle class who compiled a massive encyclopedia of the world and objects in it.

Pliny the Younger A.D. 61–112. The nephew of the elder Pliny. He was a senator whose correspondence discloses much political and personal information about Roman life.

Plutarch A.D. 50–120. A traditional Greek of the educated class who wrote about people, customs, pagan religion, and philosophy.

Polycarp A.D. 69–155. Bishop of Smyrna in Asia Minor, he had known John. Soon after Ignatius died in the very early second century, Polycarp wrote a letter to the Philippians, which is included in the collection known as the Apostolic Fathers.

Quintilian A.D. 30–100. A revered Roman teacher of rhetoric who wrote on the nature of language and classical education.

Seneca 4 B.C.–A.D. 65. A capable Roman writer-philosopher who was also minister of state under Nero.

Shepherd of Hermas Written about A.D. 155, with parts probably much earlier. The longest book in the collection entitled the Apostolic Fathers, it was written by Hermas, brother of the Roman bishop, as visions and instructions from an angel appearing as a shepherd.

Strabo 64 B.C.–A.D. 21. Careful geographer who lived in Asia Minor and reported much from personal knowledge.

Suetonius A.D. 69–130. A middle-class Roman with a distinguished career in the civil service, he wrote biographies of the first-century emperors.

Tacitus A.D. 56–115. Roman senator-historian with good sources and a deep sense of realism in evaluating the events and emperors of the first century.

Tertullian A.D. 160–220. An educated lawyer-Christian who made primitive Christianity his quest and defended its principles in biting writings.

Ulpian Prominent in the early third century. For a time the chief legal officer in Rome, Ulpian summarized criminal and administrative law from traditional materials.

Wisdom of Solomon Written just before the Christian Era. One of the books of the traditional Apocrypha, it expresses conventional Jewish devotion and wisdom.

Xenophon 428–354 B.C. A native Athenian who involved himself in national affairs and wrote on a wide variety of subjects, including the dramatic march of Cyrus' Greek army through Asia Minor.

Zadokite Document Considered to have been written in the first century B.C. One of the principle writings of the Essenes of the Dead Sea community, it outlines the struggle with evil and the rules of the sect.

Scripture References

Genesis
1:27, p. 251
2:24, p. 104
9:4, p. 53
14, p. 228 n 70
14:18, p. 212
14:27-28, p. 213
15:6, pp. 180, 222
17:7-19, p. 210
25:23, p. 189

Exodus
4:22, p. 224
7:3, p. 227 n 40
7:11, p. 388 n 103
9:12, p. 227 n 40
19:6, p. 210
20:15, p. 88
20:17, p. 88
28:1, p. 211
28:41, p. 211
24:8, p. 217
40:15, p. 210

Leviticus
16:30, p. 217

Numbers
25:13, p. 210
27:18-23, p. 211
33:55, p. 142

Deuteronomy
25:1-3, p. 26
28:58, p. 32

Joshua
22:22, p. 85

1 Samuel
15:22, p. 175

Psalm
110:4, pp. 209, 212

Proverbs
22:8-9, p. 147 n 35
22:8, p. 140

Isaiah
52:7, p. 212
64:4, p. 100

Jeremiah
1:5, p. 19
5:31, p. 377
31:31, p. 216
31:34, p. 217

Ezekiel
28:24, p. 142
36:25-26, p. 219

Daniel
12:1-2, p. 90 n 5

Habakkuk
2:4, p. 200

Zechariah
8:17, p. 123

Malachi
4:5-6, p. 271

Matthew
1:1-17, p. 320
3:11, p. 63
5:8, pp. 174, 324
5:16, pp. 194-95, 296, 328
5:17, p. 193
5:19, p. 165
7:7-8, p. 221

7:12, p. 193
7:15-20, p. 296
7:15, p. 65
7:21, p. 187
7:24, p. 187
7:26-27, p. 272
10:7-8, p. 49
10:17, pp. 20, 32
10:40, p. 62
11:30, p. 134
13:49, p. 2
16:17, p. 129
16:18-19, p. 97
16:24, p. 363
16:25, p. 136
16:27, pp. 84, 176
17:1, p. 283
18:3-4, p. 100
18:15, p. 120
18:17-19, p. 97
18:21-25, p. 240
19:5, p. 104
19:17-19, p. 194
20:1-16, p. 28
20:21-23, p. 202
22:20, p. 249
22:36-40, p. 119
23:34, p. 20
24, p. 196
24:1-3, p. 373
24:9-12, p. 374
24:9, p. 87
24:11, pp. 374-75
24:12, p. 374
24:15-16, p. 87
24:21, pp. 87, 374
24:23-26, p. 374
24:23, p. 87

24:24, pp. 87, 374-75
25:21, p. 205
25:23, p. 205
25:31-46, p. 335
25:31, p. 84
25:40, p. 140
26:28, p. 217
28:19-20, p. 276
28:19, p. 15

Mark
3:15, p. 46
7:8-9, p. 23
13, p. 196
16:15-18, p. 49
16:15-16, p. 162
16:17-18, p. 56
16:17, pp. 46, 110
16:19, p. 52

Luke
1:2, p. 41
1:4, p. 42
2:1, p. 53
2:36, p. 320
3:23-38, p. 320
6:13, p. 35
6:38, p. 140
10:1-9, p. 49
10:29, p. 159
12:49, p. 19
12:51, p. 20
15:25, p. 147 n 26
16:2-4, pp. 269,
    307 n 52
21, p. 196
22:19-20, p. 107
22:19, p. 108
22:26, p. 102
23:43, p. 406
24:20-21, p. 203
24:39, p. 129

John
1:14, pp. 249, 298
1:18, p. 324
1:35-42, p. 60
1:42, p. 95
1:47-48, p. 115
1:49, p. 115
3:5, pp. 358, 403,
    409-10
3:16, p. 137
4:1-3, p. 384 n 2
5:29, p. 127
9:2, p. 349
10:30, p. 99
12:28-29, p. 38 n 17
13:35, pp. 77, 119
14:6-9, p. 251
14:15-17, p. 165
14:15, pp. 108, 119,
    187, 361
14:27, p. 304
15:16, p. 327
15:26, p. 113
16:2, p. 25
16:13, p. 115
16:28, pp. 1, 264
17:11, p. 97
17:18, p. 97
17:20-21, p. 97
17:24, p. 264
20:17, pp. 225, 264
20:22, p. 61
21:15-17, p. 146 n 22

Acts
1:1-2, p. 42
1:1, p. 41
1:6-7, p. 80
1:8, pp. 41, 61
1:9-11, p. 323
1:15-26, pp. 327-28

2:4, p. 61
2:8-11, p. 343
2:10, pp. 13, 170
2:11, p. 110
2:38, pp. 48, 60,
    68 n 5, 162, 184,
    207-8, 225 n 8, 403
2:41, pp. 25, 49
2:42, pp. 60, 108
2:44-45, p. 139
2:46, p. 60
3:19-21, p. 267
4:4, p. 25
4:6, p. 210
4:35, p. 139
4:36-37, p. 33
4:36, pp. 45, 320
5:31, p. 225 n 8
5:32, pp. 108, 220
5:34, p. 23
5:39, p. 23
6:1-6, pp. 60, 139
6:1, p. 49
6:3, p. 45
6:5, p. 211
6:6, pp. 45, 211
6:9, p. 29
7:55-56, p. 202
7:56, p. 26
7:58, pp. 24-26,
    37 n 9, 392-93
8, pp. 319-20
8:6, p. 68 n 5
8:10, p. 384 n 16
8:12, p. 60
8:14-20, p. 208
8:14, p. 33
8:16, p. 61
8:17, pp. 60-61
8:18-19, p. 61
8:19, p. 63

8:35-39, p. 68 n 5
8:38, p. 60
9, pp. 30, 38 n 17
9:1, p. 26
9:2, p. 26
9:7, p. 38 n 17
9:15, pp. 66, 78, 233
9:17, p. 27
9:18, pp. 28, 49, 60
9:20, p. 28
9:22, p. 48
9:26-29, p. 394
9:26, p. 49
9:27-30, p. 269
9:27, pp. 31, 34
9:30, pp. 31, 394
10, p. 52
10:43, p. 225 n 8
10:48, p. 60
11, p. 52
11:19-26, p. 394
11:19-20, p. 33
11:19, p. 33
11:20, p. 33
11:21, p. 33
11:22, p. 33
11:25, p. 33
11:26, pp. 34, 394
11:27-30, pp. 394, 398 n 10
11:27-29, p. 280
11:29-30, pp. 38 n 21, 225
11:29, p. 139
11:30, p. 35
12:23-25, p. 394
12:25, p. 38 n 21
13:1-3, pp. 60, 325
13:1, p. 116
13:2, pp. 19, 43-44
13:3, p. 44

13:5, p. 45
13:6-11, p. 56
13:7, p. 46
13:9, pp. 37 n 9, 46
13:11, p. 46
13:12, p. 46
13:13, p. 46
13:16, p. 13
13:25, p. 12
13:31, pp. 47, 156
13:38-39, pp. 47, 159
13:38, pp. 48, 225 n 8
13:43, p. 13
13:46, p. 45
13:50, p. 13
13:52, pp. 48-49
14:3, pp. 49, 394
14:4, pp. 35, 49
14:8-10, pp. 50, 56
14:12, pp. 50, 401
14:14-18, p. 50
14:14, p. 35
14:19, p. 32
14:22-23, p. 50
14:22, pp. 51, 182, 315
14:23, pp. 72, 281, 311, 326, 341
14:26-28, p. 394
14:27, p. 51
14:28, p. 51
15, p. 38 n 21
15:1, pp. 51, 151
15:2, pp. 33, 51-52, 157
15:4, p. 157
15:5, p. 157
15:6, p. 52
15:10-11, p. 52
15:10, p. 164
15:12, p. 52
15:19, p. 53

15:22, p. 53
15:23, p. 157
15:24, pp. 152, 155
15:27-40, p. 67 n 1
15:28, pp. 53, 157
15:29, pp. 53, 78, 158
15:36-41, p. 394
15:36, pp. 43, 53
15:38, p. 67 n 4
15:41, p. 31
16:1-3, p. 54
16:1, pp. 149, 314-15
16:2, p. 315
16:3, pp. 151, 315
16:4-5, p. 154
16:4, pp. 43, 53
16:6-7, p. 59
16:6, pp. 43, 54, 150
16:9-10, p. 30
16:9, pp. 43, 54, 291
16:10, p. 40
16:12, p. 291
16:14, pp. 54, 68 n 5, 292
16:15, pp. 54, 60, 292
16:16-18, p. 56
16:21, p. 291
16:22-23, p. 32
16:30, p. 55
16:31, p. 55
16:32, p. 55
16:33-34, p. 292
16:33, pp. 55, 60
16:37-39, p. 22
16:40, p. 292
17, p. 11
17:1-10, p. 70
17:2, pp. 71-72
17:3, p. 76
17:4, pp. 13, 71
17:5-6, p. 71

17:5, p. 70
17:7, p. 53
17:10, p. 75
17:13-14, p. 75
17:13, p. 73
17:14, pp. 55, 73, 75
17:15, pp. 55, 73, 75
17:17, pp. 13, 57
17:19, p. 57
17:22, p. 57
17:23, p. 251
17:26, p. 263
17:28, pp. 225, 264
17:30-31, p. 84
17:30, pp. 48, 58
17:31, pp. 58, 251
17:33, p. 57
18:1-3, p. 89
18:1, p. 75
18:2, pp. 169, 171, 173
18:5, pp. 74-75, 82
18:7, p. 94
18:8, pp. 58, 60, 94
18:9-10, pp. 30, 59, 144
18:10-12, p. 391
18:10, pp. 7, 104
18:11-12, p. 394
18:11, pp. 82, 392
18:17, p. 96
18:18-21, p. 395
18:18, pp. 59, 82, 171
18:20-21, p. 43
18:21-22, p. 395
18:21, p. 395
18:23, pp. 150, 246, 395
18:24-28, p. 95
18:26, p. 171
19:1-6, pp. 61, 208
19:1, pp. 95, 246, 395
19:2, p. 62

19:5-6, p. 60
19:8-9, pp. 64, 395
19:10, pp. 64, 239, 369-70
19:12, p. 56
19:15, p. 62
19:19, p. 64
19:20, p. 64
19:21-22, p. 131
19:21, p. 66
19:22, p. 94
19:26, pp. 64, 244, 369-70
19:27, p. 260
19:29, p. 71
20, p. 196
20:1-2, p. 131
20:1, p. 395
20:2-3, p. 395
20:4, pp. 71, 149, 261
20:5, p. 41
20:6, pp. 131, 397
20:7, p. 60
20:11, p. 60
20:13, p. 41
20:16, p. 173
20:17, p. 64
20:21, p. 48
20:22-23, p. 172
20:23, p. 66
20:24, pp. 309 n 95, 378
20:25, p. 153
20:28, pp. 64-65, 282, 325, 330
20:29-30, pp. 65, 370
20:29, pp. 86, 369, 377
20:30, pp. 86, 377
20:31, pp. 65, 86, 131, 395
20:33-35, p. 89
20:35, pp. 90, 140

21:8, p. 282
21:10-11, p. 280
21:13, pp. 230-31
21:17, p. 396
21:18-24, p. 52
21:28, p. 231
21:39, p. 20
21:40, p. 22
22, pp. 30, 38 n 17
22:1-11, p. 232
22:3, p. 23
22:7-11, p. 27
22:9, pp. 27, 38 n 17
22:10, p. 31
22:14, p. 27
22:16, pp. 49, 60, 183-84
22:17-21, pp. 30, 144, 394
22:18, p. 29
22:19, p. 26
22:21, p. 31
22:25, p. 21
22:28, p. 21
23:6, pp. 22, 232
23:9, p. 232
23:11, pp. 30, 43, 60, 233
23:29, p. 232
24:17, pp. 140, 396
24:23, pp. 196, 233, 236
24:27, p. 233
25:9-10, p. 43
25:10-11, p. 233
26, pp. 30, 38 n 17
26:5, pp. 22, 181
26:9, p. 25
26:10-11, p. 25
26:10, p. 25
26:11, p. 25
26:14, pp. 26,

38 n 17, 138
26:16-18, p. 27
26:16, p. 27
26:17, p. 28
26:18, p. 234
26:20, p. 234
26:23, p. 234
26:24, p. 233
26:28-29, p. 305 n 2
26:28, pp. 233-34
26:29, p. 234
26:31-32, p. 310
27:1, p. 41
27:2, pp. 71, 235
27:6, pp. 234-35
27:7-8, p. 343
27:9, pp. 234, 396
27:11, p. 116
27:12-15, p. 343
27:23-24, p. 30
27:24, pp. 235, 316
28:3-6, p. 56
28:8-9, pp. 56, 235
28:11, p. 396
28:16, p. 41
28:30-31, pp. 236, 316
28:30, pp. 295, 396
28:31, p. 294

Romans
1:3, p. 320
1:8, p. 170
1:13, pp. 170, 172
1:16, pp. 159, 299, 376
1:17, pp. 178, 200
1:20, p. 177
1:24, p. 174
1:26-27, pp. 174, 351
1:28, p. 175
1:29-31, p. 175
1:32, p. 174
2:4, pp. 138, 176

2:6, p. 176
2:7, p. 176
2:8, p. 176
2:10, p. 176
2:11, p. 175
2:14, p. 175
2:15, pp. 175, 177
2:26, p. 175
2:29, p. 175
3:23, p. 180
3:24, p. 180
3:25, pp. 180, 203
3:28, pp. 178, 180-81
3:31, pp. 179-80
4:2, p. 223
4:3, p. 385 n 39
4:16, p. 181
4:20, p. 223
5:1-5, pp. 182, 186
5:1-2, p. 182
5:3, pp. 182-83, 340
5:5, p. 183
5:10, p. 180
5:11, p. 133
5:15-16, p. 181
6:1, pp. 184, 323
6:3-5, pp. 153, 188, 191
6:4, pp. 184, 194, 256
6:6, pp. 185, 194
6:12-13, pp. 186-87
6:12, p. 297
6:16, p. 297
6:19, p. 194
7:11, p. 181
8:4, p. 188
8:6, p. 187
8:13, pp. 188, 256
8:14-17, p. 153
8:24-25, p. 221
8:27, p. 216
8:29-30, pp. 263, 265,

307 n 43
8:34, pp. 216, 249
8:35, p. 182
9:3, pp. 171, 188
9:11, pp. 190-91
9:17-18, p. 190
9:23-24, p. 190
9:23, p. 307 n 59
10:1, p. 189
10:2-4, p. 189
10:3-4, p. 190
10:9, p. 191
10:12, p. 191
10:15, p. 191
10:17, p. 191
11:1, p. 320
11:5-7, p. 192
11:13, pp. 20, 191
11:20, pp. 192, 205
11:22, p. 192
11:23, p. 205
11:25, pp. 192, 268
11:26-29, p. 192
12:1, p. 194
12:2, p. 192
12:6-8, p. 109
12:17, p. 194
12:21, p. 193
13:1, p. 289
13:5, p. 289
13:9, pp. 153, 193-94, 270
13:13, p. 194
15:19, pp. 172, 227 n 46
15:22, p. 172
15:23, p. 169
15:24, p. 316
15:25, p. 172
15:26, p. 172
15:30-31, p. 172
16:1-6, p. 68 n 17

16:1-2, p. 171
16:1, pp. 171-73, 332
16:3-4, pp. 171-72
16:5, p. 172
16:7, p. 171
16:19, p. 170
16:21, p. 171
16:22, pp. 170-71
16:23, pp. 94, 173
16:25, pp. 268, 346
16:26, p. 268

1 Corinthians
1:1, p. 96
1:10, p. 98
1:11-12, p. 95
1:12, p. 155
1:13, p. 97
1:14, pp. 58, 94, 99, 173
1:16, pp. 94, 99
1:17, p. 98
1:18, p. 376
1:20, p. 1
1:22-23, p. 203
1:26, p. 100
1:27, p. 14
1:29, p. 356
2:2, p. 100
2:3, p. 152
2:5, p. 100
2:7, p. 1
2:10, p. 101
3:1-2, p. 200
3:6, p. 99
3:8, p. 99
3:9, p. 86
3:11, p. 86
3:16, p. 86
3:23, p. 99
4:1, p. 101
4:4, p. 101
4:14-15, p. 102

4:15, p. 239
4:17, p. 315
4:18, p. 196
4:21, p. 101
5:5, p. 102
5:7, p. 405
5:9, p. 95
5:13, p. 102
6:3, p. 203
6:9, p. 103
6:11, pp. 103, 256
6:19, p. 104
7:1-6, p. 102
7:1, p. 104
7:5, p. 105
7:7, p. 105
7:8, p. 105
7:10-11, p. 105
7:25, p. 104
7:26, p. 106
7:28, p. 105
7:29, p. 106
7:36, pp. 104-5
7:39-40, p. 105
8:10, p. 106
9:1-2, p. 142
9:1, pp. 28, 101
9:5, pp. 95, 105, 142, 155
9:16, pp. 20, 101
9:17, pp. 101, 307 n 52
9:18, p. 142
9:20, p. 190
9:24-27, p. 301
9:24, p. 303
9:27, p. 302
10:13, p. 204
10:16, p. 108
10:21, pp. 106-7
10:23, p. 104
10:25-26, p. 107
10:25, p. 107

10:28, p. 107
11:2, p. 308 n 69
11:5, pp. 111, 352
11:19, p. 344
11:21, p. 107
11:23-26, p. 107
11:24, pp. 108, 405
11:25-26, p. 218
11:27, pp. 108, 146 n 7
11:28, p. 108
11:33-34, p. 107
11:34, p. 308 n 69
12:2, p. 130
12:3, p. 113
12:7, p. 144
12:8, p. 114
12:10, pp. 109, 112, 115
12:12-13, p. 112
12:13, pp. 99, 228 n 60
12:15, p. 116
12:28, pp. 112, 116, 280-81
12:31, pp. 119, 252
13, pp. 257-58
13:1-3, pp. 117, 119
13:4-7, pp. 120-23
13:8, p. 124
13:12, p. 124
14:1, p. 115
14:6, p. 109
14:18, p. 56
14:19, p. 110
14:25, p. 115
14:26, p. 109
14:27-28, p. 110
14:28, p. 111
14:29-30, p. 115
14:30, p. 111
14:32-33, p. 111
14:32, p. 289

14:34, p. 111
15:1-4, p. 47
15:1-2, pp. 42, 91
  308 n 69
15:1, p. 206
15:3-4, p. 42
15:3, pp. 42, 126,
  133, 405
15:5-8, p. 125
15:5-7, p. 47
15:5, p. 156
15:6, p. 125
15:7, p. 156
15:9, p. 35
15:10, pp. 29, 182
15:11, pp. 42, 155
15:12-14, p. 3
15:12, pp. 125-26
15:13, p. 126
15:15, pp. 125-26
15:17, p. 126
15:18, p. 126
15:22, p. 126
15:23-24, pp. 80,
  147 n 31
15:23, pp. 81, 127
15:26, p. 126
15:29, pp. 80, 126,
  228 n 6, 403-15
15:30-32, p. 126
15:30, p. 20
15:35, pp. 127-28
15:40, p. 128
15:41-42, p. 143
15:41, p. 128
15:42, p. 128
15:43, p. 128
15:44, p. 129
15:47, p. 129
15:49, p. 129
15:50, p. 129
16:1-2, p. 131
16:1, pp. 140, 149

16:3, p. 140
16:5-8, p. 95
16:6, pp. 131, 395
16:8, pp. 130, 395
16:10-11, p. 315
16:12, p. 96
16:15, p. 94
16:16, pp. 94-95, 289
16:18, p. 96
16:19, pp. 68 n 17,
  96, 171

2 Corinthians
1:5, p. 135
1:8, p. 132
1:15-17, p. 133
1:16, p. 227 n 46
1:19, p. 133
1:23, p. 132
2:4, pp. 136, 138
2:7, p. 138
2:8, p. 138
2:12-13, p. 342
2:13, p. 132
3:6, p. 135
4:4-6, p. 324
4:4, p. 133
4:7, p. 135
4:8-9, p. 135
4:14, p. 324
4:16, p. 136
4:18, pp. 221, 324
5, p. 134
5:7, p. 221
5:8, p. 134
5:10, pp. 134, 176
5:14, p. 134
5:15, p. 135
5:17, p. 134
5:18, p. 134
5:21, p. 134
6:5, p. 136
6:6, p. 137

6:14, p. 108
6:15, p. 212
7:5-6, p. 131
7:7, p. 342
7:8, pp. 131, 138
7:9-10, p. 138
7:13, p. 131
7:15, pp. 138, 342
8:2, p. 140
8:9, p. 140
8:14, p. 140
8:16-18, p. 131
8:16, p. 342
8:23, p. 342
9:6, p. 140
9:7, p. 140
9:10-12, p. 140
10:1, p. 401
10:8, pp. 141-42
10:10, pp. 141, 401
10:11, p. 141
11:5, p. 141
11:7-9, p. 293
11:9, p. 89
11:13, pp. 141, 143
11:18-21, p. 36
11:18, p. 143
11:23-27, p. 382
11:24-25, p. 32
11:26, pp. 47, 136
11:27, p. 136
11:28, p. 136
11:30, pp. 143-44
11:32-33, p. 32
11:32, p. 233
12:1-4, p. 30
12:1, pp. 36, 143-44
12:2-4, pp. 36, 144
12:2, pp. 38 n 22,
  142-43
12:3, p. 144
12:4, pp. 144-45
12:7, pp. 36, 141-42, 151

12:11, p. 141
12:12, p. 142
12:14, pp. 133, 142
12:18, p. 342
12:21, p. 142
13:1, p. 133
13:2, p. 142
13:10, p. 142
13:14, p. 108

Galatians
1:1, p. 38 n 21
1:2, p. 150
1:8, pp. 155-56
1:9, p. 44
1:12, pp. 155-56
1:13, p. 25
1:14, p. 25
1:15-18, p. 392
1:15, pp. 19, 181
1:16, p. 129
1:17, pp. 29, 35
1:18-19, p. 29
1:18, pp. 156, 225 n 2, 393-94
1:21, pp. 31, 38 n 21, 394
1:22, p. 38 n 21
2, p. 38 n 21
2:1, pp. 38 n 22, 225 n 2, 392-93, 398 n 10
2:2, pp. 156-57, 309 n 95
2:3-5, p. 157
2:3, p. 341-42
2:5, p. 342
2:7, p. 156
2:8, p. 155
2:9, pp. 29, 155, 157-58, 269, 283
2:10, pp. 139-40
2:11-13, p. 157

2:14, p. 158
2:16, pp. 159, 162
2:20, p. 162
3:1, p. 152
3:4, p. 152
3:8, p. 205
3:11, p. 200
3:17, pp. 161, 179
3:19, pp. 216, 254
3:21, p. 162
3:26-27, pp. 162, 225 n 8
3:27, pp. 153, 184, 403
3:28, p. 288
4:4-7, p. 153
4:4, p. 268
4:8, p. 151
4:10, p. 153
4:13, pp. 151-52
4:14-15, p. 151
4:20, p. 154
4:21, p. 152
5:1, p. 163
5:4, p. 165
5:14, p. 153
5:19-21, pp. 165-66
5:20, p. 344
5:22, p. 305
5:25, p. 165
6:2, pp. 164, 168
6:8, pp. 168, 187
6:9, pp. 167-68
6:12, p. 153
6:17, p. 152

Ephesians
1:1, p. 262
1:3, p. 266
1:4, pp. 264, 346
1:5, p. 263
1:9-10, pp. 267, 307 n 52, 375

1:10, pp. 267, 269
1:11, p. 263
1:12-13, p. 307 n 43
1:13, p. 274
1:15, p. 261
1:17-23, p. 237
1:20-21, p. 272
1:22-23, pp. 272, 277
2:3, p. 273
2:4, p. 273
2:5, p. 359
2:7, p. 273
2:8, p. 273
2:9, pp. 272-73
2:10, pp. 274, 359
2:14, p. 277
2:15-16, p. 277
2:19-20, pp. 277-78
2:20, p. 280
2:21, p. 86
3:1, p. 261
3:2, p. 269
3:5, p. 280
3:9, p. 272
3:14, p. 272
3:15, p. 267
3:16, pp. 272-73
3:19, p. 273
3:21, p. 273
4:1, pp. 146 n 7, 261
4:2, p. 277
4:3-6, p. 277
4:5, pp. 154, 228 n 60, 274
4:10, p. 143
4:11-13, pp. 278-80, 282-83
4:11-12, p. 380
4:11, p. 281
4:12, pp. 50, 302
4:13-14, p. 284
4:14, p. 279

4:22, p. 284
4:23, p. 284
4:24, p. 274
4:25, p. 285
4:26, p. 285
4:28, p. 285
4:29, p. 286
4:30, p. 274
4:31-32, p. 286
5:2, pp. 287-88
5:3, p. 285
5:4, p. 286
5:5, pp. 273, 286
5:18, p. 286
5:19-20, p. 286
5:19, p. 109
5:21-22, pp. 288-89
5:22, p. 352
5:23-24, pp. 289-90
5:24–6:9, p. 237
5:26, p. 284
6:4, p. 290
6:12, pp. 287, 309 n 95
6:17, p. 287
6:19-20, p. 260
6:20, p. 237
6:21, p. 237, 261

Philippians
1:1, pp. 281, 292, 332
1:5, p. 295
1:7, p. 237
1:9-10, p. 299
1:11, p. 296
1:13-16, p. 237
1:13, pp. 237, 294,
   309 n 84
1:22-23, p. 298
1:27, p. 296
2:3, p. 298
2:5-9, p. 237
2:6, p. 298
2:7, p. 298

2:8, p. 297
2:10, p. 266-67
2:12-13, p. 296
2:12, pp. 292, 297
2:15, p. 296
2:19, p. 317
2:24, pp. 295, 317,
   396
2:25-26, p. 295
2:30, p. 295
3:1-3, p. 297
3:1, p. 299
3:5-6, p. 302
3:5, pp. 23-25
3:9, p. 302
3:12-14, p. 302
3:12, p. 303
3:14, p. 378
3:17, p. 373
3:21, pp. 298-99
4:1, p. 292
4:3, pp. 105, 292, 383
4:4, p. 299
4:6, p. 299
4:7, p. 304
4:8-9, p. 304
4:13, p. 302
4:15, pp. 227 n 46,
   293
4:16, p. 293
4:18, pp. 237, 295
4:21-22, p. 237
4:22, pp. 293, 309 n 84

Colossians
1:2, p. 249
1:3, p. 249
1:7, p. 245
1:8, p. 245
1:10, p. 257
1:12-22, p. 249
1:13-18, p. 237
1:13-17, p. 250

1:14, p. 249
1:15, pp. 249, 251-52,
   323
1:16, p. 249
1:18, pp. 249, 254
1:19, p. 252
1:22, p. 252
1:23, p. 171
1:25, p. 269
2:1, pp. 239, 246
2:8, pp. 253-54
2:9, p. 254
2:10, p. 254
2:12, pp. 207, 252, 256
2:16, pp. 109, 255
2:18-19, p. 254
2:19, p. 246
2:20-21, p. 255
2:21, p. 255
3:1, pp. 249, 252, 256
3:2, p. 255
3:5-9, p. 257
3:5, p. 257
3:7, p. 256
3:8-9, p. 256
3:10, p. 257
3:12-14, p. 258
3:14, p. 259
3:18–4:1, p. 237
3:18, pp. 288, 352
3:19, pp. 254, 290
3:21, p. 290
4:1, p. 243
4:2-4, p. 236
4:7, pp. 237, 261, 372
4:9, pp. 237-39
4:10-14, p. 237
4:10-11, p. 71
4:12, p. 245
4:13, pp. 245-46
4:14, pp. 41, 372
4:16, p. 247
4:17, pp. 237, 243

4:18, p. 237

1 Thessalonians
1:5, p. 74
1:6, p. 74
1:7-9, p. 76
1:9, pp. 71, 78
2:2, p. 76
2:4, pp. 76-77
2:6, pp. 72-73
2:9, p. 89
2:12, pp. 146 n 7, 165
2:14, p. 76
2:17, p. 75
2:18, pp. 73, 75
3:1-2, pp. 73, 75
3:1, p. 74
3:2, p. 74
3:4, p. 77
3:5, pp. 74-75
3:6-7, p. 75
3:6, p. 74
3:10, p. 77
3:11, p. 77
3:12, p. 299
4, p. 80
4:1-2, p. 165
4:1, p. 299
4:3-4, p. 78
4:3, p. 78
4:4, p. 78
4:11-12, p. 88
4:11, p. 352
4:13, p. 79
4:14, p. 79
4:15, pp. 79, 81
4:16, p. 80
5:1, pp. 80, 268, 373
5:2, p. 80
5:3, p. 83
5:5, pp. 80-81

5:9-10, p. 81
5:12-13, p. 79
5:12, pp. 72, 289
5:17, p. 78
5:19-20, p. 109
5:25, p. 78

2 Thessalonians
1:7-8, p. 84
2:2, pp. 82-83, 85
2:3, p. 85
2:4, p. 86
2:5, pp. 40, 85, 90 n 11-12, 278
2:6, pp. 85, 87
2:7, p. 85
2:8, pp. 85, 87
2:9, p. 87
2:15, pp. 90 n 12, 278
2:17, p. 84
3:4, pp. 87-88
3:6, p. 88
3:8, p. 89
3:9, p. 373
3:10, pp. 88-89
3:11, pp. 83, 88
3:12, pp. 88, 352
3:14-15, p. 88
3:17, p. 83

1 Timothy
1:2, p. 315
1:3, pp. 316-17, 366
1:4, p. 320
1:6, pp. 318, 321
1:13, p. 25
1:17, p. 323
1:18, pp. 316, 361
1:20, pp. 103, 317, 366
2:5, p. 322
2:8, p. 352
2:9-15, p. 351

2:9-10, p. 338
2:11, p. 352
2:12-14, p. 353
2:12, p. 352
3:2, pp. 280, 329, 351
3:4, p. 330
3:5, p. 332
3:6, p. 328
3:7, p. 328
3:10, p. 332
3:11, p. 332, 351
3:14, p. 317
3:15, p. 86
3:16, p. 323
4:1, pp. 268, 321, 374
4:3, p. 321
4:6, pp. 376, 388 n 98
4:7-8, p. 339
4:7, p. 320
4:12, pp. 316, 339, 341, 352, 373
4:13, p. 339
4:14, pp. 45, 325-26
4:16, p. 340
5, pp. 89-90
5:4, p. 337
5:8, p. 337
5:9, pp. 329, 335
5:10, p. 337
5:14, pp. 105, 329, 335-36
5:16, pp. 336-37
5:17, p. 332
5:22, pp. 35, 210, 326
6:3, p. 312
6:7, p. 313
6:10, p. 313
6:11, p. 340
6:12, pp. 309 n 95, 339
6:14, p. 324
6:16, p. 324
6:18-19, p. 339
6:18, p. 340

6:20, pp. 317-20
6:21, p. 318
2 Timothy
1:2, p. 315
1:5, p. 315
1:9, pp. 348, 357
1:11, p. 280
1:13, pp. 308 n 69, 369
1:14, p. 369
1:15, pp. 366, 368, 370
1:16-18, p. 397
1:16, p. 365
1:17, p. 365
1:18, p. 365
2:2, pp. 308 n 69, 372
2:5, p. 309 n 95
2:8, p. 379
2:10, p. 382
2:12, p. 382
2:15, p. 380
2:17, p. 366
2:18, p. 371
2:22, p. 379
2:24-26, p. 379
2:24, p. 379
3:1-5, pp. 370, 374
3:1, pp. 268, 374
3:2, p. 374
3:4, p. 374
3:5, pp. 374-75
3:8, p. 388 n 103
3:10, p. 381
3:11, p. 382
3:12, p. 382
3:13, pp. 370, 375, 388 n 102
3:15, pp. 315, 380
3:16, p. 380
3:17, p. 380
4:2-5, p. 283
4:2, p. 177
4:3-4, pp. 370, 376

4:3, p. 376
4:4, p. 377
4:5, p. 372
4:6-8, p. 383
4:6, pp. 365, 397
4:7, pp. 182, 309 n 95
4:9, p. 366
4:10, p. 372
4:11, pp. 67 n 4, 316, 367
4:12, pp. 261, 365
4:13, pp. 366, 378-79, 387 n 95, 397
4:14-17, p. 397
4:14, p. 366
4:15, p. 366
4:16-17, p. 367
4:16, p. 371
4:20, pp. 94, 366
4:21, pp. 365, 367, 397
Titus
1:2, pp. 346-49, 357
1:4, p. 341
1:5, pp. 343-44, 385 n 28
1:6, pp. 329-30
1:7, pp. 331, 385 n 28
1:8, pp. 329, 351
1:10, pp. 344, 360
1:11, p. 360
1:14, pp. 321, 360
1:15, p. 360
1:16, p. 361
2:2, p. 351
2:3, p. 351
2:4, p. 351
2:4-5, p. 351
2:5, pp. 352-53
2:6, p. 351
2:7, p. 373
2:12, p. 358
2:13-14, p. 358

2:15, pp. 341, 352
3:1, pp. 289, 353
3:3, p. 358
3:5, pp. 358-59, 403
3:8, p. 359
3:9, pp. 320, 360
3:10, p. 344
3:11, p. 360
3:12, p. 345
3:13, p. 345
Philemon
1:2, pp. 237, 239, 243
1:5, p. 239
1:7, p. 239
1:8-9, p. 242
1:9, pp. 37 n 12, 392-93
1:10-12, p. 237
1:10, pp. 237, 239
1:11, p. 239
1:13, pp. 237, 239
1:15-16, p. 242
1:18, p. 239
1:19, p. 239
1:21, p. 242
1:22, pp. 243, 317
1:23-24, p. 237
1:23, p. 245
1:24, p. 372
Hebrews
1:1-3, p. 250
1:2, pp. 203, 268
1:3-4, p. 197
1:3, pp. 202-3, 249
1:6, p. 250
2:3, p. 201
2:4, p. 202
2:7, p. 203
2:9, p. 203
2:10, pp. 203-4, 264
2:11, p. 203

2:17, p. 203
2:18, p. 204
3:1, p. 205
3:2, p. 205
3:6, pp. 205, 378
3:14, pp. 205, 378
3:19, p. 205
4:2, p. 205
4:14, pp. 205, 223
4:15, p. 204
5:1, p. 209
5:4, pp. 210-11
5:5, p. 209
5:7-10, p. 227 n 56
5:8-9, pp. 204, 223, 297
5:9, p. 206
5:10, p. 209
5:11, p. 195
5:12-14, pp. 195, 200
5:12, pp. 42, 206, 306 n 33
6:1-3, pp. 48, 224
6:1-2, p. 44
6:1, pp. 206, 228 n 58, 359
6:2, pp. 207-8
6:4-6, p. 209
6:4, p. 208
6:5, p. 208
6:11, p. 209
6:12, pp. 209, 222
6:15, pp. 209, 222
7:2, p. 228 n 69
7:3, pp. 213-15, 227 n 56
7:11, p. 212
7:12, pp. 211, 214
7:21, p. 215
7:23, p. 210
7:24, pp. 214-15
7:25, pp. 215-16

7:26, pp. 143, 218
7:28, p. 215
8:1, p. 216
8:6, p. 216
9:10, pp. 207, 255
9:14, pp. 218, 359
9:15, pp. 216-17
9:16, p. 217
9:20, p. 217
9:22, p. 217
10:12, p. 218
10:17, p. 217
10:21, p. 215
10:22, pp. 218-19
10:23, p. 223
10:24, pp. 223, 359
10:32, pp. 197, 223
10:34, p. 196
10:36, pp. 223-24, 339
10:38, p. 200
11, p. 200
11:1, p. 221
11:3, p. 222
11:6, p. 220
11:8, p. 222
11:17, pp. 222-23
11:40, p. 412
12:1, pp. 200, 224, 309 n 95
12:2-3, p. 224
12:2, p. 203
12:9, pp. 225, 264, 357
12:15, p. 224
12:23, p. 225
12:24, p. 216
13:1, p. 224
13:3, p. 200
13:4, p. 224
13:5, p. 224
13:7, p. 224
13:17, pp. 224, 289
13:21, pp. 224, 359

13:23, pp. 198, 396
13:24, p. 196
13:25, p. 198

James
2:21, p. 223

1 Peter
1:20, pp. 264-65
2:2, p. 200
2:9, p. 210
3:18-21, pp. 406, 414 n 18
3:18-20, p. 406
3:19, p. 407
4:5-6, pp. 411, 414 n 18
4:5, p. 407
4:6, pp. 407, 411

2 Peter
1:5-8, p. 182
2:5, p. 213
2:19, p. 360
3:15, p. 177
3:16, p. 177

1 John
2:18-19, p. 87
2:18, p. 368
4:1-3, p. 312
4:2, p. 253
4:3, p. 371
5:16, p. 209

2 John
1:7, p. 253

Jude
1:9, p. 90 n 5

Revelation
2:5, p. 370
2:7, p. 144
3:4, p. 371

3:9, p. 253
3:21, p. 324
12:12-13, p. 176
20:6-13, p. 127
20:6, pp. 174, 210
20:12, p. 272
20:13, p. 2
22:3, p. 324

Title page,
Book of Mormon
p. 5

1 Nephi
15:24, p. 287

2 Nephi
25:23, p. 183

Mosiah
18:10, p. 185

Alma
13:18, p. 213
32:21-43, p. 221
40:23, p. 128
42:8, p. 133
42:14-15, pp. 164, 216

Moroni
3:1-4, p. 385 n 37
4:3, pp. 109, 146 n 8
7:47, p. 118

D&C
1:21, p. 5
1:33, p. 274
6:3, p. 159
6:13, p. 159
9:8, p. 328
19, p. 134
19:16, p. 216

20:30, p. 177
20:32-34, p. 224
20:37, p. 185
20:77, pp. 109, 146 n 8
27:8-13, p. 228 n 72
27:11, p. 90 n 5
27:12-13, p. 283
29:26, p. 90 n 5
46:13, p. 114
46:14, p. 114
46:18, p. 114
46:27-29, p. 146 n 15
58:43, p. 139
64:9, p. 240
76, pp. 127, 145, 160
76:20-23, p. 248
76:31, p. 209
76:44-47, p. 145
76:50-53, p. 361
76:53, p. 183
76:69, pp. 183, 361
76:74-76, p. 147 n 31
76:92-94, p. 147 n 31
76:103-6, p. 147 n 31
76:114-16, p. 145
77:2, p. 144
84:14, p. 213
84:16, p. 213
84:19-25, p. 205
84:45-46, p. 177
88:27, p. 129
88:28, p. 129
88:47, p. 174
88:77, p. 114
93:7, p. 265
93:12-14, p. 227 n 56
93:29, pp. 265, 357
107:2, p. 213
107:3, pp. 210-11

121:27, p. 411
121:28, p. 411
121:35, pp. 208-9
121:41-42, p. 137
121:43, p. 137
123:11, p. 8
123:12, p. 7
127:6, p. 412
127:8, p. 412
128, p. 412
128:9, p. 413
128:15, p. 413
128:18, p. 271
128:20, p. 228 n 72
128:21, pp. 271, 401
130:2, p. 125
130:20-21, p. 361
130:21, p. 168
138:58, p. 410

Moses
1:39, pp. 137, 258
4:1-3, p. 298
4:1-2, p. 266
4:8-9, p. 353
4:17, p. 353

Abraham
3:22-28, p. 347
3:25, p. 275
3:26, p. 265
3:27, pp. 265-66

JS–History
1:17, p. 248
1:19, pp. 248-49
1:68-74, p. 228 n 72

Articles of Faith
5, p. 326
6, p. 333

Index

Aaron, 210-11
Aaronic Priesthood, 214-15. See also
  Levitical Priesthood; Melchizedek
  Priesthood; Priesthood
Abraham: faith of, 180, 222-23;
  descendents of, 189; Apocalypse of,
  357, 387 n 77, 416
Achaia, 93-94
Action, righteous, 84, 119-20
Acts of Paul and Thecla, 399-402
Acts of the Apostles: relationship of, to
  Paul's letters, 39-40; use of "we" in,
  40-41; purpose of, 41-42, 44; Paul's
  first Gentile mission in, 45-52; coun-
  cil on circumcision in, 52-53; Paul's
  second Gentile mission in, 53-59;
  Paul's third Gentile mission in, 59,
  61-66; Paul's arrest and Jerusalem-to-
  Rome journey, 66, 230-36
Administrators, 116
Advocate, Christ as, 216
Agabus, 34-35, 230
Agápē, 118, 146 n 22, 258
Age classifications, 24-25, 37 n 12
Agency, human, 188-92, 219-20, 263
Agrippa, King, 233, 294
Aiphnídios, 83
Alexander: the Great, 16; the copper-
  smith, 366
Almost, use of, 305 n 2
Anakephalaíōsis, 270, 307 n 53
Ananias, 27-28
Andronicus, 171
Angels, 203, 254
Anthropomorphism, 251-52
Antinomian, 361
Antioch: capital of Syria, 32-36,
  38 n 19, 44, 51, 156-58; in Pisidia,
  47-49
Aparábatos, 215
Apocalypse of Abraham, 357, 387 n 78,
  416
Apollos, 95-96, 99, 171, 345-47

Apostasía, 85
Apostasy: taught in Paul's farewell
  speech, 64-65; imminent, 85-87;
  problem of, 344; of Asia, 367-69,
  371-73; table on, 370; Paul and
  Christ on, 373-75; Paul prophesies
  of, 375-78
Apostates, 360, 368-69, 371-72,
  388 n 97
Apostle, use of, 35
Apostles: directed Church, 31-34,
  44-45, 53, 326-28; Paul and Barnabas called as, 35-36; settle question
  on circumcision, 52-53; greetings of,
  in letters, 72-73; before era of apos-
  tasy, 87; as Church office, 116-17;
  managed Church welfare program,
  139-41; false, 141-42; used laying on
  of hands, 211; as foundation, 277-30,
  283; jurisdiction of, 333-35; death of,
  373-75
Apostleship of Paul, 72-73, 101-2
Apostolic Fathers, 416
Appointment, priesthood, 324-28
Apprehend, use of, 303
Approval of officers, 325-26
Aquila, 96, 171-73
Archangel, 90 n 5
Archippus, 237, 243
Areopagus, 57-58
Areté, 304
Aristarchus, 71, 235-37
Aristotle, 351, 416
Arius, 323
Arndt, William F., 307
Artemis, temple of, 260
As, use of, 82-83
Aschēmonéō, 122
Asia Minor, 63-64, 368-71
Atáktōs, 90 n 6
Athens, 55, 57-58, 73, 75
Athletics, analogy of, 301-3, 309 n 96,
  339-40

Atonement: as part of missionary message, 44; of Christ, 133-35, 215-19; of Christ provides jusitfication, 159, 161-63; purpose of, 358

Augustus, 14-16, 291, 345, 417

Authority: to perform ordinances, 61-63; in Church, 137; priesthood, 141-42; of Christ, 201-4; delegation of, 210-11, 324-28; during dispensation, 269

Authorship: of Hebrews, 197-98, 200-201; of Pastoral Letters, 312-14, 384 n 3-5

Baptism: as part of missionary message, 44, 48; authority for, 62-63; as part of acceptance of Christ, 68 n 5; problems arising from, 98-99; necessity of, 162-63, 403; covenant of, 183-88; as one of first ordinances, 207-8; becoming clean through, 218-19; for remission of sins, 225 n 8; new life after, 273-74

Baptism for dead: Thessalonian concern about, 80; Paul's usage of, 126-27, 405-6; necessity for, 403, 413-14; modern commentaries on, 404-5; related to preaching to dead, 406-11, 414 n 18; instituted by Joseph Smith, 410-13

Baptismós, 207

Baptisms, 228 n 60

Barnabas: with Paul in Antioch, 33-35, 44, 51-52; takes aid to Jerusalem, 34-35, 44; separated for mission, 44; in Cyprus, 45-56; in Pisidian Antioch, 47-49; in Iconium, 49; in Lystra, 49; mistaken for Jupiter, 50, 401; close of mission of, with Paul, 51-52; at council of circumcision, 52-53, 156-58; disagrees with Paul, 54; as apostle, 73

Barrett, C. K., 9

Ben-Gurion, David, 117

Berea, 55, 73, 75

Bible, attitudes toward, 3, 5-7

Bishop: as pastor, 282; as leader, 289; Paul's search for reliable, 317; office of, 327-31, 385 n 26-28; differentiated from deacons, 332-33; types of, 334

Blindness, magician struck with, 46

Boastful, not being, 120-21

Body: in Resurrection, 127-29; physical, of Christ, 249, 251-54; resurrected, of Christ, 298-99; analogies of physically fit, 301-3, 309 n 96, 339-40; Gnostic revulsion toward, 321-22

Bond of perfection, 259

Bonhoeffer, Deitrich, 185

Bonnell, John S., 128-29, 225 n 7

Books wanted by Paul, 366-67

Bowels, meaning of, 239

Box, G. H., 387 n 77

Bragging, 120-21

Brotherhood, 77-78, 242

Browning, Robert, 264

Busybodies, use of, 83

Caesar, household of, 293-94, 309 n 84

Caesarea, 230-34

Calling: and election, 191; priesthood, 324-28

Calvin, John, 189-90, 356

Carnegie, Dale, 284

Catholic Apostolic Church, 283

Catullus, 79, 417

Celibacy, 105

Character: good, 183, 255-59, 285-87, 340-41; use of term, 202

Cháris, 178

Charity, use of, 118, 258

Cheesman, Paul R., 413

Chester Beatty Papyri, 198, 384 n 5, 417

Chiasm, 123

Children, rearing of, 290

Chrēstótēs, 120

Christians: modern, 1-2; in West Germany, 2-4; in England, 4-5; in U.S., 6-8; early Jewish, 151-54

Chronology of Paul's life, 393-97

Chrysostom, John, 38 n 19

Church, Early: management of, 31-34, 98; organization of, 112-17, 276-80, 282-83, 311, 344; Paul organized branches of, 48-49, 72; continuation of and apostasy in, 64-65, 367-69, 371-78; nature of, 66-67; standards of living in, 78-79; compared to temple, 86; practical affairs in, 88-90; efforts to fight division in, 97-98; appointment of officers in, 101-2; discipline in, 103; sacrament in, 107-9; worship services in, 109-11; women in, 111-12; discrepancy between, and modern Christianity, 116-17; authority in, 137, 141-42, 325-27; welfare program of, 139-41, 335-39; revelation in, 155-58; heresy in, 246-47, 252-55, 311-12, 318-22; Shepherd of Hermas on, 275-76; compared to body and building, 277-78; led by apostles, 278-80, 283; constitution of, 281; to perfect Saints, 283-87; bishops, 327-31; elders in, 331-32; deacons in, 332-33; apostles in, 333-35; tribulation of, 374-75; baptism for and preaching to dead in, 405-10

Church activity, 2-4, 7

Cicero, 63, 417

Circumcision: Jerusalem council on, 38 n 21, 52-53, 154-58, 341-42; problem with, 151-52; play on word, 309 n 86

Claudius, 169-70, 390-91, 397 n 5-8

Clayton, William, 400

Clement, First. *See* Clement of Rome

Clement, Second, 266, 417

Clement of Alexandria, 105, 201, 227 n 51, 417

Clement of Rome: on love, 118-19; quotes Paul, 197; on man in likeness of God's image, 202; on Paul's travels, 317; on apostles' appointments, 327; on dismissing leaders, 325-26; writes from Rome, 334; on Paul's death, 363-65; on inner division, 377,

388 n 106; on endurance of Paul, 383; about, 417

Cloak, use of, 387 n 95

Clothes, 338-39

Cole, R. A., 166

Colossae, 238-39, 243-45

Colossians, letter to: delivered by Onesimus, 238; profile, 244; reason for writing, 245-47; Godhead, 247-49, 251-52; "Paul's Testimonies of Christ and His Mission" (table), 250; errors about Christ, days, and diet, 252-55; developing celestial qualities, 255-59

Coming of Jesus Christ, 79-84, 90 n 11

Command, use of, 88

Commandments in Romans, 192-95

Common consent, 102, 211

Communication, 286

Confidence, blind, 221-22

Constitution of Church, 112, 281

Contributions, welfare, 139-41

Conversation, use of, 284, 296

Conversion, 70-72, 74, 76

Cooperation, 352-54

Corinth: Paul proselytes in, 58-59, 73-74, 82; city of, 63, 92-94, 130; Paul writes to, 91-92; Church members of, 94-95, 130; Paul revisits, 131-33; Paul plans third visit to, 132-33; resemblance of, to Kirtland, 146 n 15; Timothy sent to, 315

Corinthians, First: profile, 92; reason for writing, 95-97; appeal for unity, 97-99; revelation and man's wisdom, 99-101; Paul's apostleship, 101-2; sexual morality, 102-4; marriage questions, 104-6; true and false worship, 106-12; Church organization and spiritual gifts, 112-17; pure love, 117-20, 122-25; qualities of love (table), 121; resurrection, 125-29

Corinthians, lost letter to, 95

Corinthians, Second: profile, 130; reason for writing, 130-33; Christ's atonement, 133-35; principle of

sacrifice, 135-37; repentance, 137-39; welfare contributions, 139-41; priesthood authority, 141-42; three heavens, 142-45
Cornelius, 52
Council: on circumcision at Jerusalem, 38 n 21, 52-53, 154-58, 341-42; of Trent, 228; of Nicaea, 247-48; premortal, 265-66, 357
Covenant: of baptism, 183-88; use of term, 216-17
Creator, Gnostic reductions of, 311, 319, 321
Crete, 342-45
Cripple made to walk, 49-50
Crispus, 58, 94
Cymbals, 119, 147 n 26
Cyprus, 45-46, 67 n 3

Damascus, 27-29, 36-37
Dating: of Galatians and Hebrews, 148, 153-54; of Hebrews, 196-97; secular, 390-92, 397 n 4-8; events in Paul's life, 392-93; in chronology of Paul's life, 393-97
Days of worship, errors about, 254-55
Deacon, 332-33
Deaconess, 171
Dead: resurrection of, 79-80, 125-29 baptism for, 126-27, 403-6, 410-14; preparations for living and, 271; preaching to, 406-11, 414 n 18
Deeds, judged according to, 176
Deissmann, Adolf, 147 n 26
Delegation of authority, 210-11, 324-28
Demas, 372
Derbe, 149-50
Development, spiritual, 181-83, 255-59
Diákonos, 171, 332
Diana, temple of, 260
Diastréphō, 65
Diathéke, 134, 216-17
Diet, errors about, 254-55
Dio Cassius, 417
Discernment, 115
Disciple, use of 48-49, 62

Disputation, 352
Dispensation, last: prophecies of last dispensation, 266-67; "mystery of his will," 267-68; "fulness of the times," 268-69; "dispensation of the fulness of the times," 269; "sum up all things in Christ," 269-71
Dispensation, translation of, 307 n 52
Division of Saints, 97-99
Dokimé, 183
Drummond, Henry, 123
Duties, moral, 175

Ears, itching, 376, 388 n 105
Ecclesiasticus, 417
Eikón, 249, 251
Elder, 331-32, 385 n 28
Election, conditional, 188-92
Elijah, 271
Endurance: of love, 121, 123; as patience (hupomoné), 182-83, 222, 340, 381-82; of Abraham, 222-24; to the end, 378-82; of Paul, 383
England, 4-5
Entrusted, use of, 369, 388 n 98
Envy, 120-21
Epaggéllo, 347
Epaphras, 245-46
Epaphroditus, 295
Ephesians, letter to: profile, 259; reason for writing, 260-62; pre-earth life and foreordination, 262-66; last dispensation, 266-71; grace and works, 272-76; Church organization, 276-80, 282-83; constitution of Christ's church (table), 281; "perfecting of the Saints," 283-87; family life, 287-90; thought to be "lost" letter, 305 n 20
Ephesus: Paul forbidden to preach in, 54; Paul baptizes and confirms twelve in, 59, 61-63; Paul proselytes in, 64-65, 68 n 17; Paul warns elders of, 86, 369, 371; Paul writes from, 95-96; city of, 259-60; Timothy presides over, 315-17, 366

Epicureanism, 10-11, 57-58
Epicurus, 11, 417
Epískopos, 65, 330
Epistles. *See* Letters of Paul
Erasmus, 306 n 21
Erastus, 94, 131-32
Érgon, 176, 359
Errors about Christ, days, and diet,
    252-55
Esau, 189-90
Essenes, 348
Éthnos, 28
Euangelízō, 407-8
Eunice, 315
Euschēmonéō, 122
Eusebius, 317, 362, 417
Evangelists in Church, 282-83
Eve, 353-54, 386 n 67
Evil, thinking no, 121, 123
Existence, premortal: ancient and
    modern views supporting, 19,
    37 n 2, 190; and foreordination,
    262-66; God's preparation in,
    274-76; "trusted beforehand" in,
    307 n 43; promise in, 346-50
Exousía, 61-62, 142

Factions in Corinth, 95-96
Faith: as part of missionary message, 42,
    44, 48; as gift of Spirit, 114; grace and
    salvation through, 166-67, 356; use of
    term, 177; shown through
    faithfulness, 205-9; definition of,
    219-22; examples of, 222-24; rewards
    of, 224-25
Faith, justification by: discussion in
    Galatians, 158-59, 161-63; definition
    of terms, 177-78; salvation by grace,
    179-80; grace of forgiveness, 180-82;
    justification, 182-83
Faithfulness, 205-9
Fall of Adam and Eve, 353-54
False apostles. *See* Apostles
False teachers. *See* Teachers, false
Family, 287-90, 329-30, 336-37
Felix, 232-33

Fellowship, use of, 108
Festus, 233
Fire, Roman, 363-64
First principles, 205-9
Firstborn, use of, 224-25, 229 n 83
Food, 106-7, 254-55, 321
For, use of, 405
Foreknowledge of God, 264-65
Foreordination, 263-66, 306-8
Forgiveness: of sins, 47-48, 225 n 8; as
    justification, 159, 160-63, 180-82;
    through Christ, 218-19; is duty,
    240-44
Fornication, 78
Foschini, B. M., 414 n 5-6
Franklin, Benjamin, 285
Frontinus, 397 n 4
Fullness of times, 268-69

Gaius, 71, 94
Galatia, 148-52
Galatians, letter to: profile, 149; reason
    for writing, 152-54; gospel and
    revelation, 154-58; justification by
    faith, 158-59, 161-63; two types of
    salvation (table), 160; moral laws of
    gospel, 163-68
Gallio, 59, 390-92, 397 n 5-8
Gamaliel, 23-24, 232
Gandhi, 346-47, 356
Genealogies, 320-21, 384 n 14
Generosity, 120-21, 139-41
Gentiles, 28, 188-92, 277
Gerstner, John H., 164
Gift of Holy Ghost. *See* Holy Ghost;
    Laying on of hands
Gifts, spiritual, 112-17
Glories, three, 127-28, 143-45, 147 n 31
Gluttony, 107
Gnosticism: Pastoral Letters against
    early, 311-12; heresies of, 318-19,
    384 n 15; Simon Magus in, 319-20,
    359-60, 384 n 16; genealogies in,
    320-21, 384 n 14; marriage in, 321-22;
    antimaterialistic bias of, 371-72;
    resurrection in, 389 n 101

God: patience of, 173-77; nature of, 202; as member of Godhead, 248-49, 251-52; man is offspring of, 264, 356-57; foreknowledge of, 264-65; peace of, 304-5; Gnostic views of, 319-22; invisible, 323-24
Godhead, 247-49, 251-52, 306 n 23
Godliness, 285-87
Golden rule, 140, 193
Goodspeed, Edgar, 413
Gospel: as missionary message, 42, 44; use of term, 133; Paul condemns changes in, 154-58; moral laws of, 163-68, 192-95
Gospels of Christ, 107
Governors, Roman, 390-91, 398 n 6
Government: in Paul's world, 14-16; Church, 112, 115-17
Gôy, 28
Grace: through faith, 166-67, 178; use of term, 177-78; salvation by, 179; freely given by God, 181; Paul's experience with, 182; and works, 185-86, 272-76, 357-62; election of, 191-92; traditional view of, 355-57
Graham, Billy, 185
Gratitude, 181
Growth of Saint, 284-85
Guilt, 137

Hágios, 284
Hamlet, 90 n 13
Hanson, A. T., 322-23, 385 n 19-20
Harper, William Rainey, 301
Harvest as theme, use of, 128, 187-88
Healing, 49-50
Heaven, 142-43, 300-301
Heavens, three, 36-37, 127-28, 142-45
Hebrews, letter to: profile, 195; reason for writing, 195-97; authorship evaluation, 197-98, 200-201; Christ's authority and mission, 201-4; faithfulness and first principles, 205-9; Melchizedek Priesthood, 209-15; Christ's atonement, 215-19; faith and endurance, 219-25

Hegesippus, 318-19, 417
Helps, use of, 116
Heresy, 246-47, 252-55, 318-22
Heretic, use of, 344
Hermas, Shepherd of. See Shepherd of Hermas
Hierapolis, 245
High priest, 209-10
Holy Ghost: as source of testimony, 6-7; received by twelve Ephesian disciples, 59-63; promised by John the Baptist, 63, 68 n 15; gift of, 68 n 11, 208; as revelator, 100-101; and spiritual gifts, 112-15; grieving, 274
Home, solutions through, 354-55
Homosexuality, 103, 174
Hone, William, 399-400
Honesty, 304
Hope, 121, 123-24, 221
Humility, 99-100
Hupér, 405
Hupomoné, 183, 222, 340, 381-82
Hupóstasis, 221, 229 n 81
Hupotássō, 352-54
Husbands, 288-90, 353-55

Iconium, 49
Ideals for men and women, 350-55
Idleness, 88-90
Idol makers, 64, 260
Idolatry, 106-7
Ignatius, 253, 324, 331, 334, 418
Image, use of, 249, 251-52
Immersion, baptism by, 184
Immorality, 102-4
Imperatorship, 391, 397 n 5-8
Imposters, 375, 388 n 102
Imprisonment letters, 236-38
Imprisonments of Paul, 232-36
Infirmity of Paul, 151-52
Intercessor, use of, 216
Invisibility, use of, 252
Irenaeus: on three heavens, 127-28; on Simon Magus, 319-20, 359-60, 384 n 16; on Christ's preaching to dead, 407, 414 n 7; about, 418

Irritability, 121-23
Irving, Edward, 283
Israel, fall of, 188-92
Italy, Saints from, 227 n 46
Itching ears, translation of, 376, 388 n 105

Jacob, 189-92
Jailor, 54-55, 292
James, 29, 52-53, 157-58, 231
Jannes, 388 n 103
Jason, 71-72
Jealousy, 120-21
Jedin, Hubert, 247
Jeremiah, 19
Jerusalem: arrest of Paul in, 21-22; Paul in, before conversion, 23-26; Paul in, as new convert, 28-29; Paul's visits to, 38 n 21, 225 n 2; council on circumcision, 38 n 21, 52-53, 154-58, 342; Paul visits, after third mission, 66, 230-32; destruction of, 373-74
Jesus Ben Sirach, 349, 417
Jesus Christ: modern belief in, 3-5, 8; taught of "fire on the earth," 19-20; on Pharisees, 23; Stephen saw, 26; first appearance of, to Paul, 27-28, 36-38; appears to Paul in temple, 29-31; as fulfillment of Israel's history, 47-48; coming of, 79-84, 90 n 11; prophesies of apostasy, 87, 373-75; desire of, for unity, 97; and sacrament, 107-8; promises gifts of spirit, 113; teachings of, on love, 118-20; resurrection of, 125-26, 129; atonement of, 133-35, 180-81, 215-19, 358; letters preaching, 148; table on salvation through, 160; authority and mission of, 201-4, 254, 323; nature of, 202; first principles pertaining to, 206-7; as high priest over Melchizedek Priesthood, 209-12, 215; requires obedience, 295-99; as member of Godhead, 248-49, 251-52; table on testimonies and mission of, 250; errors about, 252-54; new person in, 256-57; premortal existence of,

264-65, 347-48; taught necessity of works, 272-73; as body and cornerstone of Church, 277-78; as model of priesthood leadership, 289-90; obedience and experience of, 297-98; Simon Magus's teachings on, 319-20; as mediator, 322-23; reveals Father, 323-24; preached in spirit world, 406-11
Jews, 12-13, 151-54, 169-73, 195-97. *See also* Judaism; Judaizers
John Chrysostom, 38 n 19
John Mark. *See* Mark
John the Baptist, 46-47, 58-59, 61-63
John the Beloved, 33, 61-62, 246, 253, 368
Josephus: on Pharisees, 22; on Antioch, 33-34; on John the Baptist, 47; uses *apostasía*, 85; uses *katéchō*, 90 n 13; on temple inscription, 231; on Caesarea, 234; on household of Caesar, 294; on Essenes, 348; about, 418
Judaism, 10, 12-13, 151-54, 188-92, 254-55. *See also* Jews
Judaizers, 152, 309 n 86
Judgment, 84
Julius, 234-35
Junia, 171
Justification: by faith, 158-59, 161-63; definition of, 177-78; through grace, 179-80; as forgiveness, 180-82; as step to salvation, 182-83; Abraham as example of, 223
Justin Martyr: on sacrament, 109, 333; refers to premortal existence, 266; on Simon Magus, 319; on Menander, 372; writings of, 384 n 15; on Christ's preaching to dead, 406, 414 n 7; about, 418
Justness in relationships, 240-44
Justus, 94
Juvenal, 169, 418

Katéchō, 87, 90 n 13
Kenyon, Frederic G., 198
Kērússō, 407-8

Kimball, Spencer W., 115-16, 290,
 308 n 74, 340, 355
Kindness, 120-21
Kirtland, 146 n 15
Knowledge, 114, 124, 318
Koecher, Renate, 4
Koinōía, 108
Kubérnēsis, 116

Labor, productive, 335-36
Laodicea, 244-46
Laodiceans, lost letter to, 246-47
Last days: restoration, 266-67; mystery
 of God's will, 267-68; dispensation of
 fullness of times, 268-69; summing up
 all things in Christ, 269-71; apostasy,
 373-75
Law: of Moses, 51-53, 151-54, 159,
 161-64, 254-55; use of, 177; of Christ,
 179-80; of harvest, 187-88; obedience
 to, 361. *See also* Mishnah
Laws, moral, 163-68, 175, 192-95
Laying on of hands: to separate Paul
 and Barnabus for mission, 44-45;
 instances of, 45; as part of missionary
 message, 48; for Holy Ghost, 59-63,
 68 n 11; as one of first ordinances, 208;
 for ordination, 325-26. *See also* Holy
 Ghost; Priesthood
Leadership: continuing, 74; missionary,
 76-79; central Church, 98; to direct
 use of gifts, 112-13, 115-17; in home,
 289-90; qualities for, 327-30
Leaving of first principles, 206
"Lectures on Faith," 219
Leith, John H., 248
Lets, use of, 87, 90 n 13
Letters of Paul: nature of, 39-40;
 relationship of, to Acts, 40, 310-11;
 early, to converts, 69; purpose of, 72;
 forged or lost, 83, 246-47, 305 n 20; of
 reconversion, 91-92; preaching
 Christ, 148-49; Roman imprisonment
 letters, 236-38; Pastoral, 310-14
Levitical Priesthood, 196. *See also*
 Aaronic Priesthood; Melchizedek
 Priesthood; Priesthood

Life, mortal, 3-4, 7-8, 78-79, 255-59,
 287-90
Life, pre-earth. *See* Existence, premortal
Linus, 365, 387 n 94
Living, ties of, to dead, 79-80, 271
Longsuffering, 120, 176-77
Lord's Supper, 107-9
Love: meaning of, 117-18;
 preeminence of, 119-20; qualities of,
 120-23; challenged to have,
 124-25; increase of, 137-38; for
 neighbor, 193; to surpass bonds of
 slavery, 242; necessary to develop,
 257-59
Lucian, 303, 418
Luke: as Paul's missionary companion,
 40-42, 54-55, 291-92; background of,
 41-42; accompanies Paul to Rome,
 235-37; after writing of Acts, 316;
 needed at Paul's final trial, 367; as
 commentator on Asia, 369, 371; as
 biographer, 393
Luther, Martin, 178-79, 186
Lydia, 54, 292
Lystra, 49-50, 149-52

Magician struck with blindness, 46
Malta, 235
Man of sin, 85-87
Mark, 45-46, 54, 67-68, 367
Marriage, 24-25, 102-6, 321-22, 329
Martyrdom of Peter and Paul, 362-65
Matthews, Robert J., 411, 414 n 18
McConkie, Bruce R., 217, 227 n 56
McDonald, H. D., 15, 186
McKay, David O., 26-27
Mediator, Christ as, 216, 322-23
Meetings, Church, 109-11
Melchizedek Priesthood: high priest,
 209-10; called of God, 210-11;
 higher priesthood, 211-12;
 Melchizedek, 212-14, 227 n 56,
 228 n 69; eternal and unchangeable,
 214-15. *See also* Aaronic Priesthood;
 Levitical Priesthood; Priesthood
Men, ideals for, 350-55
Menander, 372, 388 n 99

Mercy, 306 n 34
Merrill, Joseph F., 301
Messiahship, 207
Michael, 90 n 5
Mimētēs, 74, 76
Miracles, 56, 114-15, 219-20, 222-23
Mishnah, 22-26, 32, 161-62, 418. *See also* Law
Mission of Christ, 201-4
Missionary: message of Paul, 42, 44-47, 55, 57-58; leadership, 76-78; work and marriage, 106
Missions of Paul, table on, 43
Money, Paul's teachings concerning, 88-90
Monotheists, 248
Morality, 102-4, 163-68, 192-95, 350-51, 360
Moroni, 118
Morris, Leon, 90 n 11. 404
Mortify, use of, 256
Mortifying deeds of body, 188
Moses, 211
Moses, law of. *See* Law; Mishnah
Muratorian Fragment, 313-14, 317, 384 n 4, 408, 418
Mystery, 267-68, 307 n 50, 323
Mystery religions, 9-11
Myths, 320-21

Nathanael, 115
Neanías, 37
Nero, 311, 362-65, 371
New Paphos, 45-56
Nibley, Hugh, 283, 357
Nicene Council, 306 n 23
Nicopolis, 345
Nómos, 361

Obedience, 295-99, 352-54, 361
Obligations of family, 336-37
Offering for remission of sins, Christ as, 217-18
Offices: in Early Church, 115-17; priesthood, 324-25, 333-35; ordinations to, 326-27; appointments

to, 327-28; bishop as one of, 328-31; elder as one of, 331-33; deacon as one of, 323-33
Ogg, George, 397 n 1 and 5
Oikonomía, 269, 307 n 51-52
Oneness, 99, 378
Onesimus; background and conversion of, 238-40; as runaway slave under law, 240-44; helped Paul, 369
Onesiphorus, 365
Order of Melchizedek, 209-10, 212-14
Ordinances of salvation, table on, 60
Ordination to priesthood, 325-27
Organization of Church, 112-17, 276-80, 282-83, 311, 344
Origen, 190, 200, 362-63, 387 n 88, 418
Orr, William F., 404
Overseers, use of, 330

Paganism, 9-11, 49-50, 58, 106-7
Paradise, 36-37, 144
Pastoral Letters, 383-84 n 1-5
Pastors in Church, 282
Patience, 120-21, 173-77, 222-23, 340, 381-82
Patriarch, 282
Paul: separated for call, 19, 44-45; "fire on earth" as theme for, 19-20; in Tarsus, 20-21, 31-33, 36; Roman citizenship of, 21-22, 240; as Jew and Pharisee, 22-26; marriage of, 24-25, 105; as young man, 25, 392; as persecutor of Christians, 25-26; conversion and first vision of, 26-28, 39 n 17, 392-93; call of, as minister to Gentiles, 27; first three years of, as Christian, 28-29, 31; first meets Peter, 29; temple vision and escape of, 29-31; table on visions of, 30; directed by Church authorities, 31-34; persecutions and dangers of, 32, 135-37, 143-44, 382; in Syrian Antioch, 32-36, 44, 51-52; reunited with Barnabas, 33-34; takes welfare aid to Jerusalem, 34-35, 44, 139-41,

230-31; called as apostle, 35-36; has vision of heavens, 36-37, 143-45, 147 n 31; visits of, to Jerusalem, 38 n 21, 392, 398 n 10; missionary work of, with Luke, 40-41, 55; Gentile missions of, 41-43; missionary message of, 42, 44-47, 55, 57-58; in Cyprus, 45-46; converts Sergius Paulus, 46; rebukes magician with blindness, 46; in Pisidian Antioch, 47-49; synagogue speeches of, 47-48; baptism of, 49; in Iconium, 49; in Lystra, 49; heals crippled man, 49-50; mistaken for Mercury, then stoned, 50, 152; close of first mission, 50-51; at council on circumcision, 52-53, 156-58; sees vision of man from northern Greece, 54; in Philippi, 54-55, 70, 291-93; converts Lydia and jailor, 54-55; in Thessalonica and Berea, 55, 71-72, 76; table on miracles of, 56; in Athens, 56-58, 73-75; in Corinth, 58-59, 63, 73-75, 82, 131, 293, 391-92; vision assures safety of, 58-59; at Ephesus, 59, 61-63, 68 n 17, 89, 259-60; gives Holy Ghost to twelve disciples, 59, 61-62; farewell of, 64-66, 369, 371, 376-77; first imprisonment of, in Rome, 68, 235-36, 260-61, 293-95, 316, 338-39; personal relationships of, 69, 131-32; writes Thessalonian Saints, 69; exile of, from northern Greece, 75; love of, for Thessalonians, 77-78; avoids prophesying of time of Lord's coming, 81; letter of, misconstrued, 83; supports himself, 89-90, 101; writes to reconvert Corinthians, 91; writes from Ephesus about Corinthian problems, 95-96; baptisms by, 98-99; apostleship of, 101-2, 141-42, 155-56; as parent to converts, 102; love of, 119-20, 131-32, 135-38; as eyewitness of Resurrection, 125; again in Macedonia, 131-32; planned to revisit Corinth, 132-33; enemies of

Paul, 141-42; greets twenty-eight Romans, 170-72; nature of ministry of, 172; experience of, with Mosaic law, 181; imprisoned in Jerusalem and Caesarea, 196; name of, opening letters, 198, 201; visits of, to Jerusalem, 225 n 2; knows of impending imprisonment, 230-31; in Caesarea, 230-34; beaten and arrested in temple, 231-32; tried before Sanhedrin, 232; examined before governors, 232-33; stands before kings, 233-34; shipwrecked in storm, 234-35; in Malta, 235; survives snake bite, 235; in Puteoli, 235; converts Onesimus, 238-40; at start of third mission, 246; sends greetings to Ephesus, 261; love of, for Savior, 272-73; unwritten instructions of, 278, 308 n 69; converts members of Caesar's household, 293-94; converts members of imperial guard, 294-95; presses for prize of exaltation, 301-3; uses play on words, 309 n 86; imprisonment and martyrdom of, 310-11, 362-65; acquaintance of, with Timothy, 314-16; visit of, to Spain, 316-17; plans to revisit Macedonia, 317; acquaintance of, with Titus, 341-42; visits of, to Crete, 343; in Nicopolis, 345; foreknowledge of, about his death, 365-67; final trial of, 366-67; endured to end, 378-79, 383; birth of, 392-93; chronology of life of, 393-97; descriptions of, 399-402. See also Saul; World of Paul

Paulus, meaning of, 401
Pausanias, 301, 309 n 96, 418
Peace of God, 304-5
Perfecting of Saints, 283-87
Perfection, bond of, 259
Persecution: of Christians by Paul, 25-27; of Paul, 28-29, 31-32, 135-37, 143-44, 382; of converts, 74, 76; of apostles, 76-77; value of, 135-37; of

Christians by Nero, 363-64
Peter: first meets Paul, 29; in Samaria,
    33, 61-62; meetings of, with Paul,
    38 n 21; on remission of sins, 48; at
    council on circumcision, 52-53;
    visited Corinth, 95; misuse of name
    of, 155-56; doesn't eat with Gentiles,
    157-58; preached first principles,
    206-7; taught of Restoration, 267,
    271; martyrdom of, 364-65;
    condemns Simon Magus, 384 n 16;
    taught of Christ's preaching to dead,
    406-7
Pharaoh, 190, 227 n 40
Pharisees, 22-24, 232, 348-49
Phebe, 171-72, 332
Philemon, letter to: profile, 238; reason
    for writing, 238-40; forgiveness and
    just relationships, 240-44
Philéo, 146 n 22
Philippi, 54-55, 70, 291-93
Philippians, letter to: profile, 290,
    reason for writing, 293-95; Christ and
    obedience, 295-99; progressive
    salvation, 299-305
Phillips, J. B., 67
Philo, 19, 37 n 2, 294, 419
Phthánō, 79
Physicalness of God and Christ, 249
    251-54, 319, 322-24
Physicians, Greek, 41
Plato, 419
Pliny the Elder, 236, 260, 339, 419
Pliny the Younger, 108-9, 242, 419
Plutarch, 94, 419
Politarch, 71-72
Polybius, 9
Polycarp, 313, 331-32, 334,
    384 n 2-3, 419
Porneía, 78
Power, use of, 375-76
Praetorium, 294-95, 309 n 84
Prayer, 77-78
Prayers, sacrament, 109, 146 n 8-9
Predestination, 188-92, 262-63, 306 n 41
Preexistence. *See* Existence, premortal

Prepared beforehand, use of, 274-75,
    307 n 59
Pride, 100
Priest, high, 209-10
Priesthood: authority, 61-63, 141-42;
    restoration, 228 n 72; offices, 324-25,
    333-35; ordination, 326-27;
    appointment, 327-28; office of bishop,
    328-31; office of elder, 331-33; office
    of deacon, 323-33; organization, 344.
    See also Aaronic Priesthood;
    Levitical Priesthood; Melchizedek
    Priesthood
Principles, first, 205-9, 306 n 33
Priscilla, 96, 171-73
Prison letters, 236-38
Prò chrónōn aiōníōn, 347-48
Proconsul, 46, 67 n 3
Proetoimázō, 274-75
Profession, use of, 205
Profiles: 1 Thessalonians, 69-70;
    2 Thessalonians, 81; 1 Corinthians,
    92; 2 Corinthians, 130; Galatians,
    149; Romans, 168; Hebrews, 195;
    Philemon, 238; Colossians, 244;
    Ephesians, 259; Philippians, 290;
    1 Timothy, 314; Titus, 339;
    2 Timothy, 362
Proginóskō, 264-65
Progression: spiritual, 181-83; toward
    salvation, 299-303; qualities
    necessary for, 303-5
Prohelpízō, 307 n 43
Promise, premortal, 346-50
Proorízō, , 263
Prophecy, 115-16, 308 n 68
Prophet, 280, 380-81
Prophets, false, 374-75, 377, 388 n 102
Propitiation, 180
Proséchō, 68 n 5
Protestant minister and serviceman, 163
Puffed up, use of, 121-22
Punishment, Jewish, 32
Puteoli, 235

Qualities necessary for salvation, 255-59,
    303-4

Quasten, Johannes, 307 n 47, 408-9
Quintilian, 270, 307 n 53, 419

Race, analogy of, 301-3, 309 n 96
Rebellion, use of, 85
Reconciliation, 133
Reconversion, 91-92
Regeneration, 358
Rejoicing in truth, 121, 123
Relationships, just, 240-44
Relatives in Resurrection, 79-80
Religions in Paul's World (table), 10
Remission of sins, 217, 225 n 8
Repentance, 42, 44, 48, 103-4, 137-39
Restoration, 214, 228 n 72, 267-71, 375, 377-78
Resurrection: as part of missionary message, 42, 44, 47; Paul testifies of, to rulers, 65, 232-34; status of deceased loved ones in, 79-81; argument of, to Corinthians, 125-29; false teachings about, 371-72, 388 n 101
Revelation: as guide for Church, 53, 66-67; and man's wisdom, 99-101; gospel and, 154-58; in choosing officers, 327-28; necessity of, 412
Rewarder, use of, 220
Riches, 339-40
Rigdon, Sidney, 127
Robinson, William Childs, 356
Roman citizenship, 21-22
Romans, letter to: similarities with Galatians, 153-54; profile, 168; reason for writing, 172-73; God's patience and judgment, 173-77; justification by faith, 177-83; baptismal covenant, 183-88; conditional election, 188-92; moral laws of gospel, 192-95
Romans at Philippi, 291
Rome: Paul imprisoned in, 66, 235-36, 260-61, 293-95; city of, 169-70; Church members of, 170-72; dress styles in, 338-39; under Nero, 363-65, 371

Sacrament, 107-9, 146 n 7-9, 333
Sacrifice: principle of, 135-37; of Christ, 217-18
Saint, use of, 284
Saints, perfecting of, 283-87
Salvation: table on ordinances of, 60; types of, 158-61; use of term, 177, 309 n 85; by grace, 179, 355-57; and works, 192-95, 357-62; qualities necessary for, 255-59, 303-5; working out, 295-99; is progressive, 299-303; premortal promise of, 346-50, 357-58
Samaria, 33, 61-63, 319
Sandys, John Edwin, 244
Sanhedrin, 23-25, 232
Satan, 85-87, 208-9, 287
Saturninus, 321-22
Saul, 23, 26-27, 37 n 9, 46, 181.
   See also Paul
Schaff, Philip, 283
Scourging, 32
Scriptures, 379-81
Second Coming. *See* Coming of Jesus Christ; Last days
Secundus, 71
Self-control, 78
Self-examination, 108
Selflessness, 121-22
Self-reliance, 88-90
Seneca, 235, 241, 419
Separation of Paul for ministry, 19
Sergius Paulus, 46
Sermon on the Mount, 193-95
Servant, treatment of, 243
Serviceman and Protestant minister, 163
Sexual morality, 102-4
Shepherd of Hermas: on preaching to and baptism for dead, 214, 408-10; about, 275, 308 n 60-61, 419; on premortal planning of Church, 275-76, 308 n 63-64; on Church offices, 385 n 37
"Short time," translation of, 233-34, 305 n 2
Sick, healing, 49-50
Silas: becomes Paul's missionary

companion, 53-54; in Philippi, 54-55, 70, 291-93; in Thessalonica and Berea, 55, 71-73, 75; in Corinth, 58-59, 74-75; as Silvanus, 67 n 1; and 1 Thessalonians, 69-70; as apostle, 73
"Silence" of women, 352
Silvanus. *See* Silas
Simon Magus, 61-63, 319-22, 359-60, 384 n 15-16
Simpson, E. K., 263
Sin: man of, 85-87; sexual, 102-4; warning against, 174-75; unto death, 208-9; remission of, 225 n 8; premortal, 349
Slavery, 239-44
Smith, Joseph: on premortal existence, 19, 308 n 74, 357; on gift of Holy Ghost, 61, 63, 68; on 1 Corinthians 7:1, 104; on gift of tongues, 110-11, 146 n 15; on Holy Ghost as revelator, 113; on testimony, 113-14, 191; on pure love, 125; vision of, on glories, 127, 145, 147 n 31; on resurrection, 129; on justification by faith, 180-81; on baptism, 185; on election, 188; on not leaving first principles, 206, 228 n 58; on Melchizedek, 213; on Pharaoh, 227 n 40; on Hebrews 5:7-10, 227 n 56; on word of Jehovah, 234; on Godhead, 248-49, 252, 299; on last dispensation, 270-71; on evangelist, 282; on salvation, 300; on laying on of hands, 325-26; describes Paul, 399-402; instituted baptism for dead, 410-13; on revelation, 412
Smith, Joseph F., 410-11
Smith, Joseph Fielding, 353
Smith, William, 117
Smyrna, bishop of. *See* Polycarp
Sober, use of, 329, 351
Socrates, 382
Sorcerers, 388 n 102-3
Sōmatikós, 254
Sóphrōn, 329, 351
Sorrow to repentance, 138

Sosthenes, 92, 96
Spirit, gifts of, 112-17
Spirit world, preaching in: referred to by Peter, 406-8; in Shepherd of Hermas, 408-10; seen by Joseph F. Smith, 410-11
Spiritually minded, use of, 187-88
Stádion, 302-3
Standards, Church, 78-79, 350-55
Statistics: on Christianity, 2: on West Germany, 2-4; on England, 4-5; on U.S., 6-8
Stephanas, 94, 96
Stephen, 26
Stewardship, 101
Stoá, 11
Stoicism, 10-11, 57-58
Strabo: Tarsus, 21; on New Paphos, 46; on Thessalonica, 70; on Corinth, 93; on Laodicea, 244-45; on Ephesus, 260; on Crete, 343-44; about, 419
Strife and teaching, comparison of, 379
Stripes, 32
Style: in Hebrews, 197-98, 200-201; in Pastoral Letters, 312-13, 383 n 1
Subjection, 352-54
Submission, relationships involving, 288-89, 352-54
Submit, use of, 288
Subordination, relationships involving, 288-89
Subscriptions, 72
Substance, use of, 221, 229 n 81
Sudden, use of, 83
Suetonius, 169, 419
Suffering, examples of, 135-37, 203-4
Suffers long, use of, 120
Sugchaírō, 123
Summing up all things, 269-71
Supper, Lord's, 107-9
Synagogues, preaching in, 45-47

Tacitus, 363-64, 419
Talmage, James E., 220
Tarsus, 20-21, 31-32, 36
Teachers, false; Gnostics, 318-19; sect of Simon Magus, 319-20;

genealogies, 320-21; marriage,
321-22; truth about God and Christ,
322-24; prophecies, 374-75
Teachers in Church, 280
Teaching and strife, comparison of, 379
Telestial glory, 147 n 31
Temper, even, 121-23
Temple: Paul arrested in Jerusalem,
21-22, 231-32; Paul sees Lord in
Jerusalem, 29-31; use of term, 86,
90 n 12; destruction of, 196
Temple, William, 179
Tertullian, 362, 399, 420
Testament, use of, 134, 217
Testimonies of Christ and his mission
(table), 250
Testimony, 6-7, 113-14
Thecla, 399-402
Thessalonians, First: profile, 69-70;
reason for writing, 72-74; meaning
of conversion, 74, 76; Writing of
First Thessalonians (table), 75;
missionary leadership, 76-78; Church
standards of living, 78-79;
Resurrection and Christ's coming,
79-81
Thessalonians, Second: profile, 81;
reason for writing, 82-83; Christ's
coming and judgment, 84; imminent
apostasy, 85-87; commandment to
work, 87-90
Thessalonica: Paul proselytes in, 55, 76;
Paul writes to, 69; city of, 70, 81;
Church members of, 70-72, 82
Thinking no evil, 121, 123
Thorn in flesh, 141-42
Times: fullness of, 268-69; of apostasy,
373-75
Timothy: circumcision of, 54, 151,
315; becomes Paul's missionary
companion, 54; in Philippi, 54; in
Thessalonica and Berea, 55, 72-75;
in Corinth, 58-59, 74-75, 94, 315;
and 1 Thessalonians, 69-70; sent to
Greek churches, 130-31; with Paul in
return to Jerusalem, 149; in Rome,
171; and letter to Hebrews, 227 n 51;

Church office of, 310-11, 365-66;
background of, 314-16; Paul's reason
for writing to, 316-17, 365-67; to
attend Paul's trial, 366-67; to
counter apostasy, 368-69, 372; to be
example, 372-73; personal advice to,
379-80
Timothy, First: profile, 314; reason
for writing, 316-17; false teachers,
318-24; priesthood offices, 324-35;
earthly and eternal welfare, 335-39
Timothy, Second: profile, 362; Paul's
martyrdom, 362-65; reason for
writing, 365-67; apostasy of Church,
367-69, 371-78; Asian Apostasy
during Apostles' Lives (table), 370;
enduring to the end, 378-83
Titus: work of, with Corinthians,
131-32; Church office of, 310-11;
background of, 341-42; in Crete,
342-44; Paul's reason for writing
to, 343-46
Titus, letter to: profile, 341; reason for
writing, 343-46; premortal promise,
346-50; qualifications for bishops,
350; ideals for men and women,
350-55; grace and saving works,
355-62
Tongues, speaking in, 109-10, 115
Transgression, sexual, 102-4
Translation of Hebrews, 201
Travel in Paul's world, 16
Trial, final, of Paul, 366-67
Tribulation of Early Church, 374-75
Tribune, 231-32
Trinity, 202-3, 247-49, 251-52
Trusting, first, 307 n 43
Truth as answer to false doctrine, 322-24
Tychicus, 261, 345, 365, 372

Ulpian, 420
Unbelief, 205-6
Understanding as purpose of meetings,
110
United States, 6-8
Unity, 95-99, 276-80, 378, 388 n 107
Unseemliness, 121-22

Unselfishness, 121-22
Untransferrable, use of, 215

Values, eternal, 338-41
Vessel, use of, 78
Virtue, 304
Visions of Paul, 29-31, 143-45
Vocabulary of Pastoral Letters, 312
Voltaire, 285

Walking in spirit, 165
Walther, James Arthur, 404
Watson, S., 387
Wealth, 339-40
Welfare: in Early Church, 45, 131,
    139-41, 149-50; earthly, 335-37;
    eternal, 337-41
West Germany, 2-4
Wisdom: of world, 1, 8; of man, 99-101;
    word of, 114; of Solomon, 349, 420
Wives, 288-90, 351-55
Women in Early Church, 111-12, 292,
    350-55
Word of God as missionary message,
    45-56, 114, 287
Wordsworth, William, 350
Work, commandment to, 87-90, 335-36
Works: good, 164, 167-68, 224, 296-97;
    of flesh, 165-66; judged according to,

175-76; after baptism, 185-88; and
    grace, 272-76, 355-57; necessity of,
    357-59; false teachings on, 359-62
World, modern: non-U.S., 1-5; U.S.,
    6-8; and Paul's world, 8-9, 13-14
World of Paul: and today's world, 8-9,
    13-14; paganism in, 9-10; mystery
    religions in, 9-11; Stoicism and
    Epicureanism in, 10-11; Judaism in,
    10, 12-13; government of, 14-16;
    peace during, 16-17
Worship: idolatry, 106-7; sacrament,
    108-9; services of Early Church,
    109-11; role of woman, 111-12
Worthiness, 337-38
Worthy, use of, 146 n 7

Xenophon, 420

Yokefellow, use of, 105, 292
Young, Brigham: on testimony by Spirit,
    6-7; on authority of apostles, 102
    145 n 4; on revelation, 146 n 18;
    on being Saints, 287; on welfare,
    336; on practical religion, 338; on
    Eve, 386 n 67

Zadokite Document, 420
Zeno, 11